IN THE NAME OF JUSTICE:
THE TELEVISION REPORTING OF
JOHN PILGER

IN THE NAME
OF JUSTICE
THE TELEVISION REPORTING OF
JOHN PILGER

Anthony Hayward

BLOOMSBURY

First published in Great Britain 2001

Copyright © Anthony Hayward/Profiles 2001

The moral right of the author has been asserted

Bloomsbury Publishing Plc, 38 Soho Square, London W1D 3HB

A CIP catalogue record for this book
is available from the British Library

ISBN 0 7475 5201 0

10 9 8 7 6 5 4 3 2 1

Typeset by Hewer Text Ltd, Edinburgh
Printed in Great Britain by Clays Ltd, St Ives plc

This book is dedicated to
Deborah, Alexander and Olivia,
and to the memory of David Munro

'He has taken on the great theme of justice and injustice. The misuse of power against the powerless. The myopic, stupid cruelty of governments. The bullying and lies that shroud *realpolitik*, a mad game played at the top, which is a curse to real people . . . He belongs to an old and unending worldwide company, the men and women of conscience. Some are as famous as Tom Paine and Wilberforce . . . If they win, it is slowly; but they never entirely lose. To my mind, they are the blessed proof of the dignity of man. John has an assured place among them. I'd say he is a charter member for his generation.'

Martha Gellhorn, from
the *New Statesman*, 12 July 1991

CONTENTS

ACKNOWLEDGEMENTS

FOR THEIR HELP in researching this book, I would like to thank Janet Pitts at the Carlton film library in Nottingham and Louise Smith at the Carlton picture unit in Nottingham; staff at the British Film Institute National Library in London, the British Library Newspaper Library in London, Westminster Library, Swiss Cottage Library and the central libraries at Leeds, Sheffield and York; Katie Ekberg and Tamara Grant of *TV Week*, Australia; and Steve Anderson, Richard Creasey, Ana de Juan, Jim Howard, Richard Jeffs, Phillip Knightley, Alan Lowery, Jonathan Morris, Jacky Stoller, Ivan Strasburg, David Swift and Jeremy Wallington. Thanks also to Liz Calder and Edward Faulkner at Bloomsbury, and to my wife, Deborah, for her patience over the two years that it took me to write this book. Most of all, I would like to thank John Pilger for his time and co-operation, giving interviews and access to videotapes.

It was in the mid-1970s that I became aware of John's journalism. Seeing his television documentaries, I realized there was something about them that was 'different' from other current affairs programmes: they presented serious issues but there was a 'human reality' to them. Only later did I begin to understand that this was because of John's dismissal of the fake notions of 'impartiality' and 'balance' that were the basis for mainstream television journalism, with their roots in the Reithian 'values' that had only distanced people from reality. 'Official' truths, rooted in the agendas of those who exercised power in government and broadcasting, were being challenged by a journalist whose starting point was with those who lived with the consequences of their actions.

I think it appropriate that this book should be dedicated to the memory of David Munro, who died in 1999 at the age of 55. For twenty years, he gave his remarkable skills as a director to some of John's most important documentaries. Their professional partnership was one of like minds, with David angered by what he saw as the madness of war. In presenting me with a copy of the book based on his own 1986 documentary *The Four Horsemen*, for which he filmed wars in eight countries over fifteen months, David autographed it to me 'with best wishes and a hope for peace'. That was David, and his motivation for sanity and justice is one shared by John Pilger and evident in all of the programmes featured in this book. Lastly, I should emphasize that this is not a biography but an account of John's television journalism.

Anthony Hayward, August 2000

INTRODUCTION

J OHN PILGER'S TELEVISION documentaries, like his
newspaper reports, have often challenged those in authority
and given a very different insight into major world events
from that presented by other journalists. His style, investigative, analytical, yet humanist, has resulted in some of the most
powerful, debated and effective programmes ever broadcast.

Pilger is clear about his role as a reporter. 'I've always had a very
strong sense of justice and injustice,' he explained. 'It's one of the
themes that a journalist should address in his or her work. I believe
passionately that journalism is about lifting rocks, and not accepting the official line. One of the increasing problems in the world
of "spin doctoring" is that the official line is being packaged and
"marketed" so effectively that it's becoming more and more
difficult to resist it, but resist it we must.

'I am, by inclination, anti-authoritarian and forever sceptical of
anything the agents of power want to tell us. As a journalist, it is
my duty, surely, to tell people when they're being conned or told
lies. The idea of me crusading like some demented Christian in
pursuit of the infidel is nonsense. What I do is a job of journalism
with a respect for humanity, and for telling the stories of humanity
from the ground up, not from the point of view of the powerful
and those who, in one way or another, want to control or exploit
us.'[1]

Pilger has reported on injustices committed by both right- and
left-wing governments, his documentaries combining a humanitarian viewpoint with tirelessly researched evidence to support it.
In naming him the 1974 News Reporter of the Year, the British

Press Awards judges summed this up with the citation, 'John Pilger's field is the world and his subject humanity. His material is factual, but his expression of it powerfully emotional, and his contribution to present-day news reporting unsurpassed.'

Pilger himself explained, 'You have to legitimize before the viewer's eyes the opinion you are expressing. The Independent Broadcasting Authority [during its time as regulator for commercial television] always saw to it that I never included anything that could not be sourced and often double- or triple-sourced. I put paramount importance on making sure that the material I use has reliable sources.'[2]

Cameraman Gerry Pinches, who filmed Pilger's historic documentary *Year Zero – The Silent Death of Cambodia*, observed during the making of it one of the disciplines that he believed set Pilger apart from many others. 'In the evenings, he would not always join everyone else for a meal but occasionally ate in his hotel room and did some serious reading and research for the next few days,' recalled Pinches. 'He is very assiduous in his research. When he is doing his "camera pieces", he frequently has to speak in generalizations, so he has to be sure he is one hundred per cent right. He is a man who works with his mind. It is that simple. He thinks things through according to no particular agenda. He's often thought to be a left-winger, but he has been very critical of various governments, including the Russian one.'[3]

Over thirty years, Pilger's television programmes have highlighted America's futile war in Vietnam and Washington's threat to a democratically elected government in Nicaragua, repression in Czechoslovakia, East Timor and Burma, discrimination against the Aborigines in his native Australia, the injustice of poverty in Mexico and Japan while those countries' governments reap economic wealth, and social and political issues in his adopted country of Britain. Imperialism throughout the world, particularly that of the United States and Britain, is a constant theme – partly because he considers this an agenda unreported by the Western media.

'Imperialism is a word almost struck from the English and American lexicon,' he explained. 'It is the great unprintable and unsayable. For, once you attribute Western actions to imperialist intent, for reasons of economic or strategic advantage – it's still imperialism – you shine a light on how the world is run by the powerful. It's, of course, understandable that imperialism is a taboo – in contrast to when imperialists were proud of their exploits. Since fascism expounded its notions of racial superiority in the 1930s and 1940s, the imperial "civilising mission" has had a bad name. Since the end of the Cold War, however, the economic and political crises in the developing world, precipitated by debt and the disarray of the liberation movements, have served as retrospective justification for imperialism. Although the word remains unspeakable, the old imperial project's return journey to respectability has begun. What we are seeing now is the market testing of new brand names. "Humanitarian war" is the latest to satisfy the criterion of doing what you like where you like, as long as you are strong enough. This is why I try, from time to time, to break the silence on this important issue.'[4]

In 2000, the suffering of the ordinary people of Iraq, as a result of the Gulf War and the subsequent United Nations trade embargo, imposed ostensibly on the regime of Saddam Hussein, was a fitting documentary to mark Pilger's thirtieth anniversary of making films for television.

His most effective campaign, in 1979, was for justice in Cambodia, where two million people faced death from starvation and disease in the aftermath of the murderous Pol Pot's overthrow by the Vietnamese. Cold War power politics meant that Western governments were unwilling to give substantial aid just four years after America's defeat in the Vietnam War, but *Year Zero – The Silent Death of Cambodia* raised $45 million in relief. Alongside that humanitarian achievement was the spectacle of Western politicians and their supporters claiming that the aid was not getting through to the people, propaganda discredited by Pilger's follow-up documentary in 1980, *Cambodia – Year One*.

The theme or 'our' (Western) propaganda was explored in *The Truth Game*, Pilger's 1983 investigation into the language used to promote nuclear weapons. After the programme was given a peak-time place in the ITV schedules, it was withdrawn and delayed on the insistence of the Independent Broadcasting Authority until a 'complementary' documentary could be made. This is believed to be the first time that a specific 'balancing' programme has been ordered *before* transmission of the original.

From his first documentary in 1970, which scooped the world in its disclosure of American troop rebellions in Vietnam, Pilger discovered that the rules of television journalism were different from those in newspapers. He had written for the Labour Party-supporting *Daily Mirror* since 1963, following brief jobs as a sub-editor at the news agencies British United Press and Reuters, after arriving from Australia, via Italy, the previous year.

Born in Sydney at the outbreak of World War Two, Pilger was the son of socialists who found little political comfort during the long years of conservative government by Robert Menzies and his successors in the 1950s and 1960s. The youngster enjoyed the surfing life and egalitarianism of Bondi Beach. Taught to swim at the nearby ocean baths by Reg Clark, a notable member of the Bondi Icebergs' Club, then by the Australian Olympic coach Sep Prosser, his powerful style won him swimming medals and gave him a love of the sport, and the challenge of surfing waves, that he has taken through his life. 'I used to feel sorry for people who could not wake up and see or hear the ocean,' said Pilger. 'It is one of the quintessential joys of the Australian coast.'[5] Then, however, much about his homeland remained unknown to him and untold, such as the true history of its native population.

Having decided that a career as an illustrator was not for him, despite his love of art, Pilger completed almost four years' training as a journalist with Australian Consolidated Press and worked on the *Daily Telegraph* and *Sunday Telegraph* newspapers in Sydney, owned by Sir Frank Packer, father of future media magnate Kerry. 'The *Telegraph* was a tabloid paper, though very serious by

London standards, and very right-wing,' he recalled. 'You were allowed no more than sixteen words to the paragraph. The politics of the paper didn't bother me at the time, because I was more concerned about becoming a journalist. My own political thoughts had been influenced by my father and mother, who were anti-Establishment people.'[6]

After 'enjoying going broke' during a summer's freelancing in Italy, Pilger moved to Britain. 'I needed a job – any job,' he said. 'My father had borrowed £100 from his bookie for me, and now that was gone.'[7] Pilger became a sub-editor on the *Daily Mirror*, the biggest-selling newspaper in the Western world. Under editorial director Hugh Cudlipp, the *Mirror* was developing as a serious tabloid and presented Pilger with the opportunity to show his talent for investigative journalism and descriptive writing. He was soon beginning to realize his ambition of travelling the world.

The chance to move into television came in 1969, when actor and businessman David Swift, together with BBC documentary directors Charles Denton, Richard Marquand and Paul Watson, approached him with an idea for an independent company outside ITV and the BBC. They soon discovered the idea was ahead of its time – independents had to wait until Channel Four came along more than ten years later.

'I had an editing business through which I met Charles, Richard and Paul, who came from the BBC to put their films together,' recalled Swift. 'We talked about forming Tempest Films and it was Paul's idea to approach John. We wanted a frontman with a mind of his own, rather like another James Cameron, with whom Richard had worked. Paul thought John was very charismatic, as well as putting forward extremely original, refreshingly radical ideas. We recognized in him some-one who had the voice and charisma to put over those ideas, which we shared. So we all teamed up as partners in this co-operative. Kenneth Griffith was also a partner but there was no cross-fertilization between him and the others at the time, although he later worked with Richard.

'We then approached Robin Scott, who was in charge of BBC2, but he told us that there were no openings for independents. So we started "packaging" ideas. Jeremy Wallington, editor of *World in Action*, was very keen and took on both John and Charles.'[8]

After making two programmes for the hard-hitting current affairs series, Pilger left Granada after clashing with Wallington, who described him as really 'a poet'. But the disagreement between the two had little to do with poetry and everything to do with the politics of television, and whether a maverick could be allowed to decode the consensual language of the medium. On a one-year contract with the BBC between 1972 and 1973, he made five reports for *Midweek*, but only two were broadcast. They were uncontroversial interviews with George McGovern's wife, Eleanor, during the American senator's failed attempt to become the Democratic Party's presidential candidate, and with President Richard Nixon's brother. 'I don't think *Midweek* wanted me as me – they wanted the anodyne in disguise,' said Pilger.[9]

The opportunity to return to television came in 1974, shortly after Charles Denton became deputy head of documentaries at ATV, the ITV contractor for the Midlands, and asked Pilger to present his own series. '*Pilger* was Charles's idea,' he explained. 'It was he who encouraged me to stand up in front of the camera and say "I". He said, "Don't beat about the bush. If that's what you're saying, say 'I'." That was quite unusual, especially for one trained at the BBC. Charles commissioned a series of six films and directed half of them himself.'[10] Denton also produced the first series, before becoming ATV's head of documentaries and, later, programme controller.

The programme, *Pilger*, ran for five series – eighteen half-hour documentaries – and an hour-long special on Australia, between 1974 and 1977. It began on Sundays in a lunchtime slot, before winning peak-time slots on weekdays. When, in 1976, he made a film about the American government withholding aid from 'unfriendly' countries, the IBA insisted that his programmes should be preceded by an on-screen announcement, and a caption, declaring, 'In the programme which follows, reporter John Pilger expresses a personal view.' A similar statement was tagged on to the end. The following year, in an attempt to emphasize this point, the *Pilger* series was broadcast under the banner 'Personal Report'.

In 1976, to satisfy the IBA's demands for balance, ATV also broadcast *This Is Waugh*, three documentaries presented by right-wing journalist Auberon Waugh and directed by Derek Hart, who had been a reporter on the BBC's *Tonight* daily news magazine in the 1950s and 1960s. 'We put Auberon Waugh's films out just before John's series because the IBA wouldn't accept that we would balance his programmes,' explained Richard Creasey, who produced *Pilger* at the time. 'We argued to the IBA that we were balancing Auberon's programmes – they were completely snookered! When you consider the budget for Auberon's documentaries, and the time and commitment spent on them, compared with the much greater budget and time spent on John's, it was a sham. But, running time for running time, Auberon Waugh, right-of-centre, against John Pilger, perceived as left-of-centre, was balance.'[11]

Pilger described the series as 'contrived' and merely serving to bemuse those 'working people in pubs and northern clubs' whom Waugh interviewed.[12] However, film editor Jonathan Morris, who worked on both series, was more receptive. 'Auberon Waugh was a very nice guy,' he recalled. 'In a film about the miners, he chatted to a group of them in a pub. It was interesting because he was saying things like, "You're lazy, you don't really like the job." He was being contentious, saying what he thought, and got quite good reactions from them. The miners came out quite well and the programmes maybe didn't end up as right-wing as they were supposed to.'[13]

Morris recalled that the *Pilger* films 'livened up our department' because they received a lot of attention. 'His great asset was the ability not to write for the *Guardian* brigade but what was then the left-wing *Mirror* readership. He wrote in terrific phrases that communicated with ordinary people.'[14]

Pilger began making one-hour documentaries in 1978, when he teamed up with actor-turned-director David Munro to film *Do You Remember Vietnam*, charting his return to the country he had known through its long years of war and struggle. This allowed him to film for the first time the devastation wrought on the North, which he had previously reported only for the *Mirror*, shortly after the end of the war. 'In an hour-long documentary you can begin to make sense of a complex subject,' said Pilger. 'You can introduce a historical context, let interviews run and employ valuable texture, such as music.'[15]

The switch to one-hour films was also part of a strategy by Richard Creasey, who became ATV's executive producer of documentaries in 1977, to persuade the IBA that there was a distinction between that type of programme and current affairs. Through many 'negotiations' with the Authority, and with Pilger as his primary weapon, Creasey established the right to make 'personal view' documentaries for ITV, an idea whose subjectivity was apparently at variance with the IBA's regulations about objectivity and impartiality. After ATV became Central Television, these programmes were broadcast under the 'Viewpoint' banner. Creasey's impressive line-up of filmmakers included Antony Thomas, Adrian Cowell, Michael Grigsby, Brian Moser and, later, Ken Loach.

'I was aware that there were two, diametrically opposing views,' explained Creasey. 'One was what the IBA thought and the other was what people like John and Antony Thomas thought. Somewhere in the middle was the ATV board of directors and me. The cornerstone of the programme that would change the IBA's mind was John. He was never meant to be aware of that because, as he said to me terribly eloquently early on as I was trying to persuade him to listen to the IBA's point of view, he didn't *want* to hear their point of view. He said, "You sort out the IBA. That's *your* problem."

'John had to believe that what he was saying was true and objective. The IBA believed his films were totally subjective, completely unbalanced and "personal view". I was caught in the middle because John's greatest *strength* was that his programmes were justifiably selective – everything the IBA accused John of was exactly what we wanted. I had enormous respect for his views, but my greatest respect was that he was everything the IBA didn't want. The IBA's regulations concerning factual programmes were all about objectivity and impartiality, and didn't have any space set aside for subjectivity. It was the publisher. ATV, and then Central, could never be sued, provided the IBA had said OK. My job was to negotiate us to a position where they said just that. That was a challenge. Unlike other documentary controllers within ITV, who argued their case to the IBA and either got their programmes through or didn't, I acted as a go-between – between the IBA and John Pilger. It was a question of what I could get away with from the IBA's point of view.

'I never went in as an adversary of the IBA. Most of the programmes I took to them were untransmittable, according to the regulations. The chief escape clause was the one that John hated most – the one called "personal view". It wasn't *meant* to be balanced. My argument, which I eventually lost, was that other ITV companies were balancing John Pilger.

'However, the IBA recognized the need for subjective programmes, because television was in competition with newspapers, which could say what they liked. Once John had done his "Personal Report" series and established that as something that was present, I was able to argue that every documentary is, by definition, subjective and there is a huge difference between that and a current affairs programme, which must be balanced.

'I think David Glencross [the IBA's deputy director of television and, from 1983, director of television] really believed there was a difference between documentaries and current affairs, and the IBA couldn't ignore the fact that these big names making documentaries were winning awards. David had a stack of regulations, which there was no way he could keep. From John's point of view, he was a block. *My* job was to persuade David that this was an opportunity to sail even closer to the wind – and he did. He actually changed more than anyone I've ever known.'[16]

From 1978, Pilger made one-hour films, on average, once a year, most of them shown worldwide, in at least thirty countries. They continued to make ripples and, as the 'docu-soap' era dawned in the 1990s, with programmes showing little pretence of taking on serious issues, Pilger remained almost the only heavyweight to survive on ITV and to continue returning every year with a new documentary. 'John is a signature documentary-maker,' explained Steve Anderson, the ITV Network Centre's controller of factual programmes. 'Whenever he makes a programme, it's one of those events that stands out in the schedules. He's only earned that reputation through being a very outspoken, observant documentary-maker over many years.'[17]

Pilger's programmes have won dozens of international awards. His most prestigious broadcasting honour has been the British Academy of Film and Television Arts's 1990 Richard Dimbleby Award, conferred on him by an establishment body, yet, appropriately, with leading members of the Establishment up in arms. Still, apart from objections by the likes of David Dimbleby and Sir Robin Day, Pilger was given a standing ovation on the night he accepted the award, a demonstration of extraordinary solidarity with a dissident. 'I had a struggle to keep going right from my first documentary, in 1970, through to the mid-1980s,' he recalled. 'During that time, censorship was in the form of a bureaucracy acting on behalf of a political establishment. The ITA, which became the IBA, was only interested in ensuring that the political slant of a film, as they saw it, was towards the Establishment. This is what they called "impartiality", a word now almost Orwellian in the perversity of its opposite meaning.'[18]

The powerful response to Pilger's documentaries during the 1990s was all the more remarkable for coming at a time when people had an unprecedented number of channels from which to choose and considering that Pilger no longer had the *Daily Mirror* to use alongside his films (although he complemented his television work with reporting in the *Guardian* and the *New Statesman*). 'In the 1970s and 1980s, the combination of ITV and the *Mirror* was very effective,' he recalled. 'The two added up to an "event" on television – such as Cambodia – and this had a political impact. That is rare these days, which is a pity, because the political establishment takes more notice of television now and tries to manipulate it. My own survival in television has much to do with the support of executives who care about the medium – they are still there – and the support of the public, who have not been Murdochised, who don't suffer from "compassion fatigue", who will respond intelligently to serious issues in their thousands.'[19]

The dominance of 'infotainment' has erected more obstacles for serious documentaries. 'In the 1970s, getting documentaries on television meant getting them past the regulator,' said Pilger. 'Today, it's about fighting for slots. There is no regulator like the old ITA and IBA – the ITC [Independent Television Commission] doesn't have the same powers. These have transferred to the ITV Network Centre, which both commissions and transmits programmes, leaving the television companies as facilitators. Political censorship has disappeared – along with many serious documentaries. Censorship by a nannying regulator has been replaced by censorship by omission.'[20]

One fine irony of these changes was the transformation in the television bureaucracy's views on Pilger's films. In 1994, David Glencross, the ITC's chief executive, who in his days at the IBA was described by Pilger as 'commercial television's chief censor',[21] warned of 'the triumph of infotainment over both information and entertainment'. In commending three documentaries that had set high standards, he included Pilger's programme about Indonesian repression in East Timor. The man who, year upon year, had once demanded changes to Pilger's films, was now praising the journalist and citing him as an example of factual television at its best.[22] If nothing else, this illuminated, in retrospect, the political nature of a censorship that had dared not speak its name.

For Pilger, the irony persisted. In its review of ITV's performance during 1999, the ITC expressed its concern about lightweight factual programmes and cited Pilger's updated East Timor documentary as one of the few examples of the channel's current affairs output providing high-quality international coverage. It also singled out *Welcome to Australia*, on the continuing plight of the Aborigines, as 'one of a small number of outstanding films . . . documentaries in the best traditions of ITV', with the 'potential to expose, move and disturb'.[23]

In addition to the awards won by his documentaries, and unprecedented honours for his journalism, including the Journalist of the Year title twice, Pilger has been recognized by the academic world, with honorary doctorates bestowed by five universities.[24] The citations referred to Pilger's success in continuing to analyse world events and bring understanding to readers and viewers of issues in countries such as Cambodia and East Timor. In presenting Pilger with an honorary Doctor of Law degree at St Andrews in 1999, professor of philosophy John Haldane announced, 'One may wonder whether, had he not taken an interest in them, the places and people that now concern us would even have entered our consciousness – let alone our consciences.'

Pilger has never been one to report a story and leave it, not to return. His Vietnam and Cambodia documentaries are the best examples of this. 'I've always continued a relationship with subjects and people and countries,' he explained. 'All my films, and most of my published reporting, have sought to understand more about a subject. I keep a watching brief on all these places I have known over the years, such as Vietnam. For me, the unending job is to look behind the stereotypes, the façades, the authorized versions. That's actually my definition of journalism. It's really very simple.'[25]

I. VIETNAM

FROM HIS FIRST documentary, in 1970, John Pilger made waves by reporting the unpalatable – unpalatable to authority, that is. In *The Quiet Mutiny*, a film for *World in Action*, he broke the story of the disintegration of morale among American servicemen in Vietnam, particularly those conscripts of the anti-war generation. These revelations were, according to Phillip Knightley in his definitive study of war reporting, *The First Casualty*, among the most important ever reported from Vietnam. They also brought Granada Television into a conflict with the Independent Television Authority greater than any it had previously experienced in its run-ins with the ITV regulator over the question of balance in the current affairs series.

It seemed natural that Pilger should start his screen career with a programme on the Vietnam War. He had first visited the country in 1965, the year when US Marines landed on the beaches of Danang and the United States' bombing of the North began. He went then to write a feature in his *Daily Mirror* series 'Youth in Action', highlighting the positive contribution of young Britons around the world working for Voluntary Service Overseas. He returned the following year to report the war, and his first dispatch for the *Mirror*, headlined 'How Can Britain Support a War Like This?', signalled the paper's opposition to the war and warned Harold Wilson's Labour government of the political pitfalls ahead if it supported US government policy.

Pilger was given as his brief a six-part series of articles by the veteran American war correspondent Martha Gellhorn about Vietnamese victims of the war.[1] Following its publication in the *Guardian*, Gellhorn had been refused a visa to re-enter South Vietnam. The only American newspaper that would agree to publish the series was the *St Louis Post-Despatch*, although it rejected the feature most critical of America's involvement in Vietnam. Gellhorn later wrote that she had 'toned down' the *Guardian* reports because 'even liberal readers in Britain were not prepared for the full true story'.[2] Her theme was that this was 'a new kind of war', one against civilians. She also wrote about child victims of the war for the American magazine *Ladies' Home Journal*, with 'sugar coating on the pill', persuading the publishers that the feature's motives were humanitarian, not political.[3]

Pilger's newspaper reports from Vietnam also concentrated on the victims. At that time, television viewers in Britain and the United States had seen very little critical reporting of America's war in South-east Asia, although coverage had reached saturation point. Vietnam was the first television war. Lightweight film cameras developed in the 1950s enabled crews to cover the fighting from the frontline. At times, reporters appeared to be taking part in a *Boy's Own* adventure. The images were rarely used to explain the issues, such as why the United States had set up a government in Saigon to crush the National Liberation Front in the South and the communist government of Ho Chi Minh in the North.

'In the early days, the script was always the same,' reported the documentary series *Television* in 1985, ten years after the end of the war. 'Go out with a patrol, any patrol, and get shot at. Action film was guaranteed. It was good television. But the pictures were deceptive. Instead of sounding a warning when, inevitably, the patrol was bogged down, needing air support, television saw only spectacle.'[4] The received wisdom of the Vietnam War was that television contributed to the American public's disenchantment. However, a poll for the US magazine *Newsweek* in 1967 found that, instead of turning public opinion against the war, 'TV has encouraged a decisive majority of viewers to support the war', with 64 per cent of Americans backing it.

Few broadcasters had dared to oppose outright the United States' action, although *World in Action* had in 1964 sounded a warning. It laid out clearly the facts that, following Ho Chi Minh's defeat of the French at Dien Bien Phu in 1954, Vietnam was partitioned, with 'Uncle Ho, the Marxist-Leninist pastry cook', running the country north of the 17th Parallel and French-backed anti-communists governing the South. It was also agreed at the 1954 Geneva conference that the country would be reunited two years later after free elections for a national government, but the South's leader, Ngo Dinh Diem, was a dictator who refused to let the poll take place. When the National Liberation Front (dubbed the Vietcong by the United States) attacked, Diem secured military equipment and 'advisers' from the United States. By 1964, 20,000 'advisers' were assisting the government of the South in their civil war against Ho Chi Minh's forces, but the Vietcong proved to be a difficult enemy, living in the jungle or being sheltered by fellow villagers back in the North.

The *World in Action* team joined a patrol of gunboats and troop carriers along the Delta of the Mekong River in search of the Vietcong. The South Vietnamese soldiers were accompanied by a US Navy officer. On being ambushed, an exchange of fire followed and the troops jumped ashore, but the enemy had disappeared into the thick jungle. The programme questioned the United States' participation in this civil war and interviewed Americans back home, some of whom clearly opposed it. 'There are soldiers over there dying in this war without a name,' said one. 'We're getting nowhere, we're just sitting there. They're not doing anything . . . And you have to pay money to keep them there, so there's no sense in it.'[5]

In 1965, when a US land army invaded, British reporter James Cameron was making a television documentary in Hanoi, the capital of North Vietnam. One of the few Western journalists to report from 'the other side', he was accused of being a 'communist dupe' and his film, commissioned by the BBC, was never screened. In the same year, veteran American television correspondent Morley Safer was victim of a similar accusation after his CBS crew filmed US Marines burning down a village with cigarette lighters. His report was screened on US television and provided the first vivid glimpse of the 'war against civilians'. The US public was similarly shocked when, three years later, news film of the Tet Offensive appeared to contradict the notion that the United States was in control of its war effort. The television pictures showed its troops under siege throughout South Vietnam.

During Tet, respected American television newscaster Walter Cronkite, of CBS, had been despatched to Vietnam to present his own impressions. In *Report from Vietnam*, he stepped out of his role as 'impartial' news presenter, toured the major battle zones and noted that 5,500 US Marines were isolated in Khe Sanh, which had been built up from a small border stronghold into a 'major bastion'. Cronkite concluded that the war could not be won and the United States should 'negotiate not as victors but as an honourable people who lived up to their pledge to defend democracy and did the best they could'.

Although Pilger later castigated Cronkite for his defence of a 'democracy' (in Saigon) that was not a democracy at all, but a corrupt 'torture state', according to Amnesty International, it was a brave gesture for a high-profile television journalist to suggest that his own government's military adventure in Vietnam was not warranted. Shortly afterwards, as the siege of Khe Sanh was lifted, Lyndon Johnson announced that he would not seek re-election as president. Cronkite's broadcast was credited as a major factor in Johnson's decision.

When Pilger reported from Vietnam in *The Quiet Mutiny*, directed by Charles Denton, the *World in Action* film was announced on screen as 'a personal report by the *Daily Mirror*'s special correspondent, John Pilger, Vietnam, 1970, the frontline'. It was a rare occasion when *World in Action* was presented by a reporter in vision. Speaking directly to the camera, Pilger explained that he was returning to Vietnam for the first time in three years. 'I've come back for the final act,' he said. 'No blood, no atrocities, just the rejection of the war by those sent here to fight it, just the quiet mutiny of the greatest army in history.' This prediction of an end to the war was, perhaps, a little premature but understandable after the start of peace talks in Paris and the troop revolts that he uncovered. Thousands of American servicemen among the 400,000 in Vietnam were refusing to follow orders. 'Grunts' – conscripts – complained that they were given most of the frontline action, unlike 'lifers', enlisted men. 'Lifer' officers were being killed by their own men.

Pilger's disclosures were sensational and supported by reports that began to appear in the press the following year. In his book *The First Casualty*, Phillip Knightley wrote, 'The year 1971 saw a series of stories revealing the massive heroin problem among United States troops (about one in ten was addicted), the "fragging," or blowing up by grenades, of unpopular officers (forty-five killed, 318 wounded in 1971), the staggering desertion rate, the number of combat refusals, and the growing tendency to regard an order simply as a basis for discussion.'[6]

One of the strengths of *The Quiet Mutiny* was its irony and black humour, which were to become Pilger's trademarks. His interviews with US officers, who might have stepped out of the pages of *Catch-22*, could make viewers laugh in the middle of a film about a deadly serious issue. There was the bored Psyops [psychological operations] officer who played a 'Wandering Soul' tape from a helicopter ('the ghosts of the ancestors of the Vietcong exhorting them to surrender') while throwing out whole boxes of leaflets. 'Maybe one will score by hitting some guy on the head,' he said. Then there was the Vietcong chicken. 'On this patrol,' reported Pilger, 'we hear a chicken and the captain says it may be a Vietcong chicken . . . Only the grunts can kill that chicken.'

Back in Britain to edit the film, the chicken incident became celebrated. Pilger came face to face with television's guardians of 'impartiality' and 'balance'. In his original commentary, he wrote that the patrol had encountered a Vietcong chicken. Jeremy

Wallington, *World in Action*'s editor, asked Pilger for the source of the statement. 'He asked what proof I had that the chicken was Vietcong,' said Pilger. 'This discussion went on for a couple of days. I don't think I've laughed as much in my life, although at times it was in despair. My informant about the chicken was a US captain, so I rewrote the commentary to say that, and everyone was happy.'[7]

The film showed the arrival of Miss World and 'friends' to entertain the American troops and 'boost morale'. Their cavortings on stage were intercut with fighting from the frontline. The emptiness of the ordinary GIs' role in the war was made clear.

'The grunts are dying,' said Pilger to camera, 'at a level acceptable to both the American military and the American public – another sixty-five this week, about the same next week, and the next, and the next, until the very last American combat division is withdrawn. And so far, for all the words from Washington, only paper soldiers have gone home. The war isn't over, but it is ending. It is ending not because of the Paris talks or the demonstrations at home. It is ending because the largest and wealthiest and most powerful organization on Earth, the American Army, is being challenged from within, from the very cellars of its pyramid, from the most forgotten, the most brutalized and certainly the bravest of its members. The war is ending because the grunt is taking no more bullshit.' (The use of the word 'bullshit' became an issue when the film was sold to Australian television, causing an executive of Channel 7 in Sydney to declare, memorably, 'We can't have any bullshit in the film.' The word was taken out, leaving Pilger's lips to be easily read: a testament to the farce of censorship, with his imposed silence left to attract the attention it invariably did.)

Pilger called the daily press briefings for Western correspondents in Saigon, known as the 'five o'clock follies', a West End farce. In trying to answer his questions, the briefing officer stumbled when asked how many US troops had been wounded by mistake or accident and what the desertion rate was. 'I've never been asked anything like that,' he said.[8] In fact, more than half the US Army deaths were caused by 'friendly fire'. Beneath the circus-like exterior, there was anger among the GIs as Donut Dollies, brought in to entertain them, became, along with unpopular officers, targets of GI disaffection. 'The other day,' said Pilger, 'a Donut Dolly was blown up by a grenade and another was stabbed to death – by grunts.' The film ended with footage of wounded soldiers being stretchered from a US Army bus and The Beatles singing, 'Yesterday, all my troubles seemed so far away . . .'

World in Action editor Jeremy Wallington, who had commissioned the documentary, was enthusiastic about the result, regarding the combination of Pilger and director Denton as 'terrific' and the content as 'quite shocking in terms of its important revelations'.[9] However, an item in *The Sunday Times* almost two weeks after transmission claimed that the United States' ambassador to Britain, Walter Annenberg, had complained to Granada Television's joint chairman, Lord (Sidney) Bernstein, and 'thunderclouds of disapproval are piling up on his lordship's brow'.[10] A week later, the paper published a letter from Lord Bernstein denying that he had received any complaints about the programme. 'Whatever the nature of the reported "thunderclouds of disapproval . . . piling up on my brow",' he wrote, 'they were not caused by *World in Action* and anyway my brow is perfectly normal. Granada has not received any complaint from the United States Embassy about the programme and I was not approached by the Ambassador, Mr Annenberg, or anybody else. What is more I saw the programme and commended it.'[11]

Recalling the incident, Pilger said, 'Granada had a tradition of drama and documentaries, and Sidney Bernstein was of that Jewish-liberal generation who took pride in safeguarding Granada's independence. For the company chairman to write a letter defending a programme would probably be unheard of today, but that's how personally Sidney Bernstein felt about Granada's right to put out a dissenting view.'[12]

However, Lord Bernstein's support masked the fact that the Independent Television Authority's chairman, Sir Robert Fraser, a former civil servant, had already given a dressing-down to Jeremy Wallington and Manchester-based Granada Television's other joint chairman, Denis Forman. This came despite approval of *The Quiet Mutiny* by the ITA, which was then demanding to see all episodes of *World in Action* before transmission, believing that the venerable series carried a left-wing bias.

'In reality, they saw programmes in part and we used to manipulate the system,' recalled Wallington. 'We would say, "If you can get up to Manchester at 4am on Sunday, we can show you the film then – it won't be the final version, but it will be a rough cut." Not surprisingly, they often declined. They saw part of *The Quiet Mutiny* and approved its transmission. After it was broadcast, we got the full ferociousness of Sir Robert Fraser's temper. He had already accused us of being strongly left-wing and only the previous week told Denis Forman that this bias within *World in Action* was simply not good enough and we had to do something about it.

'After *The Quiet Mutiny* went out, Sir Robert went absolutely ape shit and we were hauled down to the ITA's Brompton Road headquarters two days later. I've never known anyone go for us quite so ferociously. He said, "This is absolutely outrageous. Do you realize what you fucking people are doing? You're exploiting the generosity of the Americans, their commitment to broad-casting and publishing. You use their helicopters and their press officers, then you go in and totally abuse the American way of life and way of war." He then said, "What about Russia? What about China? Why don't you do something about *them*?" I made the point that we could not get access to those countries. Denis then told Sir Robert, "I've heard what you have to say and taken note of it." That was the end of the meeting, but we knew we'd lost a lot of Brownie points and were in dead trouble.'[13]

Pilger was reliably told by 'a friendly US embassy official' that Sir Robert (a fellow-Australian) had received a complaint from

Walter Annenberg, the American ambassador and a close friend of Richard Nixon who had funded the American president while in opposition. Leslie Woodhead, who had been joint editor of *World in Action* until the previous year and still worked in Granada's documentaries department, recalled, 'We were quite astonished by the very strong, hostile reaction from the Independent Broadcasting [*sic*] Authority – this was a report by "a man of the hard left" . . . he had failed to do his homework . . . it couldn't conceivably be true that American soldiers were shooting their own officers, and . . . this shouldn't be seen. Of course, the strange thing is that, within months rather than years, John Pilger's view became the common currency.'[14] Also, *The Quiet Mutiny* was distinguished by being presented with several awards, including the Golden Dragon at the Cracow Festival of Short Films and another honour at the Chicago Festival.

What was not strange, of course, was that British commercial television's regulator was a man of trenchant Cold War views and that Sir Robert's notion of getting at the truth in Vietnam was to demand a series of 'balancing' programmes about the Soviet Union and China! As a result, Wallington and Woodhead found themselves discussing ways of covering events in those countries. 'We resolved to do something about it,' recalled Wallington. 'Then, we obtained the diaries of Major General Grigorenko, a Russian dissident. We couldn't get access to Grigorenko, who was being held in a mental hospital in Russia, so we invented the form of the drama-documentary with *The Man Who Wouldn't Keep Quiet*.'[15] Woodhead went on to make many more films in this genre on otherwise unobtainable subjects behind the Iron Curtain, including *A Subject of Struggle*, about the Red Guard trials during the Cultural Revolution, *Three Days in Szczecin*, reconstructing the Polish shipyard strike, and *Invasion*, dramatizing the Soviet Union's crushing of opposition in Czechoslovakia. 'For us, the dramatized documentary is an exercise in journalism, not dramatic art,' explained Woodhead.[16]

Even before *The Quiet Mutiny*, Granada had agreed with the

ITA to 'balance' *World in Action* programmes over the series as a whole, rather than to dilute the message by striving to achieve balance within each programme. One episode broadcast shortly after Pilger's Vietnam documentary was a film profile of Conservative Prime Minister Edward Heath.

After leaving *World in Action*, Pilger filmed a ten-minute report from Vietnam for the BBC2 series *Midweek*. It was never screened. He revealed that Americans were still fighting there in 1973, even though they were supposed to have pulled out following the Paris Peace Agreement in January of that year and President Nixon's announcement of 'peace with honour'. 'They had sent in private contractors who were really military in civilian dress,' explained Pilger.

'Companies were contracted by the defence department to hire "retired" American officers to do exactly what US officers were doing when they weren't retired. It made a mockery of the Paris Agreement. Moreover, with this "ghost army" in place, the Americans intensified the bombing. More Vietnamese civilians were killed in those three years to 1975 than in all the years back to 1965. The official version was that America had retired from the war and Nixon had solved everything. The truth was the opposite – they were still up to their necks in the war. That was the essence of my report for *Midweek*. Clearly, they didn't like what it was saying and they refused to broadcast it. It was reminiscent of the BBC ban on James Cameron's filmed report from Hanoi in the mid-1960s.'[17]

One of Pilger's most enduring professional characteristics is that he refuses to let go of a story that he believes should be told, and he returned to the subject in a thirty-minute documentary for his own series, *Pilger*, in May 1974. In *Vietnam: Still America's War*, he interviewed pilots and Marines disguised as civilian contractors, and pointed out that the cost of the war was still being paid by real civilians – the Vietnamese.

Pilger began, 'The war in Vietnam ended officially in January last year. American troops were seen to go home. Mr Nixon said it was peace with honour at last and those of us who had reported the war through its longest years also went home. For, as a news story, the whole boring mess of Vietnam was finished. So much for the fantasy. Since the Paris Agreement and so-called ceasefire, more than 70,000 soldiers and civilians have been killed in Vietnam. But this film is not about day-to-day slaughter of soldiers. It's about the continuing and growing and forgotten suffering of the Vietnamese people in what is still, almost incredibly, America's war.'

Pilger reported that the Pentagon still had thousands of senior officers, pilots and technicians in Vietnam, many described as 'civilians', as well as embassy officials. American secretary of state Henry Kissinger had said there were 2,300 still involved in the war. In the US embassy in Saigon alone, Pilger discovered 15,000 'diplomats'. The American military headquarters was now called the Defense Attaché's Office and most Americans there were on the payroll of sixty US companies.

One who had transferred from the United States Air Force said that, if they were not there, 'within a week to possibly a month North Vietnamese and Vietcong would possibly overrun this country'. Pilger interviewed 'Big' Will Plunkett, who described himself as an 'adviser' on a vital power plant, radar and surveillance base, equipped by the USAF. Another, asked if he thought the war had been worth it, replied, 'Every limb that was lost and every individual sitting back in a veterans' hospital now and every death – I think it was all worth it, I really do.'

Pilger reported that President Nixon had the previous month asked Congress for $2 billion in aid for Vietnam, most of which would be for military purposes. Less than half of one per cent would help civilians maimed by the war. 'There are still only three hospitals for civilian amputees in Vietnam,' said Pilger. 'They still make their own limbs and wheelchairs, and they still can't meet the demand.'

A nurse at a Quaker hospital told him that most injuries were caused by children stepping on unexploded mines and no money

allocated for this in the peace agreement had been forthcoming.
She showed him some of the children who had suffered such
wounds, said that 61 per cent of patients' injuries were still war-
related, compared with 65 per cent in 'the last year of the war',
and added, 'The biggest thing for me is that American aid
continues here and, as long as the arms flow into Vietnam at
the rate they are flowing in, people are going to go on getting
shot, new mines are going to go on being laid and people are
going to go on being injured.' Earl Martin, an aid worker with the
Menonites, showed Pilger more of the victims at a refugee village.
'People are a lot hungrier now than they were a year ago,' he said.
An American embassy official was seen awarding the Best Child of
the Month prize at a Saigon orphanage for children born illegiti-
mately of American fathers. 'If hostilities continue,' said Pilger,
'orphans are being made every day.'

At the Continental Palace Hotel in Saigon, where Graham
Greene wrote much of his novel *The Quiet American*, Pilger
mused, 'The Quiet Americans are back, doing almost exactly
what they did ten years ago, passing out millions of dollars and
favours and arms to a client regime they wish to prop up.'

Not all Americans thought the war had been worth the
carnage. 'I have seen the war here when I was here in '66 and
'67,' said one of them. 'I have seen it here as a civilian. And I don't
think it was worth it. That's my opinion.' But the majority
thought otherwise. 'Fifty-two thousand American deaths are less
than we lose in traffic in one year,' said another man. 'You don't
even miss it. It wasn't a great war, but it was the only war we had.'

Vietnam: Still America's War compared US casualties with the far
greater Vietnamese death toll and the atrocities committed against
Vietnamese civilians. At My Lai, scene of the 1968 massacre, in
which an American unit killed 130 men, women and children in
cold blood, a survivor told Pilger, 'The troops came in, rounded
up the people in this area and shot them.' Six years later, many
bodies were still in ditches. The film ended at a Vietnamese
military cemetery. 'There's a waiting list for burials at this military

cemetery near Saigon,' said Pilger. 'There are 70,000 graves . . . That's exactly the number of dead in sixteen months of "peace with honour".'

Although *Vietnam: Still America's War* was only Pilger's third documentary, it was the second to win international awards, which included a Bronze Hugo at the 1974 Chicago International Film Festival. Although he did not film the end of the Vietnam War, Pilger was one of the last journalists to leave on the day of the American evacuation, 29 April 1975, shortly before the North Vietnamese and the National Liberation Front entered Saigon, which they renamed Ho Chi Minh City after their leader, who had died six years earlier at the age of 79. Pilger's front-page report for the *Daily Mirror* the following day was headlined 'Epitaph for a dirty little war', and captured the madness and confusion of those final hours. His reports were also collected together in a book, *The Last Day*, published on 4 July 1975, American Independence Day.

Two days before Saigon fell, Pilger was notified that he had been granted a visa to North Vietnam. 'I had hoped that I would be able to enter Saigon with the winning side,' he said. 'By the time I reached Hanoi, a journey that began on an American helicopter and ended on an Aeroflot flight from Moscow, the war was over by two weeks.'[18] Pilger had tried for six years to report the war from 'the other side', as only a few Western journalists, such as Wilfred Burchett and James Cameron, had done. When he finally arrived in the North, he described in the *Mirror* a 'moonscape' created by the American bombing, which had also caused deafness in tens of thousands of Vietnamese and forests that no longer had birds or animals because of the bombs and chemicals dropped on them.

Continuing to cover the repercussions of the war, Pilger travelled to the United States to make a documentary for the *Pilger* series about South Vietnamese refugees settling in Fort Smith, Arkansas. 'I was very impressed by the way the Vietnamese were received,' he said. 'It was a sad story, really, about traumatic change. A lot of people – civil servants, soldiers in the Saigon

regime's military, movie stars, entrepreneurs, bar girls – had fled
the end of the war. It was a universal story of refugees and people
who had left their homeland with very mixed feelings, who were
completely dislocated and disaffected, in this case in the very alien
surrounds of Arkansas. But the Americans running the reception
centre were humane, imaginative and did their job very well, and
a lot of those refugees did well for themselves in the US. The
colonel who famously shot a Vietcong in the centre of Saigon
went on to run a KFC concession on the West Coast.'[19]

'To Know Us is to Love Us', broadcast in August 1975, began
with film of gravestones at Fort Smith, where the town's dead of
the war lay, and Pilger's expression of admiration for these
Americans who, unlike others embittered by the 'defeat and
humiliation', were prepared to help the Vietnamese. 'Every
day, out of the sky, came hundreds of Vietnamese,' he said.
'Twenty-four thousand of them on the edge of town, waiting for
people to come and sponsor them. But every one was a reminder
that the boys in the graveyard there died for nothing.' A surviving
American soldier told Pilger that he had not expected to see any
Vietnamese again.

When the refugees arrived, they were photographed, interviewed and finger-printed, before waiting for sponsors throughout the United States. Interviewing them, Pilger discovered that
some people had left loved ones back home, in some cases with
just two hours' notice of their departure. One woman said she was
all alone, homesick for her family and cried every day. A man said
he felt guilty at leaving his family behind. A former Saigon film
star told Pilger that he had made propaganda films for the CIA's
Phoenix Programme.

In Fort Smith, a local farmer who had sponsored a Vietnamese
woman and her nine-year-old son said they would perhaps marry
one day and the boy would probably work on his farm. A woman
said she did not understand why Americans had fought in
Vietnam and she wanted to help by sponsoring someone. Voluntary agencies vetted sponsors to ensure that they were of 'good

character and good pocket,' said Pilger. An official told him, 'The government's prime concern is that these people will not become welfare recipients. You are helping them until they become financially independent.'

Together with this generosity of spirit, Pilger found poignant tales of settling into a new country. The chief accountant of a Saigon bank, now working in a fast-food 'House of Pancakes', had 'fallen from the top of his own society to the bottom of his heap . . . dishwasher in a plastic food palace. He is now a member of a minority.' Some refugees were seen learning English parrot fashion, reciting, 'Pie is good to eat.'

Here, in the southern heartland of the United States, Pilger was able to respond to criticism thrown at him throughout the war. 'Some of us who attacked the war in Vietnam year after year were called anti-American,' he said. 'The charge, of course, was ridiculous. In their hearts, the good people of Fort Smith, Arkansas, wanted to win the war in a simple, ruthless way: to wipe the enemy, whoever they were, off the map. They weren't allowed to do this and so they knew their sons were dying for nothing, and yet today in this deeply conservative town there are no signs saying, "Go home, gooks", as I expected. Instead, there is much generosity and charity and decency and confusion. They still don't know why they couldn't win the war and why the world turned against them.'

The story of the United States' final withdrawal from Vietnam was one that Pilger was inspired to turn into a screenplay, based on those events that he covered for the *Mirror* and in his book *The Last Day*. The result, also titled *The Last Day*, eventually reached the screen as a seventy-five-minute BBC television play in March 1983, but not until after it had been turned down by major Hollywood studios. Pilger had planned it as a feature film and shown a 'treatment' to British producer David (now Lord) Puttnam, who liked it and offered it to the major studios in Los Angeles. 'I saw the assessment reports from the studios and all were highly favourable,' recalled Pilger, 'but most carried the comment that the film would never be accepted politically, that the time was wrong.'[20]

More than a year later, in February 1979, director Michael Cimino's picture *The Deer Hunter* was screened at the Berlin Film Festival, only weeks after the Chinese had attacked Vietnam, following similar incursions from Cambodia over a long period by Pol Pot's Khmer Rouge. Delegations from the Soviet Union, Cuba, Hungary, Czechoslovakia and East Germany withdrew from the festival in protest at the film's screening at such a time. But *The Deer Hunter* won five Oscars. It was certainly a powerful film, but its portrayal of the Vietnamese as 'gooks' and oriental sadists was, as Pilger later wrote, a falsehood of history and racist. In one sequence, they were seen forcing American prisoners to take part in a game of Russian roulette. Pilger had never come across this and neither had any other correspondent. Much later, Cimino admitted that it had been added for dramatic effect.

'*The Deer Hunter* was a very ambiguous film,' explained Pilger, 'but it was basically peddling the old John Wayne message that the Vietnamese were oriental demons and the Americans were fallen heroes. It presented the invaders as victims. It was one of the most manipulative films I'd seen. I went to see it in Leicester Square, in London's West End, and Scarth, my then wife, had to restrain me from protesting there and then. I was incensed by the film's rank dishonesty.'[21]

Pilger's own screenplay, which he had written 'on spec' after the idea had been rejected in the United States, was then taken up by BBC special features producer John Purdie, who had made *Sailor*, the popular documentary series about the Royal Navy, and *The Hong Kong Beat*, which followed the British Colonial Force in Britain's last colony. For budgetary reasons, *The Last Day* was shot on videotape in a BBC studio at Shepherd's Bush, with a handful of sets, over fourteen hours in just one day. This drama was mixed with actual footage.

Dan O'Herlihy played the American ambassador, David Suchet was the CIA station chief and Charles Dance a British journalist who was based partly on Pilger himself. 'He was meant to look like me, but his character was a conglomerate of four or five correspondents,' explained Pilger. 'As the production progressed, I realized that the character was becoming more and more like me. I had wanted the journalist to be a witness, not a star. So, rather embarrassed by this, I hacked away at Charles's part and reduced it to a minor character. I fear I may have upset him.'[22]

The play, shown on BBC2 in March 1983, was generally well received. Philip Jacobson, who had known Pilger as a fellow-reporter in Vietnam, wrote in *The Sunday Times*, 'Pilger's debut as a TV dramatist . . . is fairly successful in capturing the frenetic, often surreal, flavour of Saigon at the time . . . To my surprise, and pleasure, *The Last Day* resists the temptation to trumpet the broad, often irrational streak of anti-Americanism which I think has sometimes damaged Pilger's reporting from South-east Asia.'[23]

Stanley Reynolds, who had received a torrent of abuse from readers when only a month earlier he had given Pilger's documentary *The Truth Game* a scathing review in the *Guardian* (see Chapter 8), was more generous about *The Last Day*. 'It would take an extremely silly man not to be engrossed by the film,' wrote Reynolds, but he continued his earlier theme of mocking Pilger's clothes and appearance by describing Charles Dance as 'a tall, handsome man in pressed jeans, an ironed shirt and flowing blond locks' and asking, 'Was this the Bondi Bombshell himself?'[24] (A reference to *Private Eye*'s nickname for Pilger as 'the Blond Bombshell from Bondi Beach'.)

The right-wing *Daily Telegraph* still managed to continue its policy of slating almost every programme that Pilger made. 'Television's most favoured propagandist showed the Americans, especially ambassador Dan O'Herlihy, as deluded by their own rhetoric,' wrote Sean Day-Lewis. 'The Vietnamese who clung to US protection even as he flew away were labelled "scum". The Communist victory was accepted by implication as an historic inevitability that could only be opposed by the wicked and the foolish.'[25]

In 1978, Pilger had returned to Vietnam to discover the results of this victory in what became the first of his regular one-hour documentaries. For the first time, he was able to see the whole country at peace. 'When I travelled to the North just after the war ended, I knew immediately that it had to be filmed,' he said. 'It wasn't enough to write about it for the *Mirror*. I'd seen the ruin caused by the bombing and heard extraordinary stories of human survival against the "rolling thunder", the longest bombing campaign in history.'[26]

For *Do You Remember Vietnam*, Pilger teamed up for the first time with producer-director David Munro. It was a partnership that was to yield some of his best documentaries, notably those on Cambodia, Vietnam's neighbour, into which the American bombing had been secretly extended by Richard Nixon in 1969.

Munro was from a family of actors and directors. His grandfather, Ivor Barnard, was a notable character actor in many great British films of the 1930s and 1940s, as well as alongside Humphrey Bogart in director John Huston's 1953 satire *Beat the Devil*; his father, Hugh, had been a director in the early days of ITV and later switched to acting; and his brother, Tim, was also an actor. Since starting in the business in 1961, Munro had acted in the first series of the children's television drama *Orlando*, alongside film star Sam Kydd, and in the West End revue *Chaganog*.

Between jobs, he started to write and was assistant producer of the 1971 short film *Conquista*, the story of a sixteenth-century meeting between a North American Indian and a horse belonging to the Spanish Conquistadores, which he conceived with director Michael Syson. Munro made his directorial début four years later with the feature film *Knots*, which he adapted from R.D. Laing's book examining the social and psychological entanglements of a group of actors. In 1976, he produced *Eclipse*, another psychological drama in which a writer reveals to his dead brother's widow that he is not sure whether he was responsible for the death of his domineering sibling. Munro also produced and directed the television drama *Edmund Kean – The Sun's Bright Child*, starring Kenneth Griffith, but his concern for political and social issues led him into documentaries.

'In the mid-1960s, I had been quite politicized,' said Munro. 'Later, I wanted to use my craft as a filmmaker to make films about things I actually cared about. I had always been very angered and fascinated by war. Then, I read a story about a particularly horrific rape, thought something ought to be done about it, phoned Anna Raeburn, whom I'd never met, and said I wanted to do a film about the subject. As a result, we made a *Man Alive* documentary, *Rape*, for the BBC. The aim was to raise consciousness. Shortly afterwards, John and I met and made *Do You Remember Vietnam*.'[27]

It proved to be a successful first venture for the team of Pilger and Munro. 'It was a meeting of minds,' said the director. 'We have a similar temperament and ideology. I think I introduced an element of visual storytelling that hadn't always been in John's films.'[28] Pilger recalled, 'David's newness was a distinct advantage. He has a very sympathetic way of looking at subjects and sees them, as I do, from a human level, a people level. I opposed the war in Vietnam as a response to what I saw – a war of rampant technology directed against human beings for no purpose other than that of power.'[29]

With photography by Mike Dodds, Munro elicited tranquil pictures of peacetime Vietnam that included almost primitive scenes of peasants at work amid a landscape of calm far removed from the war years. This added another dimension to the tales of horror that Pilger told. 'The images capture the smell and taste of life today in Vietnam,' Munro told Carl Gardner of *Time Out*. 'In this kind of TV journalism the image has a subliminal role to play. The words are important but the image is not just illustrative. The images work their own argument.'[30]

Pilger had planned the documentary to be the first on Vietnam by a returning Western journalist, arranging the trip unofficially through a Sydney travel agency by organizing the film crew into a 'tour party'. However, Tom Mangold of *Panorama* landed at about the same time and his film was screened three weeks earlier. Pilger did write about his visit in the *Daily Mirror* in June 1978 and the *New Statesman* three months later. 'The BBC did a spoiling operation,' he said. 'They heard that we were going. They were following us everywhere! We had a wonderful guide, six-feet tall, called Tuc, who gave up trying to take us to what he thought we should see. Each day, I gave him a list of what we wanted to see – drugs, prostitutes, rehabilitation camps!'[31]

Do You Remember Vietnam opened with black-and-white still photographs of the war's wounded, including the famous image of Kim Phuc, the girl running from a napalm attack, and pictures of the American bombing, interspersed with film of children happily playing in Saigon in peacetime. In a very effective opening piece to camera, Pilger related the war to the lives of viewers who had seen its images on the television news day after day. 'Vietnam ran longer than *Z Cars* and at times had popularity ratings higher than *Kojak*,' he said.

Adding that he had returned to discover what life was now like in the country, Pilger explained, 'The film that follows is one impression. Considering that foreigners are almost extinct here now, the scope of my travels from Hanoi to Saigon has been generous. By my standards, it has been limited. Some nostalgia may creep into this film but, if it does, it will be nostalgia purely and simply for the endurance of the Vietnamese people, whom I admire. And, in case you've forgotten, let me remind you of what they endured for thirty years.'

There followed film and tales of the horrors inflicted on Vietnamese civilians. It indeed was a personal, and sometimes nostalgic, return to a country that had become dear to Pilger's heart, and it benefited from the insight of his long experience. 'The film gave a very sympathetic view of the Vietnamese people and was quite harsh on the Americans *and* the victors,' said Pilger later. 'We filmed the so-called re-education camps and were very critical of them and what I described in the documentary as Stalinist brutalities. So those looking for the "communist sympathiser" angle would have been disappointed.'[32]

It was on this visit, said Pilger, that he finally saw Vietnam as a country, not a war. 'Arriving in North Vietnam is like stumbling on the aftermath of some great, unrecorded disaster,' he said in the film's commentary. Whole landscapes had been laid to waste as the result of the Americans' Operation Hades, the spraying of the herbicide and carcinogenic poison dioxin on areas such as forests. In the former capital of Hue, where a thirty-two-day battle took place between the North Vietnamese and the American Marines during the 1968 Tet Offensive, Pilger found a vintage Austin Cambridge car, enshrined by Buddhist monks as the 'holy car' – because one of the most memorable images of the war's early days was that of a Buddhist monk burning himself to death beside an Austin Cambridge, in protest against the regime installed by the Americans in Saigon.

Bomb craters peppered Route 1 from Hanoi to Saigon, the 'Street of No Joy', as it was nicknamed by the American pilots who bombed it. As he reached the 17th Parallel, which divided Vietnam, Pilger recalled lying in mud, under fire, with US Marines in 1967. 'The helicopter that brought me was blown up in the mud as it tried to take off again,' he reported. 'Such were the appalling conditions of war – six months of mud, six months of dust.' He noted that most of the Marines were volunteers brought up on John Wayne films and escaping the ghetto, and added, 'I should say that few soldiers have endured such conditions and have resisted so bravely for so long, in the cause of nothing.' This was another indication of the lack of personal animosity that Pilger held for the Americans who pursued a war that he considered atrocious. It often translated into sympathy and affection for the ordinary Americans sent to fight for something that many did not understand.

In the northern town of Vinh, people were facing famine, with rations of only six pounds of rice per person, per month, less than that allowed to those who suffered the same fate in Bangladesh four years earlier (see Chapter 4). Food was running out in some cities and the people were being moved to new 'economic zones'. This was the result of crop failures and the enforced union of the northern and southern economies.

Pilger also discovered some of the ingenuity that helped the North Vietnamese to beat the American military. At Cu Chi, fifty miles from Saigon, he met a man known as Minh No 4, a former Vietcong leader who was now a tourist guide. There, he was shown a network of underground tunnels that had been the National Liberation Front's largest and most secret base in South Vietnam. When pursued by the Americans, they performed a vanishing act and the main tunnels were never discovered. Pilger even slid his 6ft 3in frame into one of the tunnels, in a 200-mile network, which had formed part of the unrecorded story of the Vietcong's resistance to a foreign invader. 'No wonder they won,' he said, emerging into daylight.

Visiting what had become a war crimes museum, he met a woman called Tao, a guide who had suffered terribly during the war, imprisoned and tortured in the 'Tiger Cages' on Son Son Island, run by the Saigon regime. Pilger called this a 'Disneyland of carnage', with rusted tanks and bombs, and fiendish weapons like the 'daisy cutter', a precursor to cluster weapons that sprayed minute pieces of shrapnel. Tao described how she had been paralyzed by her wartime experience in the cages. Asked how she felt when the war ended, she replied, 'It seemed that I fly! I didn't walk!'

At China Beach, near Danang, where the US Marines landed in 1965 and established the greatest single military base in the world, Pilger found rusted landing craft. He recalled flying out from Danang with Sergeant Melvin Murrell's WHAM (Winning Hearts and Minds) unit in 1967 as it distributed rice, comics, 7,000 toothbrushes and electric flush lavatories in an attempt to win the 'hearts and minds' of the Vietnamese.

Film of Vietnamese cycling peacefully along the streets of Hanoi in 1978 was juxtaposed with footage and black-and-white stills of the massive bombing of the city by the Americans over Christmas 1972, when the capital endured the greatest aerial bombardment in history. 'The bombs hit every third house, every third block of flats and a kindergarten,' said Pilger. 'After that, it was found that some 30,000 children in Hanoi alone had lost their hearing because of the bombing on that Christmas.'

In Saigon for the first time since his departure on the last day of the war, Pilger found a bustling city that had not experienced the bloodbath predicted by the Americans. This was a particularly personal moment for the reporter who had known these streets so well, and the camera followed him as he strode through them, like a tourist, recording his first impressions. He was pleased not to see crippled children selling jasmine petals and maimed veterans of the Saigon army who 'came at you like crabs' during the war. Bar girls and pimps were still evident and everyone appeared stunned to see Westerners back there.

Pilger then visited drug-addicted prostitutes at a rehabilitation centre near Saigon. One told him, 'I have accepted Uncle Ho's wisdom. Listen, mister, nothing could be worse for me than what it was.' Pilger's film crew also went to a 're-education' camp where heroin-addicted former soldiers of the South Vietnamese army were subjected to constant exercise, yoga and acupuncture. 'These are the true faces of suffering of a society colonized, vandalized and bombed,' said Pilger. One of the ex-soldiers to whom he spoke was terrified that he would say something 'out of step' with his re-education. At another camp, former soldiers were seen pushing ploughs through paddy fields.

These scenes balanced others in the documentary that portrayed the Vietnamese people's heroic struggle. Pilger pointed out that some of those taken away for re-education had not been heard of again and suicides in the camps were not uncommon.

Pilger recalled the death of 150 babies in a 'so-called mercy plane' when it crashed on take-off during the American-initiated

Operation Babylift at the end of the war. He regarded this as no more than a publicity stunt to win sympathy for the American cause in Vietnam. At the Young Flower School, an orphanage, Pilger found that children were receiving 'care that has a national priority'. They were told that their fathers were foreigners who had come to their country, but they were not denigrated.

However, he said, this benevolence had to be weighed against the horrors of 're-education' and government propaganda. In Saigon, loudspeakers told people when to get up in the morning and what they should think. 'The Vietnamese have been liberated from war, but have they been liberated from insidious, old-fashioned suppression?' asked Pilger in his final piece to camera. 'Re-education camps, loudspeakers, book burning, watchdogs in red armbands everywhere. But balance this against the civilized takeover after thirty years of bitterness and new hospitals and orphans being lovingly cared for and an absence of tension, violence and war.' Predicting that Vietnam would liberalize in the way that President Tito's Yugoslavia had done, Pilger spoke of the people's fear of becoming embroiled in the Cold War between China and Russia. This was a timely warning, with Chinese troops mounting attacks across the Vietnamese border shortly afterwards and the Vietnamese ousting that country's ally, Pol Pot, from Cambodia. 'The Vietnamese have many battles yet to win,' said Pilger.

Once film editing was completed, Pilger and David Munro made a curious decision about the documentary's title, *Do You Remember Vietnam*. 'I hate question marks in titles,' said Pilger. 'I think they say: we can't make our minds up. So we decided on a farcical compromise – we kept the question and took off the question mark!'[33] Shortly before transmission, in October 1978, Pilger contributed a two-page feature to *TVTimes*, setting the scene for viewers. He wrote that none of the film crew had previously been to Vietnam and he was fascinated by their reactions, which ranged from horror to elation. He also reported that the napalm that had disfigured children during the war was now used worldwide. He had recently seen its result in Eritrea, which he had visited for the *Daily Mirror*.

Do You Remember Vietnam was well received in Britain. In the *Observer*, Clive James described it as 'a good programme, unglib, awkward to handle, hard to ignore' and added, 'Tom Mangold of the BBC had already been back to Vietnam, so Pilger was obliged to cover some of the same ground, up to and including a tour of the war museum in Saigon. But he has been reporting on Vietnam for most of his adult life, so it was not surprising that what he had to say about what he was seeing carried the implication that he had seen plenty more.'[34]

Considering the film's broadly sympathetic attitude towards the Vietnamese, it was more surprising to see positive comments in the United States, where people were still coming to terms with their country's defeat in the war. *Do You Remember Vietnam* was enthusiastically reviewed by the trade newspaper *Variety*, which was all the more remarkable for the fact that American publications review very few British documentaries. *Variety*'s critic, 'Arro', wrote, 'It is almost impossible to be objective in reviewing this program, but the sheer expertise and dedication shown in its making demand the highest praise. Every picture makes its point and the marriage of visual images to the script, the meaningful interviews and the razor-sharp editing all combine to erect a monument to the documentary art.'[35]

True to form, the *Daily Telegraph* in Britain was almost alone in criticizing the documentary. Television reviewer Sean Day-Lewis described it as 'an anti-American sermon', although he conceded that Pilger had 'cast some doubt on the "intellectual barbarities" of the Communist "re-education" programme'.[36] (Charges of anti-Americanism aimed at Pilger are discussed in Chapter 5.)

Pilger's concern for the American veterans who had fought in the war 'in the cause of nothing' was the subject of his documentary *Heroes*, screened in 1981 and directed by David Munro, and which became the title of his best-selling book. The veterans had never been recognized with monuments and parades, as had other Americans fighting foreign wars. Pilger sought out five disabled veterans, including US Marine infantry officer Bob Muller, who in 1978 had formed Vietnam Veterans of America with the aim of raising public awareness of the neglect of the veterans. Many of the three million who had fought in Vietnam returned home to a life of unemployment, alcoholism, drug addiction and divorce, and more were dying as a result of the chemicals used in the war – especially Agent Orange – than were killed on the battlefield.

'The original idea was to compare the treatment of veterans in America and those who had fought in Ireland, and how we treat the veterans of unpopular wars,' explained Pilger. 'But the comparison wasn't right. The treatment of British troops who had served in Ireland was different – they were accepted back into the community. So the film concentrated on the special problems of the veterans of Vietnam. The film was the story of how the American establishment had shunned the greatest army of its longest war and blamed its soldiers for not winning.'[37]

In *Heroes*, Pilger and Munro illuminated the madness and confusion of the Vietnam War. It opened with black-and-white still photographs of the war and the sound of gunfire, accompanied by Buffy Sainte-Marie's wistful *The Universal Soldier*. A clip from *The Quiet Mutiny* followed, in which Pilger reported that the US Army was facing a challenge from within. In *Heroes*, Pilger described the Vietnam War as 'a constant Hallowe'en night, always growing brutally real' and 'the hours of waiting for the seconds of terror'. He reported that a poll the previous year had shown that 62 per cent of Americans believed that Vietnam veterans had 'fought in the wrong war, in the wrong place, at the wrong time and were suckers'.

'This is a film about those suckers,' Pilger said, in his opening piece to camera. 'They made up the greatest volunteer army in history, they came home not to parades but to a purgatory of silence, shame, indifference, or they came home in plain wooden boxes marked "This way up – unviewable". Today, there is not a single national monument to their dead, as if America's longest war didn't happen.' In these few sentences, Pilger summed up the veterans' case and destroyed the myth that it was a mostly drafted army who fought in Vietnam, with 80 per cent choosing to go and nineteen being the average age of American soldiers. Six years after the war, statistics showed that 60 per cent of combat soldiers were alcoholics, 40 per cent were drug addicts, 60 per cent of black veterans could not find a job, thousands were in prison and their divorce and suicide rates were the highest in America. 'The report which gives these facts was suppressed by the government,' explained Pilger, 'because what it says breaks the faith.'

He recalled seeing Muller, who had been shot through the spine, twice before. In 1972, the US Marine was thrown out, in his wheelchair, along with other protesting veterans at the Republican Party's convention in Miami Beach, after heckling presidential candidate Richard Nixon. Five years later, Pilger saw him giving a speech at City Hall, New York, on Memorial Day, talking about the public's 'guilt' and 'hang-ups' over Vietnam.

In his original research, for a *Daily Mirror* article in 1980, Pilger had found Muller in a down-at-heel office at the unfashionable end of New York's Fifth Avenue. This former Marine's eloquently stated arguments were a strand running throughout *Heroes*. 'That stigma of the war has now eroded on to the veterans,' said Muller. 'The responsibility of explaining the war has fallen on to the veterans' shoulders . . . America's uncomfortable with the Vietnam War, but you've got to heal from that war, just like a wound.' Muller revealed that 55,000 veterans had committed suicide – almost as many as had died in Vietnam.

Jay Thomas, a Marine who was badly wounded in the arm and back during the Tet Offensive, was decorated with two Purple Hearts. 'I always wanted to be a Marine and I always wanted to experience war,' he told Pilger. 'I was raised on it. Every birthday, I got cap guns and helmets and canteens, played war all the time when I was a kid. The television was always war movies – *Sands of Iwo Jima, Back to Bataan* – and I got used to that John Wayne idea that to be a Marine that's how you become a real man . . . John Wayne never served a day in his life in any military service, but he's the greatest Marine we had.' Thomas went to Vietnam out of what he saw as patriotic duty but found the reality very different from that in Hollywood films. 'When I first got there and I saw people torn to pieces, blown in half and shot through the head, I went into shock,' he recalled. He blotted out the horror by taking drugs and returned home a heroin addict and on the verge of alcoholism.

Over film of Vietnamese being interrogated by American troops, Alonza Gibbs, who was wounded by mortar fire in 1966, said, 'Some of the atrocities that went on in Vietnam really shouldn't be told. In our battalion, we had a commander that didn't know how to call in air strikes. He was too proud and too pompous to let his forward observer do it and he called in air strikes and a third of his company was either wounded or killed and, in order to cover up that fuck-up that he did, they gave him a Congressional Medal of Honor, which really just completely pissed me off. I had friends to die in that, friends to be wounded in that, and some of them are right here in Philadelphia, crazy as bed-bugs. The treatment that some of the people did to the actual people that we were fighting I couldn't go along with. I saw people interrogated and, because they wouldn't answer, they were thrown out of helicopters.'

He described watching as detonating cord was wrapped around Vietnamese prisoners and ignited. His battalion commander offered a case of whisky to the first soldier to chop an enemy's head off, and one of his men did it. Others kept ears as souvenirs. 'We're supposed to be the American fighting people,' added Gibbs. 'We don't do this kind of thing.' Although having two-thirds disability, he had received compensation of only $48 a month for the previous two years.

Dave Christian, a captain who returned home in 1969 with 40 per cent of his body burned by napalm, as well as back, leg, neck, head and arm injuries, said he was restricted to his hospital room after telling *The New York Times* that America should 'either fight a war to win or get the hell out'. Christian pointed out that, unlike the veterans of World War One, who returned en masse, those who fought in Vietnam came back one by one.

Over newsreel film, Pilger's commentary recalled the homecoming ceremonies staged for American troops returning from Europe in 1919. There was footage of the 1980 parade when fifty-two American hostages returned from Iran. 'Broken bodies and impermissible pain were not on display,' he said of that most recent event. 'Of course, they were officially approved heroes, who would embarrass no one with confessions of guilt or failure, victory in their case having been bought, conveniently, with money.'

Bob Muller's organization received little support from the government, in contrast to the official Veterans' Administration, whose huge budget, said Pilger, 'goes mostly to those who went to war and came back winners'. Those veterans of earlier wars had received special privileges from the GI Bill, which gave them employment, housing, education and medical rights. When the bill was reintroduced by President Lyndon Johnson in 1966, Vietnam veterans were awarded $10 a month less than those who had fought in Korea a decade earlier.

Mike Sulsona, a Marine whose legs were blown off by a landmine in 1971, causing him deafness and a crippled hand, had received no compensation and spent two years working on a seven-foot sculpture of a veteran with one leg. Determined not to venture on to the streets of New York in his wheelchair and to avoid arguments about the war, Sulsona told Pilger that his applications for a disabled parking permit had repeatedly been turned down. As a result, he had accrued parking fines of $7,000 over nine years by parking his car illegally. After having his car registration taken away, Sulsona visited the courthouse, walked into the judge's chambers, took his tin legs off and put them on his desk. Acutely embarrassed, the judge and his secretary walked out. The veteran made it clear that he was not moving and eventually

persuaded an official to return his registration and reduce his fines
to $1,000 – they were later cut to $75. Leaving the courthouse, a
female official told Sulsona, 'Unfortunately, you were in a war
that nobody really cared about.'

All administrations had neglected the Vietnam veterans, reported Pilger. When President Jimmy Carter assumed office in
1977, he promised 'top priority in our job-training programmes
. . . to young veterans of the Vietnam War' but had done
nothing. During the presidential campaign of 1980, Republican
candidate Ronald Reagan had criticized Carter for recommend-
ing a 'stingy' 10 per cent increase in the GI Bill and added that
'our war was a noble cause'. 'In March 1981,' said Pilger,
'President Reagan asked Congress to cut programmes specially
designed to help Vietnam veterans find jobs, finish their education
and be treated for drug addiction and alcoholism.'

The success of Vietnam Veterans of America was due to one
issue, said Bob Muller – the devastation caused by the poisonous
defoliant Agent Orange, which was used to wipe out jungles and
left a legacy of cancer and kidney and liver problems in veterans
and their children, not to mention the Vietnamese people. Pilger
explained that dioxin, the poison in Agent Orange, was 1,000
times more destructive than thalidomide, and that almost eleven
million gallons of it had been dumped on Vietnam. Film was
shown of Cu Chi, near Saigon, transformed from thick forest into
a wilderness, and pictures of deformed children from a 1979 *World
in Action* programme. 'It was the seeds of this unique horror that
the GIs brought home with them,' said Pilger. Most of the Agent
Orange used was made in Michigan by the Dow Chemical
Company, which also produced napalm, and was being sued
by veterans. Although the company insisted the onus was on the
veterans to prove their case, it had brought its own lawsuit against
the American government, claiming that the Pentagon failed to
protect its soldiers from the effects of the chemical.

The film described 'other Vietnams', notably in Central America. Turning the front pages of *The New York Times*, which traced

the United States' involvement in Vietnam, Pilger said, 'The same headlines are appearing today, the same jargon such as "escalation" and "light at the end of the tunnel", the same delusions. 'Delete "Vietnam" and write in "El Salvador", and the stories seem almost identical . . . The American ambassador to El Salvador, Robert White, has said that the war in that country is caused by social injustice and the real terrorists are the regime backed by Mr Reagan and Mr Haig, and supported, of course, by the British government.' For criticizing his government for sending military advisers to support a regime whose security forces had killed thousands of its own citizens, White was sacked. 'This is film from Vietnam and El Salvador,' announced Pilger. 'Can you tell the difference?'

Of the Vietnamese, Pilger said that they were now almost isolated in the international community, with only the waiting arms of the Russians to turn to, whom they distrusted as much as the American, French, Japanese and Chinese invaders. 'In the wake of the war's devastation, there is now famine,' he reported. 'Rations are less than even during the war years – about half the food needed for a healthy survival. There is no milk any more for children over the age of one and unexploded mines and bombs kill children every day. Like its refusal to help its own victims of the war, the American government has denied all help to the people of Vietnam and so, too, has the British government. On the other hand, both governments are building the greatest military machine ever in preparation for a war that may well end all wars, and for that one heroes need not apply.'

This final piece to camera featured a slightly more low-key Pilger than usual. It was as if he was saying the film belonged to the veterans, the story was theirs. Nigel Mercer's film editing did much to make it communicate their agonies. The programme has been screened thousands of times by the veterans on university campuses and in public halls across the United States and is so well known in veterans' circles that they have even produced a parody of it. '*Heroes* was our eloquent voice – it spoke for us,' said Bob

Muller. 'It was, in its own way, a heroic film and we are all indebted to John Pilger and David Munro.'[38]

In December 1981, seven months after *Heroes* was broadcast, Bob Muller was one of the first American veterans to return to Vietnam since the war. In a hastily arranged trip, David Munro took a film crew and made a documentary, *Going Back – A Return to Vietnam*. Pilger was unable to go. 'It all happened very quickly when John was in Australia,' said Munro. 'Bob and I had become friends while making *Heroes*. One day in New York, I was looking at *Hearts and Minds* [a 1974 American documentary film about the United States' involvement in Vietnam] and Bob was in it. We watched it and he was in floods of tears. Afterwards, I said, "The war is still going on in your mind, isn't it?" He replied, "Yes." So I said, "But don't you realize it's finished?" He said, "I know, but it's in my mind." Then I said to him, "The only way you will ever realize that the war is over is to go back to Vietnam." And he told me, "Don't be crazy."

'A year later, in October 1981, I was lying in my bath in Fulham, the phone rang and Bob said, "You're right. I want to do it, but how can I?" He came over and I called the Vietnamese ambassador here – there wasn't one in America. He was very receptive because of the documentaries that John and I had done – *Do You Remember Vietnam*, *Year Zero* and *Heroes* – and thought it was a wonderful idea. In December, I went to the Vietnam Veterans of America office in New York, where it was even more chaotic than normal, and there was a telegram saying, "You are expected in Hanoi in eight days' time." I had no one to finance the film because ATV was about to become Central Television and couldn't guarantee any film, so I took a gamble and made it on my American Express card. It changed the lives of the four vets.'[39]

In 1982, a monument to the American dead in Vietnam was finally erected in Washington and, three years later, a parade was organized in their honour in New York. Ronald Reagan appointed a special presidential envoy to Vietnam and discussions began on the American MIAs – those missing in action – although the Library of Congress in 1985 listed only 2,477 of them, compared with tens of thousands from the country's other twentieth-century wars. That year, the Vietnamese handed over the remains of twenty-six American servicemen and material evidence relating to six others.

In 1995, Bob Muller travelled with Pilger and Munro when they returned to Vietnam to reflect on the changes in that country twenty years after the end of the war. Pilger had been back again in 1989, when he discovered a more open society. South Vietnam was then producing enough rice to feed the whole country. Now, in this new documentary, he was able to tell the story of a country facing its 'last battle' – against the pressures of 'globalization' and 'the market'. 'It was about the terrible ironies that were besetting Vietnam, how it was being drawn into the great, globalized economy and the loss of many of the gains it had fought for against invading powers,' explained Pilger. 'Another form of imperial control had exerted itself through the World Bank, the International Monetary Fund and the other global institutions. This had produced a very visible consumer class in the south and Saigon was beginning to look the way it did before 1975, with all the old divisions of rich and poor. I found that disconcerting.'[40]

The opening of *Vietnam – The Last Battle* combined film of the American bombing and Vietnamese victims with the voices of American presidents extolling the virtues of the war, including Ronald Reagan insisting, 'It's time that we recognized that ours was, in truth, a noble cause,' and Richard Nixon talking of 'peace with honour' in 1973 and adding, 'Let us be proud of the young Americans who served with honour and distinction.' This was followed by film of the 1975 American evacuation.

'Twenty years ago this week, I reported the end of the Vietnam War from here, the American embassy in Saigon, where the last American troops fled from this helicopter pad on the roof,' said

Pilger, from the embassy rooftop. 'Vietnam had marked the last stage of the longest war this century, a war in which the greatest tonnage of bombs in history was dropped, in which more than two million Vietnamese were killed and a bountiful land devastated. This film is not just about an anniversary but will try to rescue something of Vietnam's past and present, from Hollywood images that have pitied the invader while overshadowing one of the epic national struggles of the twentieth century. Above all, it's about a remarkable people who've paid a high price for their victory over a superpower. Indeed, the terms of their long-awaited peace are still being negotiated.'

On China Beach, near Danang, Bob Muller sat in his wheelchair recalling that his original belief that he had gone to Vietnam 'to repel this massive communist invasion from the North on the freedom-loving people of the South' was a myth that was soon exploded by the experience of fighting there. This was the reality that America's three million servicemen who went there had to confront.

Recalling that twentieth-century epic struggle of America's enemy there, Pilger spoke of Ho Chi Minh's declaration of independence from the French in 1945 after being freed from the Japanese invading force during World War Two, which was intended to align his country closer with the United States. Instead, the Americans opted to interpret it as part of a Chinese-led conspiracy. He interviewed Mrs Thai Thi Tinh, a Vietnamese woman from Hanoi who had lost five of her eight children – her two elder sons dying in the subsequent war against the French and her youngest son killed fighting the Americans – as well as her doctor husband in the French war. Pilger and Munro filmed Mrs Thai visiting the grave of her eldest son, wearing the medals won by her husband and children.

Overlooking the Gulf of Tonkin, a coalminer recalled the devastation caused by the American bombing, which Pilger explained was greater than that inflicted on Dresden. Moving on historically, film of the countryside was accompanied by Pilger's commentary about the United States' post-war trade embargo, which the British government joined after Margaret Thatcher became prime minister, making Vietnam more reliant on the Soviet Union.

The international embargo was broken only after the Vietnamese government's announcement, in the late 1980s, that it was embracing the free market and foreigners would be welcome. On the streets of Hanoi, the traditional bicycle was joined by the motor car as foreign investors arrived. 'America effectively runs the currency, Japan dominates the money lending, Singapore the property market and Taiwan and Korea the sweatshops,' said Pilger. 'The French and Australians are doing nicely, too, with the British not far behind. And, as the roads fill up and the air pollutes, the Vietnamese sink deep into debt to those who once profited from their suffering.'

A Vietnamese sociologist told Pilger that life was happier but capitalism posed the danger 'of losing what we have gained with so much sacrifice, losing this ideology, of justice, of equality and so on'. 'Market socialism' was being embraced, explained Nguyen Xuan Oanh, a senior economic adviser to the Vietnamese government. People were speaking more openly, said Pilger, but the price being paid for foreign investment was in the Vietnamese being used as a cheap labour pool, with wages as low as £20 a month. In the countryside, the system of rich landowners and tenant farmers was returning, with co-operatives closing down. Cheap labour was commonplace and education was no longer free.

Much of the health service had also been privatized and a doctor at Hanoi's Bach Mai hospital, who had survived President Nixon's 1972 bombing campaign, showed Pilger around the crowded building in 1990s Vietnam. Throughout the country, there was a higher proportion of underweight and stunted children than in any other in South-east Asia, apart from Bangladesh.

In another world of wealth and privilege, foreigners could spend their money on golf clubs and exclusive resorts that were

opening in Hanoi and Saigon. An Australian property developer
told Pilger that his target market was Australian, British, American
and Canadian expatriates. 'I make no apologies for the fact that it's
exclusive, because these things will only work if they're exclusive,' he added. Pilger held up a British Department of Trade and
Industry guide for investors in Vietnam, which described the
country as a goldmine because of its low wages. The Vietnamese
government economic adviser preferred to describe this as 'in-
expensive labour'.

A happier development was the return of many Boat People
under a programme sponsored by the European Community. A
fisherman said he had missed his 'motherland' and felt secure back
in Vietnam. A 'regreening campaign' was also spawning success,
with film of people planting trees to reclaim millions of hectares of
forest destroyed by the chemicals dropped on the countryside by
the Americans.

However, a reminder of the continuing horror caused by this
was the sight of deformed babies in a Saigon hospital, where the
vice-director revealed that 266 had been born there the previous
year and the proportion had been the same since the early 1970s.
'Deformed babies are more likely to be conceived in Vietnam
than almost anywhere in the world,' said Pilger. 'In 1994, the link
between the herbicide known as Agent Orange and cancer was
confirmed by the Australian government. American and Australian veterans have now been compensated for what Agent Orange
did to them. The Vietnamese have received nothing.'

Pilger returned to the network of tunnels at Cu Chi and found
that they were now a tourist attraction and had been widened to
make them more visitor-friendly. How was Vietnam perceived by
the rest of the world, he asked. Recalling that the 1968 My Lai
massacre was not reported in the United States for more than a
year, and then represented as an American tragedy, Pilger tackled
the way in which Hollywood consistently depicted the war. Film
producer David (now Lord) Puttnam said that the biased images
of pictures such as *The Deer Hunter* would take 'generations and

generations to eradicate' but blamed the United States, not Hollywood – 'This is a nation that can't deal with complexity,' he added.

The Vietnamese sociologist said that her people were beginning to look to the future and forget 'about this period', although the Americans 'had not recovered from this failure'. Pilger noted that Vietnam had finally been granted a place in the New World Order, at the price of a society based on exploited labour and divisions between rich and poor. 'Perhaps the most difficult battle of all has only just begun,' he said, 'and, this being Vietnam, it is far from lost.'

2. BRITAIN

ALTHOUGH PERHAPS BEST known for his foreign reporting, some of John Pilger's most incisive documentaries have been made in Britain, where he has lived since the early 1960s. (Interestingly, *he* says 'based', not 'lived', as if he is about to move on.) Starting on the *Daily Mirror* as a sub-editor, he was sent as a feature writer to the North of England for two years. To some of his colleagues in London, this was like being exiled to outer Mongolia. For Pilger, it was an experience similar to that of George Orwell, who in the 1930s was commissioned to write *The Road to Wigan Pier*, about the unemployed in the industrial North, and discovered another world.

'Those two years sharpened my understanding of industrial history and struggle,' said Pilger. 'I also discovered English people with an unfettered warmth and tolerance who were able to express emotions, politically, like the miners of Durham. It was my grounding for life in this country. Most of all, it gave me a strong sense of the class divisions and social attitudes that still dominate this country. In Britain, there are two histories. There's the written history for the élite – and I don't necessarily mean the toffs. The élite can change, as under Tony Blair. Then there's the partially written history of ordinary people.'[1]

Pilger returned to London in 1965 and began his travels around the world, but invariably balanced foreign assignments with his reporting of issues in Britain. In 1971, he travelled to the West Yorkshire industrial town of Keighley to make a second documentary for *World in Action*, about the life of a dyehouse worker. *Conversations with a Working Man*, directed by Michael Beckham, featured twenty-six-year-old Jack Walker and was intended to present the views of a rank-and-file trade unionist: his life, struggle and hopes.

'Jack Walker represents the silent core of this country,' said Pilger at the beginning of this documentary, 'those millions of average Britons who feel they have no voice in 1971, who have little power to control their way of life. People who belong to and believe in trade unions. People whom politicians and many of us in the press and television now readily blame for this country's economic problems. It is the Jack Walkers who pay the majority of this nation's taxes and yet take home a wage which barely accounts for a decent existence.'

Pilger followed this family man and trade unionist's daily life, leaving his council house to catch a bus at 6am and arriving at the textile dyehouse half-an-hour later, 'in the confinement of steam and fumes and pipes', with only roof windows providing light. Walker, who had worked in factories for fifteen years, talked of his attachment to the machines, including 'Big Bertha', and working in temperatures of up to 120 degrees centigrade. Alongside this, Pilger juxtaposed the monotonous working day of Walker's wife, Audrey, on a pram factory production line.

Outside work, Walker showed pride in his garden, where he grew marrows, leeks, potatoes and flowers. 'I'm a bit of a Dahlia man, like,' he said. 'In fact, last year I won the best award in the Shipley Show for my Dahlias.' With £20 a week take-home pay, the best labouring wage in the area, and his wife earning £10 a week, Walker acknowledged that he was better off than many people. His biggest hope was for his daughter to get well educated and not have to work in the mills.

'Probably the only way to keep her out,' he said, 'is if she turns out to be a grammar girl and a fella with a Jaguar comes along and she's gone into the middle class or something like that. I'd like her to be a lot better than we are.' Walker talked of his own aspiration to run a small gardening shop but the likely reality of spending the rest of his working life in the dyehouse. Husband and wife were shown going through their household budget, with weekly bills amounting to £22.85, leaving 'a couple of quid spending money' and the challenge of finding the cash to buy a dress for daughter Beverley.

Walker had never been on strike, but he and 250 other employees were sacked eight years earlier by Denby dye works, near Shipley, for being members of a trade union. The lockout that followed, with pickets watching as non-union labour was bused in for less money, had been the longest industrial dispute in British history. Resentment and bitterness at 'blackleg' labour was still strong.

'The Denbys, at that time, did not want the trade union movement in the works,' explained Walker. 'They came and said that if you want to work here after today it's a non-union shop, on our conditions. And the very next day each man, of the 250 of us, was sacked . . . I think it's diabolical that, after our fathers, like my father, served in the trade union movement for all the years that he did, that any management in this country can turn round and say, we don't want a trade union movement at all and you're sacked . . .

'You've got a job, one's married, one's got a family. All of a sudden, you feel secure and then you get a thing like Denby where they say every one of you is sacked, not for bad work, not for stealing or anything like that. All of a sudden you're sacked and, believe me, John, the bottom's dropped out of your life. From once where you felt secure, you've no longer got security. You're just something that's stood on a picket line. A lot of people said we're lazy buggers. You're stood there sixteen months. I have pride and I think that most people in our firm have pride in their work.'

Pilger joined the Walker family in Bridlington, on the Yorkshire coast, which was their traditional holiday destination for two weeks of the year. Their budget would not run to hotels on the front. Instead, they stayed in a guesthouse on a 'bed and cruet' basis, where the landlady cooked the food that they bought.

Asked by Pilger about 'all these people who go to the Costa Brava and Majorca', Walker replied that in his factory 'you could count them on one hand'. He had been 'off the island' only once himself, for a holiday on the Isle of Wight.

'If Audrey's money didn't come in,' he said, 'there would be very little difference between my father's way of life and my way of life.' Walker had saved £100 during the previous three years, the only money he and his wife had been able to put aside after putting in a combined working week of eighty-two-and-a-half hours. He hoped to accumulate £500 to give daughter Beverley on reaching the age of 21 or for getting married, 'so that she's got a better start than me and her mother had'.

Conversations with a Working Man was Pilger's second film for *World in Action* and his last. Although the series was renowned for its radical, uncompromising style and crusading zeal, as well as 'the appearance and drive of a self-confident editorial', according to acclaimed documentary-maker Norman Swallow,[2] Pilger clashed again with the programme's editor, Jeremy Wallington. This time, he was told that use of the description 'working class' had a political bias and must be changed to 'working heritage', and that the term 'the people' could not be used because it was Marxist. Pilger put the incident in the same league as the 'Vietcong chicken' debate after filming *The Quiet Mutiny* (see Chapter 1). 'It was farcical,' he said, 'but it had a serious meaning.'[3]

David Swift, as Pilger's business manager, was used as a mediator. 'I think Jeremy was frightened by John's radicalism,' said Swift. 'I was hauled in by him and told to ask John to revise some of the script by taking some words out and putting others in. Jeremy was concerned that the programme would reflect on him. He felt he was employing a subversive who was going to undermine his company and his own position.'[4]

In fact, Wallington later claimed not to have been enthusiastic about the idea of *Conversations with a Working Man* from the beginning. 'John Pilger had discovered the working man!' he said.

'I felt there was an intense naïveté about it. We had an enormous row over the programme in the editing stages. It was then that I formed the view that John was a poet rather than a journalist. That's no disrespect to him, but the kind of factual journalism to which I was dedicated at that time, with everything copper-bottomed, wasn't John's world at all. John was part of the "new journalism" of that time, where opinion had to be part of the story.'[5]

However, Wallington failed to acknowledge the shadow of ITA chairman Sir Robert Fraser and the unspoken ideological pressure that his earlier carpeting at the Authority's headquarters, over *The Quiet Mutiny*, had represented. Ironically, there was no backlash from the Independent Television Authority over *Conversations with a Working Man*. Pilger refused to work with Wallington again. 'At that time,' said Pilger, 'British television was pushing out the boundaries of free speech, tentatively. Those like Charles Denton were bold. Those like Jeremy Wallington put a toe in the water and ran away. It had absolutely nothing to do with poetry versus journalism – although I'd recommend Jeremy read a bit of Shelley – and everything to do with the principle of journalists and filmmakers as agents of people, not authority.'[6]

When, in the 1980s, acclaimed filmmaker Ken Loach made *Questions of Leadership*, a four-part series giving trade unionists a chance to air their views and their charges of betrayal to a Conservative government by some of their leaders, he ran into far greater difficulties with the broadcasting establishment and the programmes were banned. Both Loach and Pilger had run into trouble because they had given ordinary people an opportunity to speak on television in their own terms. (See Chapter 8.) There had been few such opportunities.

John Boorman, who went on to become a successful film director, made *Citizen 63* for the BBC in 1963, although this five-part series about the day-to-day lives of five different people concentrated mostly on those whose jobs carried some authority. The following year, in *The Newcomers*, Boorman recorded over six months the lives of a young married couple awaiting the birth of their first child. Then, in 1975, producer Paul Watson and director Franc Roddam made their acclaimed fly-on-the-wall series *The Family*, about the working-class Wilkins clan of Reading.

In the 1990s, this observational-type programme was transformed into the 'docu-soap', which rarely gives true insight into serious issues affecting people and whose overriding aim is to entertain, rather than inform. As a result, programme-makers exploit the passiveness of viewers and allow themselves to be exploited by the willingness of their subjects to 'perform' for the cameras.

Back in 1970, when Pilger started making television documentaries, Britain had a new Conservative government. One of its main policies was 'expansionism', which resulted in more exports for British firms and a buoyant time for financial companies and property speculators. But the boom was followed by bust and the government faced bitterness from the workers as strike actions loomed. In January 1974, Prime Minister Edward Heath faced a dispute with the miners at the same time as coping with the international energy crisis that resulted in much of British industry working a three-day week. Unemployment was rising and, within a year of the new Labour government taking office in 1974, it exceeded one million for the first time. Eventually, Labour imposed cutbacks in public expenditure, which were extended drastically when the Tories returned to office in 1979.

In the 1960s and 1970s, in his work for the *Daily Mirror*, Pilger regularly reported on the stark realities of working people's daily lives. A year after making *Conversations with a Working Man*, he wrote about a forty-eight-year-old agricultural worker in Dorset who earned just £16.20 a week. Then, in January 1974, Pilger joined miners underground at Murton colliery, in County Durham, when pit men nationwide banned overtime in an effort to get a better wage. He observed the cramped, filthy and dangerous conditions endured by the miners, just a month before they called a national strike. The Tory prime minister, Edward Heath, called an election and lost. At the time, this was heralded as a victory for the miners, although Pilger would later lament that the price was paid during the bitter strike of the 1980s, when the miners lined up against the Conservative government of Margaret Thatcher.

In 1974, during the first series of *Pilger* for ATV, he returned to the theme of injustice suffered by ordinary people. In *Guilty Until Proven Innocent*, directed by John Ingram, he tackled the subject of 'the imprisonment of people without trial, of innocent people, first offenders, petty offenders and children', who represented 'many thousands who, almost unnoticed in the last few years, have been caught in the system which has become almost as chaotic and repressive as in countries without even the pretence of our Bill of Rights'.

Treatment and conditions inside prisons for those who had committed no crime was the subject of this documentary. Out of about 50,000 people remanded in custody by magistrates each year, Pilger reported, more than half were found not guilty, fined or given a conditional discharge. He was, he said, not questioning the right of magistrates to remand villains in custody but the judgement of those who were overcrowding prisons with people who should not be there 'on a whim or in keeping with the politically inspired climate of law and order'.

The Home Office gave Pilger access to a typical prison, where he found remand prisoners kept three to a 12 foot by 7 foot cell, 'airless and stinking, with only a slop pot each', for twenty-two hours a day and mixed with villains. One woman complained that a request to a prison warder to see a booklet setting out her rights was ignored. A man compared staying in a prison cell for fourteen weeks with living 'in a pig sty'.

Pilger highlighted the case of 'Helen', who had been remanded in Holloway Prison, North London, on charges of stealing a pair of slippers, although she had never previously been convicted of any crime. Eventually, she was given a conditional discharge. 'Helen' gave an account of her prison day, starting at 7am, dressing, rushing with ninety-six other remand prisoners to use four toilets, eating breakfast and returning to her cell. The toilet conditions were 'disgusting' and the food 'revolting'. Between then and lunchtime, all prisoners were locked up, apart from being let out for half-an-hour's exercise, which consisted of walking anti-clockwise round a large yard. Lunch was eaten in cells and, at 3.30pm, prisoners were given a tea meal of bread with margarine and jam, plus a cup of tea. They were then locked up until the following morning.

Another remand prisoner, eighteen-year-old Edward Shapell, had spent fourteen months in prison before being acquitted. He saw others as young as fourteen who had been refused bail. On subsequently signing on the dole, Shapell was told that he could not be credited with unemployment stamps for during that period and, as a result, could not claim benefit or get work. 'When I came out, I'd lost an awful lot of weight, I looked very ill,' he said. 'But I'd seen kids who'd been much worse off than me.'

One of two sisters who spent four weeks in Holloway before being acquitted of drugs charges said she had been denied necessary medicine for most of her time there. A psychiatric patient, who had suffered two nervous breakdowns and attempted suicide three times, was remanded to Winston Green prison after being charged with petty theft. A magistrate refused him bail, disregarding the fact that he was being treated with drugs at the time and could not remember what he stole or why. He spent eight weeks in a cell with two hardened criminals and, when his case came to court, was given a suspended sentence.

London solicitor Peter Sherrett, pointing out that British law presumed accused people to be innocent until proven guilty, claimed that some magistrates felt their task was 'to teach people a lesson' and tough sentences would act as a deterrent. 'My own experience, from the contact I've had with people after they've come out of prison, has been completely to the contrary,' he added. 'People come out with feelings of resentment and bitterness if they've been treated unfairly.'

A judge, Crown Court Recorder Victor Lisseck, agreed that
the remand system had to change. 'There are far too many people
at the present time who are remanded in custody,' he said. 'I think
one of the reasons is particularly the person who is arrested and
brought before a court very quickly . . . and the bench or the
magistrates concerned are prepared to remand in custody without
really investigating the matter in any great depth.'

Asked why some magistrates accepted police objections to bail
on 'the flimsiest of objections', Lisseck replied, 'A good magistrate
. . . would not necessarily accept police objections to bail just on
the face of it.' He blamed 'inexperienced' magistrates and ones
who were prepared to let it 'all be sorted out later on'.

At the end of the film, Pilger reported that an average of
twenty-seven prisoners had attempted suicide each year between
1969 and 1971 at Risley Remand Centre – 'the final despair of
people on remand, who have no one to reassure them of their
rights and to whom British justice must seem as remote as their
freedom'.

The documentary was immediately followed by a short statement from the secretary of the Magistrates' Association, A.J.
Brayshaw. He acknowledged it as 'a profoundly disturbing programme' and agreed that the subject of prison conditions needed to
be tackled. However, on the issue of remand, he considered the
film to be 'slanted and tendentious and emotive'. Brayshaw said
that viewers had not been told the reasons for those featured in
Guilty Until Proven Innocent being denied bail.

He then read out the conclusions of a Home Office working
party's report, just published and 'full of sensible suggestions',
which included more information being made available to courts,
breaking bail becoming a specific offence and the idea of creating
more bail hostels for accused people with no fixed address. He
concluded, 'There are cases where it's necessary to keep people in
prison until their trial, but it should only be done when it is
necessary to get a fair trial. And, if the programme put that point
over, it's a very good thing.'

This 'official' response, presented in the style of a pre-war BBC news programme, when even the radio presenters wore dinner jackets, was seized on by the *Guardian*'s television critic, Peter Fiddick. 'I don't know whether the secretary of the Magistrates' Association feels pleased with his performance after yesterday's John Pilger report but from where I sat he simply hammered another well-balance nail in his own side's coffin . . .' wrote Fiddick. 'I know not by what backstage expressions of outrage he contrived this access but it seems a proper function for a television critic to observe that in terms of communication he might have better saved his breath.' [7]

In fact, the Magistrates' Association response was added to keep the IBA happy over its rules about impartiality. 'We had completed the film and Charles Denton said that we had to have something from the Magistrates' Association,' recalled Pilger. 'That probably came from the IBA. But, like Granada, throughout the *Pilger* series ATV would try to second-guess the IBA. I was never sure which one it was.'[8]

Then there was the related issue of the conspiracy laws, the subject of a film in the *Pilger* series the following year. In *A Nod and a Wink*, again directed by John Ingram, he demonstrated how the charge of conspiracy was used as a means of political suppression in Britain, comparing this with statutes in police states such as Brazil and the Soviet Union, which used 'a vague law' to silence and imprison people for their political or religious views.

'You may be surprised to know,' Pilger said in the film's introduction, 'that we have begun to use almost exactly the same kind of law in Britain. The law is conspiracy . . . A law made before the Middle Ages and never sanctioned by Parliament has been dug up quite recently to be used virtually unchanged as a tool of suppression. Let's be quite clear – this law can affect us all. To be charged with conspiracy, you need not have committed any crime or have even been associated with a crime. Indeed, it's likely that all you will have done is committed, or thought of committing, a trivial civil wrong like trespassing. But, if there are more than two of you, the trivial offence of trespassing, which is not a criminal offence, can suddenly become conspiracy, for which you can get a huge fine and up to life imprisonment. And at your trial you can be convicted on rumours, on who you are, on how you live, on what your friends are. "Conspiracy," an English judge said recently, "can amount to a nod and a wink." '

Over black-and-white film of then Young Liberal Peter Hain, a white South African exile, taking part in anti-apartheid demonstrations and a still photograph of him being carried away by police at a 1969 Davis Cup tennis match in Bristol, Pilger talked of the student's campaign to draw attention to racism in his native country and his conviction at the Old Bailey three years later on a charge of conspiracy to trespass, for which he was fined £200.

In answer to his question as to why a conspiracy charge was used against him, Hain explained, 'It was the only way that they could prosecute me . . . They would not have been able to get me on "trespass" on its own without sticking "conspiracy" in front of it because trespass is a civil offence and it would have required the owners of the ground to sue me for damages. Since there wasn't any damage, nothing could have been done about it. It showed people that there isn't really a right to demonstrate in Britain . . . I don't think there's any doubt that it's had a restraining effect on my colleagues and other people involved in the field.'

Pilger then turned to industrial action and the case of Shrewsbury building workers who, in 1973, went on strike to protest against the use of non-union labour and its acceptance of dangerous work conditions, resulting in pickets being charged with conspiracy to intimidate and imprisoned. One of those was Ricky Tomlinson, later to become a successful actor in television programmes such as *Brookside*, *Cracker* and *The Royle Family*, as well as two Ken Loach films.

'Our view was that it was something that was brought up on the spur of the moment to try and deter the working-class people from getting a decent living and decent conditions,' said one of those who was charged. 'There hasn't been any strikes or union action at all since the trial itself. Now the conspiracy law's been used against union members, union leaders, nobody wants to be a leader, nobody wants to be in the union. Therefore, the safety regulations on building sites are now deteriorating very badly.' A solicitor told Pilger that conspiracy charges were increasingly used in new areas, including industrial relations, and 'that terribly dangerous concept of guilt by association so easily gets translated into a conspiracy', so that everyone involved was treated equally, whatever their part in the alleged charges.

The distributor of a contact magazine, *His & Hers*, explained that, although a charge brought under the Obscene Publications Act was dismissed in 1971, he was still prosecuted. His solicitor told Pilger that a conspiracy charge was the only means of prosecution left, although it, too, failed in court. 'It was used, perhaps, as a political end,' he said. 'Pressure had been put on Parliament in 1974, and Parliament wasn't going to pass any further legislation to deal with obscenity or anything to do with public morals.'

Film followed of nine protesters trying to stage a sit-in at Broadcasting House, in London, to demand more BBC Welsh-language television programmes, a decade before the creation of S4C (Sianel Pedwar Cymru) gave them their own channel in their own country. At the time, in 1973, the nine Welsh Language Society demonstrators were charged with being equipped to cause criminal damage, carrying a roll of Sellotape and two glass cutters. Six months later, conspiracy charges were brought against them and, when the case eventually reached court, it was thrown out after just two days.

Twenty-one Iranian demonstrators who staged a peaceful sit-in inside their country's London embassy in protest at the Shah's murder and torture of political prisoners were charged with conspiracy to trespass. Pilger pointed out that Iran was one of Britain's major trading partners, as a major supplier of oil.

Fourteen people were about to be put on trial, he reported, charged with conspiracy to incite disaffection among soldiers, after

Special Branch officers had raided the offices of *Peace News* and discovered leaflets belonging to the British Withdrawal from Northern Ireland campaign. Monsignor Bruce Kent, later to become chairman of the Campaign for Nuclear Disarmament, and nine other people including a professor of law and an Army brigadier had written to the *Guardian* newspaper stating their intention to hand the same leaflet to soldiers at the Army recruiting office in Bradford in an attempt to demonstrate their support for those charged and for freedom of speech. After they did so, the chief superintendent of West Yorkshire Police informed Kent that the police would be taking no action. 'Why was their case so different?' asked Pilger. 'Why weren't they charged, like the others? Are the conspiracy laws reserved for certain groups only?'

Summing up, and relating the issue to the making of his programme, Pilger said, 'If the Director of Public Prosecutions, a civil servant, decided that the film you have just seen was not in the public interest, he could prosecute the producer, the cameraman, the sound man, the lighting electrician and me under the laws of conspiracy. That sounds absurd, doesn't it? But, as I see it, the laws of conspiracy are so loose and all-embracing that it could happen.

'You see, these laws are a dragnet, the perfect weapon to use against critics of the prevailing order and political opposition. Shouldn't Parliament be more concerned with the fairness of the law, under which a person can be found guilty of one crime without any proof that they've actually committed a crime? And is it not fundamental to our democratic system that politically contentious laws like conspiracy should be strictly defined by Parliament and not left to the mercy of policemen or civil servants to use as they wish? A great many lawyers are appalled by the use of the conspiracy laws and the Law Commissioners recommended the abolition of conspiracy to trespass because of, and I quote, "its vagueness and unfairness". But the laws of conspiracy are still being used in this country. They're used to intimidate and silence all kinds of dissent. As I mentioned at the beginning, that's exactly how the system works in dictatorships.'

A Nod and a Wink finished, rather bafflingly, with Tom Harper of the *New Law Journal* explaining to the camera what he believed to be the official justification for wider use of the conspiracy laws. Even if an activity did not constitute a specific criminal offence as defined by Parliament, 'its consequences may be so socially harmful when it is done by several people acting together that the courts should be able to deal with it', he said. 'They have used the offence of conspiracy for that purpose.' Harper cited a statement by Lord Hailsham, who had recently retired as Lord Chancellor, that statute law was notoriously easy to evade and, by using the law of conspiracy, the courts could act quickly in 'unforeseen' circumstances where Parliament could not. 'However,' he added, 'the overriding issue in the administration of the law of conspiracy is whether the purpose of a particular getting-together is socially harmful.'

Harper's section was added to the film, Pilger explained later, as 'yet another sop to keep the IBA happy'.[9] It served only to create confusion, not even making sense as a 'response' to what had gone before. Unlike the official response in *Guilty Until Proven Innocent*, which was added after the end credits had finished rolling, this one was made part of the documentary. 'Establishment subversion', Pilger later called it. 'It had no impact,' he said. 'People *know* when the Forces of Light are lecturing them and that it usually means there is something to hide.'[10]

For Peter Hain, there was an interesting legal postscript to *A Nod and a Wink*. In October 1975, two months after its transmission, he was arrested and falsely charged with committing a bank robbery. It was a case of mistaken identity, the title of Hain's subsequent book, but a shopping trip to buy a typewriter ribbon from the Putney High Street branch of W.H. Smith resulted in a nightmare scenario that began with his being held in a police cell and ended with his being tried at the Old Bailey, Britain's highest criminal court.

Several schoolboys had joined bank employees in a chase after the real thief and, after he disappeared, saw Hain rush in and out of Smith's. Believing him to be the robber, they reported his car's registration number to the police. An identity parade, held after charges had been made and the consequential press publicity, resulted in one of five witnesses, the bank cashier from whom the money had been stolen, positively identifying Hain. This spurred the police to press ahead with the prosecution and Hain opted for committal proceedings.

A packed Old Bailey heard all the evidence over two weeks in March and April 1976. The police case began to collapse when the bank cashier, their critical witness, expressed uncertainty about Hain's similarity to the thief, saying that the man she had picked out of the identity parade had shorter and thinner hair, and she admitted getting only a 'split-second' glimpse of the robber. The descriptive evidence of the schoolboys was also shown to be flawed and there was an unidentified print on one of the stolen banknotes. Hain's six-month ordeal ended with a 'not guilty' verdict, which caused pandemonium to break out in court, with the public cheering and clapping.

However, he remained bemused by the police's decision to charge him. 'The reality is that their primary concern is to ensure that a prosecution is brought,' Hain subsequently wrote. 'They are "prosecution" orientated rather than "investigative" orientated, not over-bothered to uncover the truth about a case so long as they can make a charge stick.'[11] There was later evidence to suggest that the South African security service, BOSS (Bureau of State Security), had framed Hain.

Lack of justice in the legal system was also at the centre of Pilger's campaign to get compensation for almost a hundred victims of thalidomide who had not been included in the 1973 settlement under which the Distillers Company set up a £20 million trust fund. It was public recognition that the 342 'lucky' ones, who featured on the X-list of children drawn up by a firm of solicitors, had suffered deformities as a result of their mothers taking the drug. However, another ninety-eight children on the Y-list did not receive any compensation because their mothers lacked written proof that they had taken thalidomide – even though some on the X-list had no proof, either – or their deformities were not typical of those caused by the drug.

Thalidomide: The Ninety-eight We Forgot, broadcast in the *Pilger* series in 1974 and directed by Christine Fox, was allied to a Pilger campaign that ran in the *Daily Mirror* for four years, which helped to achieve a partial victory for many of the 'forgotten' victims. 'I expect it will surprise almost all of you, perhaps even shock you, that the thalidomide affair is not over,' Pilger said in the film's opening sequence. 'Last year, after eleven years of struggle, the children won their compensation. But there are still ninety-eight children whose mothers believe they took thalidomide who've got nothing.'

He explained that thalidomide, made by the manufacturers of Johnnie Walker whisky, had been introduced as a 'wonder drug' in 1958 to cure headaches, act as a sleeping pill and calm nerves. It was withdrawn two-and-a-half years later, after reports of deformities in new-born babies. Some parents in Britain took legal action against Distillers, but it was not until a major campaign by *The Sunday Times* in 1972 that public pressure mounted, Parliament intervened and the slow cogs in the legal process started moving towards a conclusion. (Pilger began writing about the Y-list at that time.)

However, the struggle was to continue for some parents of teenaged victims. 'The Y-list parents are those who, when they came to look for proof, found their doctor had died or retired or the medical records destroyed or missing,' explained Pilger. 'In some cases, the doctor denied giving the drug although the mother remembers taking it, or the mother got the tablets from a friend or directly from a chemist. Anyway, like most of us, most of them didn't know what they were taking.'

Interviews followed with some of the mothers, as well as their champion, the Labour MP Jack Ashley, a veteran of the disabled's rights who is himself deaf. 'They were an uncoordinated group of parents spread all over the country,' said Ashley. 'They didn't quite know where to turn to.'

Some of the children were also featured. They included Sandra Tootle, who was born without legs and with two crooked feet that were later amputated, as well as deformed hips and a left hand with just three fingers. Her mother, Margaret, told Pilger that her GP had twice given her tablets in envelopes, without prescription, on home visits during her pregnancy. She remembered the name Distaval, one of the brands under which thalidomide was marketed, appearing on them. Of the long battle to achieve compensation, she said, 'I'm not a person that likes arguing . . . We're very timid, actually.' The impression was of parents, who had passively accepted their situation, lined up against a giant business.

Eleven-year-old Sonya West's mother had been given tablets by the doctor when she suffered from 'nerves' during pregnancy but could not remember which tablets. Her husband, Mike, explained that his wife had experienced a history of nervous disorder shortly after they married and took many pills. When his daughter was born, he assumed that Sonya was a thalidomide victim because the publicity highlighted exactly the kind of drug his wife was prescribed.

Keith Lewis, chairman of the Y-Group Parents' Committee and father of an eleven-year-old, Mark, born with arm and shoulder deformities, explained why parents of those on both lists had signed the Distillers settlement, under which the company would pay compensation if the majority agreed to it and no future claims could be brought against it. 'If all those children who were on the Y-list held out, it would only slow down proceedings for the people who were on the X-list who could receive compensation,' he said. The parent of an X-list child told Pilger that the Y-list parents' 'situation is unsatisfactory'.

David Brookes, a Lancashire solicitor acting for a Y-list family, told Pilger, 'There seems to be very little difference between the evidence which got some children on to the X-list and some children on to the Y-list. It seems to me that somewhere along the line, possibly unknown to that person at the time, somebody has been asked to almost play God.'

Dr David Poswillo, a world-renowned authority on birth deformities who had just completed five years' research into thalidomide, provided Pilger with some of the evidence that was finally to help the Y-list children to get compensation. 'You really cannot put a jigsaw puzzle together if many of the pieces are missing,' he said. 'So much depends on the clinical history. If one can establish that there has been thalidomide intake by the mother during the sensitive period, then I think it's impossible to decide whether a malformation was definitely caused by thalidomide or not . . . I think the onus of proof is to prove that thalidomide didn't cause it.'

Five days after *Thalidomide: The Ninety-eight We Forgot* was screened, Pilger wrote a front-page story for the *Daily Mirror*, illustrated with photographs of two children suffering almost identical deformities, one on the X-list and the other on the Y-list, and headlined, 'For the sake of humanity, help these youngsters NOW!' As a result of the documentary and this article, the Conservative MP Dr Gerard Vaughan, chairman of the thalidomide assessment panel and a future junior health minister, agreed to have reassessed those who had not been part of the Distillers settlement. However, few children were examined and, by December 1977, only thirteen of the Y-list ones had been transferred to the X-list and received compensation.

In 1978, Pilger telephoned American consumer champion Ralph Nader, who agreed in principle to arrange a boycott of Distillers' products in the United States. When he reported this in the *Mirror*, Pilger received an anxious telephone call to him from a company official. He now felt that he was close to achieving something for the children and wrote an 'open letter' to John Cater, headlined 'Dear Sir, in the name of humanity' and including a reproduction of a 1960 advertisement espousing the 'safety of Distaval'. The *Mirror* published this across two pages – and it worked.

Pilger's direct appeal led Distillers to agree to abide by the recommendations of an inquiry conducted by Sir Alan Marre, which reported its findings a few months later, in August 1978. The remaining seventy-four youngsters on the Y-list were split into two categories, 'A' and 'B', with just twenty included in the 1973 settlement, forty-nine offered £10,000 compensation and five told that they must await further reports.

There is no doubting that this was one of Pilger's most effective campaigns and *Thalidomide: The Ninety-eight We Forgot* was one of the first pieces of ammunition in it. 'As a campaign, it was as successful as you could make it,' said Pilger. 'For press and television campaigns to be successful, or even partially successful, they have to be tenacious. It was unusual for a popular newspaper to sustain such a story for years – that was the kind of paper the *Mirror* was. It was both humane and willing to fight. To achieve that success rate with the thalidomide victims was extraordinary. Not even *The Sunday Times* campaign resulted in full compensation until some years later.

'Having said that, as a journalist, one needs to hold a very modest, cautious view of whether campaigns can actually succeed. Some do and some don't. And you must never underestimate the power and ruthlessness of the forces you're up against, especially corporations like the Distillers company. The nice, woolly liberal idea is that these organizations will behave decently in the end. If they're the John Lewis Partnership, they might. But, generally speaking, they don't – that's the nature of corporate power. Companies like Distillers have to be severely embarrassed and their shareholders identified. This takes time. Look at the campaigns against the foreign companies in South Africa. For years, people boycotted banks such as Barclays and nothing changed. But they kept going and, finally, it worked.'[12]

Another social scandal involving Britain's youngest people, in this case the physically and mentally handicapped, was the subject of *Nobody's Children*, a 1975 documentary in the *Pilger* series, directed by John Ingram. The recent census had revealed that one-third of all mentally handicapped children in institutions were given no intelligence testing for more than ten years, reported Pilger, and MENCAP, the Royal Society for Mentally Handicapped Children and Adults, which represented them, believed that many should not have been locked away in such places.

'This is one of the many cold and damp corridors in Leiston Mental Hospital, near London,' said Pilger, inside a long-stay institution. 'The other day when I was here, this corridor was partially flooded and its patients and staff said it wasn't at all unusual. Of course, Leiston has been tarted up here and there with Formica and coats of paint in order to comply with the latest institutional standards. But its main purpose remains as insidiously, if not exactly, the same as when it was built last century, and that is as a place not so much to treat or to salvage the mentally handicapped and children especially, as indeed many of them can be salvaged, but as a place to confine them, to dump them, to isolate them from our so-called safe society.

'Perhaps you think these children should never have been allowed to live. I believe you're wrong. The question, surely, is, how sane is a society that shuts away children who can be part of the life of the community?'

Citing a 1971 Department of Health White Paper that had found only one nurse to care for up to sixteen children in many institutions, Pilger said that at Darenth Park Hospital, in Kent, he discovered one nurse looking after twenty-five. This care was officially restricted to getting children up in the morning, dressing, washing and feeding them, and putting them back to bed at night. According to the White Paper, this staff shortage resulted in 'boredom, tension and occasional violence', and 'the children become apathetic and sink into a state of complete physical and social dependence, and nurses become deeply frustrated by having no time to use the psychiatric skills in which they've been trained'. The White Paper had been 'largely ignored' and, in the four years since it had been presented to Parliament, staff shortages had worsened.

At Harperbury Hospital, near London, Pilger interviewed Dr Derek Rix about his efforts to help the children in his care. The doctor introduced him to children who had shown progress, such as a boy who could sit more stably and was starting to feed himself after help from an orthopaedic surgeon, with the result that he was using his hands and becoming more aware of the world around him. 'He was a piece of wreckage,' said Dr Rix. 'To nurse him and help him to recover from the operation and to get him moving in the way that we've done was a full-scale exercise involving a lot of people most of the time.' The doctor added that it was possible to make such children 'manageable in community placements' but there was nowhere for them to go.

Moving to the Hilda Lewis Centre for Specially Handicapped Children, in London, with film of youngsters singing happily, Pilger found an institution where each child had one-to-one care, 'to stimulate him, to play with him, to make him laugh'. Some of the twenty-four children at this experimental centre returned home in the evenings and staff did not wear uniforms, contributing to an informal atmosphere. There was continuing assessment of disabilities and how they could be treated. 'The children are taught to be functioning human beings, how to go to the toilet, how to wash, how to use the hair brush – the simple, vital things that will bring them back into the community,' explained Pilger. 'The children here are never allowed to vegetate.'

Paddy, one of those at the Hilda Lewis Centre, was given as an example of someone who had come from a big institution where he had been classified as severely retarded. In fact, he simply could not make himself understood. 'He was trapped in his own little prison of silence and should never have been accepted into an institution,' said Pilger. 'Paddy realized his dilemma and this made him very angry. Paddy seldom gets angry now.'

The film switched back to Leiston Hospital, with Pilger commenting that most children never escaped from this system and grew up with little chance of getting a job. Despite a 1970 Act of Parliament giving all children the right to education regardless of handicap, by May 1974 only two projects approved by the Department of Education provided classes for mentally handicapped children in ordinary schools.

Pilger introduced seven-year-old Stephen Kingham as one child destined for a life in large institutions. The dilemma facing parents of such children was starkly revealed by his mother, who spoke of her reaction when Stephen was born handicapped. 'I didn't want him, I wouldn't look at him and I wouldn't touch him,' she said. 'I begged them to put him away, I begged them to kill him. That's all I could think . . . But now I couldn't part with him for the world.'

One of the hospital's officials told Pilger that children were seen rocking backwards and forwards much of the time simply because they were bored, a result of a lack of staff. 'The pressure on us is simply to be custodial and to keep the children quiet and appropriately contained,' he said.

Pilger was seen giving attention to a boy, who responded with a smile. He then quoted the UN Declaration of Human Rights, signed six years earlier and a copy of which was posted on a wall at MENCAP's offices, which gave every mentally handicapped child the right to 'such education, training, rehabilitation and guidance that will enable him to realize his potential to the fullest possible extent' and 'to live in surroundings as close to a normal life as possible'.

'Such fine, correct, noble words,' added Pilger, 'but they are only words, just as this film is only words and images that will dissolve and go away in a minute or two. But the children you'll have seen in this film won't go away. They exist, they feel, they are aware, they laugh, they need. They are everybody's children.' This served to connect his subjects' lives with viewers – a constant aim in Pilger's filmmaking. True to another aim, of 'taking away the veil', he had shown the mentally handicapped as human beings just like those watching. The sound of a child crying softly was heard over the film's end credits.

Much has changed in the system since *Nobody's Children* was broadcast. 'Long-term institutions were already on the way out,' said Pilger. 'The policy of David Owen as health minister in the mid-1970s was to put people back into the community, which was the right way to go. The problem has since been matching the principle with funding. Community care itself has too often become a front behind which mentally inadequate people are dumped on the streets and one of the reasons for the large number of homeless in our cities.'[13]

A citation for one of Pilger's press awards included the observation that 'the thread through all his work is an abiding concern for children'.[14] They were also the subject of *Smashing Kids, 1975*, another report in the *Pilger* series, this time about youngsters growing up in poor families. From the opening titles, it was hard-hitting, with whole sequences of black-and-white still photographs by John Garrett providing an innovation in documentary-making. Standing in a street, Pilger said, 'A young mother called Christine McKenzie lived in this house in Wolverhampton not long ago. While she was here, pregnant with her second child and without a husband, she filled in this questionnaire. She was asked, "In the past two weeks, have you gone a whole day without a meal?" She answered, "Yes," and added, "The baby had some porridge." She was asked to list a typical day's meals. She wrote, "Breakfast: nothing. Midday: toast, jam or an egg. Supper: nothing." "Have you any general comments?" she was asked. "I don't feel very well," she wrote.

'Christine McKenzie is one of the people you will hear about in the next half-hour. They are people who represent the true crisis in this country. Tonight, more than two million parents will go to bed hungry in order to give their children something to eat and already many of these children are suffering a degree of malnutrition and diseases, like rickets, related to malnutrition. But please don't get me wrong. This is not a documentary about the perennial poor. In all the numbing, mostly middle-class debate about falling living standards in Britain, one truth has been excluded. It is this: for the first time since the Great Depression,

Britain – the so-called Welfare State – is deliberately cutting back the means of survival of its poorest, and their children.'

In the late 1960s and early 1970s, documentaries and television plays about poverty were commonplace. One of the first to alert people to the issue of those falling through the net in the Welfare State was director Ken Loach's 1966 BBC television play *Cathy Come Home*, most memorable for its scene of a mother being evicted from a hostel for the homeless and having her children taken away by social services. Written by Jeremy Sandford, *Cathy Come Home* had the effect of a punch in the stomach and was credited with helping to bring about the creation of Shelter, the charity for the homeless, and ending the policy of separating homeless husbands from their families.

However, poverty persisted as the Labour government of 1964-70 effectively pursued Conservative economics of austerity and wage restraint in response to the large balance of payments deficit left by the previous Tory administration. The sterling crisis of 1966 led to a devaluation of the pound the following year. By the time the Conservative Party returned to office in 1970, Britain was back in the black. Then a boom in the property and finance sectors was followed by bust and those without a voice were not heard. Recession was already under way as Labour once more took power in 1974.

Among those featured in *Smashing Kids, 1975* – a pun intended to relate the idea that children in poor families were being hit badly – were the Hopwoods of Liverpool, who survived on £30.53 a week, including benefits. Hunger, said Pilger, had become a way of life for the family of five during the six months that father Harry had been unemployed. The Hopwoods were living on £1 a day when he visited them and his commentary was accompanied by pictures of an empty larder.

Interviews with Harry and Irene Hopwood spelled out the reality of living in poverty – they had potatoes only on Sundays and had not eaten a 'decent' Sunday meal in seven weeks, the wallpaper in their council house was torn, there were no clothes in the wardrobe and no sheets on their bed. Asked by Pilger what her happiest times were, the Hopwoods' daughter replied, 'I don't think any, really.' She told him that she had never been on holiday. Irene herself had only been on holiday once, during her schooldays. 'What do you think your children's future will be?' Pilger asked Harry. 'Well, they've got no future here,' he replied. 'None of us have. It would be easier to serve time than to put up with this. It's just like a prison. It's worse, in fact, because you're paying for this.'

Over John Garrett's searing, yet sympathetic still photographs of impoverished youngsters, Pilger reported that an increasing number of parents could no longer afford to feed their children. Frank Field, director of the Child Poverty Action Group, who later became a Labour MP, told him that benefits for the unemployed were falling in real terms.

One family that had to face this were the Brunsdens of Hackney, East London – Jim, Irene, son Derek and daughter Rachel – who lived on benefits of £28.22 a week. Following the same line of questioning as with the Hopwoods, Pilger asked Irene what food she had in the house. 'I've got about half a loaf of bread, two eggs and a little bit of cornflakes for the children,' she replied. Two-year-old Rachel had eaten only cornflakes, bread and fish-and-chips bought with borrowed money the previous day. Irene had only five pence in the house and would have to borrow more money to feed her children that evening. Asked by Pilger whether Rachel complained of hunger, Irene said, 'She doesn't tell me she's hungry. She just moans all the time and I get that feeling like she's hungry. If I've got anything, I'll give it to her. If not, I'll just give her milk.'

The Brunsdens had received notice to quit their council house for not paying the rent. 'If you're evicted, what will happen?' asked Pilger. 'They will probably either put me and the baby into a halfway house and my husband will have to find somewhere to sleep or else they will take the baby away from me,' said Irene. Here were echoes of *Cathy Come Home*. Pilger noted that it would cost the local authority at least £70 a week to keep the family in temporary accommodation. 'That doesn't make sense, does it?' he said, to camera. 'But that's the way the Welfare State operates in Britain today. Indeed, the smashing of the Brunsden family, especially of the baby, is typical of these times. First Jim Brunsden loses his job as a lorry driver, through no fault of his own, and then his family tries in vain to draw their full social benefits from a maze of forty-six means-tested handouts, and now they are hungry and in debt to a tallyman and fast approaching a point of desperation. But, of course, that's the way it was in Ramsay MacDonald's Britain in 1931, when mothers in desperation contemplated taking up prostitution to feed their children.'

Shockingly, Irene Brunsden told Pilger, 'I wouldn't go on the streets, not if I could help it. But, if my baby really, really needed something to eat and I didn't have a penny, whether it cost me my marriage, my life or anything, I would have to do it, for my baby's sake . . . We're getting closer to it. If I done this sort of thing, I would lose my husband, I know that for a fact. But we're getting so close to it now that it's going to be that way before long. I'm just going to have to go out to keep my kids.'

Feeding children remained the question at issue when Pilger met the Stock family. Their larder was filmed on a Monday and by Thursday, the night of the programme's transmission, there would be nothing left, he said, with two days to wait for their benefits. Mrs Stock said that she did not mark her younger children's birthdays because 'they're too young to know anyway'. She gave the older ones 'a couple of bob' when she could afford it. Melanie, the eldest of four daughters, said her friends were very accepting of their poverty. The family had no hot-water facilities, which meant they never had baths – they simply 'washed down' with water heated in saucepans and kettles, said Mrs Stock.

Putting the film's examples into perspective, Pilger quoted a Child Poverty Action Group report published just a month earlier. It stated that five million people in Britain had no more than £1.60 a week to spend on food. 'That is,' said Pilger, 'one pound and sixty pence for each of these children who are the future.'

Returning to the story of twenty-one-year-old Christine McKenzie, Pilger explained that she had not been featured in the programme because she was now dead, having suffered a rare infection shortly after the birth of her second child. 'Her miserably low social benefits could not keep pace with the uncontrolled rise of food prices . . .' he said. 'This government's minute increases in social benefits planned for November will be wiped out by inflation and are effectively cutbacks, imposing a direct threat to the survival of the growing number of the poor. Unless we regain our sense of priorities, which amount to our civilization, there will be more and more Christine McKenzies.'

Smashing Kids, 1975 was a disturbing insight into the human face of poverty. 'As a documented, unrelenting reminder that economic winter is hardest, first, on poorer people with less protection, the programme could not be faulted,' wrote Shaun Usher in the *Daily Mail*. 'But it did seem curiously negative even by television's doom-laden standards. It is all very well to beat the breast and shake the head over State indifference towards walking wounded in the money war – but some mention of schemes to improve the situation would have been a sound idea.'[15]

Usher would have heard the response if it had not been censored. 'In the original final piece to camera,' recalled Pilger, 'I said that the Labour Party had come to power pledged to end the kind of poverty that was shown in this film. Why hadn't they done so? The film posed a direct challenge to the Wilson government. But that was cut out, one of the few examples of crude censorship of my films.'[16] In the complete version of that piece to camera, Pilger had also said, 'The commercials that you'll now watch will be advertising and promoting products that will not be available to the people you've just seen.' This connected poverty with consumerism and its promotion through television and this, too, was edited out. 'It would have been hypocritical of me had I not challenged the commercial ethos of television itself,' explained Pilger. 'Commercial television is part of consumerism, and independent journalism has a duty to raise the issue of consumerism and its complicity with poverty.'[17]

Like the *Mail*, its right-wing bedfellow, the *Daily Telegraph* sought to denigrate the emotive approach of *Smashing Kids, 1975*, criticizing the decision to highlight the plight of three families. 'This is not in my view the most effective way to present social problems with real urgency,' wrote Sylvia Clayton. 'Such programmes as Jenny Barraclough's *Gail is Dead*, which traced the tragedy of a girl drug addict, had a basis of careful research focused on an individual case . . . An angry compassion, however genuine, is no substitute for real information about social conditions.'[18] This seemed to be a mixed-up argument, pleading on the one hand for a single case study, which is not necessarily typical, and on the other for wider information. All it did was to voice the newspaper's prejudices against a reporter who did not share its view.

Although he did not return to poverty in Britain in his television documentaries, Pilger continued to write about the issue, first in the *Daily Mirror*, then in the *New Statesman*. In 1980, a year after Margaret Thatcher brought the Conservative Party back into government, with inflation hitting 19.8 per cent and the number of unemployed reaching one-and-a-half million, he reported for the *Mirror* on shocking conditions reminiscent of the 1930s in Birkenhead. Four years later, following the Thatcher government's abandonment of a national housing programme, he wrote frequently about increasing homelessness and the profits being made by hotels and hostels in providing accommodation for them, sometimes in the most squalid of conditions. For three years, Pilger traced every suicide in Britain related, in any way, to unemployment. He started collecting reports of coroners' courts in 1980, the year in which the unemployment figures passed three million, and the shocking stories were published in the *Mirror*. Pilger also wrote about the poverty imposed on miners' children whose fathers were on strike.

Poverty was rarely reported on television throughout the 1980s and 1990s, despite official figures constantly showing one-quarter of the population to be living on or below the breadline and the 1997 United Nations Human Development Report stating that no other country had experienced such a substantial rise in poverty since the early 1980s and that those in 'income poverty' had risen by almost 60 per cent under the Thatcher government. One notable exception was director Michael Grigsby's shocking 1987 Central Television documentary *Living on the Edge*. Pilger has included poverty in programmes on other issues, such as that on the British arms trade, *Flying the Flag – Arming the World* (see later in this chapter), but, during the 1990s, most of his films were set in other countries.

Poverty was a central issue in *Dismantling a Dream*, Pilger's 1977 documentary about the state of Britain's health service, at a time when a Labour government was imposing cutbacks. It was allied to a campaign that he ran in the *Daily Mirror* during which, at a press conference in a decaying Northampton hospital, he had a stand-up argument with health secretary David Ennals over his responsibility for conditions there.

In the film, Pilger recalled the establishment of the National Health Service in 1948 and health minister Aneurin Bevan's declaration that the 'silent suffering' of the old, young, chronically sick and handicapped had no place in a civilized society. But, in December 1976, an official report had revealed that thousands of children who could be saved were dying and, quoted Pilger, 'Twice as many children of unskilled workers die in the first month of life as the children of professional workers, and the gap between the social classes in health care has been widening for twenty-five years.' In that same week, fifty senior doctors at a Northampton hospital had issued a statement saying that patients were dying as a result of financial cutbacks.

'The doctors' statement, issued in desperation, was the first of its kind in Britain,' explained Pilger. 'It was also the first real evidence that the silent suffering to which Nye Bevan referred had come back as a direct result of public spending cuts by this

government. The examples that will follow are not the most
sensational or the most shocking – they are typical. Nor is this
report merely about cutbacks. It's about a dismantling, a tearing
down of whole sections of what was once Britain's most civilizing
post-war achievement – your health service.'

Dismantling a Dream was filmed mostly in Murray House, a
Surrey hospital for the mentally and physically handicapped, and
Hackney General Hospital, in London. Pilger described the first, a
former workhouse, as a 'typical slum hospital' and a member of
staff said that minimum safety levels were not met and patients
were unstimulated. Many needed physiotherapy, but there was
only one physiotherapist for 150 patients and he was available for
only half a day every week. 'The situation is so desperate here,'
said Pilger, over film of one patient, 'that this severely handicapped man seized upon the presence of our camera to cry out for
more staff. There is seldom anyone with the time to push him into
sunlight.'

This had echoes of *Nobody's Children*, Pilger's documentary on
the handicapped, two years earlier. 'They've taken down the old
workhouse plaque,' Pilger noted, 'and yesterday, just for our
benefit, they painted this rotting wall. This morning, a nurse told
me there were no toys here for the kids in the hospital.' He
reported that the government spent just 4 per cent of the National
Health Service budget on the mentally handicapped while an
increasing amount was being spent on drugs.

Hackney General's forty-five junior doctors had described the
hospital as 'a public showplace of how squalid the health service
can be'. Expectant mothers were farmed out to the Salvation
Army's Mothers' Hospital, with no resuscitation time or a full-
time anaesthetist. 'It puts the mother and the baby in an extremely
dangerous position, which might very well lead to foetal death,'
said Hackney's senior consultant anaesthetist, Dr Frederick Lancaster. One still birth experienced might have been caused by the
delay. The previous week, Dr Lancaster had been called to the
Mothers' Hospital when one woman in labour had a seizure and

there was not the correct equipment. 'I've never felt that I might lose a patient ever, except at The Mothers',' he said. The anaesthetist added that he would not allow his own family to be treated under such operating conditions – a shocking public admission at that time. Hackney's infant mortality rate, said Pilger, was twenty-five per cent above the national average.

Some people in need of urgent operations and in constant pain were having to wait, said the hospital's orthopaedic registrar, Dr Françoise Eagleton. Patients with much needed hip and knee replacements were waiting up to three years, according to the Arthritis and Rheumatism Council, said Pilger. A senior consultant, Thomas Wadsworth, explained, 'Most of the patients that are suitable for total hip replacement are old people whose lifespan is not very extensive. They may have several years to live and a year is probably a long time to be in a lot of pain. They are suffering and will be suffering for longer periods of time now because we won't be able to get them in in anything like the time we've been able to until recently. Instead of improving facilities here, the situation is getting worse.'

A surgeon at Hackney General, Dr Peter Burke, told Pilger that he had just sent home five people suffering from cancer of the bladder who were due for their annual review operation, an examination under general anaesthetic. He simply did not have the beds. They were told to return in the morning.

In 1973, said Pilger, the Hospital Advisory Service had described Hackney's psychiatric wards as some of the worst for the care of mentally ill patients that it had seen. Earlier in 1977, a consultant psychiatrist, Dr John Reed, had spoken out in the press after sewage poured down the wards for a third time. 'There were two people who should have been in hospital and who did commit suicide out in the community,' Dr Reed told Pilger. 'I suspect strongly that the service here will break down, in the sense that we will find ourselves in a situation where there are people who must come in when there are no beds and no way of finding beds for them . . . It's always more difficult in the winter months. We did close on many occasions last winter.'

Pilger also mentioned Rainhill Mental Hospital, near Liverpool. He said that wards were locked that should be open and some nurses believed that patients were deliberately being oversedated. Over one picture, he explained, 'This floor was left covered with faeces – shit – because there were no cleaners. Finally, the overworked nurses had to scrape it off.'

A consultant in Oldham, Dr Brian Shepheard, said his hospital was lacking diagnostic facilities. This meant that bladder cancer, for example, was taking up to four months to diagnose. Although cancer patients could then be operated on within two to three weeks, the disease would have spread during the four-month wait and there was the risk of unnecessary deaths.

Dismantling a Dream provoked controversy even before its screening, in September 1977. 'There was pressure on key witnesses [and] doctors, from the [hospital's] administrators and public relations people, [and] attempts to stop us filming people because they were said not to be representative of the hospital,' said Pilger.[19] The City and East London Area Health Authority threatened ATV with a court injunction to prevent transmission of the programme, but this turned out to be no more than a threat.

At the end of the film, Pilger told viewers, 'You would not have seen this report if a number of people whom you employ in the health service bureaucracy had had their way. Since last June, certain health officials have co-ordinated their efforts to prevent us filming, to obstruct our filming and to stop tonight's transmission. For example, at Rainhill Hospital, near Liverpool, our film crew was barred, over the objections of people who work there who wanted us to see the scandalous conditions of the hospital. At Hackney Hospital, unrelenting pressure has been applied to doctors and especially to one consultant, a sick man [Dr Frederick Lancaster], to withdraw from the film. Also at Hackney, the hospital secretary has demanded that a doctor sign a statement that she did not write disclaiming an interview about the dangers to mothers and babies at Hackney.

'All this amounts to a cover-up of the damage being done to your health service by expedient and unplanned cuts. Make no mistake, the people who actually care for the sick – the doctors, nurses and ancillary staff – are among the most efficient and productive workers in the country. But, while the beehive of adminstrators and deputy administrators and assistant administrators and their public relations protectors has doubled in the last twelve years, it is the doctors and nurses and their vital support people that are being cut back. And it is the doctors' and nurses' modest demands for life-saving equipment, for beds, for basic standards of hygiene that are being denied.'

Shaun Usher, the *Daily Mail* television critic who had previously criticized Pilger for being 'negative' in his film about children living in poor families, was more enthusiastic about *Dismantling a Dream*. 'Obviously anxious to avoid spoiling its case by overstatement, the programme chronicled scandalous states of affairs in a notably restrained way,' he wrote. 'Which made some of its findings all the more shocking somehow.'[20] Presumably, if the case *had* been 'overstated', Usher would have branded it negative or not typical of the problems facing the health service.

Over at the *Daily Telegraph*, Richard Last continued that paper's assault on Pilger. 'He invited us to believe that the whole system, Aneurin Bevan's postwar "dream", was falling apart,' wrote Last. 'Now I know, both as a citizen and a customer, that in many areas, quite possibly in most, the NHS functions pretty well. Imperfectly, but that is the nature of human institutions.'[21]

Pilger responded to Last's accusation that he claimed the health service was 'falling apart' with a letter to the paper. 'I did not say this,' wrote Pilger, 'nor is there any mention of this in the transcript of my film. I referred only to "sections" of the National Health Service and at no time suggested the absurd notion that the whole of the NHS was on its way out. Using this sloppy little lie about my film, Mr Last went on to question my credibility and, in doing so, effectively destroyed his own.' Last was unrepentant, simply replying, 'Mr Pilger claimed that "whole sections of the Health Service were being torn down" and entitled his programme *Dismantling a Dream*. If that is not a case of something "falling apart", then it would be hard to know what is.'[22] With this, Last had reduced 'the whole system' of his review to 'whole sections'. In the years that followed, the British public watched in dismay as increasing pressures effectively dismantled sections of the health service and, by the time a Labour government was returned to power in 1997, it was accepted that health and education were the country's most urgent priorities and needed vastly increased funding.

Dismantling a Dream and Pilger's *Daily Mirror* campaign were among his most successful. He succeeded in getting the Mothers' Hospital at Hackney closed down and a commitment to a new maternity unit, which has since been built. His newspaper reports contributed to his being named Campaigning Journalist of the Year in the British Press Awards for 1977. The judges praised Pilger for his attacks on declining standards in some of Britain's hospitals and his continuing crusade for thalidomide children, noting that he showed 'a passionate concern for standards of social responsibility'.

The television film had other repercussions when, in 1981, Pilger reported for the *Mirror* on the plight of the ailing health service as the result of cuts under Margaret Thatcher's Conservative government. Liverpool Area Health Authority complained that he and photographer Eric Piper entered two of its hospitals without permission. The Press Council dismissed the complaint on the grounds that Pilger believed, as a result of the earlier television programme, that he would not be given free access if he requested it. Members of the National Union of Public Employees had invited Pilger to interview staff, and the Press Council praised him for performing a service in the public interest.

Back in 1974, for the final programme in the first series of *Pilger*, he tackled an issue that had been particularly sensitive in Britain

during the previous decade – race. West Indians had begun to
enter the country after World War Two and immigration
continued apace throughout the 1950s. They, along with Indians,
Pakistanis and Africans, were full British subjects, a legacy of the
country's imperial past. However, during the 1960s, successive
governments started to restrict their entry into the country. The
1964 general election produced a sharp swing from Labour to the
Conservative Party in Smethwick, attributed to the race issue in
Britain's 'most colour-conscious town', resulting in the seat
switching to the Tories despite a win nationally for Labour. In
1968, at the time a new Race Relations Bill was being discussed in
Parliament, the Conservative Opposition MP Enoch Powell's
'rivers of blood' speech, delivered in Birmingham, prophesied a
dramatic increase in immigration of non-whites. Despite many
Britons being sympathetic to Powell's views,[23] they were regarded as inflammatory and Edward Heath sacked him from his
job as Shadow Cabinet defence spokesman.

In *One British Family*, Pilger focused on Gus and Julie Gill, who
arrived in Britain with their family from Trinidad in August 1961.
'The Gill family aren't meant to typify the black population of this
country,' said Pilger. 'Tyneside doesn't have ghettoes like Brixton
and Bradford, but what is typical about them is their journey
through a racial minefield that is our society and through all our
racist fantasies, like the one that accuses immigrants of living off
the dole and taking all the jobs. The Gill family, like the overwhelming majority of immigrant families, have given more to
Britain than Britain has given to them. They take less from the
social services than the equivalent white families. They're not on
any council's housing lists and they've never been out of work. I
suppose it's a cliché to say that they're a family of our times, but
that's what they are. Because, even though most of the media
regard race as something that's best left ignored, race is still the
issue. At least one British family knows that.'

Film of the family – nineteen-year-old son Errol and daughters
Julie, seven, Andrea, nine, and Wendy, fourteen – at home

singing along with Gus's guitar-playing presented viewers with a 'normal', 'happy' image of them. Errol, who was seven when he arrived in Britain, said he missed the climate of Trinidad, while father Gus first encountered racism when he was called a 'black bastard'. 'I was shocked,' he said. 'I never thought that I would hear such a remark from people from a civilized country.'

Gus found casual work with British Railways, at just £7.10 a week, while living in the West End of Newcastle, a black ghetto. Then, he was rejected by Dunlop because of his colour but finally found a job as a night packer at a packing company. Seeking acceptance in white society, he bought a house in Moor Street, helped by a loan from community worker Rocky Byron, his oldest friend in the West End. The Gills were the only black family in the street. Winning a singing competition made Gus feel accepted, and he reflected that his younger children did not regard themselves as immigrants. Now, Gus was a foreman at a bakery, earning little more than £40 for a six-day week, working from 7pm to 7am. 'The white world has given Gus what he regards as precious acceptance,' said Pilger over film of him at work.

Son Errol, who had grown up in Newcastle and worked as a clerk, regarded himself as no different from other young Geordies and did not crave acceptance. Rocky Byron predicted problems to come as a result of growing up in an exclusively white, European society. 'This is where the father has to bring him back into reality,' said Byron.

Asked about Enoch Powell's famous speech, Gus recalled that television reports of it were followed one night by a group of whites telling him in the street, 'Why don't you go back to your country? We don't want the likes of you here.' Now, son Errol was planning to marry a nineteen-year-old white woman, Susan, with whom he was expecting a baby. They had kept this news to themselves for a month and had only told Errol's mother that morning. 'She was stunned, but not as much as Susan's mother,' he said.

Rocky Byron felt that the white response to a mixed marriage depended on where the couple lived. In some places people were more liberal-minded, but in others residents 'will turn their noses up'. This place was probably the latter. Asked by Pilger about white women going out with blacks, Susan said, 'Respectable ones always think twice. I thought, "What would my mam say about this?"' Her mother was shocked, but Susan felt that attitudes were changing and there was the possibility of a truly multiracial society, 'amongst the younger generation, but not the older generation, because they want to be more dominating and want the younger generation to do what they do'.

Summing up, Pilger said, 'If Errol is lucky and Susan has no illusions, then their unborn child must take his chances. But he'd better get lucky, too. For in the last ten years, the number of black people in mental hospitals has increased four-fold, from 6,000 to 24,000, and most of them are young and many of them are suffering from schizophrenia, personality splits between black and white. Yes, their child had better get lucky. But, of course, if he does get lucky, he'll be starting something.'

Another contentious issue in Britain during the 1970s was nuclear power, which had been developed for military purposes during World War Two and subsequently adapted to generate energy for civilian purposes. Work began on a nuclear plant, at Windscale, on the Cumbrian coast, in 1946 and Britain's first nuclear power station, at nearby Calder Hall, began producing electricity ten years later. By the early 1970s, nuclear power stations had proliferated. In exploding a test atomic bomb in 1952, Britain became the world's third nuclear power, after the United States and the Soviet Union. The first bomb, of course, was unleashed by the Americans at Hiroshima, in Japan, in August 1945.

In *An Unjustifiable Risk*, screened in 1977, Pilger tackled the potential dangers of nuclear weapons and the new breed of plutonium-fuelled reactors that were planned. He opened with the words:

This film is about atomic power, so please don't switch off. This time, it does concern you directly. Let me start with three facts. Number one: anyone with an expert knowledge of physics can make an atomic bomb with just that much of a substance called plutonium. Number two: a speck of plutonium causes cancer. Number three: there is no absolutely safe way of storing, protecting or transporting plutonium . . . And yet plutonium is what you're going to get if the government go ahead and build the first commercial nuclear power station fuelled by plutonium, the first of many so-called fast-breeder reactors that will solve all our energy problems – according to the salesmen of our nuclear industry, but not according to an independent royal commission. The head of the royal commission, Sir Brian Flowers, said, 'We believe that nobody should rely on an energy process as dangerous as plutonium, unless he is absolutely convinced that there is no reasonable alternative course of action. I am bound to say that we are not convinced that this is the case by the evidence submitted to us.'

Most of the documentary was filmed in Japan, 'where the world's first human nuclear guinea pigs live, people whose experiences and suffering might help us to understand'. Film followed of hundreds of doves flying over a square in Japan and of wreaths being laid on the thirty-second anniversary of the Hiroshima bomb, then of the bomb exploding.

After one American weapons expert predicted the odds of a global nuclear war increasing if the plutonium fast-breeder reactor programme went ahead and another nuclear expert pronouncing nuclear power safe, Pilger described the legacy of Hiroshima, where about 200,000 people had died. And people were still dying as a result of the fallout, with 1,600 deaths the previous year, from injuries and diseases linked to the atomic bomb. Witnesses and victims remembered the day the bomb fell on them. A woman told how a midwife tried to help a woman having a baby, then died, covered in blood. 'I don't know what happened to the baby,' she said. A man recalled his whole body being 'covered in pus, flies and maggots crawling over me' and the agony of his back being stuck to a rush mat when women tried to pull him up to bathe his wounds.

Pilger read from a Health and Safety Executive report, prepared at the request of the then energy secretary, Tony Benn, describing what might happen in the event of an accidental explosion at a plutonium-fuelled nuclear reactor in heavily populated Britain, with tens of thousands of people dying from cancer over several decades. The nuclear industry claimed that the possibility of a nuclear accident was remote, said Pilger, but the previous November a Soviet scientist had published evidence of an explosion at a nuclear dump in the Soviet Union, killing hundreds, and which 'turned a region as big as an English county into a contaminated wilderness'. There had been at least one near-disaster at Windscale.

Selling nuclear power to the British people was, said Pilger, the end of a long line of nuclear salesmanship. 'The atomic bomb was sold to us as the means that ended World War Two,' he explained, 'and yet its other purpose was research, to find out what would happen if a Russian bomb was dropped on America . . . The salesmanship reached its peak in 1963 with the Test Ban Treaty. Of course, this did not interfere with nuclear testing or with free enterprise. In 1973, President Nixon finally lifted the veil when he ruled that private American companies could trade directly in nuclear merchandise. Today, we are once again being sold the atom, reconditioned, low-mileage, new price tag, new name – plutonium.'

The secret London Suppliers Group, consisting of fifteen members from Europe, the United States and Japan, had sold nuclear power to thirty-six countries – Argentina, Austria, Belgium, Brazil, Canada, China, Czechoslovakia, East Germany, Egypt, Finland, France, Hungary, India, Iran, Israel, Italy, Japan, Mexico, the Netherlands, Norway, Pakistan, the Philippines, Poland, South Africa, South Korea, the Soviet Union, Spain, Sweden, Switzerland, Taiwan, Thailand, the United Kingdom, the United States, West Germany, Yugoslavia and Zaire – which now had the atomic bomb or the means to build it by 1980.

Film of a child walking with a frame at the Atomic Bomb Hospital in Hiroshima was accompanied by Pilger's account of the extremely high incidence of leukaemia among victims exposed to low levels of radiation. 'This could mean that the former guidelines from Hiroshima are wrong,' he added. 'It could also mean that the acceptable levels of radiation around nuclear plants in Britain like Windscale are already too high.' A doctor at the hospital told Pilger about the long-term effects of radiation, passed from one generation to another.

'Dalek-like' machines at Ravenglass, near Windscale, monitored radiation in the atmosphere. A Lancaster University professor had reported to the Windscale Inquiry the previous week that fish caught in the Irish Sea contained enough radiation to cause genetic damage to humans as a result of radioactive isotopes being released by the nuclear industry.

'There's big money involved,' said Pilger, 'and, already, Britain's first major nuclear deal is being worked out with Japan. The deal is to reprocess four thousand tons of Japanese nuclear waste, at Windscale, but the problem is: how do we get it back to Japan? Last June, the managing director of British Nuclear Fuels admitted that this huge dump of highly radioactive waste could remain in Britain indefinitely.'

Alternatives to nuclear energy included tidal, solar and wave power, which were renewable, harmless energy sources but accounted for only one per cent of the energy development budget. One of the Hiroshima survivors said of nuclear power and weapons programmes, 'These developments are very dangerous and we're afraid of this dependence on nuclear energy. We know the dangers better than anyone else in the world and all the survivors are getting old. Soon, there will be no one left to tell what really happened.'

To the camera in Hiroshima, Pilger said, 'There will be some scientists and politicians who will say that this film is emotional.

But, unlike them, almost all the witnesses in the film actually took part in the first nuclear experiment using human beings, here in Hiroshima. Please be clear about one thing: those who want the British government to build the nation's first commercial-scale nuclear power station fuelled by plutonium want you and your children to take part in an experiment. In other words, in order to save an industry that has been many times proven uneconomic, inefficient and dangerous, they want you to take a risk. Do you really want a future of nuclear installations that are not completely safe, of waste dumps radioactive for thousands of years, of atomic policemen ruthlessly guarding these poisons? And do you want to spend hundreds of millions of pounds on this unjustifiable risk, when just a fraction of that amount could make our coalmines safe and more productive, and develop other sources of energy of which Britain has an abundance? And are we that hard up that Britain now needs to export to other countries the means of making the atomic bomb?

'These questions have to be answered by you and not by nuclear salesmen in jargon which only they can understand. Sometime this autumn, the government will decide whether or not to commit you to a fast-breeder plutonium reactor and, perhaps, to a new atomic age. Those politicians, they know that this is what's called a sensitive public issue and *you* are the public. Isn't it up to you to speak out now, before the next Hiroshimas?' At the end of the programme, an announcer said, 'Since this report was filmed, the government has postponed its decision on fast-breeder reactors, pending further public inquiry.'

The film was broadcast only after ATV resisted pressure from the Atomic Energy Authority to drop it. Despite a public campaign of opposition, fast-breeder reactors were introduced in Britain. In 1980, Pilger reported for the *Daily Mirror* on how Americans were adjusting to living with unsafe levels of radiation after experiencing the horror of the world's worst civilian nuclear accident, at Three Mile Island, Pennsylvania, the previous year. Already, there was a higher incidence of babies being born with deformities. In Britain, Windscale, renamed Sellafield as part of a public relations exercise to soften its image, was responsible for a string of nuclear leaks and, in 1985, its owner, British Nuclear Fuels, was fined £10,000 with £60,000 costs for failing in its safeguards to minimize exposure of humans to radiation and in keeping radioactive discharge as low as possible.

Fifteen years later, it was revealed that British Nuclear Fuels had falsified safety data for customers worldwide, including Kepco of Japan. When that company demanded that suspect nuclear fuel unloaded at a plant in central Japan be returned to Britain, the British government refused. In 2000, three damning Health and Safety Executive reports highlighted the lack of safety measures at Sellafield and revealed that British Nuclear Fuels staff had falsified plutonium safety data.

Pilger would revisit the theme of nuclear weapons in *The Truth Game*, in 1983 (see Chapter 8), but the issue of selling another dangerous commodity, arms, was one he tackled in *Flying the Flag – Arming the World*, screened in ITV's week of 'War Machine' programmes eleven years later. The film traced the British government's history of selling weapons to countries with appalling human rights records and told the story of arms sales to Iraq, which was the subject of the Scott inquiry which was still due to report. In researching the programme, Pilger was given an insight into the way in which the arms manufacturer Astra had been mysteriously taken over by British intelligence so that it could break the Thatcher government's reluctant embargo on arms sales to Saddam Hussein's regime.

'Jonathan Aitken was on the board, nodding all this through,' explained Pilger, 'and Gerald James was having his company taken away from him by IMS, a front company for the Ministry of Defence. It was a way of getting round the ban on arms sales to Iraq. Suddenly, Jordan was getting masses of arms that it hadn't asked for. They went to Iraq.'[24]

Pilger started and ended the documentary by relating the build-up of a military economy during the years of the Thatcher government in Britain to the running down of manufacturing industry that accompanied it. From inside the ruins of British Leyland's Lancashire factory, he said, 'Industrial deserts like this are not hard to find. With the exception of one industry in which Britain is still a world leader. Indeed, it has 20 per cent of a world market, second only to the United States, and this industry is considered so important by the government that it consumes almost half of all research and development funds. Strangely, it produces not consumer goods that people want, but machines that hardly any of us use or want to use. Moreover, for all its pre-eminence, its future is uncertain and depends to a large degree on secret deals with some of the most corrupt and brutal regimes on earth. One of the biggest manufacturing industries in Britain at the close of the twentieth century is arms.'

The British economy had been militarized during the Thatcher years, explained Pilger, and one in ten employees now worked on military material. The Ministry of Defence was industry's biggest customer, spending more than £23 billion a year. Outside the Ministry of Defence, Pilger outlined its inner workings. DESO, the Defence Services Organization run by the MoD, was a 'hard-sell' international arms broker overseeing 80 per cent of Britain's arms exports to developing countries, 'many of them run by unsavoury dictatorships'.

Its forerunner, the Defence Sales Organization, had been set up by Labour defence secretary Denis Healey in 1966 to 'secure its rightful share of this valuable commercial market', at the same time as aiming for arms control. Healey told Pilger, 'I don't feel all that happy about it, but remember this was at the time when the Cold War was really at its height. There was an enormous amount of arms sales by the Soviet Union all over the world . . . for me, the main thing was to reduce the unit cost of British weapons by selling some of them abroad.' A former government arms sales-man, Robert Jarman, said that Margaret Thatcher made it obvious on becoming prime minister that 'she personally thought that defence exporting was good for the United Kingdom'. A former

Cabinet Office clerk, Robin Robison, said that Thatcher was the only prime minister ever to attend joint intelligence committee meetings at which discussions took place about arms deals between foreign countries and potential sales for British firms. He never recalled any discussions about human rights and concluded that 'the intelligence information that should have been stopping the arms trade was possibly helping it'.

In 1985, reported Pilger, Thatcher negotiated the Al-Yamamah deal with Saudi Arabia, worth up to £30 billion in exports of fighter aircraft, missiles and ships. Her son, Mark, was accused of making £12 million in 'commissions' from the deal, but he denied the charge. Howard Teicher, a Middle East diplomatic analyst, told Pilger that intelligence and diplomatic messages from Saudi Arabia that he had studied included Mark Thatcher's name. 'There was no doubt in my mind that Mark Thatcher was a principal in the group of individuals promoting the UK arms transaction and he undoubtedly would benefit economically,' said Teicher. His name appeared 'tens of times' on documents dated between 1984 and 1986. When Pilger produced a document about competition between the United States and Britain over the Saudi deal, mentioning Thatcher in a $4 billion deal, Teicher verified its authenticity. In the United States, this could bring about the impeachment of an elected official, he added.

Pilger explained that commissions on arms deals were not illegal under British law, but in Saudi Arabia women were executed for adultery and others publicly beheaded for changing their religion. 'Thousands of British jobs depend on a single arms deal with this regime, whose viciousness the British government has worked hard to disguise,' said Pilger. He then listed a catalogue of deals with some of the world's worst human rights violators: a torture chamber supplied to Dubai; armoured cars that took part in the Sharpeville massacre in South Africa; communications equipment that assisted Idi Amin's reign of terror in Uganda. Today, said Pilger, Britain was arming Turkey, where MPs were jailed for speaking out and journalists murdered,

Nigeria, which staged public executions and meted out torture, Chile and a list 'too long for inclusion in this film'.

Britain was Indonesia's biggest arms supplier. Since Pilger's documentary earlier that year about East Timor, whose invasion by Indonesia in 1975 was followed by genocide, thousands of people had written to their MPs and the government to voice their concern (see Chapter 6). They had been sent a standard Foreign Office reply claiming that Hawk aircraft sent to Indonesia were only 'trainers'. Mark Higson, who worked as a clerk on the Foreign Office's Iraq desk in 1989, told Pilger, 'Everyone knows that the Hawk aircraft can be utilized in an offensive way. Assurances from the Suharto regime in Indonesia that the Hawks were not being used in East Timor were,' said Higson, 'about as worthless as the piece of paper that they're written on.'

Turning to Sir Richard Scott's inquiry into British arms sales to Iraq, Pilger was told by Labour MP Michael Meacher that throughout the 1980s billions of pounds of British arms were exported to both Iran and Iraq with the government's knowledge, in contravention of its guidelines. In 1989, said Pilger, the Thatcher government denied that it had changed its policy on arms sales to Iraq, although she had underlined words in official papers suggesting that such sales should be subject to 'more flexible interpretation'. On taking power, Thatcher's ministers had courted Saddam Hussein, reported Pilger. The flow of arms did not stop despite a 1985 ban. At the time Foreign Office minister David Mellor visited Sadam Hussein three years later, the Iraqi dictator ordered the gassing of 5,000 Kurds in the town of Halabja, and trade with Iraq subsequently increased.

Firms responsible for arms sales to Iraq were being investigated by the Scott inquiry. One company that sold to that country was Astra Holdings, which had been taken over by MI6, according to its former chairman, Gerald James. Astra's former acquisitions adviser, Tim Laxton, told Pilger that a subsidiary, PRB, was involved in contracts other than those stated on the documentation. 'Our notepaper and our name were being used for contracts which were really being operated by other people,' said James of the Jordan deal, whose arms were passed on to Iraq and probably used in the Gulf War. 'I think it was IMS, the company that was owned by the Ministry of Defence. It was a separate organization from Defence Sales which handled what I would term perhaps the more covert activities of the government.'

'This is the carnage of the Gulf War,' said Pilger over film from that conflict, which included dead bodies being collected together. 'A shop window for the arms trade. The official truth of the war was that, thanks to hi-tech weapons, few people had been killed. But up to 200,000 people died.' (See Chapters 4 and 8 for further coverage by Pilger of the Gulf War.)

Turning to the 'glossy' way in which British companies traded on the international market, Pilger and director David Munro filmed arms fairs in Farnborough and Paris. Pictures of salesmen pitching to potential buyers were reminiscent of Munro's earlier documentary, The Four Horsemen, which related the upbeat, almost surreal way in which arms were sold like washing machines or cars, and regardless of their drastic results thousands of miles away.[25]

'Gaining access to the arms bazaars was no problem,' said Pilger. 'They had no grounds for refusal. In Paris, we came upon a British salesman trying to sell a Russian missile to a group of Chileans. He was well into his pitch about how wonderful the thing was when we moved in with the camera and a sound boom. He carried on regardless, then marched over to me and said, "You're not being very helpful." I replied, "It's not my job to be helpful to you." '[26] Wandering through the arms fair, asking salesmen what this or that weapon did and how many people it could kill or maim, clearly appealed to Pilger's black sense of humour. Nodding sagely, he was told by one salesman how a new type of cluster bomb sprayed lethal dust on its victims. 'How ingenious,' said Pilger. 'Did you always want to be a salesman?' The representative of a Birmingham razorwire company told him of his pride in his product, which was used in detention camps 'all over the world'.[27]

Over an idyllic scene of Cambodian children running through fields of mustard flowers, Pilger said that unexploded landmines caused 500 amputations to be performed every month in that country. 'Throughout the world, there are more than a hundred million of them waiting to explode,' he said, 'and yet the British government has planned a military strategy of scattering mines from the air.'

United Nations figures showed that 2,000 people a month were maimed or killed by mines, said Rae McGrath, of the Mines Advisory Group, UK. The British government had voted at the UN Security Council in favour of an international moratorium on the export of landmines as long as it did not apply to British mines. Conservative MP Roger Freeman, the minister for defence procurement, told Pilger that the mines were part of Britain's weaponry that was needed for the self-defence of the nation.

At Gairloch, in Scotland, and with the Trident nuclear submarine base behind him, Pilger said, 'The government claims that Trident cost £10 billion. Greenpeace says the real figure is more like £30 billion over twenty years. Last year, the National Audit Office revealed that £800 million had been wasted building facilities for Trident. That's more than the entire costs of the cuts in Britain's conventional forces this year.' Built for the Cold War, Trident was now said to have a new role – 'sub strategic capability', which meant that 'a new threat has been found'. Professor Paul Rogers, of Bradford University, said that the new threats came from the Middle East, Latin America and other countries in the southern hemisphere.

The Labour Party effectively had the same nuclear policy as the Conservative government, said Pilger. Shadow defence spokesman Dr David Clark told him that there were dictators 'who could actually cause damage on what we call our civilized West', and countries in the Middle East and parts of Africa that 'already have missiles which can reach halfway up Europe', such as Iraq and Libya. Asked by Pilger why they were likely to fire them at Britain, Dr Clark replied, 'Well, we don't know.'

'This is the real cost,' said Pilger, over black-and-white still photographs of homeless people. 'It has been estimated that the money spent over the years on nuclear submarines would restore a national housing programme and virtually end homelessness. It would also restore the transport system and stop the haemorrhage of teachers from schools by raising salaries to a decent level. And it would pay every outstanding bill in the health service and ensure that no one died waiting for an operation. It would also allow non-military research and development to catch up with the best in Europe and what was left over could be invested in converting industry to peaceful production.'

Professor Michael Cooley, formerly a leading design engineer for Lucas Aerospace, said this could be phased over a ten-year period. Answering the allegation that jobs would be lost, he said, 'One of the choices is to use the skill and ability we now have, large amounts of it concentrated in the defence industries, to produce products and services which would be caring for humanity and the environment, and I don't think that's really very Utopian.'

Returning to the theme of Britain becoming a military economy as whole industries were dismantled, Pilger said, 'Who authorized the illegal sale of arms to Saddam Hussein? Who has made a fortune out of deals with other murderous dictators? And what exactly was the role of supersaleswoman Thatcher and her family? Of course, for people in other countries the issue is one of life and death – death from British cluster bombs, life denied by money squandered on British arms they don't need. Is the end of this century going to mark the British as people whose great manufacturing reputation has been reduced to that of making magnificent tools of death?'

Flying the Flag – Arming the World caused many questions to be raised in the House of Commons, especially about the Astra revelations. However, Lord Justice Scott's report concluded that, in spite of the evidence before his inquiry, Cabinet ministers had acted 'honestly and in good faith' in the arms to Iraq affair. In *Paying the Price – Killing the Children of Iraq* (see Chapter 4), Pilger returned to the subject and reported for the first time from Iraq.

By the 1990s, the British press had changed almost beyond recognition since Pilger had joined the *Daily Mirror* in 1963. The entrance of Australian media magnate Rupert Murdoch in the 1960s with his purchase of the *News of the World* and then, most significantly, the *Sun* not only altered the character of those newspapers but had the effect of making their rivals go more downmarket. At the *Mirror*, Pilger had seen the beginnings of this decline, which accelerated after Robert Maxwell took over the paper in 1984. Pilger was sacked on New Year's Eve 1985 while on holiday in Australia – although he had planned to resign on his return to Britain, having had a string of stories and ideas rejected. His uncompromising journalism, including unrelenting attacks on the Thatcher government, was not an ingredient that Maxwell wanted. The *Mirror* was no longer the paper of the people, who could rely on it to look after their interests and call governments and politicians to account.

Pilger had long wanted to make a documentary about the changing fortunes of the paper that he had worked on for twenty-three years. The result was *Breaking the Mirror – The Murdoch Effect*, directed by David Munro and broadcast in 1997. However, it did not come to screens until after a battle with the ITV Network Centre, which had commissioned the Pilger film. The Network Centre was a centralized, statutory body responsible for ITV programmes and schedules. 'I had an uneasy relationship with John Blake, who was deputy controller of factual programmes,' recalled Pilger. 'He questioned whether people would be interested in watching a "nostalgic film about the *Mirror*", as he put it. I said it wasn't to be at all nostalgic – it would be a film about what a newspaper had been and why it had declined so rapidly. It would address the whole issue of press freedom and monopoly. We had an exchange of letters and I said that, if ITV didn't want the idea, I would withdraw it and take it somewhere else.'[28] The programme was accepted.

Clearly regarding the paper he had worked on for so many years as having passed away and worthy of mourning, Pilger began and ended *Breaking the Mirror – The Murdoch Effect* in St Bride's, the 'journalists' church', off Fleet Street, which had been abandoned over the previous eleven years as newspapers moved out. 'It's a place where journalists come to say goodbye to their own, someone they were proud to know, someone with humanity and humour that touched millions of lives, who gave voice to people and fought their battles,' said Pilger inside the church. 'There have been newspapers like that and this seems a fitting place to celebrate the best of them, and the *Daily Mirror was* the best of them. It was a tabloid when "tabloid" still meant a people's paper that respected its readers and earned their trust and affection.'

Whatever his old loyalties and coloured views, it was true that the *Mirror* had been the most popular newspaper in the land, and biggest-selling in the Western world, when he joined it. Along with the broadsheet *Daily Express*, it was one of two papers that journalists queued up to join more than any others. 'This film is a personal tribute,' said Pilger, 'but it's also the story of what happened to the once popular *Mirror*, how the reporting of the blood, sweat and tears of ordinary people has changed out of all recognition. Above all, it's the story of the rise of a new kind of tabloid and a new kind of media power, now set to dominate much of the world.'

Tracing the *Mirror*'s history from its beginnings in 1903 as a newspaper written by women for women to that of one explaining the significance of political events in Britain and around the world and campaigning against injustice and oppression, Pilger recalled that it was a lone voice in opposing fascism throughout the 1930s and the Vietnam War three decades later, and in the 1970s it was the only paper to call for the withdrawal of British troops from Northern Ireland.

Hugh Cudlipp, the *Mirror*'s great editorial director who gave Pilger much of his freedom to write in the 1960s, explained that his predecessor, Harry Guy Bartholomew, had pioneered the use of pictures in the paper and shaped its character. 'The modern technique of the big picture, of the splash on the front page, just wasn't thought of then,' said Cudlipp. It was Cudlipp, said Pilger, who then transformed the post-war *Mirror* into Britain's 'first quality popular newspaper'. The paper urged its readers to 'Vote for Them', the ordinary men and women who had beaten Hitler and did not want a return to the economic depression of the 1930s. This resulted in a landslide win for the Labour Party, although Cudlipp explained that at the time the directors of the *Mirror* would not have tolerated a direct call for its readers to vote Labour. 'Half of the directors would have dropped dead,' he told Pilger.

The 'Shock Issue' was invented by Cudlipp, with much of a single day's paper devoted to a subject such as housing, class or racism, intended both to shock and offer solutions. Notable campaigns included sports writer Peter Wilson's opposition to apartheid in South Africa. Other great journalists in the 1960s included the columnist Cassandra (William Connor) and the entertainment writer Donald Zec, who never paid for a story. By the end of that decade, said Pilger, the *Mirror* was read by more people of every social class than any other newspaper. It provided a 'window on the world'. He cited his own story that revealed the legacy of Pol Pot's terror in Cambodia, which was spread over more than half of an issue that sold out. The *Mirror*'s success, said Cudlipp, arose from its 'bond with its readers and the quality of its journalists'.

Marje Proops, who spent more than forty years as the *Mirror*'s agony aunt, told Pilger that Cudlipp had congratulated her on making history by being the first journalist in a national newspaper to use the word 'masturbate'. She recalled that letters from female readers in the 1950s were often about 'submitting' to their husbands. Paul Foot, who survived Maxwell's regime while Pilger did not, said that he received more than 150,000 letters from readers asking him to investigate various issues during his fourteen years on the *Mirror.*

This 'nostalgia' was interrupted by the appearance of graphics showing a red planet rising, labelled 'The Sun'. Accompanied by the sound of 'Also sprach Zarathustra', it was a dramatic and typically David Munro way of introducing the threat posed to the *Mirror* by the revitalized, Murdoch-owned *Sun.* Ironically, the *Sun* had been owned by the Mirror Group as a serious broadsheet but was loss-making, so it was put up for sale. The unions opposed Robert Maxwell's bid because he had promised redundancies, so the *Sun* was sold to Murdoch. Over pictures of Page Three Girls, which were soon adorning the relaunched *Sun*, Pilger reflected that the paper had become 'a crude copy of the *Mirror* itself, with the added ingredients of soft-porn, gossip and cheap fantasy'. Murdoch had refused to be interviewed for Pilger's film, but his biographer, Thomas Kiernan, described him as 'very mild, self-effacing, shy in public in company', with high standards in his family life, although in his newspapers and other media 'he lowers standards, he destroys standards'.

As an increasing number of people bought the *Sun* and others simply gave up reading popular newspapers, said Pilger, ITV programmes such as *World in Action* 'began to fulfil the role of the *Daily Mirror* in its more confident days'. The rapid rise in the *Sun*'s readership presented the *Mirror* with the dilemma of whether to maintain its standards and character or compete on the same, 'low' ground. Opting for the latter, it failed and was eventually over-taken in circulation. When Robert Maxwell bought the *Mirror*, the paper lost more than a million more readers in just eighteen months.

Pilger offered a personal insight into Maxwell's maverick, questionable ways of running the newspaper. Declaring himself the 'Houdini of Fleet Street', he described vanishing whenever

Maxwell tried to find him so that he could send him on assignments to Bulgaria, Poland and China. These all involved the
proprietor's attempts to 'promote some huge and often dodgy
business deals'. In 1984, Pilger feigned a life-threatening malady
when Maxwell ordered him to accompany him to the Ethiopian
famine, to report his 'philanthropy to the world's starving' – in
reality, his usual exercise in self-aggrandisement.

Former editor Roy Greenslade reflected on Maxwell's con-
tinual interference in editorial matters. On his first day in the job,
he was ordered to run a story accusing miners' leaders Arthur
Scargill and Peter Heathfield of using Libyan money donated to
the National Union of Mineworkers to pay off their mortgages.
The story proved to be entirely false. Maxwell himself was
unmasked as a crook after his mysterious death at sea. 'Not only
had he robbed the *Mirror*'s pension funds, he had made off with its
self-respect,' said Pilger.

Back in the Murdoch camp, Pilger reported Murdoch's removal of his News International empire to Wapping, East
London, in 1986 after sacking more than 5,000 workers on
the pretext that the print unions were obstructing manning
and new technology agreements. Murdoch was effectively backed
by the Thatcher government, said Pilger, when a massive police
operation safeguarded distribution of the *Sun* and other Murdoch
papers in the face of picketing outside 'fortress' Wapping. It
almost seemed out of place when Hugh Cudlipp told Pilger that
he forgave Murdoch 'a lot' for defeating unions who at times had
made it impossible to produce newspapers. ('I disagreed passionately with this statement by Cudlipp,' said Pilger later, 'but the
wily old genius challenged me to use it and I did so out of great
respect for him.')[29]

Over photographs of confidential documents, Pilger said, 'The
unions had worked hard to negotiate an agreement with Murdoch which he clearly had no intention of keeping.' In one letter,
Murdoch's lawyer outlined the most convenient way of sacking
the maximum number of people. Dismissing employees while on

strike would be the cheapest way, advised one letter. Half of those sacked were, in fact, workers such as cleaners and secretaries. The 'flowering of independent newspapers' predicted by Murdoch as a result of agreements on new technology had not happened, with the *Independent* the only survivor of four national papers launched in the mid-1980s.

Murdoch's power, which had never been greater, said Pilger, was illustrated by *Independent* editor Andrew Marr, who spoke of the price war launched by the owner of *The Times* in an attempt to put his paper and the *Daily Telegraph* out of business. It was, explained Marr, financed by Murdoch's huge profits from his satellite television service Sky. In turn, Pilger explained that Murdoch had been able to launch Sky in 1988 through the increased profits enjoyed by moving his newspapers to Wapping. He now exercised great power over television as well as the press but had paid almost no British tax on News International profits of more than £1 billion since 1991. Christopher Hird, author of *Murdoch: The Great Escape*, said that Murdoch's global empire enabled him to escape tax. His Australian newspapers and tele-vision stations were owned by companies in countries with low tax rates, such as the Netherlands. Hird added that the Labour Party in Britain had 'abandoned any idea of trying to discipline the Murdoch press'. Labour broadcasting spokesman Dr Lewis Moonie told Pilger that he did not seek complete deregulation and described Murdoch as a 'visionary' who put a lot of money into satellite television before seeing any return on his investment.

Returning to the theme of how events affected ordinary people's lives, film of a rundown housing estate in Liverpool was accompanied by sombre music and Pilger's contention that their struggles were no longer reflected in the *Mirror* and the *Sun*. He cited their failure to report the long-running Liverpool dockers' strike and two national conferences of pensioners – a quarter of the electorate – and contrasted this with a week-long campaign for Britain's most senior citizens in 1963. The *Sun*'s claim that fans had caused the Hillsborough football tragedy of

1989, in which ninety-six Liverpool supporters were crushed to death, proved to be completely untrue, said Pilger. A subsequent inquiry blamed lack of police control. Eddie Spearitt, father of fourteen-year-old victim Adam, explained that he had not only lost a son but had to defend him 'against all the rubbish that's been printed by the *Sun*'.

Since 1992, the *Mirror*'s offices had been in Canary Wharf, 'a sort of vertical Fleet Street', said Pilger, and the Mirror Group had been run by former Murdoch editors – chief executive David Montgomery, editor Piers Morgan, managing director Charles Wilson and L!veTV boss Kelvin MacKenzie. On some days, continued Pilger over pictures of front pages, the paper was indistinguishable from the *Sun*. 'The *Mirror*, as imitator, has been the loser,' he said, 'with its falling circulation down to less than two-and-a-half million.' Students at Pimlico School, in London, told him that they regarded the *Sun* and the *Mirror* as 'superficial' and 'sensationalist'.

Perhaps interviews with some of the millions who read those papers every day might have shed more light on their success and why people buy them, but Pilger could not be faulted for his exposition of the way in which the *Mirror* had changed its content and values to compete with the *Sun*. He also kept his usual 'editorials' to camera to a minimum in this film, perhaps compensating for the very personal nature of it. However, he finished with a piece at St Bride's Church. Over photographs of James Cameron, Martha Gellhorn and Ed Murrow, he asserted that 'journalism is not a product looking for a niche market – it is a vital extension of democracy and, without diversity, journalists are merely the agents of power when they should be the agents of people'.

The final words of *Breaking the Mirror – The Murdoch Effect* went to Hugh Cudlipp. Quoting his own speech at the funeral of a former *Mirror* editorial director in 1988, Cudlipp said that Sydney Jacobson had been fortunate to retire in 1974, 'the dawn of the dark age of tabloid journalism . . . playing a continuing role in public enlightenment was no longer any business of the popular press, information about foreign affairs was relegated to a three-inch, yapping editorial insulting foreigners . . . nothing, however personal, was any longer secret or sacred and the basic human right to privacy was banished in the interests of publishing profit, when significant national and international events were nudged aside by a panting, seven-day and seven-night news service for voyeurs and the one-night stands of pop stars with teenage delinquents'. Cudlipp added, 'Some of these foolish things are worthy of mention in the popular press. Now, it's overkill.'

The documentary was certainly a lament for a once-great newspaper and was no doubt written off by some as sour grapes. Pilger's sadness at the 'loss' of the *Mirror* came through but, more important, he placed the fate of his old paper in a wider context, demonstrating that standards had fallen as 'infotainment', cheap voyeurism and the insidious effect of public relations diminished much of journalism. It was a subject he expanded on in his book, *Hidden Agendas*, published a year later.

3. CAMBODIA

J OHN PILGER'S LONGEST-RUNNING and most
effective television campaign has been for justice in Cambodia. Having reported from the South-east Asian country for
the *Daily Mirror* in 1967 while covering the Vietnam War, he
returned twelve years later, after the Vietnamese had thrown out
Pol Pot and the murderous Khmer Rouge. Not only did he reveal
that possibly more than two million people, out of a total
population of seven million, had died as a result of genocide
or starvation under the previous regime, but he also laid part of the
blame on the United States, which had secretly and illegally
bombed the country and created the turmoil that allowed Pol Pot
to seize power.

Now, the beleaguered Cambodians faced famine, and Western
politicians and aid agencies were refusing help because they did
not recognize the new government set up by the Vietnamese,
who had only four years earlier defeated the Americans in the
longest war of the century and recently thrown out the Khmer
Rouge after repeated attacks across their border. The story was
dramatic enough, but director David Munro's pictures of emaciated children and Pilger's suppressed anger at power politics
denying help to a starving population made *Year Zero – The Silent
Death of Cambodia* a memorable piece of filmmaking with some of
the most stunning images ever contained in a Pilger programme.
It is one of the most watched documentaries ever made.

News from Cambodia, in the Pol Pot years, had filtered out
through refugees. Father François Ponchaud, a French Jesuit priest
who lived for ten years as a missionary in the country until leaving

three weeks after the Khmer Rouge takeover, pieced together an account of life under the murderous regime in his 1977 book *Cambodia Year Zero*, based on his own experience, the stories of almost a hundred refugees, and radio broadcasts from inside Cambodia. Prime Minister James Callaghan's Labour government in Britain sent a report to the United Nations Human Rights Commission containing shocking reports of atrocities. However, none of this prepared the outside world for the reality of what had been done to the people of Cambodia and it took more than six months for it to wake up to what had actually happened and the need for urgent aid.

Two French doctors who were trying to save some of the children in the main hospital in the country's capital, Phnom Penh, were instrumental in getting Pilger to Cambodia. Jean Yves Follezou and Jean Michel Vinot, representing the Comité Français d'Aide Médicale et Sanitaire, had in May 1979 gone to Cambodia with the Paris-based journalist Wilfred Burchett, another Australian renowned for his uncompromising reporting, but Burchett's subsequent features in the *Guardian* went almost unnoticed.

The doctors returned to Paris with a list of the Cambodian people's needs, drawn up in consultation with the new, Vietnamese-installed government in Phnom Penh, but they failed to generate any significant response. In July, Burchett travelled to London with the list and read out most of it at a packed, all-party meeting in the House of Commons, stressing that the country was in dire need of help. But his moving speech failed to spur any government action in Britain.

For more than a month before this, Pilger had been receiving telephone calls, almost on a daily basis, from Madame Louise Vidaud de Plaud, an elderly woman of Dutch-Flemish origin but later French citizenship, by then living in Oxford. During five years in Cambodia during the early 1970s, she had arranged for civilians to be trained in Vietnam to make artificial limbs for amputees and met many of the leaders of the different factions in the civil war. 'I read Wilfred Burchett's articles in the *Guardian* and then met him,' said Mme Vidaud. 'He said to me, "Isn't it sad that the poor Vietnamese have had to put their uniforms on again and help the Cambodians?" They didn't want any more trouble and they had to reconstruct their own country. In June 1979, I called John Pilger and said, "You must go to Cambodia and do this story."'[1] She put Pilger in touch with the two French doctors. He told them that he would go if he could take a film crew with him.

At the same time, Jim Howard, senior technical adviser for the British charity Oxfam, put into motion a relief plan despite being told by a Ministry of Overseas Development official in London that the government's boycott on Vietnam now extended to Cambodia. Howard, who had organized relief in Biafra, India, Bangladesh, Latin America, Ethiopia, the Sudan and Asia, had heard Burchett's House of Commons speech. The overseas aid official also told him that the Cambodian authorities had blocked aid from the Red Cross and UNICEF (the United Nations Children's Fund). Howard was sceptical of this, and his own experience was to show that they were willing to allow in aid and its distribution.

Oxfam had also been badgered by Mme Vidaud, who lived near the charity's Oxford headquarters. 'She told me that, if I went to Paris with her, she could make some introductions that would get me into Cambodia,' recalled Howard. 'So we flew to France and I met an extraordinary professor, Henri Carpantier, an old, left-wing intellectual who had known Mao Tse-tung, Chou En-lai and Pol Pot, when they studied in Paris. We all had a meal, and Dr Follezou was there, too. He said that the medical situation in Cambodia was dire. Carpantier then showed me a garage where he and others had been collecting drugs to send. I told him that Oxfam would be prepared to lay on a plane to fly into Cambodia as long as I went with it. Carpantier took my passport and obtained a visa from the Vietnamese embassy in Paris that very day.'[2]

While Howard was setting up this operation, Pilger, director David Munro, cameraman Gerry Pinches, sound recordist Steve Phillips and *Daily Mirror* photographer Eric Piper flew to Vietnam to negotiate with the government there the terms under which they could film. Pilger laid down three conditions: they must have their own van, their own fuel and the right to travel wherever they wanted. All three were accepted and, a day before leaving for Cambodia, Pilger interviewed Vietnam's foreign minister, Nguyen Co Tach, who explained that the Vietnamese had entered the country in January 1979 following almost four years of attacks on their border by the Khmer Rouge and, finally, an invasion on their northern border by China, Pol Pot's ally and the United States' newest trading partner.

It was now August, and Pilger and his team flew over the border to see for themselves the results of four years of Khmer Rouge rule. Their first sight of the landscape was enough to make them realize that something of enormous proportions had happened to this country. There appeared to be no movement, not even animals, and towns and villages were completely deserted, but they were to find an even more deep-seated devastation when they landed in the country that had been turned back to 'Year Zero' by Pol Pot in his attempt to create a society that had no connections with the modern world. The evidence of murder was everywhere, including cracked sculls dug out of mass graves near Angkor Wat by villagers who had lost relatives. 'What I saw,' recalled Pilger later, 'was something I had never imagined. I expected to see devastation, but not such a cultural devastation and the ripping apart of the fabric of a whole society.'[3]

In his subsequent film, *Year Zero – The Silent Death of Cambodia*, Pilger contrasted this with the Cambodia he had known in 1967. Pictures of Phnom Penh's deserted streets – 'as if in the wake of a nuclear war that spared only the buildings' – were followed by archive footage from 'the capital of a land of plenty, of markets everywhere, a land that produced three annual harvests and a variety of fruit renowned in Asia'. Pilger recalled Phnom Penh as being 'the most beautiful city in South-east Asia' but admitted that it was perhaps too easy for a foreigner to romanticize such a place.

This was the idyllic view held by many foreign visitors. The French director Marcel Talabot made a film about Cambodia entitled *The Smiling Country* as part of the *Connaissance du Monde* travel series in the 1960s. The British author William Shawcross, who reported the Vietnam War for *The Sunday Times*, but spent only a week in Cambodia, wrote that Phnom Penh's 'fine white and yellow-ocher buildings, charming squares and cafés lent it a French provincial charm that gave it a considerable edge over its tawdry neighbours Bangkok and Saigon', and that 'the country-side, where 90 per cent of the people lived in villages built around their Buddhist temples, seemed, if anything, even more attractive than the capital'. However, Shawcross added ominously, 'It was never quite the smiling, gentle land that foreigners liked to see.'[4]

Pilger explained in his documentary that, under the rule of Prince Norodom Sihanouk – who had preserved Cambodia's independence 'like an absurd juggler in a cockpit of war' – there had been feudalism and corruption, but neutral Cambodia was thrown into turmoil when he was deposed by his prime minister, the anti-communist General Lon Nol, in a bloodless coup in March 1970. This came a year after the United States' secret and illegal bombing of the country had begun as an extension of the Vietnam War.

Details of this bombing, contained in Shawcross's book, *Side-show: Kissinger, Nixon and the Destruction of Cambodia*, which was published shortly before Pilger's trip to the stricken country, were accompanied by still pictures of top-secret military cables, obtained by Shawcross under the United States' Freedom of Information Act while researching his book. These provided evidence of the cover-up that had begun in the spring of 1969, when the American president and his national security adviser ordered American B-52s to bomb Cambodia under the guise of removing Vietcong bases inside its borders, without any reference to Congress. Pilger insisted, 'President Nixon's aim was to show the Vietnamese

Communists just how "tough" he could be – a policy he once described as the "Madman Theory of War".'

A month after Lon Nol's coup, which plunged the new republic of Cambodia into civil war, the United States' land forces invaded the country and the bloodshed continued for five years. Pilger laid the blame for the devastation, and the conditions that allowed Pol Pot and his Khmer Rouge to emerge as victors, firmly at the feet of Nixon and Kissinger. When 'peace' finally came, new horrors were visited on this 'passive, docile people'. Pilger's opening piece delivered direct to camera in *Year Zero* is the most hard-hitting of his television career. After colour film of B-52s bombing the countryside and black-and-white still photographs of frightened civilians and victorious Khmer Rouge troops entering Phnom Penh, Pilger addressed the camera from the verandah of the former Air France residence in the capital:

At 7.30am on 17 April 1975, the war in Cambodia was over. It was a unique war, for no country has ever experienced such concentrated bombing. On this, perhaps the most gentle and graceful land in all of Asia, President Nixon and Mr Kissinger unleashed 100,000 tons of bombs – the equivalent of five Hiroshimas. The bombing was their personal decision. Illegally and secretly, they bombed Cambodia, a neutral country, back to the Stone Age, and I mean Stone Age in its literal sense.

Shortly after dawn on 17 April, the bombing stopped and there was silence. Then, out of the forest came the victors, the Khmer Rouge, whose power had grown out of all proportion to their numbers. They entered the capital, Phnom Penh, a city most of them had never seen. They marched in disciplined, Indian file, through the long boulevards and the stilled traffic. They wore black and were mostly teenagers, and people cheered them, nervously, naïvely. After all, the bombing, the fighting, was over at last.

The horror began almost immediately. Phnom Penh, a city of two-and-a-half million people, was forcibly emptied within hours of their coming, the sick and wounded being dragged from their hospital beds, dying children being carried in plastic bags, the old and crippled being dumped beside the road, and all of them being marched at gunpoint into the countryside and toward a totally new society, the like of which we have never known.

The new rulers of Cambodia called 1975 'Year Zero', the dawn of an age in which there would be no families, no sentiment, no expressions of love or grief, no medicines, no hospitals, no schools, no books, no learning, no holidays, no music, no song, no post, no money; only work and death.

Cambodia. 'Where is Cambodia?' some of you might ask. Unlike Vietnam, its neighbour, Cambodia has been virtually sealed for four years, its suffering invisible. In a world of saturation news, there has been no news of what was really done to more than seven million people, of whom at least two million are missing, believed murdered. That's about a third of the entire population. Proportionately, it's Birmingham, Manchester and London exterminated.

For me, coming here has been like stumbling into something I could never imagine, and what follows is the first complete film report by Westerners from the ashes of a gentle land. And I have to say there are scenes which may upset some of you.

The most shocking pictures were those of Cambodian children fighting for their lives in hospital, but most of these were left until the second half of the documentary, allowing Pilger to explain how this crisis had come about. When the scenes arrived, they were literally overwhelming. The majority of the 558 patients in Phnom Penh's main hospital were babies and children, and their cries could be heard in the street outside. Most were dying from starvation or nutrition-related illnesses, which are preventable and curable in the West. Antibiotics, milk, antiseptics, anti-malarials, vitamins, painkillers and anaesthetic were all that was needed, but there was almost nothing – all modern equipment had been destroyed by the Khmer Rouge and the dispensary was bare.

Jacques Beaumont, UNICEF's representative in Phnom Penh, told Pilger that Heng Samrin's Vietnamese-backed government in the capital had in July requested help for 2,250,000 people threatened by famine. Although not seen on screen – or, some might say, not exploited – the interview had to be stopped several times while the clearly emotional Beaumont, relating his experiences of the suffering children, composed himself.

On camera, Beaumont told Pilger that he had visited the hospital at Kompong Speu on 18 July. 'In one of the very poor barracks with practically nothing, there were already fifty-four children dying,' he recalled. 'One of them was sitting in the corner of the room with swollen legs because he was starving. He did not have the strength to look at me or to anybody. He was just waiting to die. Ten days later, four of these children were dead and I will always remember that, saying, "I did not do anything for these children, because we had nothing."'

The Cambodian government's request to UNICEF and the International Red Cross was for 100,000 tons of rice and medical supplies. When Pilger and Munro filmed in Kompong Speu, they found that people had only four scoops of rice each per month, and this came from Vietnam, which itself was facing famine. 'Up to the middle of October,' Pilger's voiceover told viewers, 'the International Red Cross and UNICEF had sent 200 tons of relief, which effectively is nothing.'

After his emotive interview in Phnom Penh, Jacques Beaumont of UNICEF led Pilger to a similarly distraught François Bugnion, the International Red Cross representative. Bugnion asked Pilger if he had a contact in the Australian government who could arrange for the dispatch to Cambodia of just one C-130 Hercules aircraft with a truck, food and drugs, which could unload itself at the airport in the absence of forklift trucks, which had been destroyed, and save thousands of lives. Pilger asked Bugnion why the Red Cross itself could not arrange this. The shameful reply was that the politics had to be 'ironed out' before a relief operation could be mounted by the Red Cross.

This interview was not shown in the documentary, but Pilger – standing outside the hospital in Phnom Penh – spoke of a starving boy whose screams could be heard in the street 'rising and falling in agony', then reported the previous incident straight to camera in perhaps the most anger-filled commentary he has ever delivered. 'The United Nations, Britain included, still recognizes the murderous regime of the Khmer Rouge and it's difficult to get official help for a people whose new government still does not diplomatically exist', he said. 'In other words, three million people are beginning to starve to death in Cambodia and the International Red Cross and the relief agencies and governments are doing virtually nothing because the new leaders of this country have yet to be recognized, to be approved of. Of course, if you're in Geneva or New York or London, you can't hear the screams of the little boy I just mentioned.'

When Pilger and his film crew returned to the hospital the next day, six more children had died. They had on their first day there filmed a ten-year-old called Kuon lying still on an iron bed after being discovered starving on a rubbish tip and in need of penicillin. On their return, the camera filmed from exactly the same position, but Kuon was no longer there – he was dead. The two pieces of film merged into one another before moving to scenes of children with stick-like legs and large abdomens.

The camera then switched to a convoy of trucks from Vietnam – 'Cambodia's only guaranteed lifeline,' said Pilger – ferrying in food. As this tracking shot of the trucks continued, he explained that Vietnam itself was facing famine but had already sent 25,000 tons of food, whereas the major international aid agencies, the International Red Cross and UNICEF, had insisted on imposing strings to their offers of charity, such as the right to supply 'the other side', who were mostly the remnants of Pol Pot's army now based in camps along the Thai border. As a result, aid was being withheld from 90 per cent of the population. Pilger then reported that Western governments – including Britain – had in September voted to continue recognizing Pol Pot's representative at the

United Nations, in support of a motion by China, which was the West's newest ally and trading partner, as well as Pol Pot's principal backer.

By now, the picture had changed to scenes of the rice from Vietnam being scooped out. Pilger pointed out that Oxfam had attached no political strings to its aid. Then, as the film showed more of the starving in hospital, Pilger quoted Oxfam's director-general, Brian Walker, as saying that the charity had enjoyed 'complete and honourable co-operation' from the Cambodian and Vietnamese governments. Now, said Pilger, the denial of aid meant that both governments were being pushed deeper into the waiting arms of the Soviet Union.

Pilger's recollections of colourful, bustling Phnom Penh in 1967 were heard over film of the city's deserted streets twelve years later, with a few children seen foraging in the rubble. But some hope was offered in scenes of youngsters at an orphanage playing with the first toys they had ever seen and in a classroom at the capital's first school to reopen. But a return to shots of the city's hospital brought the realization that this hope was threatened by the continued denial of aid. Jacques Beaumont, the UNICEF official, told Pilger that there was just six months to save this nation.

The other recent horrors − of the destruction wreaked on Cambodia by Pol Pot between 1975 and 1978 − were explained in the first half of *Year Zero*. Pilger showed how the Khmer Rouge had razed a Roman Catholic cathedral, destroyed the National Library's books and, as the Vietnamese approached in December 1978, blown up the National Bank. He also found bank notes, carried by the monsoon rains, littered through the streets of Phnom Penh − all of them worthless.

'Every family I met had lost at least six members, killed or starved,' reported Pilger over film of refugees tramping along roads in search of their villages, some of which had been razed. Backed by China, which saw Cambodia as a future colony, Pol Pot had enslaved the population. *Year Zero* included rare Khmer Rouge film showing hundreds of people dressed in black at work, with yokes on their shoulders, moving in a long chain through paddies.

A visit to Tuol Sleng extermination centre, a former school where men, women and children were tortured and killed by a gestapo called S-21, was a reminder for Pilger and photographer Eric Piper of Auschwitz, which they had visited only two months earlier while covering Pope John Paul II's historic return to his native Poland. Like the Nazis, the Khmer Rouge kept meticulous records of their atrocities, which showed that 12,000 Cambodians died at Tuol Sleng between 1975 and 1978. Haunting black-and-white photographs of some of the victims were interspersed with tracking shots filmed inside the building. There was still blood and tufts of hair on the floors.

One of only eight survivors found by the Vietnamese at Tuol Sleng – four men and four children – Ung Pech, whose crime was being an engineer, told Pilger that between ten and fifty people were killed there every day in 1975 and 1976, and this rose to between 100 and 150 during the following two years. 'First they killed the children, then the wives and then the men,' he explained of S-21's torture methods, as he sat outside the barbed wire of Tuol Sleng. His wife and five of his six children had died through being denied food and his own hand had been crushed in a vice and the finger nails pulled out with pliers.

In a remarkable scene, Pilger spoke to two captured Khmer Rouge soldiers at a barracks outside Phnom Penh who had taken part in mass murder. One admitted to being in a group of eight who killed 250 people, the other in a group of fifty responsible for murdering 2,500. 'Would you ask this man here if he must have thought, when he was killing all these people, that he was killing fellow human beings, fellow countrymen?' Pilger asked, through his Cambodian interpreter. 'He says that if he does not kill these people, the higher command would kill him,' she replied. Pictures of some who died were now interspersed with film of the eight clearly happy survivors walking and playing in the grounds of Tuol Sleng.

After the shocking film of starving children in the second half of the documentary, Pilger pulled the strands of the story together in his final piece to camera:

> If the horrors in this documentary are to have any purpose, it is not just to assault your emotions. It is to end the silence and in-difference contrived by governments and relief agencies, and to put Cambodia back on the human map. When the Vietnamese army threw out the Khmer Rouge, they rescued this country, for whatever reason, from slavery and possible extinction. Western governments may not wish to recognize that fact, but nothing is more obvious to the Cambodian people. On the day of liberation, my interpreter, a young girl, was due to be killed.
>
> The British government knew all along what Pol Pot and his fanatics were doing to these people. Mr Callaghan's government presented a report to the United Nations Commission on Human Rights with information as shocking as anything you have seen tonight. And yet people here are being allowed to die for want of the simplest things – food, drugs, transport – because govern-ments, including our own, are bent on isolating and punishing the Vietnamese. In other words, saving Cambodia would mean co-operating with Vietnam.
>
> Both the Cambodians and Vietnamese have told me at the highest level that any relief plane can come without conditions. At the time of our filming, three planes had come in nine months. America and Europe hold most of the world's surplus food. We feed it to animals. In Britain, we are treated with penicillin as a matter of right. All of us who made this film have never seen anything like Cambodia today. The cries of children have fol-lowed us everywhere. There are six months to save a nation of mostly children. Is that impossible?

The public's response to *Year Zero* was unprecedented, but major hurdles had to be overcome before the documentary reached the screen. Pilger and his team left Cambodia shortly after Oxfam official Jim Howard arrived to launch the charity's rescue operation. They were able to appraise him of the gravity of the human disaster. 'John spent almost two days talking and giving me the full picture,' recalled Howard. 'The information he gave me was immensely valuable, including the names of a number of contacts. When John and his crew left, I was the lone Englishman there.'[5]

On driving into Vietnam, Pilger and the others stayed a night in a Saigon hotel before flying to Thailand, where David Munro received a message from ATV in London that ITV technicians were on strike and *Year Zero* could not even be edited. In Bangkok, Pilger phoned the Australian embassy to pass on François Bugnion's request for an aircraft with aid. He was told that the ambassador was unable to speak to him. Instead, upon his return to London, he wrote an article for the Melbourne newspaper the *Age*, on 21 September 1979, reporting Bugnion's appeal.

This came just over a week after Pilger's two dramatic 'world exclusive' reports appeared in the *Daily Mirror* on 12 and 13 September, produced over twelve pages with 6,000 words and fifteen of Eric Piper's shocking photographs. The response was immediate. Within a few days of its publication, thousands of readers telephoned Oxfam and other charities, donating more than £50,000. The money continued to flood in and, just two weeks after Pilger's reports appeared, a Cargolux DC-8 plane took penicillin, vitamins and milk that was estimated to save the lives of 69,000 children.

On his return to London, Munro approached ATV film editor Jonathan Morris, who explained that he could not work on the Cambodia footage because of the technicians' strike. 'I was the union rep in the film department,' recalled Morris. 'David said, "We have to get this programme on television as quickly as possible. We need some kind of dispensation." I went to the shop stewards at Elstree. David came with me and said we needed to screen the documentary as soon as possible after the strike to try to save lives and, for compassionate reasons, wanted dispensation to edit it. They pushed it through with the heads of the union within days, but we couldn't edit at Elstree because there were pickets, so we hired a cutting room in Soho. We did eight weeks' work in ten days. It was harrowing, fascinating and extremely stimulating because we were doing something we really felt could make a difference. We knew when we were editing *Year Zero* that we would probably never work on anything more important.'[6]

Editing began on 1 October, from the twelve hours of footage brought back from Cambodia, and it was ready for transmission once the eleven-week industrial action ended. *Year Zero – The Silent Death of Cambodia* was screened at 9pm on Tuesday 30 October, following an evening of ITV entertainment that featured 'time detectives' *Sapphire & Steel*, the celebrity sports contest *Star Games* and the situation comedy *George and Mildred*. The fifty-two-minute film was not only an antidote to all that, but was considered so shocking and important that ITV screened it with no interruption for commercials. As the final credits finished, viewers saw a postscript that had been added just a day earlier. Pilger reported directly to the camera:

> Since this film was made, more relief has reached Cambodia from Vietnam, the Eastern bloc countries, Australia, Britain's Oxfam and some other Western charities, and the food situation has slightly improved. But throughout Cambodia hunger and disease and trauma are widespread. Three months ago, the Cambodian government requested 100,000 tons of emergency food. As of yesterday, the total Western aid sent through UNICEF and the Red Cross amounted to 1,300 tons of food. Effectively, that's almost nothing. And this situation is likely to continue as long as Western governments recognize and give international comfort to Pol Pot, the Asian Hitler. You can assume that most of the people you saw in tonight's film are now dead.

An announcer, speaking over the address caption, then invited viewers to send donations to the Cambodia Fund. More than

26,000 letters arrived in the first postbag and, within two weeks, donations topped £1 million. Just one day after the film's transmission, the children's programme *Blue Peter* – broadcast on the rival BBC – launched an appeal as a direct result of *Year Zero*. Clips from *Year Zero* were shown and Pilger was interviewed on the programme, which asked children to 'bring and buy' toys at Oxfam shops, eventually raising £3.5 million. The documentary, screened in fifty countries and seen by 150 million viewers, was credited with raising more than $45 million in aid for Cambodia. It also won more than thirty international awards, a record for any documentary, including the Broadcasting Press Guild's Best Documentary honour and the International Critics Prize at the Monte Carlo International Television Festival. Pilger himself won the 1980 United Nations Media Peace Prize for 'having done so much to ease the suffering of the Cambodian people' and, for his *Mirror* reports, the British Press Awards' Journalist of the Year honour, for the second time.

'It wasn't just *Year Zero* that had such an effect,' explained Pilger. 'It was the film combined with the reports in the *Mirror* and others that followed it up. It was also the *Blue Peter* appeal. All this helped to launch a rescue operation where there wasn't one.'[7] But Jim Howard, of Oxfam, had no doubt that Pilger's newspaper and television reports were the most important factor in enabling his organization to mobilize public support. 'It was all possible because of him,' said Howard. 'John and David Munro did a fabulously professional job in capturing the terrible tragedy of what had happened in Cambodia. The effect was astonishing and outstanding. They brought into focus the tragedy that Oxfam was trying to cope with so that a major effort was possible. I think a little nation would have gone under, otherwise.'[8]

Despite the obvious magnitude of the disaster facing Cambodia, the immediate response to Pilger's documentary by television critics was mixed, perhaps saying more about the state of TV criticism than its subject. In the *Daily Telegraph*, Sean Day-Lewis claimed that 'Pilger's angry allegiance to Vietnamese Communism, or nationalism as he sees it', his version of Cambodia being 'liberated' by Vietnam and his view of that country as a 'paradise' before the American bombing amounted to a 'half-history'. However, Day-Lewis admitted that 'his lugubrious delivery was for once entirely justified and his accusatory editorials delivered to camera came as a visual relief from emaciated, tortured bodies and their patient, haunting eyes'.[9] The *Daily Mail*, also politically right-wing and a staunch supporter of the Conservative government in Britain, might have been expected to echo similar sentiments, but Herbert Kretzmer kept his review to reporting the horror of what had happened to Cambodia and the need for action to avoid further disaster.

Meanwhile, Nancy Banks-Smith, in the *Guardian*, concentrated on the lack of aid being sent to Cambodia and the children who faced death. 'An extraordinary feature of the film is that I mistook several sequences for stills,' she wrote. 'There was no smile, no cry, no word, no movement or flicker of an eyelid from the children in their makeshift hospital. Only when the flies moved on their faces could you see that the film moved too. The camera held steady on this child with legs thin and feet curled as a bird. Evidently he was dead. Then an eyelid moved . . . I found myself covering my face at one point, not that I should not look at them but that they should not look at me.'[10]

In the *Observer*, Clive James admitted that most of what Pilger featured in *Year Zero* was 'hard to look at' but accused him of portraying the Vietnamese as 'philanthropists', who 'have recently taken to offering their internal enemies the opportunity of going on long yachting expeditions', and added, 'Pilger loudly accused the international relief organizations of playing politics, but forgot to mention the possibility that the North Vietnamese might be playing politics themselves.'[11] Pilger responded with a letter to the newspaper:

In suspecting that I went to Cambodia merely to put Vietnam's official view Clive James . . . attempts a McCarthyite smear. He invokes the tragedy of the Boat People. But my TV documentary was not about Vietnam: it was about Cambodia. For four years, I have been speaking up for the Boat People, and have described their persecutions as brutal, in no way to be condoned. By attempting to smear me, James contributes, in his mean little way, to the Cold War bigotry that has allowed so many people to die.[12]

The controversial issue of Western governments and relief agencies denying aid to Cambodia had already been raised in the weeks between the publication of Pilger's reports in the *Daily Mirror* and *New Statesman* and the screening of the television documentary. Pilger was one of twelve signatories – including the journalists Jonathan Dimbleby and William Shawcross and politicians such as Robin Corbett and David Owen – to a letter from the London-based International Disaster Institute published in the *Guardian* on 29 September. They appealed to the British government 'to extend its traditional humanitarian assistance either directly or through the United Nations and voluntary relief agencies' to 'allow humanitarian attitudes to supersede political barriers' and thereby set an example to the world.[13]

Three days later, on 2 October, Pilger followed this up with his own letter pointing out that only two weeks earlier the United States had 'orchestrated the charade of support for a Chinese motion to continue recognition of the Pol Pot regime' and Britain also lent its support to China. While the International Red Cross and UNICEF were still attaching conditions to the supply of relief, Oxfam and Medical Aid for Cambodia were sending as much as they could and receiving complete co-operation from the Cambodian and Vietnamese authorities.[14]

Evan Luard, of St Antony's College, Oxford, and a member of the United Nations Human Rights Commission, also wrote to the *Guardian*, pointing out that the British government and most of the UN had immediately recognized the new administration in

Uganda after its overthrow of Idi Amin's brutal regime earlier that year but had not done the same in Cambodia.[15]

After John Gee, of Sutton Coldfield, complained to the *Guardian* letters page about Pilger's 'sympathy with the Vietnamese invasion' and questioned whether Pol Pot had been responsible for genocide,[16] Pilger responded by writing that 'the UN Human Rights Commission, Amnesty and governments including the British government all have documented the barbarism of the Khmer Rouge' and added that 'British newspapers published similar letters in the 1930s apologising for the Third Reich and there are those today who deny that Hitler exterminated millions of Jews'. On the same page, David Munro wrote of his disgust at the 'self-righteous posturing of UNICEF and the International Red Cross'.[17]

The story of several million Cambodians threatened with death through starvation had turned into one of power politics and why governments and relief agencies would not give immediate assistance. Shortly afterwards, Pilger wrote a feature in the *New Statesman* headlined 'The "filthy affair" of denying relief', pointing out that most of UNICEF's budget came from the US government, and that the Red Cross depended mostly on Western administrations for its finance. 'Last week Robert McNamara, the head of the World Bank, said that political strings demanded by the American government were preventing food aid from reaching one and a quarter million people throughout the world,' reported Pilger.[18]

However, public pressure was growing and hundreds of people wrote to the British prime minister, Margaret Thatcher, about their concern. To deal with questions posed by the press and public, the Foreign Office launched a propaganda campaign intended to make it appear that the Vietnamese-installed government in Phnom Penh was blocking aid. This was shown to be untrue two weeks after *Year Zero* was broadcast, when money donated by the British public as a result of the documentary and Pilger's press reports was used to pay for a huge barge to take food and medical supplies to Cambodia, as well as other equipment that would help the devastated country to rebuild itself. The cargo comprised rice, maize and vegetable seed, a chemical to clean out Phnom Penh's water system and give it fresh running water, a cotton yarn for clothing, diesel pumps to irrigate fields, hoes for tilling, cold storage cabinets to preserve drugs such as penicillin and eight tons of nylon cord that enabled a factory to make thousands of fishing nets. The barge also carried 100 'orphanage kits', containing blankets, water-purifying tablets, mosquito nets, towels, soap, cooking pots, brightly coloured clothes, needle and thread, blackboards, pencils, crayons, paints and footballs.

The double standards of Western governments and relief agencies were highlighted a week earlier when ITV's *News at Ten* included a report showing the Khmer Rouge – which had regrouped around the border with Thailand – carrying boxes of Western aid across the border into Cambodia without any of the 'monitoring' that agencies had insisted must accompany aid sent direct to the Vietnamese-backed government in Phnom Penh. The International Red Cross, which had formed a partnership with UNICEF for a 'joint mission' in Cambodia, continued to insist that it had to demonstrate its 'neutrality' and could not help those inside the country unless it supplied 'the other side', which in reality consisted of Khmer Rouge troops who had escaped across the border and some refugees. However, this did not stop the Red Cross sending aid to Pol Pot's army, which enjoyed the backing of Thailand.

Although, by the end of November, the Red Cross and UNICEF finally began to respond to public pressure and send aid to Phnom Penh, the British Red Cross Society had already sought to exact revenge for Pilger's attacks on the organization. Its chairman, Sir Evelyn Shuckburgh, wrote to IBA chairman [*sic*] Lady Plowden a week after transmission of *Year Zero* in Britain, complaining about the 'allegations' contained in the documentary and trying to stop it being screened in other countries. Lady

Plowden, whose job was government-appointed, replied that *Year Zero* was unsatisfactory 'in certain respects', supposedly relating to 'the truth', although she did not specify what these respects were. However, she admitted that the programme had been viewed in advance by two IBA officers, who approved it after asking for several points to be clarified. Lady Plowden added that she could not reassure Sir Evelyn about 'wider circulation' of the programme because the Authority had control over only that which was transmitted in Britain.[19]

Despite supporting the United Nations vote in September in support of China's motion to continue recognizing Pol Pot's 'Democratic Kampuchea' as the legitimate government of Cambodia – thus denying the country aid from the United Nations Development Programme, the Asian Development Bank, the International Monetary Fund and the World Bank – public pressure resulted in Britain becoming the first Western government to 'derecognize' it, on 6 December 1979. The Australian government, similarly, withdrew its recognition of the Pol Pot regime after *Year Zero* was screened there and Pilger was invited to brief the foreign affairs minister, Andrew Peacock. However, the documentary was never screened in the United States.

During the first half of 1980, there were accusations by Western governments claiming that relief was not getting through to people inside Cambodia. Power politics and its propaganda resources sought to discredit the government in Phnom Penh while it was backed by the Vietnamese. Moreover, Western aid was going to Pol Pot and his Khmer Rouge troops on the Thai border, and China was sending arms. Six years later, it was revealed that the newly installed Ronald Reagan administration was directly funding Pol Pot in secret. Among those duped by the 'disinformation' at the time was the respected broadcaster Alistair Cooke, who in one of his *Letter from America* programmes for BBC radio in December 1979 had referred to a CIA report – to be published five months later – claiming that the Vietnamese and Russians were blocking aid. The report turned out to be bogus and was aimed at journalists sympathetic to the US administration.

Another journalist who, wittingly or not, went along with the American government's line was William Shawcross, author of the acclaimed book *Sideshow: Kissinger, Nixon and the Destruction of Cambodia*. He wrote in the *Washington Post* of aid being diverted to Vietnam and, in the *New York Review of Books*, claimed that the Vietnamese themselves were committing genocide in Cambodia. This second allegation was based on information passed to Shawcross by François Ponchaud, author of *Cambodia Year Zero*, who had been told stories of Vietnamese barbarism by anti-communist Khmer Serei groups in the refugee camps on the Thai border, although Ponchaud had warned that their credence was questionable. Shawcross himself had not been to Cambodia for nine years.

Pilger sought to find out what was really happening by returning to Cambodia almost a year after his previous visit, taking with him the same film crew and *Daily Mirror* photographer Eric Piper. He was also joined by Jim Howard of Oxfam and Jean Yves Follezou and Jean Michel Vinot, the only Western doctors in Cambodia during the months following the Vietnamese rout of Pol Pot.

Inside Cambodia, away from the pronouncements of governments with political axes to grind, Pilger discovered a people who were staging a remarkable return from the abyss. Howard, who had been travelling to and from Cambodia over the previous year, confirmed that 90 per cent of aid was getting through, which flew in the face of accusations that the Vietnamese were blocking it. 'We wanted to be in a position to refute that,' Pilger said. 'I was staggered to find alive several children I had seen in a particular orphanage the year before. It was, in many ways, an uplifting experience – here was human resilience at its best.'[20]

David Munro was struck by the tinkling of bells on pony traps – a stark contrast to the quiet and emptiness of the previous year. Phnom Penh now had buses, electricity, telephones, markets and reopened factories, and children were back at school. In *Cambodia – Year One*, Pilger opened the film by describing the aid that had flowed into the country after his 1979 report:

> Following its showing throughout the world, some £19 million was raised in relief for Cambodia, much of it from those of you who could least afford to give, who gave up pensions, family allowances, life savings, holiday money, pocket money, dole money. The film you are about to see will show what your compassion and generosity have achieved. It will also show, in the first report both from here in Cambodia and the camps in Thailand, why this suffering nation is being kept in shadow, isolated by power politics; why its future and survival are still very much in question; and why the most thorough mass murderers in memory are being actively sustained by the United Nations and by Western governments. But first, in the hope that it will never be forgotten, let me remind you of what was done to the people of Cambodia.

There followed a five-minute flashback to *Year Zero*, then the now bustling streets of Phnom Penh. Freshwater supply was thanks to British money and the work of a British engineer. A pharmaceuticals factory had opened. 'The generosity of the British people has literally put colour back into people's lives,' said Pilger. 'With the money sent to us by viewers following last year's report, Oxfam were able to reopen this textile factory . . . When we passed your money to the relief agencies last year, we insisted that it went to actual projects and this is but one of them. More than 300 people are employed in this textile factory.'

Film from *Year Zero* of the hospital at Kompong Speu, which had been consumed by disease and starvation, was accompanied by Dr Jean Yves Follezou's observation, 'We are very surprised by the very low rate of malnutrition. Now, there is no plague, no anthrax.' Examining a nine-month-old boy with gastroenteritis, Dr Jean Michel Vinot said the child would survive. New-born babies appeared to be healthy, although both doctors pointed out that many problems remained. Pilger remarked that there were more equipment and beds in the hospital, and that the drugs were coming mainly from the Soviet Union and Phnom Penh's pharmaceuticals laboratories. He recalled it as 'a house of death' a year earlier.

One of Pilger's 'delightful surprises' was a child, seen in *Year Zero*, battling for life, with flies on her face, now 'growing into a healthy little girl'. In a very moving scene, Pilger was joined by a group of children. 'This is Ock,' he said. 'When we last saw him, he was spreadeagled on a bed, thin, malnourished, very close to death. And look at him now – look at that wonderful pot tummy! People who think they can never help children that they see in a film like ours should look at these healthy children and know that the mosquito nets and the drugs and many of the things that have helped them grow into the bonny children they are becoming were sent by them and paid for by their money, including the toys and the footballs and all the other things that are now starting to make their life liveable.'

At a newly reopened school, Pilger found new equipment such as desks, paper, pencils and toys, 'much of it paid for in Britain', and Jim Howard confirmed that there had been 'no misuse whatsoever' of supplies arriving at the docks in Phnom Penh as Pilger and Munro filmed rice seed arriving there. 'Every bag of that will grow twenty, thirty or fifty bags of rice,' said Howard. Having arrived at the docks unannounced, they then followed the seed from the barge to the railway yards in the capital, where it was loaded on to a train for Battambang province, 350 miles north-west of the capital. Three days later, the seed arrived in Battambang.

'The government has given priority to seed over food, which is being rationed and stored,' said Pilger, who quoted Bill Yates, Oxfam's chief representative in Cambodia, as saying, 'Everyone who needs to work and has no source of food . . . is getting rations. As for the countryside, the government has trusted in the peasants' natural instinct to live off the land. They are gambling to achieve self-sufficiency and it may well pay off.' But many were still on the edge of famine, Pilger added.

Returning to film the train arriving back in Phnom Penh two days later, Pilger and Munro discovered that it had been attacked by Khmer Rouge troops with rockets and automatic weapons, killing more than 150 people on board. Pilger himself, who had been put on a Khmer Rouge death-list since the transmission of *Year Zero*, was lucky to escape with his life when he, Munro and their crew were ambushed as they were travelling in a van, followed by an Oxfam Land Rover, back to Phnom Penh one evening. Rounding a bend, they saw a truck parked across the road, then caught sight of armed men wearing black, lying on their stomachs and firing at them as their Vietnamese driver screamed for them to get down and sped towards the verge and around the road block to safety. Only two months earlier, journalist Wilfred Burchett had survived a similar fate. Jim Howard was not with Pilger and Munro when they were ambushed but, knowing the hazards of travelling widely in Cambodia, he later looked back on their return to the country with admiration. 'They were amazingly courageous to have gone into such a danger-ous situation,' he said. 'They might have disappeared and we would never have seen them again.'[21]

The Khmer Rouge had regrouped across the border in Thai-land, where Pilger visited the town of Aranyaprathet, which he compared to 'old Saigon'. He explained that Thailand was one of China and the United States' proxies. 'China wants Pol Pot back in power, with a new, respectable image, of course,' said Pilger, 'and America does not wish to displease China, for its current Cold War enemy is also the Soviet Union.' The United States had created an organization called KEG (Kampuchean Emergency Group), whose refugee co-ordinator, Lionel Rosenblatt, told Pilger that its aim was 'to track the overall situation of refugees', of whom there were 150,000 Cambodians camped on the border, and to monitor American funding. Pilger identified various KEG officials and their links to the US government. All of them reported to the US ambassador in Thailand.

Then, Pilger travelled in a UNICEF Land Rover, at the head of a convoy of forty trucks loaded with food, seed and other supplies, to Phnom Chat, a camp inside the Thai border controlled by the Khmer Rouge, whose strength had doubled to 30,000. This meant that United Nations relief was going to the Khmer Rouge leadership. After a bumpy ride over ground littered with land-mines, Phyllis Gestrin, an American university psychology professor leading the convoy, admitted her disquiet at where the aid was headed and said, nervously, 'We always position the car so that we can get out fast.' Pilger added, 'The beneficiaries were clearly not the civilians in the camp.'

He interviewed the camp's Khmer Rouge commander, Nam Phann, asking how international relief had helped him. He replied that the ASEAN (the Association of South-east Asian Nations) countries provided most help, along with the United States, China and the United Nations. In a piece to camera, Pilger reported that the aid agencies were 'deeply embarrassed' by their presence there. He added, 'The British government is the only Western government to have ended its recognition of Pol Pot and yet we still support Pol Pot through the back door.' Jim Howard, who had done more than most to organize relief aid for the Cambodian population, said, 'To allow that force to come back in here will be one of the crimes of history.' Pilger summed up:

> If the West supports what President Carter himself described as the vilest regime in history, there is the real possibility that China, with American approval, will attempt to restore Pol Pot to power under a different name, and that is what the people of Cambodia fear more than anything . . . I find it difficult to cope with the thought that the children in this film may have survived, only to face war and famine yet again because your generosity has never been matched by a political generosity from so-called civilized governments.

The message was one of relief that the Cambodian people were getting back on their feet again, but a warning about the threat still posed to them by power politics. David Munro, who fell ill with dysentery during the filming, could at least feel a satisfaction at having seen what *Year Zero* had helped to achieve. 'In the market of Phnom Penh, among all the fruit and meat, was a laughing-faced woman selling fresh-baked bread from an enormous basket,' he recalled. 'I caught sight of her out of the corner of my eye and was about to pass by when I had to look again. The bread was fresh and plentiful, and she was well fed: how *ordinary* and *normal* it seemed, until I remembered that a year ago there was no flour, no bread, no laughing faces.'[22]

Despite the evidence of this second film, some television critics insisted on repeating the propaganda of the British Foreign Office. Clive James, who in 1979 had accused Pilger of being too kind to the Vietnamese, wrote in the *Observer*, 'In my review of the programme *Year Zero* I said that there seemed to be a lot of independent evidence to suggest that the Western relief agencies were being denied access to Cambodia by the North Vietnamese. Pilger wrote a letter to the *Observer* calling me a McCarthyite for saying this, but in fact subsequent evidence proved that he had indeed been wrong on this very point.'[23] Again, Pilger responded with a letter to the newspaper, pointing out that James's review of *Year Zero* had said 'nothing of the kind' but implied that he was simply putting the Vietnamese line. Pilger added:

> To this distortion, he now adds that I was wrong all along and 'there can no longer be much doubt that they (the Vietnamese) were obstructing then'. Let Clive James produce the complete 'independent evidence' that backs up this statement – *not* in his usual few glib words, but with sources, places, dates: documented eye-witness evidence. For this is what I and many others, who work within the widest constraints of reporting, have to do continually.[24]

When Pilger and Munro returned to Cambodia in 1989, ten years after their first trip, the essential story had changed little. The West was still punishing the country by continuing an international embargo, making it the only country not eligible for United Nations development aid. A World War One law, the Trading with the Enemy Act, prevented US humanitarian organizations from sending aid, and the EEC followed the same line. At the same time, Western governments continued to support Pol Pot's representative at the United Nations and its troops in Thailand. They had become the dominant partner in a three-party coalition called the CGDK (Coalition of the Government of Democratic Kampuchea), along with the Sihanoukists, under Cambodia's former ruler, Prince Norodom Sihanouk, and the KPNLF (Khmer People's National Liberation Front), led by his former prime minister, Són Sann.

On the eve of the Vietnamese withdrawal in September 1989, Pilger and Munro made *Cambodia – Year Ten*, broadcast around the world the following month, exactly ten years after their first film. In this film, they reflected the fears of the Cambodian people that the Khmer Rouge would now return. After recalling the horrors that had befallen that country, Pilger told viewers, 'This film is about extraordinary events which have allowed Asia's Hitler to rise again and the prospect of the previously unthinkable happening again.' Personalizing this report, he said, 'I felt deeply uneasy about returning to Cambodia. The memories of ten years ago are indelible and, now that the Vietnamese have left, almost everybody I know is in fear of their lives again. And yet there's a normality here. It has a seductive quality. A moment is just long enough and deceptive enough to suspend fear.'

This 'normality' was evident in scenes of the bustling Phnom Penh streets, but pictures of rows and rows of skulls at Tuol Sleng extermination centre were a reminder of the horrors that Pilger had reported in the aftermath of Pol Pot's rule. 'Ten years later, I find myself shocked again and seriously doubting if the enormity of what happened here is understood outside,' he said. 'How *can* it be understood when those responsible are not only allowed to go free and unpunished, but are living comfortably with expense accounts?'

Pol Pot was living a life of luxury near the Thai town of Trat, sustained by the United States and United Nations. British Prime Minister Margaret Thatcher had supported US policy in secretly backing the Khmer Rouge in the border camps. 'Mrs Thatcher's government warned off relief organizations from supplying aid directly to Cambodia in 1979,' said Pilger. Oxfam's communications director, Bill Yates, confirmed that his charity had consistently been told that aid would not be distributed. 'Ultimately, of course, we were vindicated,' he said. 'Supplies not only were getting through then, they continue to get through now. This was a distortion of what was happening.'

Dith Pran, subject of the Oscar-winning film *The Killing Fields*, was interviewed by Pilger in *Cambodia – Year Ten*. 'We were keen to have a Khmer speaking in English, directly to viewers,' said Pilger at the time. 'He lives in America, is highly articulate and is at the forefront in campaigning to alert people to what is now happening in Cambodia.'[25] Pran told Pilger that his country had almost no army and very few guns before 1970, and the West, led by the United States, had 'helped' by sending B-52 bombers and killing so many Cambodians. The Vietnamese had invaded and liberated Cambodia from Pol Pot's terror. With them now leaving, Cambodians wanted to hear that the world would prevent the return of the Khmer Rouge.

At a military hospital in Saigon, Pilger visited a Vietnamese soldier who had been terribly injured in Cambodia. US Congressman Chester Atkins explained that the Khmer Rouge had been used as a 'lever' to force the Vietnamese out of Cambodia, without any thought about what would happen in the long term. A recent Khmer Rouge defector, Yang Channa, said that 6,500 Khmer Rouge troops were waiting for the Vietnamese to leave. 'They will be engaging in full-scale attacks throughout the country in order to try and take over the country,' he said. Film shot by the Khmer Rouge themselves and obtained by Munro showed a raid on a village thirty kilometres inside Cambodia, carried out by Pol Pot's men along with troops loyal to Prince Sihanouk. They terrorized the villagers, destroyed a hospital and took a tractor, which would prevent land being farmed.

Outside the United Nations' headquarters in New York, Pilger explained that the Coalition of the Government of Democratic Kampuchea, recognized by the UN, was 'not a coalition, it's not a government, it's not democratic and it's not in Kampuchea'. It was simply a cover behind which Pol Pot's defunct regime could represent their victims. 'Just imagine if West Germany's seat in the United Nations were still occupied by Hitler's Third Reich in exile and that the Swastika flew high in the United Nations Plaza in New York,' he added. 'And imagine if this barely credible state of affairs was largely the result of pressure by the major democracies such as the United States and Britain. Well, that is exactly what has happened in Cambodia.'

President Bush had distanced himself publicly from Pol Pot while campaigning for American arms to be sent to the so-called non-communist members of the coalition, knowing that they would end up with the Khmer Rouge. Sihanouk, who had always been 'all things to all people', had collaborated with the Khmer Rouge after his overthrow in 1970 and now demanded a part for them in a Cambodian government. This was supported by the United States and Britain.

An interview that Pilger conducted in London with Lord Brabazon of Tara, Britain's minister of state for foreign affairs, ended in a farce that was itself revealing. Asked whether he was aware that Sihanouk's army fought side by side with the Khmer Rouge, his Lordship paused before replying, 'Well, that may well be the case.' Pilger quoted to him a remark made by Prime Minister Margaret Thatcher on a *Blue Peter* television programme the previous year. She said that Pol Pot and some of his supporters could not go back to Cambodia but a 'more reasonable' faction within the Khmer Rouge certainly could.

Asked by Pilger exactly who these 'more reasonable' people were, Lord Brabazon answered, 'I don't know their names.' Pilger responded, 'Surely it's rather important, isn't it, if Britain is supporting their inclusion in a future government of Cambodia. Who are they?' 'Well, there are obviously some more reasonable than others,' said Lord Brabazon. 'These are the ones who Prince Sihanouk can work with.' Pilger persisted, 'But you must know their names, really?' At that point, Foreign Office official Ian Whitehead stepped in front of the camera, shouting, 'Can we stop this now? John, this was not the way that we were led to believe the line of questioning would go.' As the picture went blank but the sound remained on, Whitehead continued, 'I think the minister is doing remarkably well under an aggressive line of questioning that we were not told that we had to brief the minister for.'

Cambodia – Year Ten showed that the denial of development aid was having a disastrous effect on the infrastructure of the country. Buildings, bridges and roads were collapsing. Every day, two people were killed by exposed electrical wires. Highways were impassable because they had been mined by the Khmer Rouge, affecting food distribution.

In Battambang Hospital, Pilger despaired that there were scenes reminiscent of his first visit in 1979. Tuberculosis and cerebral malaria were now afflicting the majority of the population. Malnourished children lay in the corridors. One in five children in Cambodia died of malnutrition and preventable diseases such as diarrhoea, 'and they die for political reasons', added Pilger. One such child was an eleven-month-old baby girl called Ratanak, whose mother watched her suffering from dengue fever at the hospital. All she needed was basic equipment such as a respirator, as well as plasma and drugs. 'But these items are subject to international embargo,' reported Pilger. 'An hour after we filmed her, the baby died.' After the film was shown, the Ratanak Project was set up by Brian McConaghy, a forensics expert with the Royal Canadian Mounted Police. It established a network of health centres throughout Cambodia that saved the lives of thousands of babies and today funds large areas of regenerated agricultural land for poor farmers.

Bill Yates, of Oxfam, said that viewers should write to politicians, urging them to 'take the action of outlawing the Khmer Rouge from the international community'. It was necessary, he said, to expel them from the United Nations. 'Everybody watching this programme can help that to happen,' he added.

The response to *Cambodia – Year Ten* proved that viewers had been moved to take the action suggested by Yates. Tens of thousands of people wrote to their MPs to protest at British policy on Cambodia. The Swedish foreign minister phoned Pilger to tell him that, having seen the film, he had recommended to his government that it should no longer support Pol Pot's allies at the United Nations. Such was the public and political response that a follow-up programme, *Cambodia – Year Ten Update*, was broadcast three weeks later. Pilger presented it live from Thames Television's studios in Euston Road, London, hired by Central Television. (As the ITV franchise holder for the Midlands, it had no London studios.)

He began by describing the 'unprecedented' public reaction to the suffering of Cambodia. He also disclosed that British SAS troops had been training guerrillas allied with Pol Pot's army since 1985. Following the screening of *Cambodia – Year Ten*, British foreign secretary Douglas Hurd had insisted that the government had 'never given and will never give support of any kind to the Khmer Rouge'. Pilger described this as misleading. Not only had Britain given military support, but it had voted in favour of Pol Pot's representative at the United Nations. Frank Judd, director of Oxfam and former minister of state for foreign affairs, told Pilger that Hurd's claims were 'just not true' because Britain supported 'the other factions of the Khmer Rouge'. In the studio, Pilger said, 'No member of the US administration would even state Washington's position to us. Never in my experience as a journalist has there been such a silence, never has a policy been so indefensible.'

Of the previous week's session on Cambodia at the United Nations, Pilger said, 'A majority of the world voted, in effect, for the return of Pol Pot. Why? Many of these small nations have little choice. If they defy the United States, for example, they may well lose vital loans that help to keep their people alive.' The UN result was: 124 in favour, 17 against and 12 abstentions.

Frank Judd described the UN vote as 'one of the low moments of international history'. In a satellite link-up to Sweden, whose government had opposed support for any coalition including the Khmer Rouge, the deputy foreign minister, Pierre Schori, talked of the cynicism 'among those who on one side say they are in favour of peace and national reconciliation but on the other hand either provide arms or accept arms deliveries to the Khmer Rouge'. From Bangkok, *New York Times* correspondent Steven Erlanger said that a secret organization called the Working Group funnelled all aid through the non-communist resistance. This had been set up by ASEAN, 'in which the Americans also play a part', and had no direct connection with the Khmer Rouge. 'This is certainly a war that's funded by the CIA with secret money,' said Erlanger. 'There is also some covert money voted by Congress.'

Conservative MP Jim Lester told Pilger in a recorded interview that Douglas Hurd's statement on British policy in Cambodia was 'helpful' in indicating that 'the diplomatic wheels are now turning'. However, he admitted that the stumbling block was Hurd's backing for an interim administration that would include the Khmer Rouge. In the studio, Ann Clwyd, shadow minister for overseas development, Dr Peter Carey of Trinity College, Oxford, and Brian Walker, director of Oxfam at the time of *Year Zero* and now director of Earthwatch, were interviewed. Walker criticized the 'absence of morality' in British policy, Carey said the return of the Khmer Rouge would probably lead Cambodia to become 'a Lebanon of South-east Asia' and Clwyd demanded a ceasefire and that the West 'stop pushing Sihanouk on the people of Cambodia'.

Pilger and Munro returned again to Cambodia the following

year for a film that reported on the continuing danger of Pol Pot's return following the Vietnamese withdrawal. They revealed the covert means by which British and American companies supplied weapons to the Khmer Rouge and their allies, and provided evidence that the British SAS was training them.

In *Cambodia – The Betrayal*, Pilger urged viewers not to be deceived by recent reports of peace talks. 'There have been no agreements,' he said, 'only the imposition of the strategic aims of great powers upon a suffering nation.' The latest peace plan demanded the resignation of the Hun Sen government in Phnom Penh, which was Cambodia's only opposition to Pol Pot, said Pilger. There was fear on the streets and 'when the curfew comes, the night belongs to the prospect of a second holocaust'. 'Genocide' had been erased from United Nations Security Council references to the Pol Pot years in an attempt not to offend China, while American and other Western documents referred to 'human rights abuses'. American government officials had mounted a campaign to persuade people that the Khmer Rouge had changed out of all recognition.

'We have evidence of Pol Pot's secret plans to fool Western governments and to take power, as he did before,' said Pilger over pictures of hand-written documents. 'These notes are of secret speeches made by Pol Pot and discussions with his leadership. Pol Pot's spokesman, Khieu Samphan, who has smiled his way around the world of so-called peace conferences, made the following declaration to Khmer Rouge commanders. "The outside world," he said, "keeps demanding a political end to the war in Cambodia. I could end the war if I wanted because the outside world is waiting for me, but I am buying time to give you comrades the opportunity to carry out all the military tasks." At this point, Pol Pot added that to end the war politically would make his movement fade away and this must be prevented from happening.'

Following the screening of *Cambodia – Year Ten*, reported Pilger, Western governments indicated that they were beginning to bow to public opinion. Sweden changed its vote at the United Nations, Australia launched its own peace plan and Britain sent diplomats to Cambodia for the first time in fifteen years. But this masked the reality of the West demanding a 'comprehensive settlement', which meant that the Khmer Rouge must be given a share in power before elections. Pol Pot eventually had a veto over peace.

In Kompong Speu province, Pilger found that villages were no longer immune to the threat of the Khmer Rouge, as they had been a year earlier. Several villages had been captured, those trying to escape had been shot and others had died or been injured after stepping on Khmer Rouge mines. 'The situation is deteriorating and, still, no large-scale aid is going from the West to assist the people of that country,' said Oxfam director Frank Judd.

Pilger walked down the same hospital corridor as he had a year earlier to find children suffering from the same preventable diseases, victims of the West's trade embargo. In the past year, said Pilger, Cambodians had also become the most disabled people in the world, along with the Lebanese. Stepping on mines resulted in eighty new amputees each day. Pilger and Munro filmed victims at a hospital. Tea Banh, Cambodia's vice-premier and minister of defence, told Pilger that weapons used against the government by the Khmer Rouge and its allies were supplied by Western countries such as France, Sweden and West Germany, as well as China. 'All three factions, including the Khmer Rouge, are using the same weapons,' he said. Pilger was shown some of the arms that had been captured on the battlefield and he and Munro filmed others shortly after they had been taken.

'The discovery of these arms, which include American weapons, set us off on a journey around the world, revealing direct American and British involvement in the return of Pol Pot,' said Pilger. In Bonn, the capital of Germany, he spoke to Michael Sontheimer, South-east Asia correspondent of *Die Zeit*, who told him that his government was in the 'immoral position' of supporting the Khmer Rouge. A German anti-tank missile called

Ambrust was supplied to them. Pilger telephoned the manufacturers, MBB, with the serial number of a weapon he had seen in Cambodia and was told that it was not their serial number. The company had sold a licence to make the weapon to a Belgian company called PRB, in Brussels. There, Pilger revealed that PRB was owned by the British company Astra, which had made part of the supergun that ended up in Iraq. Astra would later figure in his documentary *Flying the Flag – Arming the World* (see Chapter 2). 'In 1981–82, the company [PRB] arranged for Chartered Industries of Singapore to produce the German Ambrust weapon,' said Pilger, but PRB denied all knowledge of the weapon and of having anything to do with arms at all. Raol Jennar, former adviser to the Belgian Senate, said that a commission of inquiry in the country had discovered that PRB had been 'involved in a series of important contracts with South-east Asia' for arms.

In Singapore, the United States' and China's most active ally in the region, Pilger revealed that the government-owned Chartered Industries made Western arms under licence and shipped them directly to the Cambodian guerrillas. This allowed US President George Bush to continue sending arms through Singapore, 'aid' that broke a law passed by Congress only the previous year. From Singapore, they were shipped to Thailand, where Pilger and Munro travelled to their destination, a Khmer Rouge munitions warehouse, with a United Nations aid convoy. 'Our sources tell us,' said Pilger, 'that the land is owned by the United Nations Border Relief Operation and leased to the United States Government . . . a humanitarian agency renting its property to a foreign government, which allows the Khmer Rouge to use it as a military base.' Pol Pot lived nearby.

Following the screening of *Cambodia – The Betrayal*, Unbro complained to the Broadcasting Complaints Commission that the allegation about this warehouse was false. The BCC dismissed the complaint. Much more serious was a libel action taken against Pilger and Central Television relating to the revelation that the

SAS had trained the Khmer Rouge and others in mine-laying (see Chapter 8 for full details of the libel case).

Sue Elliott, who had worked with Cambodian refugees, spoke to Pilger on the telephone from New Zealand on behalf of a former Cambodian guerrilla who insisted on remaining anonymous for fear of his life. In Malaysia, he and others from the three groups of the non-communist resistance, including the Khmer Rouge, were trained by American and British advisers, she said. One of the skills they were taught was mine-laying. In Phnom Penh during September of the previous year, said Pilger, international observers to the Vietnamese withdrawal included British MPs Ann Clwyd and Jim Lester. Clwyd recalled meeting two British men who claimed to be on holiday but, said Pilger, the official list of observers included the names of 'Anthony Norman' and 'Christopher MacKenzie', representing the British Ministry of Defence. When Clwyd tried to discover the identity of the men back in London, she was told that the information was classified. Pilger alleged that Captain Anthony de Normann and Christopher MacKenzie-Geidt had both been members of the SAS. The men subsequently claimed that the programme implied that they had been linked to training the Khmer Rouge and its allies.

'The SAS has given secret training to the Cambodian guerrillas for five years,' said Pilger, 'and, as we can now reveal, British support for Pol Pot has never been more crucial.' Simon O'Dwyer-Russell, the *Sunday Telegraph*'s diplomatic correspondent, who investigated the issue with Pilger and Munro on condition that he could publish the story two days before the screening of their film, had spoken to two SAS trainers. The Official Secrets Act prevented them telling their own story, so he spoke for them on screen, explaining that training had started along the Thai–Cambodian border 'around 1985' for 'both the Sihanoukists and the Khmer Rouge'. After October 1989, when this was revealed in *Year Ten* and O'Dwyer-Russell's reporting, support became 'very much more covert in its nature, so it passed very clearly to being an MI6 Operation', with former SAS men on contract 'to provide training and mines technology to the Khmer Rouge'. Over film of child victims of unexploded bombs, O'Dwyer-Russell explained how 'anti-personnel mines' embedded themselves in people's bodies. 'My understanding is that the British are still involved in supplying these sort of mines,' he added, referring to his sources in the government and the SAS.

Frank Judd suggested that viewers should write in protest to their governments, as they had after Pilger's previous film. Summing up, Pilger said that, in the year that the Berlin Wall was being torn down, the Cold War was still being fought with the blood of faraway people in poor countries. 'The Khmer Rouge must be stopped,' he said. 'They *must* be brought to trial at the International Court of Justice and expelled from the United Nations. All aid and comfort to Pol Pot and his allies – guns, mines, bombs, uniforms, training, food and so-called diplomacy – must stop and their bases in Thailand closed down, and the wall built around Cambodia must be torn down and aid to rebuild this country denied no more. Every day these steps are not taken, every day that governments appease and deceive, is a day lost for the people of Cambodia.'

Foreign secretary Douglas Hurd was swift to deny the claim that SAS men were training the Khmer Rouge, writing (or putting his name to) a half-page feature in the *Independent* three days after the screening of *Cambodia – The Betrayal*. The following year, Pilger and Central Television settled out of court with the two former officers but emphasized that the aim of the film had been to bring attention to the fact that the SAS was still training forces that included the Khmer Rouge. A feature of the brief court hearing was the use of Public Immunity Certificates – gagging orders – by John Major's government to prevent the defence calling the armed forces minister, the commanding officer of the SAS and other senior political and military figures to be cross-examined.

On the day the libel case finished, Pilger and Munro began

making their sixth documentary on Cambodia, *Return to Year Zero*. They interviewed witnesses such as the former Cambodian guerrilla who had been trained by the British in Malaysia and worked undercover with the Khmer Rouge, and whose story had been told in the previous film by Sue Elliott. General Tea Banh, Cambodia's defence minister, was interviewed again, this time revealing intelligence information about the British training of Khmer Rouge troops. The 'Deep Throat' former British intelligence officer who had anonymously provided much of the information about SAS training agreed to be interviewed as long as his face was hidden and his voice distorted. He explained that British training had continued for ten years, despite the government's claim that it had finished in 1989.

Return to Year Zero took almost two years to make and was screened in April 1993, a month before internationally supervised elections. Pilger and Munro had filmed in Cambodia during October of the previous year, when 22,000 United Nations troops and other personnel were a permanent presence on the streets, there to see through the UN 'peace process', which would culminate in elections. The documentary also focused on the increasing number of limbless people in the country's streets and hospitals, the ever-present prospect of a return by the Khmer Rouge, who had control of more areas of the country than at any time since their overthrow, and the evidence of British complicity in training them.

Pilger opened the film by asking, 'What will happen when the United Nations leaves? Why has Pol Pot's organization grown stronger and more menacing since the arrival of the UN? Indeed, has a Trojan horse been built for the return of Asia's Hitler? This film will look behind the façade of the so-called peace process and ask: Has the unthinkable for Cambodia at last been made acceptable for the rest of the world?'

The 1991 UN peace plan would allow the Khmer Rouge to return with the backing of the United Nations, said Pilger. Khieu Samphan, 'Pol Pot's chief henchman', was given a veto and on his return to Phnom Penh there was rioting on the streets and he was attacked in his villa. The Khmer Rouge then refused to comply with the Paris Agreement. 'This year,' said Pilger, 'the UN will hold elections, which will almost certainly produce a government that includes allies of the Khmer Rouge. The UN says the elections will be held in a neutral political environment. Meanwhile, Pol Pot waits in the countryside.'

Lieutenant-General John Sanderson, the UN force commander, insisted that he was neutral. Disarming all the factions and demobilizing 70 per cent of them was part of the process intended to bring that about. But the UN Special Rapporteur in 1986 had described the Khmer Rouge as genocidal, pointed out Pilger. 'They may well have, but I'm not going to,' said the general, with a smile. This was followed by familiar film of skulls piled up and scenes from inside the Tuol Sleng extermination centre, with Pilger pacing through the corridors recalling his first visit there, in 1979. A filmmaker, Yvon Hem, recalled that the Khmer Rouge killed 10,000 people during the evacuation of Phnom Penh in 1975, then forced the rest into slave labour. His wife and four children were all killed. Shortly before liberation by Vietnam, he was forced to dig his own grave. 'If the Vietnamese liberation hadn't happened, they would have exterminated all of us,' he said. A journalist, Khieu Kanarith, told Pilger that eighty-one of his relatives had been murdered.

United Nations spokesman Eric Falt explained the transformation of 'the Khmer Rouge' to 'the National Army of Democratic Kampuchea' and said that 'the peace process was aimed at allowing them to gain respectability'. Over film of the Royal Palace, Pilger explained that Prince Norodom Sihanouk had returned after denouncing the Khmer Rouge, having supported them in exile throughout the 1980s. Behind Sihanouk's palace was a Khmer Rouge fortress, erected in 1992 and now the home of Khieu Samphan, Pol Pot's second-in-command. 'I never thought I'd see the day when the so-called international community contrived to bring back the Khmer Rouge to Cambodia under United Nations protection,' said Pilger, as he walked past the building's walls. Film followed of Khieu Samphan as a guest of honour at a UN military parade in Phnom Penh, the day before Pilger's interview with General Sanderson, who told him that the UN had wanted 'maximum participation by Cambodians' and 'they were one of the factions that signed the Paris Agreement'.

Pilger visited Kompong Thom province, where the Khmer Rouge 'controlled the roads, the paddies, the towns and villages by night' and where the UN was to conduct its 'free and fair' elections. 'It has been estimated,' said Pilger, 'that the amount of territory controlled by the Khmer Rouge has more than doubled.' UN military observer Ed Pyne, who was responsible for rounding up and disarming those troops, said that they had refused to comply.

Returning to the subject of unexploded mines, previously featured in *Cambodia – The Betrayal*, Pilger said, 'The war in Cambodia may be the first in history in which landmines have claimed more victims than any other weapons. No other country in the world has a higher percentage of physically disabled people; no other country has a higher percentage of amputees.' Most of the seven hundred amputations performed a month by doctors were caused by mines and, for every one wounded, another was killed.

A report by Asia Watch, an American human rights organization, stated that China and Britain trained Cambodian guerrillas in the use of mines and explosives. Rae McGrath, author of the report, explained that Britain, through the SAS, had given the Khmer Rouge-dominated KPNLF (Khmer People's National Liberation Front) training that included a three-month demolition course. This amounted, he said, to 'the very things that we reviled in the IRA, the very things that we call terrorism when they happen in Oxford Street'. Pilger reported that the British government had for two years denied any involvement in training Khmer Rouge forces or their allies. 'In July 1991, the government finally admitted that British soldiers had indeed been secretly training allies of Pol Pot,' said Pilger. 'It meant that the government had consistently misled Parliament and the British people over its complicity in Cambodia's civil war. And it was almost certainly designed to stop further disclosure that the SAS had directly trained the Khmer Rouge.' The interviews recorded in July 1991 with Tea Banh, Cambodia's minister of defence, and the former British intelligence officer confirmed this fact. Pilger added that Tea Banh had subsequently stated that British training had continued until August 1991.

'The British are back in Cambodia as part of the UN operation, ensconced with the Khmer Rouge,' said Pilger. 'They are now teaching them to clear mines.' A serving British soldier in Phnom Penh, filmed secretly with his face out of vision, explained why Pol Pot's troops had asked for the British. 'I believe it goes back a bit during the war, when it was the British SAS that taught them mine warfare then,' he said. Pilger said that the UN had done little to rid Cambodia of the mines and General Sanderson explained that the policy was to train Cambodians to do so. 'This is a Cambodian problem,' he insisted. Sergeant-Major Joost Van Den Nouwland, of a UN mine-clearing unit, told Pilger that mines had been destroyed but none cleared in the province where he was stationed. It had been estimated, said Pilger, that there was a mine for every one of Cambodia's seven million people.

As in his previous film, Pilger visited amputees in hospital and established that there had been no attempts to clear the mines in that area. He also discovered the fruits of a humanitarian effort inspired by *Cambodia – Year Ten*. The Jaipur Limb Centre, where prosthetic limbs were made and fitted, was founded by the Indo-China Project, an offshoot of Vietnam Veterans of America, whose driving force, Bob Muller, was previously featured in Pilger and Munro's 1981 film *Heroes*, about US veterans of the Vietnam War. Muller was seen in *Return to Year Zero*, along with fellow-veterans Dave Evans and Ron Podlaski.

The international community had pledged $880 million in development aid to Cambodia as part of the peace plan, but 'not a single dollar has arrived', said Uc Kim An, adviser to the country's prime minister. Edouard Wattez, of the UN Development

Programme, said that $400 million-plus had been committed over the next two years and only $2 million of $60 million pledged by the United States had arrived. In his final piece to camera, Pilger said:

> Like Hitler, Pol Pot must and can be stopped *before* the United Nations leaves Cambodia. Of course, only Cambodians can do it, but the international community *can* bring pressure on countries like Thailand that continue to give vital backdoor support to Pol Pot. And is a serious, co-ordinated attempt to clear Cambodia's mines and to restore its roads, bridges and clean water supply beyond the capacity of the world body that mobilized so spectacularly for war in the Gulf? And those who've argued for an international tribunal to try Pol Pot and his gang for genocide surely deserve our support. But time is short. You saw Tuol Sleng extermination centre in this film. It holds unique records of Khmer Rouge crimes. Pol Pot has demanded its closure. Clearly, he's looking ahead to destroy the evidence and the truth of history. 'If understanding is impossible,' wrote Primo Levi of the Jewish Holocaust, 'knowing is imperative, because what happened could happen again.' The simple truth is that no peace was ever built on unrepudiated genocide and the words 'never again' remain the cry of civilization.

After the end titles finished, Pilger added a postscript: 'Since this film was made, the Khmer Rouge have withdrawn from their compound in Phnom Penh and abandoned any pretence of complying with the so-called peace process. This means they have declared open war on the UN operation, which has allowed them to double the territory they now control. In the last month, they've killed at least a hundred people, including seven UN personnel. Their aim is clearly to disrupt the forthcoming elections. In the meantime, thousands of people are fleeing Cambodia, just as they did in the months before Year Zero.'

Events seemed to have turned full circle in Cambodia, although the policies of Western governments had, in reality, changed little from the time when Pilger made *Year Zero* in 1979. Much of the success of that documentary lay in its ability to raise consciousness about the millions starving in that country, causing people world-wide to donate money. More than any other British organization, Oxfam ignored political considerations to mount a relief effort that saved lives and helped the country back on to its feet. Like Pilger, the charity put humanitarian issues first, but it paid a heavy price by voicing its criticisms of power politics in the West.

Oxfam continued to speak out against governments, culminat-ing in a 1988 book, *Punishing the Poor: The International Isolation of Kampuchea*, by Eva Mysliwiec, the charity's chief representative in Phnom Penh. This blamed the American bombing for beginning the carnage in Cambodia and contended that the country was being punished still for being on the 'wrong side'. In 1990, an American group, the right-wing International Freedom Founda-tion, complained of 'political bias' to the Charity Commission in London and drew the support of backbench Conservative MPs. The following year, the commission censured Oxfam for its campaign warning of the threat of Pol Pot's return. Since then, the charity has been less vociferous in the political elements of its campaigning, wary of the threat to its charity status.

Twenty years after Pilger's campaign for justice in Cambodia began, Pol Pot was dead and the country was enjoying a fragile peace under Hun Sen's elected, fairly stable government in Phnom Penh, and the Khmer Rouge had been largely defeated in the countryside – although leading members of the Khmer Rouge remain free and its cadre has infiltrated every corner of political and military life. There are tentative plans for a war crimes tribunal. 'This is a step forward,' reflected Pilger, 'and, until the evidence suggests otherwise, we might even allow ourselves a modicum of hope.'[26]

4. FLASHPOINTS

A LONGSIDE THE IMAGES of Vietnam, human tragedies around the world provided some of the most vivid television pictures of the late 1960s and early 1970s. Those of the famine in Bangladesh in 1974 were a reminder of scenes from Biafra five years earlier. John Pilger's documentary *An Unfashionable Tragedy*, with pictures of starving Bangladeshi children, had overtones of Jonathan Dimbleby's 1973 *This Week* programme about the Ethiopian famine and was a forerunner to his own film *Year Zero – The Silent Death of Cambodia*, particularly in its revelation that power politics was holding up Western aid.

Bangladesh had emerged from the state of East Pakistan. In 1970, a year before independence, Pilger reported from there for the *Daily Mirror*, when up to one million people died in a cyclone. His eyewitness reports were world exclusives, along with his reporting from inside East Pakistan, where he travelled with Bengali guerrillas. On the day that the territory became Bangladesh in December 1971, one of the guerrilla leaders held up a copy of Pilger's report on the front page of the *Mirror*.

Pilger's despatches emphasized that Western governments did not wish to upset Pakistan's ruling generals, in the same way that years later they would not want to displease China by helping the Vietnamese-installed government in Cambodia. Previously, in 1969, the British Labour government had withheld aid from the starving Biafrans to avoid upsetting Nigeria, a major oil supplier. So the rescue operation mounted by the British government in East Pakistan as a result of media coverage was small and amounted to little more than a triumph for public relations.

Pilger's newspaper reporting of the violence that had preceded independence won him many friends in the new state. Justice Abu Sayeed Choudhury, who was to become the first president of Bangladesh, wrote to the *Daily Mirror* in July 1971 offering his government's gratitude 'for bringing to the notice of the world the massacre of the unarmed civilian population of Bangladesh by the army of West Pakistan' and 'appreciation of the services rendered by your distinguished correspondent, Mr John Pilger'.[1]

After independence, Pilger was a frequent visitor to Bangladesh. In late 1974, he returned with director John Ingram to make *An Unfashionable Tragedy*, the first in his second series of *Pilger* documentaries, starting the following January. 'In the film which follows,' an ITV announcer intoned before the programme started, 'there are scenes of famine and its results, which some of you may find distressing.' Following the opening titles, Pilger was seen speaking to the camera, telling the story of a boy's death from diarrhoea after eating poisoned leaves because there was no food. 'In other words, he starved to death,' said Pilger. 'The cost of keeping him alive was inflationary. Milk powder and a handful of grain every day would cost at least 20p. I must apologize. This really isn't appropriate for New Year television, is it, especially with all our own problems of inflation in Britain? Indeed, before I came here I was told many times, "Don't do Bangladesh. People won't watch it. They'll switch over." And of course I can sympathize with people who do switch over, because I realize that I and other reporters have helped to immunize people against Bangladesh by reporting their horrors year after year. But I do ask you to watch this film because I believe that possibly the greatest famine in recorded history has now begun here, with tens of thousands of people already dead and dying and suffering.'

With this direct approach to television viewers, acknowledgement of his own part in bombarding the public with images of tragedy and the skill of being able to relate the value of a

Bangladeshi boy's life to viewers at home, Pilger clearly captured the imagination of many, who did not switch channels. The audience figures were high, taking *Pilger* into the Top 20 of the week's most watched programmes, and £30,000 in unsolicited donations was sent to ATV.

Once again, Pilger placed the suffering of a society in a wide geo-political 'big picture'. *An Unfashionable Tragedy* told how Bangladesh fitted into the age of power politics. 'I also believe,' said Pilger to the camera, 'that Bangladesh could become the world's most ignored tragedy, because Mr Kissinger and Mr Brezhnev have now agreed on a world doctrine in which a country like Bangladesh is expendable. It has no oil, it has no real strategic value, it has no military power, it has no practical purpose. All it has is people, who now wish to live.'

The film showed bodies being collected in the streets of Dacca, the Bangladeshi capital, including an eleven-year-old girl who had starved to death. 'Why have these children been allowed to starve?' asked Pilger, over more pictures of dead bodies. 'For some of us who came here at the birth of this country, Bangladesh was no more than a source of good copy. We were too concerned with oil to notice that in 1974 food became a political weapon.' Kissinger, the US secretary of state, had directed the distribution of the United States' surplus food abroad, but none of the countries on his priority list was in desperate need. These included Chile, Cambodia, South Korea and South Vietnam, all US client states. This was to be the main theme of Pilger's 1976 documentary *Zap!! The Weapon Is Food* (see Chapter 5). In *An Unfashionable Tragedy*, he revealed that a secret US State Department report had been leaked, disclosing how food was used to shore up some regimes and blackmail others.

In a piece to camera, Pilger – standing in front of human skeletons piled high – said angrily that there had been 10,000 victims in this one cemetery over the previous six months. 'Many of these children died because they couldn't get milk,' he explained. 'Last year, the UN in Dacca stopped feeding starving children a powder made from milk and soya beans, simply because the Common Market countries had bought up all American soya bean stocks to use as cattle feed. And yet the EEC Council of Ministers haggle for months before releasing a miserable £63 million as relief and an eighth of what they'd promised to twenty-five hungry countries, of which Bangladesh is just one.'

Footage of a World Food Programme Conference in Rome being told that 'no children must go to bed hungry' was intercut with black-and-white stills by *Daily Mirror* photographer Eric Piper of starving children at a relief camp near Dacca. A US State Department official had said, off the record, that there was no strategic value in Bangladesh.

Pilger travelled to a village forty miles from the Bangladeshi capital, where everyone was starving. Some women were naked because they had sold their clothes for food, so he could not film them. One man, a farmer who had sold all his land for food, said that he was now eating flour. In scenes that bear comparison with the later documentary *Year Zero – The Silent Death of Cambodia*, film of a small, starving boy was accompanied by Pilger's words, 'He has the distended belly and he probably has about every kind of parasite and disease. He's existing on the root.'

Bangladesh's prime minister, Sheikh Mujibur-Rahman, told Pilger that some villages had no food as a consequence of floods and 27,000 people had died. Over film of two helicopters standing idle, Pilger explained that they had been sent by the British government but needed vital parts. The Soviet Union had lent Bangladesh nine 'creaking' helicopters. Still, he pointed out, there had been no shortage of American, Australian and British aircraft to relieve the victims of a cyclone in Darwin, Australia. He talked of 'the world's culpable neglect of this ravaged country' and said there were only seventy-five hospital beds for children in all of Bangladesh – about one per million of population.

Over film of graves being dug, Pilger reported that Bangladesh had declared a state of emergency on 28 December 1974. He criticized the United Nations for ignoring its charter by its 'meanness', the Soviet Union, 'which heaps friendship on Bangladesh but little else', Australia for 'not sending its surplus wheat', and Britain, 'with its traditional goodwill and two idle helicopters'.

At the end of this harrowing report, Pilger said, 'If you've been horrified by what you've seen, then good. No doubt the commercials in a minute's time will offer reassurance to those who feel they need it. The truth is that Bangladesh and Britain have been caught in the same blizzard of inflation, energy crisis and shortage, with the one difference – when prices go up in Britain no one dies, when prices go up in Bangladesh thousands die. You see, it's no longer a question of pity and charity – to hell with that! *Their* struggle to survive is *our* struggle. Beat it in Bangladesh and you beat it in Britain. It's really a simple choice that has simply to do with the brotherhood of man. The alternative is that we are all expendable.'

The compassionate response of viewers to *An Unfashionable Tragedy* was an early example of the effectiveness of Pilger's documentaries. Bangladesh has had a rocky history since, marked by war, poverty and natural disasters. Sheikh Mujibur-Rahman, the prime minister, was murdered in a 1975 coup and a struggle for power followed within the army. Presidents have come and gone, as has the imposition and lifting of martial law. Floods in 1988 left three-quarters of the country under water.

Like Bangladesh, Israel had emerged from a different state in the twentieth century. As with the new war in Ireland in 1969, the Six Day War of two years earlier reignited flames that had already been fanned and it brought Israel and its Arab neighbours back into the world spotlight.

The British had ruled Palestine under mandate from the League of Nations since 1919 and after World War Two, under pressure from Arabs concerned about Jewish immigration, asked the United Nations to make a decision on the country's future. In 1947, the UN declared that it would be divided into two states, one Jewish and one Arab, with Jerusalem as an international city.

The Arabs would not agree to this and, although the Jews gave their public acceptance to the plan, they secretly plotted the annexation of the Arab land.

Violence followed and in 1948, when the British surrendered their mandate, the Jews declared the state of Israel. Thousands of Palestinians fled to refugee camps on both banks of the Jordan, and to Syria and Lebanon. From 1950, Israel aligned itself with the United States and other Western powers, such as Britain and France. Israel, spurred into attacking Egypt six years later when President Abdul Gamal Nasser nationalized the Suez Canal, received British and French military support. However, the United Nations ordered a ceasefire and sent an international peace force to the Middle East.

The Six Day War followed a series of border incidents between Israel, Syria and Jordan. Egypt became involved after demanding the removal of a UN patrol on its frontier with Israel and blocked the Israeli port of Eilat. Israel struck first and, once a truce was arranged after six days, had added to its lands Jordanian territory on the West Bank of the River Jordan, the rest of Jerusalem, the Gaza strip on the west coast and Egypt's Sinai peninsula. Refugees fled in their thousands to camps in Syria, Jordan and Lebanon, and the seeds of the Palestinian Liberation Organization were sown. Soon, they were conducting raids across Israel's border. The Yom Kippur War of October 1973 saw territory won and lost by both sides when Egypt and Syria attacked Israel on the Jewish holy fast-day. Ultimately, the Arabs emerged stronger.

Pilger had visited Israel for the *Daily Mirror* since 1966, seen refugee camps in Jordan and met children in a kibbutz who were raised to fight. In 1973, he wrote about taking a Palestinian refugee back to see his former home in Israel, and he reported the Yom Kippur War, becoming the first British correspondent to reach Cairo after a journey across the desert from Tripoli, in Libya. The following year, he made the documentary *Palestine Is Still the Issue*. Since the fourth war between the Arabs and the Jews, the word 'earthquake' had become part of everyday language in Israel, said Pilger, in the ruined capital of the Golan Heights. 'For what happened here and on the Suez Canal was indeed an earthquake that shook Israel as never before, causing illusion after illusion to crumble,' he explained.

'The illusion that wars could always be won, and quickly, the illusion that the Western world, and especially America, would always bear Israel's burden, regardless of oil, what it costs, or what was right or wrong. The earthquake, neither victory nor defeat, has left Israel in almost a manic state of confusion and self-doubt. The old unity which once drew strength from war after war, and from a permanent feeling of siege, is in question now. People are hurt and bitter. They no longer see generals as heroes or politicians as leaders and, because of this, there is now among some of them the faint beginnings of a new realism, almost a revolutionary thinking that may, just may, bring peace.'

The film showed a kibbutz where seven people were killed during the Yom Kippur War. Dr Israel Shahak, a Holocaust survivor who founded the Israeli Civil Rights League, told Pilger about the fears of his people. 'You have to look around and be careful all the time,' he said. 'Somebody might stab you from behind.' Pilger noted that Dr Shahak and other Israelis had begun to talk about 'Palestinians', 'to say the unthinkable'. Palestinian Arabs living within the expanded Israeli borders would one day outnumber the Israelis. 'In other words,' said Pilger, 'the Jewish nation will have a clear Arab majority unless the occupied lands are given up and form part of a new neighbour called Palestine. Until this happens, Israel is liable to go on suffering atrocities.'

At a United Nations refugee camp near Jerusalem, where children were seen collecting meagre food supplies, Pilger explained that many of them were the second generation born in the twenty-six years since the first Palestinians became refugees in their own land. They still regarded Palestine as their homeland and talked about going home. 'If there's really to be a chance of peace, it won't be Egypt or Syria with whom the Israelis will do their final deal,' he said. 'It will be these people.'

However, one Israeli told him, 'Non-Jews, who happen in the majority to be Palestinians here or Arabs, are not regarded in this country as human beings.' Dr Ben Meir, a member of the Israeli Parliament, said, 'We have no doubt that we can maintain, as long as we can see in the future, a Jewish majority in Israel.' Against this, Pilger quoted a recent poll in one of the country's newspapers revealing that 320,000 Israelis were considering leaving the country.

Likening the segregation resulting from Palestinian refugee camps to apartheid in South Africa, Pilger pointed out that an increasing number of Israelis relied on Arabs to do menial jobs. 'I've been coming here on and off for eight years,' he said direct to the camera, 'and nothing ever changes, only the mud for dust, the dust for mud. The children still get their 1,500 calories of supplementary food every day in summer, 1,600 calories in winter, which is almost exactly what they need to survive and no more. And, of course, that's all the world community and the world's conscience can afford.

'No, nothing ever changes here, certainly not the irony that the position of the Palestinians now is so remarkably like that of the Jews before the birth of Israel. Both people were Semites, of course. Both were dispossessed and dispersed, and most became someone's problem. How ironic that the Palestinians, the Jews of the Arab world, have become Israel's problem. From the aftermath of the October war, while Israel does her deals with Egypt and even with Syria, her greatest and most neglected problem, as well as her greatest and most neglected chance of peace, still resides here in a wretched camp like this.'

A group of young Israelis told Pilger that they craved an end to conflict, one pointing out that Egypt had signalled the same desire. 'I must tell you how much we want peace,' said one young man. Shulamit Aloni, a member of the Israeli Parliament, said, 'If President Sadat is ready to hear us, as I believe he is, maybe we will have peace in not too many years.'

Pilger explained that the Jews, who had come to Israel from

places as far apart as Damascus and Miami, had justified their nation and settlement of Arab lands taken during the Six Day War by citing the Old Testament. Over film of a rabbi from Boston taking his flock on a tour of Israel, Pilger said that the United States government was giving annual grants and loans equivalent to £400 for every Israeli, but this would not cover the cost of the last war.

He asked Nathan Yalin-Mor, former leader of the Stern Gang, a terrorist organization operating in Palestine before the founding of the state of Israel, whether he could see a similarity between his group's murders and those carried out recently by the Palestinian Black September group. 'We didn't murder people,' said Yalin-Mor. 'The difference is that we killed people only in the conflict between the Hebrew nation and the British occupation power.' He insisted that his organization did not attack those out of uniform, although some inevitably died. 'Liberation for people can't come without using armed force,' Yalin-Mor added. 'I justify the right of every people to fight for its own independence with arms.'

Dr Israel Shahak, of the Israeli Civil Rights League, said he sought security for both Jews and Arabs. 'Security must be mutual,' he told Pilger. 'There is no security for a single community. Jews will never have a security if they insist only for their own security, and the same goes for Palestinians.'

Abdul Amin, a Palestinian who had become a grocer in a refugee camp near Jerusalem since being expelled from his home, was taken by Pilger back through the Jordan valley to the farm he had not seen since the Six Day War. 'This sad old man, wandering through his land, to which he can never return, is not just a pawn in a confused political situation,' said Pilger. 'He and thousands of Palestinians like him are the problem.' Through an interpreter, Amin told him that, if both Arabs and Jews, Palestinians and Israelis, had equal human rights, there would be a lasting peace. 'He said that the Arabs forgive easily and they forget easily,' explained Pilger.

'It seems to me,' summed up Pilger, 'that Israel now, and perhaps for the first time in her history, has been handed a clear choice. She can choose to cling to the old fears and to an uncertain mortgage in Washington or she can face a new reality, and that new reality is the recognition of a Middle East where Israelis and Palestinians, Jews and Arabs, are equals and partners, perhaps even part of a rich, developed, flourishing, undreamed-of Middle East, perhaps even a peaceful one. And that's not as forlorn a hope as it may sound, for in the end there's no other way.'

Palestine Is Still the Issue became one of the most viewed Pilger documentaries. 'Time and again, I've run into people in the Middle East and elsewhere who've seen it,' he said a quarter of a century later. 'In telling a very simple story of a man trying to go back to his land, in half-an-hour, it justified the title – that, whatever you say about the Middle East, whatever side you take, Palestine and returning the Palestinians to their homeland is still the issue. It's about justice. The so-called peace process has changed little; Palestinians have been given no more than the equivalent of the South African homelands under apartheid, a tiny proportion of their own country.'[2]

Pilger never returned to Israel for television as 'peace talks' dragged on during the 1980s and 1990s. In his writing, he pointed out that Israeli forces repeatedly invaded the Lebanon and committed massacres, with press coverage in the West generally placing disproportional blame on the Lebanese 'terrorist' group Hizbollah. 'In Palestine, as elsewhere,' he wrote, 'the victims, not the oppressors, are the terrorists: a perception widely held, according to Richard Falk, because of "the domination of *fact* by *image* in shaping and shading the dissemination of images that control the public perception of reality".'[3]

In late 1999, Pilger filmed in Iraq for his 90-minute special *Paying the Price – Killing the Children of Iraq*, broadcast at peak-time on ITV the following March. The documentary was a powerful indictment of the largely unreported effects of United Nations sanctions on Iraqi civilians following the 1991 Gulf War. The most striking was the fact, verified by UNICEF (the United Nations Children's Fund) and other UN agencies, that 500,000 children were among more than one million Iraqis who had died in almost ten years of sanctions. Pilger described it as 'the most comprehensive embargo in modern history against a country' and asked why twenty-one million people were 'being punished for the crimes of a dictator, Saddam Hussein'.[4] Iraq, which in 1989 had one of the lowest infant mortality rates in the world, as well as universal, free health care and education, now had one of the highest.

In the south of the country, he reported on another lethal result of the Gulf War, which had followed Saddam Hussein's invasion of Kuwait in August 1990. The Americans used depleted uranium in shells and missiles fired by their tanks and aircraft. Wind and dust carried the radiation across the towns and villages of southern Iraq. The subsequent embargo denied Iraq the equipment and expertise needed to clean up the former battlefields, as well as equipment for diagnosing cancer and drugs for treating it. A specialist described to Pilger 'a cancer epidemic that is likely to strike almost half the population'.

Paying the Price also reported that the United States and Britain were continuing to bomb Iraq, almost every day, and that a third of the casualties were civilian. This 'forgotten war' cost the British taxpayer £4.5 million a month. Pilger interviewed United Nations and US government officials, but Britain's Foreign Office would not agree to foreign secretary Robin Cook taking part in the film without guarantees: his interview had to be broadcast 'as live', in full, at the end of the programme and for a minimum of ten minutes. Not surprisingly, Pilger would not accept this. He did, however, guarantee that an interview with Cook would be given substantial time in the documentary, that most of the questions would be supplied in advance and that the editing would be rigorously fair. The Foreign Office rejected this.

'For two months, we requested an interview with the foreign

secretary, Robin Cook, and were told he didn't want to appear in a film with dying babies,' said Pilger in a camera piece with a large picture of Cook in the background. 'I wanted to ask Mr Cook if he agreed with his American friend, Madeleine Albright [the US secretary of state], that the death of half a million children was a price worth paying for sanctions. I wanted to ask him why Iraqi children are denied vital medical supplies like vaccine and why British and American bombs rain down on children. Only two people were unavailable to appear in this film: Saddam Hussein and Robin Cook. This raises an important issue. Unlike all the others you've seen interviewed, only the Foreign Office demanded special treatment: an exclusive screening of the film, followed by a ten-minute, uncut contribution by Mr Cook right at the end. In other words, they wanted editorial control. Is that how accountability in a democracy works these days? What is the British government frightened of? What have they got to hide?'

Pilger had consulted Steve Anderson, the ITV Network Centre's controller of factual programmes, before rejecting Cook's demands. 'We both agreed that accepting them would be the wrong course because it would question our integrity,' said Anderson. 'Our worry was that he would filibuster his way through the last ten minutes and not answer the questions, and we would be forced to run everything he said. We were certain, through hard experience with politicians, that he would take a set amount of time and use it to say what he wanted to say rather than answer the questions. We were prepared to supply him with a detailed list of question areas and to guarantee that he would be represented fairly, and to make him more familiar than any cabinet minister had ever been with the content of a film. That still wasn't good enough for him, so we walked away from it.'[5]

Because sanctions prevented flights to and from Iraq, Pilger, director Alan Lowery and their crew entered by road. Accompanying them was Denis Halliday, former assistant secretary-general of the United Nations, who had resigned in protest against sanctions. It was his first trip back to Iraq, where he had been the senior UN official. The team drove two vehicles from Amman, Jordan: a hazardous, sixteen-hour journey along a road that was Iraq's only lifeline to the outside world. 'It was bizarre,' recalled Lowery. 'As you travel from Amman it's a two-lane highway, but when you cross the border into Iraq there's a six-lane motorway all the way to Baghdad, yet it's falling apart. Then you see the rest of the infrastructure of the country has crumbled as a result of the bombing first during the Gulf War, then by Britain and the United States since.'[6] Cameraman Preston Clothier and sound recordist Grant Roberts had to take great care to ensure that their equipment was not damaged by dust and faulty power supplies.

On Pilger's return to London after the two-and-a-half-week trip, he immediately contacted the ITV Network Centre and sought an extension of the 50-minute film to 74 minutes (broadcast in a 90-minute slot). Steve Anderson requested twenty minutes of 'rushes'. 'After looking at the material and assessing its strengths, we felt that this was going to be a very, very powerful story,' said Anderson. 'It's very rare that you get a documentary that can justify such an extensive slot, especially in ITV peak-time. But we thought that this was so important that, by giving it 90 minutes, it would get showcase status, stand out in the schedules and alert a lot of the world to what was going on in Iraq. There are certain programmes you do not simply to get ratings but because the story matters. This was one of those.'[7]

With Anderson's go-ahead, Pilger flew to Washington to interview James Rubin, assistant secretary of state and spokesman for the Clinton administration, Kofi Annan, the UN secretary-general, other senior UN officials and a leading member of the Iraqi opposition in exile.

The documentary opened with scenes of suffering Iraqi children, interspersed with the pronouncements of former US President George Bush and British Prime Minister Tony Blair that their 'quarrel' was with the Iraqi leadership, not its people, as well as Robin Cook's statement of an 'ethical' foreign policy. The implication could not have been clearer – whatever these politicians' words, their actions were devastating.

Going straight to the principal cause, Pilger explained that in August 1990, four days after Iraq's invasion of Kuwait following a dispute over shared oil fields, the United Nations Security Council imposed economic sanctions. For eight months, food and medicine were completely embargoed. 'Today, ten years later, sanctions are still in place,' reported Pilger, 'and the United Nations reports widespread chronic malnutrition and death among young children, an unprecedented human rights disaster.' Clean water, fresh food, soap, paper, pencils, books, light bulbs and life-saving drugs were either no longer available or extremely limited in supply, and people often sold furniture to buy food and medicines. Sanctions had killed more people than the two atomic bombs dropped on Japan. Before this, Iraq had been a developed country whose oil had brought great wealth, but also a dependency on imported food.

Over film of malnourished and dying children in a hospital in the city of Basra, Pilger reported that at least four thousand more Iraqi children under the age of five were dying every month than before sanctions. Scenes of him walking around the hospital ward and meeting these young victims were reminiscent of those in his Cambodia documentaries. Dr Jinan Ghalib Hassen, a paediatrician, told Pilger that a nine-year-old boy's course of treatment for leukaemia was affected by the intermittent supply of drugs. Professor Karol Sikora, former head of the World Health Organization's cancer programme, interviewed in London, explained that drugs were needed 'at the right time and in the right sequence, usually over a period of about six months' and that the success rate of treatment was dramatically lower if they were 'given in the wrong sequence'. He poured scorn on the claim by the US and British governments that life-saving drugs could have a 'dual use', in building weapons of mass destruction.

The Iraqi paediatrician showed Pilger an example of an eleven-year-old girl with a malignancy on the nervous system, which had once been rare but was now common. Other children shown were suffering from Hodgkin's disease and leukaemia. Most of those in the ward were malnourished and Dr Jinan Ghalib Hassen could barely control her emotions as she reflected that all of them looked like 'our daughter or my son' and she had to watch them dying. She told Pilger that families who could afford drugs bought them and their children survived, but others often died. 'What crime have the Iraqi children done to receive this punishment?' the doctor asked. In another hospital, in Basra, cancer specialist Dr Jawad Al-Ali, a member of Britain's Royal College of Physicians, showed Pilger a woman with breast cancer who could not be cured, and painkillers such as morphine were not available. Many of the doctor's own family had cancer, as did a disproportionate number of the medical staff at his hospital.

Over film of the Security Council chamber, 'centre of power at the United Nations in New York', Pilger outlined how Iraq in 1996 had been allowed to sell some of its oil reserves to buy food and other basic needs. This was known as the Oil for Food Programme. A special Security Council committee, dominated by the United States, which with Britain took a hard line on Iraq, controlled this oil revenue and had consistently blocked the restoration of power, light and clean running water in Iraq. 'For the children of Iraq, oil means food,' said Pilger. 'Although the Iraqis have been told they can repair their damaged oil industry, contracts for vital equipment have been blocked or delayed in New York. Currently, more than a billion-and-a-half dollars' worth of desperately needed shipments are on hold, including food, life-saving medical equipment, such as equipment to diagnose and treat cancer, and X-ray machines, heart and lung machines, firefighting equipment, agricultural equipment and toilet soap. The stated aim of the sanctions is to eradicate Iraq's weapons of mass destruction. Just before last Christmas, the department of trade and industry in London blocked a shipment of vaccines intended to protect Iraqi children against yellow fever and diphtheria. The vaccines, said the minister, are capable of being used in weapons of mass destruction.' This was illustrated with official documents, showing the lists of vital items 'on hold'.

Pilger introduced Denis Halliday, who in 1998 had resigned from the UN after two years in Iraq, setting up the Oil for Food Programme. Halliday had accused the West of 'destroying a whole society'. In a cancer clinic in Baghdad, he was reunited with a girl whose life he had helped to save. Halliday said he had brought in drugs from Jordan illegally and these had checked her leukaemia over a two-year period. The girl, Saffir Magib, stood with her father and Halliday, all of them smiling in one of the most moving scenes in the film. 'Today, she looks wonderful, beautiful,' said Halliday, 'and she has only now treatment once every month, so I think she's almost cured of leukaemia.' He had also intervened to help three other children but two had died for lack of drugs.

Halliday was a powerful witness in *Paying the Price*, bringing to the film an informed, eloquent anger. 'I think in this hospital we've seen today evidence of the killing that is now the responsibility of the Security Council member states, particularly, I think, Bill Clinton and Tony Blair,' he said, almost straight to the camera. 'They should be here with us, they should see the impact of what their decisions and their sustaining of economic sanctions means. The very provisions of the Charter and the Declaration of Human Rights are being set aside. We are waging warfare through the United Nations on the children and people of Iraq.' Halliday added, 'We are targeting civilians. Worse, we are targeting children.'

Pilger quoted US secretary of state Madeleine Albright, who was asked on US television whether the deaths of more than half a million children were a price worth paying and answered, 'We think the price is worth it.' This quote was the film's original title, but Pilger was concerned that, in isolation, its bleak irony might be misunderstood. In Washington, James Rubin told Pilger that Albright had been quoted out of context and his government did not accept the World Health Organization figure for children dead. Pilger produced the full transcript of her remarks and passed it to him. In making policy, said Rubin, the United States had to 'choose usually between two bad choices and, unfortunately, the effect of sanctions has been more than we would have hoped'. What was striking about the interview with Rubin was his obvious surprise at being challenged. He later told colleagues he had never encountered an interviewer like Pilger. 'He was so well prepared,' he said, 'and he wouldn't let go, as if he really believed in the issues he was raising.'[8]

The film made clear that sanctions had not hurt Saddam Hussein and his 'rich cronies', who received first-class treatment in well-stocked clinics. Asked by Pilger why ordinary people should suffer and the innocent held hostage to the compliance of a dictator, Peter van Walsum, the chairman of the UN sanctions committee, replied, 'Sanctions are one of the coercive measures that the Security Council has at its disposal under Chapter Seven . . . Sanctions are the measure just short of military action and obviously they hurt.' 'But *who* do they hurt?' asked Pilger. Van Walsum replied, 'Military action has collateral damage. Sanctions are short of military action but they also have, of course, effects that one doesn't want.' Why, then, asked Pilger, were there not sanctions imposed on Israel, which had the only known nuclear weapons in the Middle East and attacked the Lebanon 'almost every day of the week', or on Turkey, which had displaced three million Kurds and killed thirty thousand. Van Walsum seemed at a loss for a reply and, shaking his head, said, 'There are many countries that do things that we are not happy with, but this is the situation which has come into being due to the invasion of Kuwait.' Pilger asked him if he believed that every person had human rights, regardless of where they lived. 'Yes,' he replied. Asked whether sanctions were violating those human rights, he insisted that the UN did not want to hurt the population and, tellingly, admitted that 'the major powers' disagreed on that while ensuring that there were 'guarantees that Iraq will not again develop weapons of mass destruction'.

Denis Halliday, interviewed by Pilger on the floor of the UN General Assembly, said there was no democracy in the Security Council and he believed that the General Assembly would overturn the sanctions if the issue were ever presented to it. Pilger reported that, in February 2000, weeks before the programme's transmission, another UN official had resigned. Hans von Sponeck, Halliday's successor as senior UN representative in Iraq, said that he could no longer tolerate the suffering caused by sanctions. Interviewed by Pilger in Baghdad the previous October, von Sponeck had said, 'I do not think it is fair, after such a long period of time, to make the civilian population subject to bargaining.' Pilger reported that the head of the World Food Programme in Iraq, Jutta Burghardt, had also resigned. 'The United Nations has not known a rebellion like this,' he said.

Halliday and Pilger walked along a street in nineteenth-century Baghdad where, in the colonnades, people sold books in order to buy food and medicine for their families. Halliday pointed out that this was a particular tragedy because the art of writing had been developed in Iraq. To this effect of sanctions could be added the increase in violent crime and children being taken out of school to beg. Halliday spoke of 'a downward spiral of life' in Iraq as people were being denied access to travel, technology, education and books. Pilger visited a school where there were no desks and he was 'overwhelmed by the stench of raw sewage in the playground', the result of water and sewage treatment facilities being bombed and parts needed for the repair of them being delayed or denied by the UN sanctions committee.

UNICEF's representative in Iraq, Anupama Rao Singh, told Pilger that there had been a 125 per cent increase in children seeking psychiatric help and homes had been 'virtually denuded of the very basic stimulation play materials because most families, in order to cope with the present situation, have sold everything except the bare essentials'. Hans von Sponeck said that Iraq now had what someone had described to him as 'a young generation that is in the refrigerator, waiting until better times come'.

Because Iraq's electricity supply was limited – again because of a UN ban on infrastructure repairs – people often had no choice but to use paraffin heaters for cooking. A somewhat surreal sequence was a rehearsal by the Iraqi National Orchestra, conducted by Mohammed Amin Ezzet, whose hand and arm had been badly burned in an accident with a paraffin heater that had set his wife alight. She died from her injuries, an accident common under the conditions imposed by sanctions. The orchestra, said Pilger, sounded 'a bit tinny', because the violins needed new strings and the clarinets new reeds. Along with sheet music, these were now almost impossible to import. In the studio of the distinguished Iraqi sculptor Mohamed Ghani, the artist showed Pilger works symbolizing life under sanctions and bombing. A line of seven heavy blocks each placed on a sculpted figure, representing a day of the week, symbolized the burden placed on ordinary people by the embargo. A figure of a child pleading with his mother for milk from breasts that had none was, said the sculptor, 'exactly the situation in thousands of our homes', where food was extremely scarce.

As for the 'threat' of Saddam Hussein used by Britain and the United States to justify sanctions, Pilger recounted that the Iraqi dictator had been supported and nurtured by those Western countries, who had an interest in controlling the oil of the region. In 1921, Britain had set up a 'desert monarchy' in Baghdad with a compliant king, but the real power remained in London and the profits of oil continued to flow to the West. A popular nationalist government that took over in 1958 was soon overthrown in a coup engineered by the Central Intelligence Agency. The new regime, dominated by the Ba'ath Party, eventually produced a leader in Saddam Hussein, whom Presidents Reagan and Bush courted. Robert Gates, CIA director between 1991 and 1993, told Pilger that Saddam was known to be 'a thug who had very good ideas about how to perpetuate himself in power'. Said Aburish, author of the biography *Saddam Hussein: The Politics of Revenge*, said that the dictator could thank the United States for helping him to power, keeping him there and providing him with financial aid during the country's war with Iran. 'It's a love–hate relationship,' he said.

Similarly, British Cabinet ministers offered Saddam loans and trade deals, reported Pilger over a gallery of images of Conservative Cabinet ministers Lord Carrington, Cecil Parkinson, John Knott and David Mellor, who were regular visitors to Baghdad. 'They sold him ammunition, they sold him electronics, they sold him anti-nuclear, biological and chemical warfare suits and boots,' said Aburish. A leading member of the Iraqi opposition in exile, Laith Kubba, explained that Britain sided with Saddam Hussein in the war against Iran and simply 'brushed aside' his human rights violations against his own people. 'He used chemical warfare against the Iranians and against the Iraqis,' said Kubba.

The ingredients for Saddam Hussein's biological weapons included anthrax made at the British government's Porton Down laboratories and botulism developed by a company in Maryland, in the United States. As a result, when sanctions were imposed, the UN Security Council insisted that he destroy his weapons of mass destruction. Scott Ritter, a former chief UN weapons inspector in Iraq, told Pilger that 'by 1998 the chemical weapons infrastructure had been completely dismantled or destroyed by UNSCOM [the UN inspections body] or by Iraq in compliance with UNSCOM's mandate'. The biological, nuclear and long-range ballistic missile weapons programmes were also 'eliminated', he added, concluding that there was no threat posed by Iraqi weapons of mass destruction.

One of the extraordinary sequences in *Paying the Price* was an explanation of why the Iraqi people had apparently never risen up against their tyrant. This was not so, reported Pilger. Moreover, they were crushed with the help of the West. In March 1991, revealed Said Aburish, the Bush administration, having called on Iraqis to overthrow Saddam, secretly aided his counter-revolution and betrayed the popular movement. 'They [the Americans] denied them shelter . . . they gave his republican guards safe passage through their lines to attack the rebels,' he said. 'They did everything, except join the fight on his side.' Over pictures filmed in secret by two rebelling Iraqis, one of whom was killed, Pilger quoted an adviser to President Bush as saying, 'The United States could not allow the overthrow of Saddam Hussein without knowing that his replacement would support American policy.'

Filming in southern Iraq, close to the battlefields of the Gulf War, Pilger reported that dust was a permanent problem in that part of the country and 'carried the seeds of cancer'. A 'hidden' effect of sanctions was that Iraq was prevented from cleaning up its battlefields, where the United States and Britain fired shells coated in depleted uranium, a source of radiation used in nuclear weapons. A former US Army health physicist assigned to clean up Kuwait in 1991, Professor Doug Rokke, himself became a victim, with 5,000 times the recommended level of radiation in his body. He told Pilger that the radiation was 'throughout all Iraq and Kuwait' and in parts of Saudi Arabia. 'The contamination was extensive, the casualties were grotesque,' he said, adding over a horrific picture of a charred victim that some of those who died were 'burned to a crisp'. Many of those who survived were suffering respiratory problems and cancer.

In the southern city of Basra, explained Dr Jawad Al-Ali, up to 48 per cent of the population would get cancer as a result of the depleted uranium used during the Gulf War. Dr Jinan Ghalib Hassen said that some of the deformities she had seen among children had not been apparent before the war and sanctions. As after the atomic bombing of Hiroshima, she said, there was a dramatic increase in congenital malformations, leukaemia and brain tumours. Before sanctions, all the drugs needed had been available to her. Now, they were severely limited or non-existent.

In commentary that followed, Pilger said, 'Smashing Iraq gives the United States greater control over the Middle East as the West expands across a vast new oil protectorate stretching from the Persian Gulf to the former Soviet Union. Iraq may well be the blueprint for policing this new order, with the weapons of sanctions and bombs.' The camera moved across still photographs, like terrible icons, of two small sisters killed and buried in the rubble of their homes when a missile hit the centre of Basra in January 1999. The scale of the Anglo-American bombing campaign was, said Pilger, 'a well kept secret'. The US Air Force and Navy had flown 36,000 'sorties', including 24,000 combat missions, over southern Iraq between May 1998 and January 2000. Britain had spent £60 million over the previous year on its part in the bombing. Little of this had been reported in the West.

At a Christian monastery in the north of Iraq, where St Matthew is entombed, Pilger spoke to priests who reported constant bombing. Over footage of dead sheep, British journalist Felicity Arbuthnot explained that she had heard about flocks being bombed in the north and south. When she visited the village of Mosul, she found one such incident, in which four children, their father and grandfather, who had been minding the animals, had been killed by bombs. 'This is a totally isolated, desolate place,' said Arbuthnot, 'and it would have been visible as that from the air.' Pilger quoted an internal UN report revealing that almost half of the victims of the bombing in one five-month period were civilians.

Television news pictures from January 1998 of Robin Cook talking about the determination to 'leave Saddam Hussein in no doubt about our resolve to win this struggle' and Madeleine Albright declaring that 'the United States and Great Britain stand shoulder to shoulder' were followed by Pilger's explanation of how Cook had refused to give him an interview.

The film closed with Pilger in an empty Security Council chamber at the United Nations. He said:

At the dawn of the new millennium, how is Western civilization to be judged? By the fine words of the Declaration of Human Rights, words like 'the right to life', or by the denial of that right to a whole nation? Do the representatives of the powerful who sit here in the Security Council ever think beyond their so-called interests and manoeuvres and about their victims, small children dying needlessly half a world away? And do those politicians who tell us about their 'ethical policies' and 'moral crusades' ever ask the question, by whose divine authority do they punish twenty-one million people for the misconduct of a dictator? We think the price is worth it, says Madeleine Albright. No, it is not and it never will be, and it's time we reclaimed the United Nations. While you've been watching this film, countless children have died silently in Iraq. How many more will die before the silence is broken?

Paying the Price proved to be one of Pilger's most powerful films, and the extra airtime allowed him to present all the issues with great clarity and time to breathe before moving from one to another. Although the right-wing *Daily Telegraph* dismissed the documentary in its usual fashion, other right-wing newspapers at least took on board the horrors presented and the logic of its argument. One example of reluctant, grudging praise came from A.A. Gill in *The Sunday Times*, who described Pilger as 'the guilt fairy' who 'comes in the night and pours thick Third World guilt into your ear' and asserted that 'this was just another round in Pilger's long war of attrition against capitalism'. However, he added, 'Much as I despise his retro, student-poster politics and his scavenging of others' misery to further an old cause, I'm pleased he's back on the box. Television is a good medium for committed first-person essays, and we don't get anything like enough. A programme like this raises more pertinent questions and gets more of the grey matter fizzing than any number of balanced studio discussions.'[9] Most pertinently, Jamie McCallum wrote extensively in the *Guardian* about the issues raised and praised Pilger and Denis Halliday's revelations: 'Through their words, and the pictures of children malnourished and bug-eyed with disease, children being punished for crimes perpetrated before they were even born, *Paying the Price* was a stark portrait of what our political masters think is a fair price worth paying for keeping the world safe for us.'[10]

As with *Year Zero* and *Death of a Nation*, the response to *Paying the Price* proved that factual television can realize its full potential when such powerful films are allowed to blaze their way across the small screen. The political and public response was both immediate and dramatic. ITV, British MPs, the Foreign Office and the prime minister received a torrent of letters, e-mails, faxes and phone calls. Asked about the film during Parliamentary question time, Prime Minister Tony Blair deflected all the blame for Iraq's suffering to Saddam Hussein, without responding to the film's principal charge: that the British and US governments had led the United Nations in its punishment of millions of innocent people, especially children, for the misconduct of a dictator over whom the population had no control – indeed, a dictator whom Iraqis had tried to depose, only to be betrayed by the West – and that the embargo was actually strengthening Saddam's inner circle by centralizing the regime's control.

In long, defensive statements, neither foreign secretary Robin Cook nor his junior minister, Peter Hain, addressed the issue that sanctions that hurt the civilian population ought to be separated from a legitimate embargo aimed at preventing the regime from reconstituting its so-called weapons of mass destruction. Asked by Labour MP Tam Dalyell why he had not appeared in the film, Cook explained that Pilger had rejected his 'format' of an unedited 'right of reply' at the end of the transmission, begging the question why he alone had demanded this privilege when the secretary-general of the United Nations, other senior UN officials and the chief US state department spokesman had been prepared simply to be interviewed.

On the day of the programme's transmission, Victoria Brittain, the *Guardian*'s deputy foreign editor, who had attended a preview at the National Film Theatre, suggested that the executives and writers attending the paper's morning news conference watch it. The *Guardian* had given qualified support to the sanctions policy, just as it had supported the Gulf War and the NATO action against Serbia. The impact of *Paying the Price* on the most sceptical at the *Guardian* effectively changed editorial policy. Two days after it was broadcast, the paper ran a major leading article declaring sanctions to be inhuman and wrong. Headlined 'The policy isn't working – Saddam prospers while his people suffer', the editorial demanded the suspension of 'non-military sanctions' and declared, 'In vain do US and British officials insist that it is Saddam who is responsible for his people's agony. The finger of blame is pointed at them.'[11]

In response, Peter Hain wrote to the paper, 'It is a lie propagated by Saddam that sanctions are responsible for the suffering of the Iraqi people . . . Saddam plays politics with suffering. He believes TV pictures of malnourished Iraqi children serve his interests so he makes sure there are plenty of malnourished children to film.'[12] Hain repeated this claim in a letter to the *New Statesman*.[13]

There followed an extraordinary exchange between Pilger and Cook in that magazine. It began with a cover depicting the foreign secretary as a long-nosed Pinocchio and, under the headline 'Iraq: yet again, they are lying to us', Pilger described a 'culture of lying' at the Foreign Office that had hidden the truth from the public on all the major issues he had reported: Vietnam, Cambodia, East Timor and now Iraq. He wrote that Hain had 'metamorphosed in the depressingly time-honoured way from a principled political activist to yet another Foreign Office mouthpiece' and added, 'Tens of thousands of malnourished children need no setting up: they are everywhere.'[14]

Cook responded that Saddam Hussein was responsible for the suffering, there were 'no sanctions on humanitarian goods' and that he had been denied 'a right to reply' in *Paying the Price*.[15] Pilger asked why the British government had cast doubt on United Nations reports detailing the humanitarian tragedy, why it had not listened to the two senior UN officials who had resigned rather than administer a policy described by one of them as 'immoral and illegal' and why it had even withheld vaccines from children. He also challenged Cook to take part,

alongside Denis Halliday and Hans von Sponeck, in a public
debate on British government policy on Iraq.[16]

When Cook wrote back to the *New Statesman* that there was no
ban on vaccines,[17] Pilger accused him of meeting 'the Irving
standard' of lies (historian David Irving had just lost a libel action
following accusations that he was a Holocaust denier). Pilger
reported that Jon Davies, head of the Foreign Office's Iraq desk
and supervisor of Cook's letters, had told a visiting Iraq specialist
[Dr Eric Herring, of Bristol University] that the British government
must be 'reassured that the use of every batch of vaccine ordered by
Iraq was not for weapons'. However, this reassurance could be
given only by UN weapons inspectors, who had been expelled
from Iraq in 1998 after it was discovered that the US government
had used their presence to spy. 'No "reassurances" equals no
vaccine equals children dying from preventable diseases,' wrote
Pilger. He added that Professor Karol Sikora, head of the World
Health Organization's cancer programme, had found 'no possibility of converting these drugs into chemical warfare agents'.[18]
Cook wrote personally to Pilger, declining the invitation to take
part in the public debate on Iraq 'because I will be in Brussels'. As
political theatre and a rare glimpse of television journalism challenging government to account for its actions on a momentous issue of
life and death, this affair was probably unprecedented.

Denis Halliday sent a copy of *Paying the Price* to every member
of the UN Security Council before a debate on Iraq. Sitting in on
the debate, he heard several representatives refer to its power –
'this moving film I have seen' – and the French representative
declare that the council's 'liability has been proved'.[19] Halliday
also showed it to the Canadian and New Zealand parliaments,
resulting in a shift in policy in both countries away from sanctions.
After Kofi Annan, the UN secretary-general, had viewed a copy
sent to him by Halliday, he announced that the UN was losing the
'war of words' on sanctions. On 6 May, exactly two months after
the documentary's screening, 700 people packed Kensington
Town Hall for the public debate, entitled 'A Day for the People

of Iraq', and gave Halliday, von Sponeck and Pilger a standing ovation. At least half the audience were Iraqi exiles bitterly opposed to Saddam Hussein.

'I was conscious of the risk of being labelled Saddam's dupe,' said Pilger, 'although James Cameron once told me that "when they call you a dupe, you know you've got it right". For that reason, I wanted *Paying the Price* to be unrelenting in its exposé of Saddam's barbarities while demonstrating that Saddam and the Iraqi people were *not* one and the same – just as Suharto was not the Indonesian people and Pol Pot was not the Cambodian people – and that ordinary people had once again been swept up in power politics beyond their control. The balance was probably right, or as right as we could make it within the limits of the editing period. I think most viewers separated the tyrant from those who were his victims, and those who were the victims of Western governments. When provided with hard evidence, made accessible and vivid and without the usual vocabulary of deference to British official thinking, public opinion becomes a wonderful, almost rogue force and, although it is important not to overstate the impact, once people are touched and informed, anything can happen – often for the best.'[20]

5. UNCLE SAM

I N HIS FILMS and writing, John Pilger has sometimes been accused of 'anti-Americanism', even though he has never been critical of the American people, only their governments, institutions and corporations, whose power is universally felt. Indeed, the issue, as he sees it, is not criticism of any society, but of the imposition of great power by élite structures. This he has consistently exposed and analyzed, regardless of its source. For example, he opposed Soviet intervention in Eastern Europe, Afghanistan and Ethiopia. In his undercover film *A Faraway Country*, he described Soviet imperialist oppression in Czecho-slovakia as fascist. As a young correspondent, the Vietnam tragedy was perhaps the most important imperial adventure he witnessed at first hand. Yet he was careful to separate the responsibility of Washington's policy-makers and military ma-chine from the role of those sent to fight in the paddy fields. His 1981 documentary *Heroes* (see Chapter 1) was a sympathetic and intensely moving disclosure of the plight of returning American veterans, including those brutalized by the atrocities they had seen and participated in.

'I'm as anti-American as those legions of Americans who changed the world during the civil rights campaign of the 1960s and have struggled, against great odds, to enlighten their democracy and change the policies of their governments,' he said. 'I am no more anti-American than I am anti my own country, even though I have reported trenchantly on the policies of Australian governments towards the Aborigines, or anti-British because I have reported on the struggles of ordinary people in this country. Why is a loyalty oath required when discussing American actions? Is it because the defenders of American power dare not confront the truth that "our side" is capable of great crimes? The American establishment has always coated itself in a gloss of selective patriotism. The "anti" charge hardly applies anywhere else in the world. Indeed, the term "anti-American" begs interesting questions. Historically, it is not unlike the "anti-German" abuse encouraged during the extreme nationalism in Germany before and during the First and Second World Wars.'[1]

Pilger's own relationship with the United States began 'on the other side of the tracks', he recalled. 'I went to live in and report from the US in the late 1960s. The Americans who impressed and influenced me were those once described by Martha Gellhorn as "that life-saving minority of Americans who judge their government in moral terms . . . people with a wakeful conscience, the best of America's citizens".[2] Martha, one of my oldest friends, was one herself, of course. I worked with the great civil rights activist and *Life* photographer Matt Herron, with whom I shared many assignments in the Southern states. There were many like him, inspiring people, people of wakeful conscience. One of my real pleasures was writing about and filming small-town America, where I still keep in touch with people who invited me into their homes.'[3]

In his book *Heroes*, Pilger wrote about one such town, Beallsville, in Ohio, during the Vietnam War. This passage illustrates what he says is his understanding of and sympathy for the American heartland:

Beallsville, Ohio, June 1970. The first hot winds of summer blew through the American heartlands, where the town of Beallsville had slept beneath its magnolias and elms for two centuries, ever since George Washington himself farmed here. There is one main street, which is also State Highway 556, coming in from the hills of Appalachia, West Virginia, going on to Jerusalem, Hannibal and Cincinnati. Some seven hundred people live here, beneath scarred slopes and in sour little hollows over which hangs the fleck of coal: the 'dust of darkness' as an eloquent soul wrote on a memorial near the pit-top at the Ogilby-Norton mine.

There are two major sources of income: the mines operated by the North American Coal Company and the Ornet aluminium plant in Hannibal, where the 'swing shift' (through the night and dawn) is worked by poor dirt farmers. During the 1960s and early 1970s the plant thrived on making shells for the war in Vietnam. In 1970 40 per cent of the families of Monroe County, which has Beallsville at its centre, subsisted below the official government poverty line of $3,000 a year.

For this reason Beallsville is not attractive in the style and manner of so much of small-town America. It has a few splendid multi-gabled buildings, but most are of gaunt grey and white clapboard, like a western film-set about to blow down. There is a general store run by Dewey and a barber shop run by Kelly and a hairdresser's over which hangs a sign, 'Dior wigs made to order'.

And beyond the junkyard is the high school from which fewer than 3 per cent of the pupils go on to college; the rest go to the mines or to the service industries of Cincinnati or are idle. In 1970 they went to the military draft, and when the seventeen young men of the 'senior class of '70' received their diplomas, they strode ritually across the football field and up the hill, to where many of the classes of '65, '66, '67 and '68 were enshrined: in the grave-yard.

Jack Pittman and Bob Lucas, Charlie Schnegg, Rick Rucker and Duane Greenlee: all of them born here and grown up here; all of them killed in places their parents could never pronounce. At the height of the war in Vietnam the national ratio for Americans killed was one in 6,000. For Beallsville it was one in ninety.[4]

Pilger reported from the United States in the late 1960s for the *Daily Mirror*, most notably on the 1968 election campaign. Earlier that year, he was only yards away from Robert Kennedy as the Democratic Party candidate was shot dead. 'My political education got under way in the United States,' said Pilger. 'I made friends with the best Americans and I brushed against the worst, many exercising great power over the rest of humanity.'[5]

His documentary *The Quiet Mutiny* (see Chapter 1) broke the story of US troop rebellions in Vietnam and he returned to the domestic scene for *The Most Powerful Politician in America*, in the first series of *Pilger*, in 1974. In this film, he looked at the likelihood that George Wallace, governor of Alabama, would run for president in the 1976 elections. Pilger had followed him on the campaign trail during the two previous elections. Wallace had made his name in Alabama as a segregationalist and was remembered for standing 'in the schoolhouse door' of the University of Alabama in 1963 in an attempt to stop the enrolment of black students.

In 1972, after running as an independent and winning primary elections in Maryland and Michigan, Wallace was shot by would-be assassin Arthur Bremer, leaving him paralyzed and in a wheelchair. After polling 35 per cent of the national vote in the primaries, he was the one person who might have reduced Richard Nixon's majority in the White House. Now, all parties were courting him and there was even talk of an Edward Kennedy–George Wallace Democratic 'ticket', with Wallace running for vice-president.

'It was a very colourful story of political power in the American South,' recalled Pilger. 'Wallace had been an outspoken racist and "good old boy", but he was also a politician who would actually tell you things. I first interviewed him in 1968, a few years before he was shot and seriously disabled. In 1974, I based this programme around getting an interview with him and I learned never to do that again. He was forever promising to see me, then not turning up, and we were running out of time. So, at one of his campaign revival meetings, I ambushed his wheelchair in a car park outside and did the interview there. I also spoke to his wife, Cornelia, who played a very powerful role in his political life.'[6]

The public face of Wallace had now been transformed from the governor of Alabama who insisted, 'Segregation now, tomorrow and for ever', to a politician who courted all sections of the voting public, including blacks. Ten years earlier, most blacks in Alabama had been unable to vote – 'largely thanks to George Wallace,' said Pilger. Now that they could, the old tormentor needed them. He was second only to Edward Kennedy as the popular choice for a Democratic president in 1976.

Harold Martin, publisher of the *Montgomery Advertiser*, declared himself unsure whether Wallace had changed or not. Wallace was now saying that he had never been for segregation, only for upholding the law. 'Anyone with any intelligence at all can see that this is not true,' said Martin. There followed a 1963 television clip of Wallace defending segregation as 'in the best interest of all concerned'. President Kennedy had sent federal marshals to confront Wallace's steel-helmeted troops and forcibly integrate the University of Alabama. This had brought Wallace to national attention, said the publisher. A black woman newly enfranchised told Pilger she did not believe the governor. 'He's putting on a front,' she said.

Pilger told Wallace, 'I've never seen you so mellow.' He replied, 'Well, I suppose all of us mellow with age a little bit, in the sense that we don't need to shout as loud as we did to get your [the media's] attention . . . People in this state never have supported politicians who oppose people because of the way God made them. They oppose the heavy hand of big government trying to run everything at the local level.'

Pilger asked how Wallace could have changed his segregationist views. 'I think you are obviously a very intelligent person,' the governor replied, 'and whether you asked me that question to bait me or not, or whether you asked that question because you're not familiar with the abilities of most successful politicians to blow and suck at the same time, and talk out of both sides of their mouth – maybe that'll answer your question.' Asked whether he wanted to be president, Wallace replied, 'I don't rule the thing out, but I don't rule it in.'

Pilger then described the role of Wallace's second wife, Cornelia. She had 'plotted his comeback', was always at his side and would do anything to change his image from that of 'a little punk to something rather more presidential or, at least, vice-presidential'. Cornelia told Pilger that the gunman Bremer had been photographed with one of the leading Watergate conspirators shortly before the shooting. 'We know Bremer wasn't alone,' she said. 'We know something smells about the whole affair.'

Then, Pilger turned to Wallace and asked, 'Who really shot you?' He said he had no knowledge of Bremer but he questioned how an unemployed man could save up enough money to buy a car and guns, travel to New York, stay in a luxury hotel and rent limousines. 'He kept a diary,' said Wallace, 'and he'd never kept a diary before, and it seems that all these political assassination attempts and assassinations are made by people who keep diaries. So I'm not satisfied in my mind that he was a loner.'

On 4 July 1973, reported Pilger, Edward Kennedy had visited Alabama 'to pay homage to the power of the man whom he once described as representing all that was wrong with America, but now Ted needs George Wallace because Ted wants to be president and George has all those folks and all those votes'. Pilger summed up Wallace as 'a political conman second to none'.

Wallace, of course, never reached the White House. Democrat Jimmy Carter took over from Gerald Ford, Richard Nixon's successor. In his 1975 film *Mr Nixon's Secret Legacy*, Pilger examined American defence policy under Ford. He reported:

There were two historic events in America last year. The first was the removal of the crook Richard Nixon. The second was something you will have almost certainly heard nothing about. For the first time since the beginning of the atomic age almost thirty years ago, the United States formally and quietly abandoned its policy of Ultimate Nuclear Deterrent. In other words, the old game known in Washington as MAD – Mutual Assured Destruction – is out and the new, more insidious and dangerous game is in. It is called Counter Force. Counter Force means that the United States is now prepared not merely to deter its enemies by the threat of annihilation but to actually wage a flexible, acceptable nuclear war.

For the first time, said Pilger, military thinkers in Washington were 'thinking the unthinkable', and the breakthrough in Strategic Arms Limitation Talks with the Soviet Union announced by Ford and Dr Kissinger had been 'no more than a sham'. Nixon had been responsible, during his last year in the presidency, for giving generals in the Pentagon what other presidents had refused them, a flexible strategy that would blur the distinction between conventional and nuclear warfare. Pilger asked a B-52 bomber crew based in North Dakota, which had just returned from Vietnam, about the risk of killing civilians. 'In any operation, you're going to have some collateral damage,' one of the pilots replied. 'Just as in Vietnam,' commented Pilger, 'the language is sterilized and dehumanized so that war, even nuclear war, is somehow made more tolerable, more acceptable.'

He then explained, 'It would not be possible to make this kind of film in Russia or even in Britain, because both countries are closed societies compared with the United States.' But the paradox of that country was that alongside a democracy that exposed the Watergate scandal was a technocracy in which economic pressures generated by the military stimulated the international arms race more than the threat from Russia. Almost all of the federal government's research budget went to the military.

Pilger and his crew filmed in the Underground Command Post at Strategic Air Command's headquarters in Nebraska. In the event of a nuclear war, this would be filled with generals and other top-ranking officers. The commander-in-chief would speak to the joint chiefs of staff in Washington, and probably to the president himself. On receiving his orders, he would transmit them to 'the men downstairs manning the consoles' and the world would almost certainly be at war. Here, Pilger's fondness for black humour was given an outlet. 'Irony and humour run through most of my films,' he said later. 'It's often a serious humour, but it allows people to look at the absurdity of power. True humour is the truly ridiculous.'[7]

Over film of a US Air Force plane taking off, Pilger said this was called 'Looking Glass', a flying command post with a general always on board. If everything below were wiped out in a 'flexible, limited nuclear war', the general would open a sealed envelope and, by coded radio signals, launch the United States' underground missiles. 'But, by then, it would be no more than a spasm from the nuclear ashes,' Pilger added.

Arms limitation talks had accelerated the arms race, with each side building more nuclear weapons as bargaining power. The United States was about to scrap its Polaris nuclear submarines and replace them with Trident. If Britain wanted to 'keep up', it would have to do the same, at a cost of £1 billion for each Trident submarine. A report delayed by Nixon disclosed that more than seven thousand nuclear warheads were stored in Europe, of which two-thirds were controlled directly from Washington.

Lieutenant Gene Moseley, a 'missilier' trained to launch the Minuteman 3 missile from its silos across North Dakota, was seen leaving home for a shift in his bunker. Pilger sat with Moseley as he received a briefing. With his fellow missilier, Captain Leroy Wayman, Moseley drove to the Launch Control Center to take charge of ten Minuteman missiles buried beneath more than seven thousand square miles of farmland. 'The first thing they must do is load their revolvers, which they wear in case one of them goes mad,' said Pilger, warming to the absurdity. 'And, if that happens, the other man must shoot him. This is official policy.'

The two men were filmed taking an elevator down to the launch capsule forty feet below, which was suspended within 'a huge concrete egg', hanging from four gigantic shock absorbers designed to withstand a nuclear attack. Moseley's wife, Barbara, told Pilger that she did not worry about her husband being underground if a nuclear war happened. 'He is here to defend his country and that's just fine with me,' she said.

Pilger joined the men in the Strategic Air Command launch capsule, along with the missile squadron leader, Colonel Donald Crutchfield. 'Now, what happens if these two men are the last left?' Pilger asked Crutchfield, who replied that there were back-up systems to support them. 'I cannot discuss the procedures involved,' he said. 'Does that mean the two-man crew in the end could have the capability of launching a missile?' asked Pilger. Again, Crutchfield shook his head.

Pilger explained the procedure on receipt of the signal to go to war. The two men would each take a key from a red box and insert it in his own keyhole. The two would turn their keys simultaneously. 'Although Colonel Crutchfield refused to answer my question,' added Pilger, over film of the pair going through the exercise, 'there is, in fact, a plan for a surviving two-man crew, or even one man, to launch a missile. That is why each man must wear a gun and why each man must always watch the other.' He then asked the two missiliers why they each had a gun and was told that they had classified material in the capsule. Moseley was reluctant to be drawn on the idea that it was to shoot one another. 'We're not authorized to use the weapon unless there's absolutely no other way,' he said. 'That is *the* last resort.'

Of thirty-three major accidents involving US nuclear weapons between 1950 and 1970, two missiles with nuclear warheads were launched by accident in 1968, reported Pilger. They were shot down 'just in time'. Black-and-white still photographs of the atomic bombing of Hiroshima and film of the victims, shown with no sound, brought into focus the reality of what a finger on the trigger could mean.

Pilger relished making *Mr Nixon's Secret Legacy*, which was nominated for an Emmy Award. 'It was a joy, wonderful to do,' he recalled, 'but we had one obstacle. I had been writing about US nuclear policy for some time, and we held our breath that my name would not register at the Defense Department. But it finally did, on the day filming began. We were ensconced in a hotel in North Dakota, in the middle of a freezing winter, when my director, Richard Marquand, received a call from the Pentagon saying the whole thing was off and we would get no co-operation. Julie Stoner, the production assistant, broke the news to me. "Richard says that, whatever you do, don't answer the phone, don't say anything," she said. "There's a problem and he's handling it, he hopes."

'Richard was a very funny man and capable of being very theatrical. His first reaction on the phone to Washington was, "This is shocking! I didn't know this about Pilger. I'm extremely upset about this. I can assure you I'm going to look into this." Somehow, he persuaded them to believe him and told them, "I'll keep that man in order. I'm in charge here." So we were allowed into the bunker and the military press officer who came along was nodding and winking to Richard, expecting him to deal with any transgressions by me.

'Colonel Crutchfield could have been invented by Stanley Kubrick. I asked him whether the policy of missiliers shooting each other if one went crazy had ever happened. This was, of course, the very question they dreaded. The press officer looked grimly at Richard and, when I had finished the interview, Richard said to me, "John, I told you we were not going to do that. It's *not* good enough!"

'In Omaha, I asked the commanding officer of Strategic Air Command to confirm that a missilier had indeed gone crazy. The press officer exploded and, again, Richard upbraided me. "John, I told you not to go too far," he shouted, before turning to the press officer and lamenting, "I'm sorry, I just can't control him!" That evening in the motel bar, Richard and I laughed ourselves silly.'[8]

Pilger later tackled the very serious issue of nuclear weapons and the West's 'selling' of them to the public in *The Truth Game* (see Chapter 8). Before that, the 'selling' of US policies around the world, with heavy penalties if they were not supported, was at the centre of the first documentary in his 1976 three-part *Pilger* series, directed by Marquand and filmed in the United States. *Zap!! The Weapon Is Food* revealed secretary of state Henry Kissinger's policy of seeking support for the US government's foreign policy by refusing aid to countries that did not vote with it in the United Nations.

'It was about the power of American multinational food corporations,' explained Pilger. 'Three of them control the international trade in food grain. Kissinger was denying food to countries that failed to vote with the United States at the UN. He had a Zap Office specially set up in the State Department that monitored voting patterns. Zapped countries were warned and, if they continued to vote against the United States, were denied shipments of American food.'[9]

Pilger opened the documentary by explaining that the United States controlled half of all the world's wheat, two-thirds of all cereal foods and 95 per cent of soya beans. President Harry Truman had called the country 'the bread basket of the world', extolling a generous spirit that was mythical. Pilger quoted a member of Kissinger's staff as saying publicly, 'To give food aid to countries just because they are starving is a pretty weak reason.' Food had been a decisive factor in every major deal recently concluded by Kissinger. 'For agreeing to détente, Russia got American food,' said Pilger. 'For signing a Middle East peace agreement, Egypt got American food. For prolonging the war in Vietnam, the generals of Saigon got American food, which they sold to buy arms. In the last few years, the world has been much obsessed with the oil weapon. But, as the following half-hour will show, there is a new, more powerful weapon – food. And this one is lethal.'

Over film of Americans eating, Pilger reported that each citizen of that country ate almost a ton of grain a year on average. In 'the hungry world', less than one-fifth of this amount was eaten. In the United States, obesity was now officially listed as a cause of death. 'In Britain, we don't eat quite as much,' said Pilger. 'But, like the

Americans, we feed most of our grain to meat-producing animals – grain that would feed some twenty million hungry people. In effect, we choose to feed animals rather than people.'

Alongside film of starving children, Pilger explained that one of the least understood reasons for people dying was the denial of food for motives of politics and profit. There were sixty-five indictments outstanding against American food companies. In April 1976, a New Orleans federal court found two of the largest US food companies guilty of shipping deliberately short-weighted grain to poor countries. Since 1971, the US secretary of agriculture, Dr Earl Butts, had evolved a policy of high food prices to satisfy the farmers' lobby. With the Stars and Stripes behind him, Dr Butts told Pilger that he was 'not very sympathetic with the food needs of a nation where their governments and their leaders are constantly demeaning the United States', aligning themselves with the Soviet Union and condemning it for being 'imperialist'. He explained that the concept of 'agro-power' had evolved alongside 'petro-power' and the challenge in the coming years was how to feed more and more people in the world. Peter Henriot, a director of the Washington-based Center of Concern, which monitored US food policy, told Pilger that this power could be used to influence the activities of recipient nations, so food could be used for political purposes. In the early 1970s, most of this went to South Vietnam and Cambodia as military, not humanitarian, aid.

Kissinger's claim that most food aid *was* humanitarian was not true, said Pilger. In 1974, the General Accounting Office in Washington had found that most American food aid did not go to starving countries but to regimes politically acceptable to Washington and to Kissinger. Cutting food aid was one of the weapons that brought down the democratically elected Allende government in Chile. It was restored following the military coup that brought General Pinochet to power.

Not far from Kissinger's state department office was the so-called Zap Office, which monitored the voting of countries in the UN. 'If certain small and poor countries which are dependent on

American food aid vote against the policies of the United States, they are zapped,' said Pilger, 'which means simply that their food aid agreements can be suspended and, of course, many of their people will go hungry, and some of them may die.'

Dr Butts refused to admit knowledge of the Zap Office, whose official title was the Office of Multilateral Diplomacy. A senior State Department official, John A. Baker, had publicly admitted its existence in March 1976. Its policy was not to 'zap' immediately countries opposed to US policies but to play a 'cat and mouse' game, said Pilger. Peter Henriot gave Sierra Leone as an example of a country consistently voting against the US at the United Nations and not receiving food aid, despite its great need. He added that the Soviet Union had become increasingly dependent on the United States for large amounts of food grain. Dr Butts admitted that the government had interrupted sales to the Soviet Union for three months the previous year by using the commodity of food as 'a diplomatic tool', gaining a long-term commitment from the Soviets to buy a minimum amount of wheat and corn. 'This was the use of "agro-power", I think, to produce a desired end,' he said.

Clips followed from *An Unfashionable Tragedy*, Pilger's documentary on Bangladesh, screened the previous year (see Chapter 4). Nothing would change there or in similar countries, said Pilger, while they were dependent on the 'fickle and political charity of a great power'. 'Agro-power' forced the poorest countries into an endless cycle of poverty, and this kept countries weak and ineffectual internationally. 'If this film has attacked only your emotions, then it has failed,' Pilger said, 'because starvation is not caused by hopelessness or fatalism, but by political decisions taken by those who control most of the world's economy.' He ended:

For too long, the rich world, and that includes Britain, has salved its conscience with convenient myths about hunger. Myth number one is that the world is running out of food. In fact, two-and-a-half times the present cultivated land of the world is not being farmed properly or even farmed at all. Why? Because the wealthiest nations, and especially America, control and waste most of the food and do not seriously help or even allow the poor nations to develop themselves and to kick the habit of having to sift the crumbs in the so-called free markets of the West.

Myth number two has to do with population control, which we preach endlessly. The truth is that rapid population growth will stop only when people are freed from a system that keeps them poor and powerless. The 'agro-power' of Dr Earl Butts is the pillar of such a system. Do the Buttses and the Kissingers have to actually see a child starve to death on colour television before they understand what kind of dangerous and pointless world they are passing on to all our children?

The revelations in *Zap!! The Weapon Is Food* were considered so controversial, despite all the information being on the public record, that the Independent Broadcasting Authority insisted on viewing the programme. It then demanded that a 'disclaimer' be attached to this film and the rest of the *Pilger* series. The result was a caption and voiceover at the start and end of each documentary. 'In the programme which follows, reporter John Pilger expresses a personal view,' were the words used before the opening titles. Then, at the end, an announcer intoned, 'In the programme you've just seen, reporter John Pilger was expressing a personal view.' The IBA had originally wanted to interrupt the half-hour programmes in the middle with similar words, even though there was no commercial break.

The next documentary in the 1976 *Pilger* series, complete with disclaimer, highlighted the demise in the culture of native Americans. 'I've had a lifelong interest in indigenous peoples,' explained Pilger, a white Australian whose own people were responsible for the demise of the Aborigines. '*Pyramid Lake Is Dying* was about the theft of resources that belonged to people and their struggle to get them back. The lake was being drained off into Lake Tahoe. It was, physically, the most haunting part of the world that I've visited.'[10]

Pilger had reported on the Indians for the *Daily Mirror* eight years earlier, when he travelled to see the Navajo in the deserts of Arizona and New Mexico, and wrote of these 'forgotten people' who had been more mythologized than any other. They earned less than half that of even a black American family and died twenty-seven years earlier than whites.

In 1972, Pilger met Red Cloud, Chief of the Sioux, at Wounded Knee, South Dakota. Four years later, in Nevada, Pilger and his film crew visited Pyramid Lake, which had once boasted two-feet-long salmon trout and was described as 'one of the few remaining unspoiled natural wonders in the American West'. The lake took its name from a pyramid-shaped rock precipitating from it. Now, the pyramid was joined to the shoreline and, beyond this, another lake had been formed. Lake Winnemucca relied on water from its neighbour, but it had now dried up. The same was beginning to happen to Pyramid Lake, whose principal source was the Truckee River, which started almost a hundred miles away, at Lake Tahoe. Its fisheries and wildlife were disappearing for ever.

'In the words of the Indian people who lived here, it was murdered,' Pilger reported to the camera. 'It was murdered by the white man. What happened to Lake Winnemucca is about to happen to one of the world's last great and beautiful inland seas . . . It's a story that not only tells again the plight of the American Indian . . . The story of Pyramid Lake is much more universal than that, for it tells very simply what we all achieve when we knowingly and culpably destroy the partnership between man and nature.'

Pilger explained that this process had begun when, in 1905, the government built a dam across the Truckee River to feed white squatters nearby. The water left was not enough to save Winnemucca from extinction or prevent the slow death of Pyramid Lake, which had belonged to the Paiute Indians for 4,000 years.

An old woman from the tribe told Pilger about the good life they had led there and recalled her father fishing in the lake. She said that 'the white man' had taken the Indians' best land, in California, and pushed the Indians away into the rocky mountains. Today, she added, the native language had disappeared, too, with all children speaking English.

'The evidence of Pyramid Lake's imminent murder is here for everybody to see,' said Pilger. 'Eighty feet of water has already gone since the government's dam was built.' As the tribe's fisheries expert took him out on a boat, Pilger remarked that 'another eighty feet will turn the lake into a useless, lifeless salt bed'. The Paiute had secured a Supreme Court order that water should be filtered back into Pyramid Lake, 'but only a trickle followed'.

In the town of Fallon, where much of the water had been diverted into a failed irrigation scheme, Pilger and his crew filmed a 'sportsmen's reserve' to which most of the wildlife had fled. The biggest user of water in Nevada, a state without water controls, was on its biggest ranch, owned by state senator Carl Dodge. He told Pilger, 'I've always felt the proper thing to do would be to settle with the Indians by the federal government paying them in money damages.' But he insisted that the water should stay where it was. Asked how that would preserve the Indians' life, Dodge responded, 'No, money won't buy that, but it's a case of balancing the interests . . . Where does the public interest lie? . . . We make a lot better use, more of a multiple use, of the water with this irrigation district . . . We have an enormous amount of recreational use – swimming, boating, water-skiing, picnicking, overnight camping and fowl hunting and that sort of thing.'

Pilger reflected on the changing culture for native Americans. 'The Indians are having to come round to the ways of the white man,' he said. 'They now eat the new breed of automated, tasteless fish, which they hate, and Kentucky Fried Chicken, and their menfolk go to the white man's wars. In Vietnam, more Indians died proportionately than any other Americans.' An Indian woman in her seventies, called Kate, took Pilger to a graveyard where her husband and son, killed in World War One and Vietnam, were buried. 'They were all drafted – they had to go,' she said. A school had been built on the edge of the reservation in the 1960s because whites living nearby wanted it. Only the whites' way of life was taught. 'This represents defeat at last for the Paiute,' said Pilger.

The white man's ways were the subject of *The Street of Joy*, about advertising, the last in Pilger's 1976 US trilogy. 'I compared the selling of a politician with the selling of a new product, a wet toilet paper called Fresh'n,' recalled Pilger. 'This same agency was responsible for a leading politician, a state senator, and a new type of toilet paper, and sold them all in much the same way.'[11]

In 1974, a record $26 billion had been spent on advertising in the United States, Pilger explained at the beginning of the film. At the same time, the country was undergoing recession, with high unemployment. Madison Avenue, the centre of the United States' advertising industry, had risen to the challenge of these hard times. The Skally McCabe Slowes agency, founded just nine years earlier and responsible for promoting products such as caffeine-free coffee, was now marketing wet toilet paper. 'Can they sell the ultimate in the unnecessary?' Pilger asked. 'Can they sell Fresh'n?'

An agency executive insisted, 'We are not selling it to replace dry toilet paper.' It was 'a new concept in bathroom care . . . God's answer to anal problems'. Pilger got into the mood of things with the words, 'It cleans better, it's flushable, it's biodegradable.' But was such an unnecessary product fair to sell in the middle of a recession, with nine million unemployed, asked Pilger. 'I don't think our job is to be a censor on what the American people should have,' answered another executive.

So what would the agency *not* sell? Marvin Slowes did not expect anyone there to work on any political campaign if they did not believe the politician or the cause were 'just and fair'. Five years before Ronald Reagan's inauguration as president, one of the agency executives cited him as an example. 'He put himself right into a box, and it's like distribution in every supermarket,' said the advertising man. 'The whole world is waiting and you open up the box, it turns out there's nothing in it.'

Half of the $300 million spent on choosing a new president in the United States that year would go to advertising agencies and image makers, reported Pilger. He recalled 1968, when 'the new Richard Nixon' was sold, in contrast to his previous image as a person from whom no one would buy a used car. 'They gave him that magic ingredient – believability,' said Pilger. Now, Jim Sprouse was campaigning to become governor of West Virginia but he lacked that same magic ingredient, so he had hired the man who helped to change Robert Kennedy's image from carpet-bagger to 'all-American hero'.

Highlighting Jimmy Carter, who went on to win the US presidential election, Pilger explained that the politician's claims about his past were 'never exactly right'. Carter said he was a farmer who worked the soil himself and had been a nuclear scientist. In fact, said Pilger, he was a commodities broker, the commodity being peanuts, and an ordinary navy engineer – 'not exactly a lie, but not exactly the truth, either'. An ad man told Pilger he would find Carter difficult to sell. 'He rarely takes a definitive stand on important issues,' he said. And was there a warning in 'what happened to Nixon and J. Walter Thompson', asked Pilger, because 'that product turned out to be a bit of a no-no, didn't it?' The advertising executive simply replied that Roosevelt and John F. Kennedy both had the support of advertising people.

Image-making had begun with Kennedy, and Carter's campaign bore an uncanny resemblance. In 1960, the Democratic Party had estimated that the use of television advertising had made just a few per cent difference in the electoral vote but that was enough to give Kennedy a narrow victory. 'Nixon had never really understood the image game, but he learned quickly from Kennedy,' explained Pilger. 'Eight years later, he sold himself like soap powder and he won with a margin of only a few per cent. Once again, Madison Avenue had made all the difference.'

Describing 'the $26 billion Madison Avenue game', Pilger said, 'It would take just one billion of those dollars to put all the poor farmers in the world on their feet, to make them self-sufficient and independent of our charity. But $1 billion is actually the amount of money that Americans are expected to spend on freshened, pre-moisturized toilet tissue and some presidential campaign. Need I say that both products – pre-moisturized toilet tissue and some politicians – have those two magic ingredients: believ-ability and flushability.'

Eight years later, consumerism was also the subject of *Burp! Pepsi v Coke in the Ice Cold War*, Pilger's examination of the long-running battles between Coca-Cola and Pepsi-Cola to establish dominance in the soft-drinks market. This gave him another chance to inject humour into a documentary, although politics, and the rivalry between the two companies, was the central theme. Pilger showed how they had influenced American politics, with Democrats usually supporting Coke and Republicans opting for Pepsi. Richard Nixon helped Pepsi to gain entry into coun-tries such as the Philippines, Taiwan and Russia. Throughout, the documentary – the first in which representatives of both Coca-Cola and Pepsi-Cola had agreed to appear together – was enlivened with colourful advertisements and commercials used by both companies down the years.

The film was inspired by a book called *The Cola Wars*.[12] It was the first of Pilger's to be directed by Alan Lowery (although *Nicaragua* was screened first) and opened familiarly, with Pilger standing in front of an American war monument, saying:

This is a film about war. A world war. A war which in all my years as a correspondent has somehow escaped my attention. It is a war fought in more than a hundred countries regardless of ideology, in communist and capitalist countries, in Moslem, Buddhist and Christian countries. It's a war that has directly involved President

Eisenhower, President Johnson, President Nixon, President Carter, Chiang Kai Shek, Mao Tse-tung, the Dalai Lama, Mr
Khrushchev and Father Christmas . . . According to one side,
the entire American army has adopted its name as the very symbol
of freedom and the American way. One side claims to have
captured China. The other side says that it has taken Russia . . . I
refer to the bittersweet war behind those giants of carbonation and
regurgitation, Coca-Cola and Pepsi-Cola.

Their story began shortly after the US Civil War, when the
Yankees defeated the Confederates. In 1886, the Ideal Brain
Tonic was invented by chemist John Pemberton, who claimed it
could cure ailments. Later, it became known as Coca-Cola and he
sold the formula and title for only $2,300 to prosperous Atlanta
chemist Asa Candler, who marketed it 'as the very symbol of
American wholefulness'. It was perfect for those times of temperance and prohibition. 'God was happy, Coca-Cola was happy
and the consumers were happy,' reported Pilger.

Atlanta remained the world headquarters of Coca-Cola, which
Pilger described as 'the centre of a uniquely American empire,
covering 147 countries'. In almost a century, Coca-Cola had
survived and grown richer while wars had been fought and
regimes overthrown. Through advertising, it persuaded generations that its product was more than just 'sticky, sweet, coloured
water'. A Coca-Cola executive was once asked, said Pilger, which
came first – the United States or Coke? 'Let me put it this way,' he
said. 'When you don't see a Coca-Cola sign, you have passed the
borders of civilization.' Those borders were first extended into
Cuba in 1906 by Candler's Methodist bishop brother, after
American troops invaded the Caribbean island.

Wilbur Kurtz, Coca-Cola's retired archivist, explained that the
company had never patented its name because the secret formula
would have passed into the public domain after fifty years. Those
who dared to imitate 'the real thing' had been taken to court, but
Pepsi-Cola – invented in 1893 by Carolina chemist Caleb B.

Bradham – survived to challenge it and find a market in 145 countries, with headquarters in New York State. Both companies' franchise systems had made them huge multinationals. Each provided the ingredients of their drink to local bottling companies in different parts of the world, promoted and sold according to local conditions and politics.

Pepsi went bankrupt when sugar prices collapsed. 'Meanwhile,' said Pilger, 'God-fearing Coca-Cola launched a new bottle, wickedly shaped like a woman.' It also had a new owner, with Robert Woodruff's consortium of Northern banks buying out Candler in 1919 for $25 million, the biggest business deal the South had ever known. Establishing a foreign department, Woodruff set out to sell Coke to the world. In the 1920s, in its most inventive advertising campaign so far, Coca-Cola featured St Nicholas in the modern image of Father Christmas dressed in the colours of the company.

During the Depression of the 1930s, Pepsi fought back by projecting an image of being the drink of 'the little guy down on his luck'. It offered twice as much as Coca-Cola, for the same price. 'The war was now on,' enthused Pilger. 'During the Thirties, Coke sent its undercover agents, called Soda Spooks, on a series of raids to discover if Pepsi was being served to customers who had ordered "the real thing".' When, in 1939, Coke sued Pepsi in Canada over the use of the word 'Cola' and lost, it appealed to the Privy Council in London. Pepsi won because, it was reported, Britain 'did not want to strain its wartime ties with the Empire'.

Pepsi, said Pilger, had made the world's first 'singing commercial' in 1939. During World War Two, Coca-Cola made much of a letter from a GI telling his wife that the one thing he wanted apart from her was 'a bottle of Coca-Cola'. 'It was a symbol of home, love, family, the fireside and all that,' said Kurtz, the Coke archivist. The company offered to ship bottling plants to the frontline and the US war department picked up the bill. Dispensers were installed in tanks, submarines, even fighter planes.

In the post-war period, Coca-Cola grew rapidly and its first international challenge was the Cold War. In Stalinist Poland, it was attacked as 'a nest of American espionage', but the Polish Temperance Union declared it preferable to the 'ideologically pure' vodka. Meanwhile, Pepsi aligned itself with 'Red seeker' Senator Joe McCarthy, who called sugar rationing 'anti-American'. Film star Joan Crawford, wife of Al Steele, Pepsi's chairman in the 1950s, became a 'Pepsi ambassador'.

Pepsi portrayed a youthful, 'alive' image and invented something called 'the Pepsi generation', aimed at teenagers and the affluent middle class. John Sculley, until recently president of the Pepsi-Cola Company, told Pilger that the firm concentrated on how the drink could articulate the aspirations of these people, 'because most of our Americans at that time were gaining affluence but they didn't have much experience of how to spend this money'. In the 1960s, Pepsi's advertising portrayed a young, 'sporty' generation. A decade later, people were given 'the Pepsi Challenge', and asked to choose which drink they preferred, Pepsi or Coke.

A talking Coca-Cola vending machine told Pilger, 'You need to put in more money.' As his can was dispensed, he said, 'Machines such as these are the latest, ingenious weapons in the long war of attrition between Coca-Cola and Pepsi. You'll be pleased to know that they also speak French, Spanish and Japanese.' Coca-Cola's 'secret ingredient', missing from the list on the can, was '7X', which included a blend of the Brazilian cacao leaf and the African coconut, and whose details were locked away in a trust company bank in Atlanta. Pilger described the myths that had grown up around Coca-Cola and described it as a religion, adding, 'Think how popular God would have been if only his image people had thought of a slogan like "The Real Thing". He might even have been as popular as Coca-Cola.'

Outside the White House, Pilger described the influence that Coca-Cola and Pepsi-Cola had over American presidents. Alongside photographs of Franklin D. Roosevelt, Harry S. Truman,

John F. Kennedy, Lyndon Johnson and Jimmy Carter, he ex-
plained, 'Only Democratic presidents have been the patrons of
Coca-Cola, with the notable exception of Dwight Eisenhower.
President Johnson had a button on his desk which gushed Coca-
Cola.' Republican Richard Nixon was the most famous Pepsi-
Cola president. As vice-president at a Moscow trade fair in 1959,
he was approached by salesman Donald Kendall, who told him
that his aim was 'to get a bottle of Pepsi into the hands of
Khrushchev'. Nixon did exactly that and, on being beaten to the
presidency by Kennedy in 1960 and losing the election for
governor of California two years later, he became Pepsi's lawyer.

Kendall, then chairman of PepsiCo Inc, said that Nixon had
'tremendous contacts' around the world and, in particular, helped
the company enter Taiwan. Nixon's world travels, during which
he promoted himself as the next president, were bankrolled by
Pepsi. Within a month of becoming president in 1968, he
appointed Kendall head of the National Alliance of Businessmen.
In 1971, Kendall travelled to Moscow and struck a deal with
Prime Minister Kosygin that gave Pepsi the distinction of being
the first US consumer product to be made and sold in the Soviet
Union, in return for marketing vodka in the United States. Nixon
and Kendall considered that totalitarian countries could best serve
US interests as monopoly markets rather than adversaries. 'It
became the symbol of détente,' said Kendall.

Another Republican president, Ronald Reagan, saw soft drinks
as 'an obstacle to establishing total American superiority', said
Pilger. He pointed out that Reagan had advertised many products
over the years before entering the White House, including
cigarettes, soap and shirts. 'But is he a Pepsi president or is he,
like his predecessor, a Coke president?' asked Pilger. Jimmy
Carter, the former governor of Georgia, brought in image-makers
to help his campaign for president (as Pilger reported in his film on
advertising). Tony Schwartz, who had made 300 television
commercials for Coca-Cola, saw no difference in marketing
Carter, said Pilger, 'as long as you kept to the rules and didn't

mention what the product contained'. At the White House, Carter changed the vending machines from Pepsi to Coke. He authorized a $300 million loan to Portugal, where Coca-Cola had been banned, and it was no longer banned. In China, which had also turned away Coke, an agreement reversing this was signed a week after the Carter administration recognized the Chinese government.

Indeed, many of Coca-Cola's foreign deals were closely tied to US foreign policy. In South Vietnam, the company closed its operation well before the departure of American troops in 1975. Both Coke and Pepsi had bottling plant franchises in Latin America, 'America's backyard'. In Guatemala, which had an appalling human rights record, the local Coca-Cola bottler, John C. Trotter, paid his workers less than $2 a day. When they unionized, three of them were murdered and two union lawyers kidnapped. Coca-Cola refused to intervene. In 1980, following embarrassing publicity, the company sacked Trotter but kept its franchise in Guatemala.

The overthrow of Chilean president Salvador Allende also had a Cola connection. Augustin Edwards, the Pepsi bottler there, also published the influential newspaper *El Mercurio*, which became a CIA front, according to a Senate report. After Allende's election, Edwards flew to Washington and conferred with Henry Kissinger and CIA director Richard Helms.

Advertising in developing countries encouraged people to consume soft drinks every day and natural products such as fruit were eaten less, according to a survey of malnutrition. In 1973, a Senate select committee concluded that soft drinks were the biggest cause of sugar intake in the United States and recommended a marked reduction in their manufacture. This did not happen. It was estimated that Americans would soon be drinking more soft drinks than water, and that would be mostly Coke and Pepsi.

Donald R. Keough, president of the Coca-Cola Company, told Pilger that he went to bed every night believing that his company added 'a little brightness to life'. He gave the example of an imaginary poor, young woman in Colombia buying a drink of Coke. 'For a moment,' he said, 'she's got her hand around the same thing that the president of that country is drinking or that people of every walk of life drink. And I think that's terribly valid.'

6. TYRANNIES

FROM HIS EARLY DAYS covering world events for the *Daily Mirror*, John Pilger's constant theme was the struggle of people against repressive power and, citing Milan Kundera, 'The struggle of memory against forgetting'. This was woven through his documentaries on Czechoslovakia, East Timor and Burma, all of which were filmed under cover.

The streets of the Czech capital, Prague, were the scene of some of the most memorable television news pictures of the 1960s, at the height of the Cold War, as Warsaw Pact tanks rolled in following President Alexander Dubček's attempts to relax the communism of his Eastern Bloc masters. The Soviet-led invasion of 1968 was filmed by Czech cameramen who used mobile transmitters to beam their pictures across the border to Austria, from where they were transmitted worldwide. Parts of Czecho-slovakia could pick up pictures screened in Austria, although strict censorship followed once the Soviet Union had put down Czech resistance. This momentous event was later re-enacted in *Invasion*, one of Granada Television's drama-documentaries that resulted from the *World in Action* team's agreement with the ITA (later IBA) to report on events in the Eastern Bloc, following their grilling over Pilger's alleged 'anti-American' report on troops turning against their commanding officers in Vietnam (see Chapter 1).

Nine years after the invasion, when Czech dissidents formed the Charter 77 movement to demand freedom of speech and worship and protest at human rights violations, Pilger set out to make a documentary that would allow them to speak to the outside world. Jan Patocka, a philosopher, had died suffering a heart attack and a brain haemmorhage, after undergoing police interrogations for daring to speak to the Dutch foreign minister in Prague. This was part of the government tyranny and repression that accompanied the first months of Charter 77, which the authorities immediately banned. Patocka's funeral was attended by thousands and demonstrated the support that he and the movement enjoyed, with its members including teachers, journalists, clerks, factory workers and housewives, with wide-ranging ideologies. Pilger entered Czechoslovakia shortly after his reports for the *Mirror* on dissidents in the Soviet Union as part of a series on life there, published in June 1977.

For *A Faraway Country . . . a people of whom we know nothing*, a title taking the words that Neville Chamberlain used to describe Czechoslovakia dismissively in 1938 when it was invaded by the Nazis, Pilger and his television crew filmed secretly under the light of 60-watt bulbs in table lamps. The sometimes grainy images were reminiscent of some of *World in Action*'s documentaries of the time, from behind the Iron Curtain at the height of the Cold War.

The first obstacle was entering Czechoslovakia. Film crews from the West were effectively banned. However, Pilger obtained a three-day tourist's transit visa from the Czech embassy in Austria. He, cameraman John Davey and sound recordist Christian Wangler drove in from there in a camper van, while director Alan Bell entered by train, and researcher Ed Harriman flew in as a tourist. Harriman organized the passage of film stock into and out of the country. Pilger's idea for distracting the border guards was one that he had previously used to enter Ghana during a coup. He scattered copies of *Playboy* and *Penthouse* across the floor of the camper van, concealing film equipment underneath a mattress. The three men also made the van look decidedly uninviting, with food leftovers and the personal debris of itinerant travellers.

'The idea was to film over the weekend, when there were

fewer secret police on the streets,' recalled Pilger. 'I flew to Austria and set off for Czechoslovakia on the Friday in the van with John and Christian, who had driven there from Britain. The plan was to disguise ourselves as politically harmless travellers. When we arrived at the border, two guards approached us. The senior man picked up a *Playboy* and said, "What's this?" We exchanged knowing smirks, then, to my amusement, he delivered a lecture, distinguishing between the two titles, saying *Penthouse* was illegal in Czechoslovakia because it was pornographic and *Playboy* was illegal because it was political. So he confiscated the lot – with a smile on his junior's face. They waved us through.'[1]

Once in Czechoslovakia, the film team had to work quickly and carefully. Charter 77 supporters acted as lookouts while Pilger interviewed members of the movement in their homes. The documentary opened with pictures of Dubček and the Soviet invasion of 1968, and this camera piece from Pilger:

This is Prague, Czechoslovakia, and this film is being made in secret. Just to get into Czechoslovakia as a television team, we've had to join up with an underground movement and smuggle in cameras normally used for home movies. That's why the picture you are watching is not perfect. And the people I interview in this film know they are taking great risks just by talking to me, but they insist on speaking out. Such is their courage and their commitment to freedom in Czechoslovakia. Isn't it strange that, for all the ringing speeches in Brussels about European unity and our own, obsessive concern with inflation, millions of our fellow Europeans are still not free to talk or read or write or sing or argue or travel as they would wish? And how long is it since we in Britain assumed that a European people like the Czechs willingly surrendered their democratic heritage for an imported fascism disguised as socialism? The people you will hear from are not an isolated few. They represent a peaceful struggle for freedom as widespread as it was against the Nazis, as widespread as it was against the Kremlin when Russian tanks smashed into Prague in that summer of 1968. Do you remember? Please listen carefully to what these brave Europeans have to say.

As in much of his television and press reporting, Pilger was clearly identifying with the subjects of his work and asking viewers or readers to listen to their case. Those who spoke to him included teacher Julius Tomin, who was incarcerated in a psychiatric clinic for two years after refusing the military draft and could subsequently not find work, and clerk Jitka Bidlasova and electrician Jiri Pallas, both of whom lost their jobs after signing the Charter 77 document.

Pallas told Pilger that, on losing his job, he tried to place an advertisement in a newspaper offering himself for work and announcing that he was a signatory to Charter 77. 'They passed me from one to another, right up to the editor-in-chief,' he explained. 'They all refused to accept the ad and they refused to explain why they wouldn't accept it. They also refused to confirm in writing that they had refused to accept it.' Tomin said that Charter 77 called for a combination of freedom and socialism in Czechoslovakia, but that should not necessarily relate to the Western democratic experience. 'We must develop new concepts of freedom which come from our own situation,' he insisted.

Pilger quoted the author Zdener Urbanek, whose books had been banned in Czechoslovakia since 1948, as saying, 'I have lived with censorship for so long that the censor is no longer at his desk – he is in my head.' After signing Charter 77, Urbanek was interrogated for twelve hours, his house was searched and his typewriter taken away to be registered, which meant that the authorities would be able to identify anything he wrote.

'The courage of the few is personified by this man,' said Pilger. 'He speaks good English, but often slowly and with hesitation because the price of his courage has been a nervous breakdown.' Referring to the period after 1919, when the new country of Czechoslovakia was created, Urbanek told Pilger, 'It is quite important to remind British people that we had democracy during twenty years of freedom.' But part of the country, German-speaking Sudetenland, was ceded to Hitler under the 1938 Munich Agreement and, said Urbanek, 'All that happens here now began at that time.'

Over a Movietone newsreel reporting the Munich pact, Pilger said, 'The British people could hardly know about the betrayal of Czechoslovakia. Like so much of what is called objective information, the news then was mostly shrill propaganda for government policy, and that policy in 1938 was to appease Hitler.' He continued, over newsreel footage of Neville Chamberlain shaking hands with Hitler, 'And here is the British prime minister preparing to give Czechoslovakia to the Nazis . . . What the admiring crowd did not realize was that his efforts were a prelude to World War Two.'

Film followed of Chamberlain announcing, 'Incredible it is that we should be digging trenches and trying on gas masks because of a quarrel in a faraway country between people of whom we know nothing.' Pilger explained that the Czechs resisted the Nazis bravely but were powerless to stop them, 'just as they were powerless to stop the great powers carving up Europe in 1945, just as they were powerless to stop the Russian invasion in 1968 and the Helsinki Agreement in 1975, which, with the backing of the government of Harold Wilson, further legitimized the Russian empire and once again dismissed that faraway country'. In the Prague Spring of 1968, Dubček and the Czechoslovak Communist Party had tried to transform society from the bureaucratic class system imposed by the Soviet Union in the post-war years to a socialist democracy, but this attempt was crushed. Urbanek told Pilger that Czechoslovakia had been handed to the Eastern bloc, 'to which we don't belong by what I would call our democratic traditions'.

In a village near the Austrian border, on their way out of Czechoslovakia late on the Sunday night, Pilger and his crew filmed an interview with the country's most popular female singer, Marta Kubisova, who, a month after the Soviet invasion, had performed at a concert in Prague and sung, 'O my country, let not fear and violence establish themselves on your soil; keep yourself faithful and true to yourself', which was known as 'Marta's Prayer' and was an anthem for the people. The following year, the Czech authorities tried to discredit her by circulating fake photographs of a nude woman whom they said was Kubisova. Her records were subsequently banned and she was unable to find work.

Kubisova told her story to Pilger in broken English and explained that her twenty-two-month-old child would suffer an inferior education because she had signed Charter 77. 'I'm afraid that's how it is,' she said, switching to her native language and using an interpreter. 'Of course, I'm still fairly young, so I still believe that it won't turn out quite like that. I hope that, before those eight, nine or ten years are up, before these things really begin to affect her, she will have a fair chance of an education. But, even if she doesn't, we will have to arrange something else because I don't share the view of most of the people in this country that we should keep quiet on account of the children. On the contrary, I am convinced that, on account of the children, we should speak out.' Summing up, Pilger said:

> For many, the views in this film will no doubt fit the conventional Western image of communist Europe. What does not fit this image is what the Czechs themselves want. It seems to me that the last thing they want is to rush from the Soviet camp to the American camp. Many don't trust the human rights campaign of President Carter and already they see the American and Soviet delegates to the Belgrade conference on human rights agreeing not to be too critical of each other and of each other's imperial backyards. You see, the Czechs look back at their history and they know that any alliance between great powers, whether it's called Munich or détente, is bad news for them because it means that small countries in the middle like Czechoslovakia are expendable, no matter what camp they're in.

Like most small nations, the Czechs want to go a third way, their own way. In spite of all the years of oppression, they've never forgotten their democratic traditions and it's fair to guess that a majority of them want their country to be socialist, democratic and fiercely independent. Charter 77, a new beginning of this democracy, was partly inspired by the courage of a Czech pop group called the Plastic People of the Universe, which was banned and brutalized by the regime. In one of their last songs, the group sang these words about their oppressors: 'They' – that's the regime – 'are afraid of the old for their memory; they're afraid of the young for their innocence; they're afraid of the graves and the flowers people put on them; they're afraid of those who aren't in the party; they're afraid of singers, tennis players, Santa Claus, archives, each other; they're afraid of truth; they're afraid of freedom; they're afraid of democracy; they're afraid of socialism. So why the hell are we afraid of them?'

The film finished poignantly with Marta Kubisova singing 'Marta's Prayer', cutting from black-and-white footage of the singer's powerful performance for Alexander Dubček to her voice breaking as she sang in her garden at the end of her secret interview with Pilger. It was now Sunday night and Pilger and the film crew headed for the border. Having got through the weekend without having their covers blown, their luck faltered. 'At the checkpoint, John Davey couldn't find his passport,' recalled Pilger. 'We were held for two hours, still with the camera and film concealed beneath the floorboards – but this time with no copies of *Playboy* and *Penthouse* to distract official eyes. Their suspicions were clearly aroused, but it was late and John finally found his passport and we were through. Filming had taken exactly forty-eight hours.'[2]

Pilger had been concerned about the risk taken by the Czech dissidents who talked openly to him. 'Their courage in speaking out was undisputed,' he said, 'but what was not so clear cut was whether I should have allowed them the exposure that put them at risk with the regime. It was a risk we all tried to calculate. They argued convincingly that the decision was theirs. "There is no point us saying anything," Julius Tomin had said, "if the world cannot hear us. If you deny us our public voice and identity, you, too, are censoring us." It was a view which, on balance, I went along with, although I remained uneasy. The same principle arose in East Timor, but there I was in no doubt – dissident faces had to be masked and their voices changed. Unlike the East Timorese, the Czech dissidents were not in fear of losing their lives – although we couldn't be absolutely certain about that – and they considered their day-by-day persecution by the state a bearable price to pay for their determination to bring freedom to Czechoslovakia. Fortunately, all survived. Most went into exile.'[3]

Following the screening of *A Faraway Country*, Pilger was denounced on Prague Radio as a 'dupe of the reactionary forces of the London and Washington axis'. 'I am proud of my official enemies,' he said, 'and that citation was most appreciated. What upset the dreadful satellite regime in Prague was the shining decency of the Charter 77 people and the irrefutable reason of their arguments. I understand my description of Soviet totalitarianism as "approaching fascism" was considered beyond the pale. It was certainly accurate.'[4]

A constant factor in Pilger's television career has been the presence of danger and the personal risks he has taken, often life-threatening. His attempted assassination in Cambodia by the Khmer Rouge is the best-known example, although he considers his filming in East Timor in 1993 'the most challenging to my sense of self-preservation'.[5] Two Australian television crews had previously been murdered by the Indonesians while filming in the occupied Portuguese colony.

Death of a Nation – The Timor Conspiracy proved to be Pilger's most effective film since *Year Zero – The Silent Death of Cambodia* in 1979. Like that programme, it told millions the story of genocide, this time committed behind the closed borders of a speck of a place that most people would have difficulty finding on a map. Little had been reported on the events in East Timor since

Injustices from within and without were featured in *Welcome to Australia* (1999) and *Paying the Price – Killing the Children of Iraq* (2000), made by (left to right) director Alan Lowery, Pilger, sound recordist Grant Roberts and cameraman Preston Clothier.

Pilger's powerful film *Paying the Price – Killing the Children of Iraq* (2000) highlighted the injustice of United Nations sanctions on Iraq after the Gulf War and included victims of the continued American and British bombing. (Photographs: John Pilger)

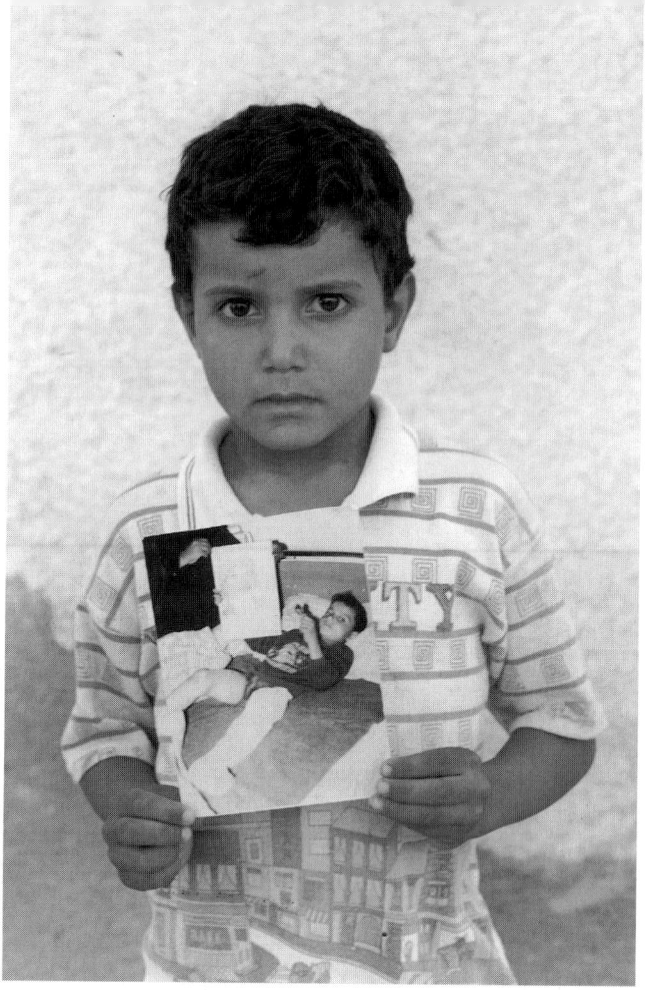

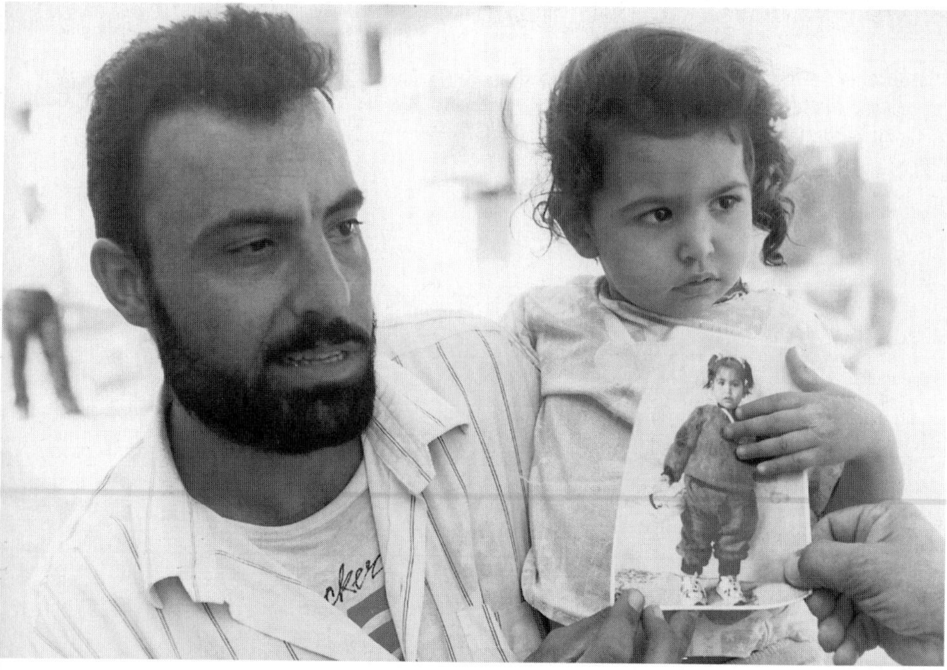

Report by
JOHN PILGER

Wednesday, September 12, 1979   8p

Death of a Nation

AN INCREDIBLE human disaster has happened in Cambodia, a once peaceful and gentle land in South East Asia. Perhaps more than two million people—a third of the population—have been killed by a fanatical regime whose apparent aim was to wipe out anyone and anything connected with the modern world and to return a whole nation to "Year Zero": the dawn of an age of slavery, without families and sentiment, without machines, schools, books, medicine, music.

The evidence of murder is plentiful. Like the cracked skulls, above, which were dug out from mass graves near Angkor Wat by villagers who had lost relatives.

For four years there has been almost no contact with people inside Cambodia; its borders were sealed. JOHN PILGER, in Cambodia, sends the first of two world exclusive reports.

Recollections of the *Daily Mirror* and its skill at reporting important issues to a wide audience during his time on the newspaper were featured in *Breaking the Mirror – The Murdoch Effect* (1997). Pilger's own original Cambodia reports were just one example, featured over two days and twelve pages. Now, he lamented, Rupert Murdoch's dominance of British newspapers had resulted in a very different popular press.

Pilger and Munro organized their trip to Burma with almost military precision, arranging for couriers to fly in and out with their film.

A centrepiece of *Inside Burma – Land of Fear* was Pilger's interview with Aung San Suu Kyi, the country's democracy leader. When he updated the documentary two years later, Pilger was unable to get through to her on the telephone in her home, where she was held under virtual house arrest. (Photograph: David Munro)

While filming *Inside Burma – Land of Fear* (1996), Pilger and director David Munro travelled to the south of the country and discovered child labour forced to work on an extension to the World War Two 'death railway'. When a wheelbarrow of clay tipped into a hole where a ten-year-old boy was working, they both rushed to rescue him. (Photographs: David Munro)

In *Death of a Nation – The Timor Conspiracy* (1994), Pilger reported on the genocide committed by the Indonesian military since that country's dictators had invaded the Portuguese colony of East Timor almost twenty years earlier. (Photograph: David Munro)

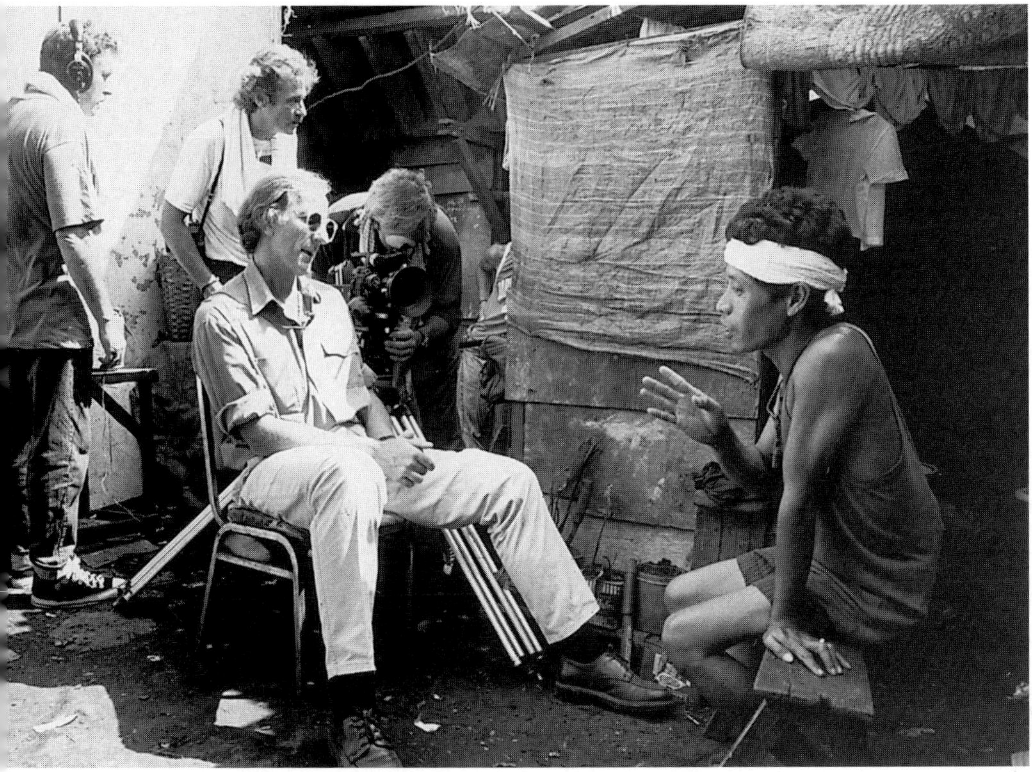

Examining Third World debt in *War by Other Means* (1992), sound recordist Mel Marr, director David Munro, Pilger and cameraman Noel Smart filmed on Smoky Mountain, a giant rubbish tip that was the refuge of thousands of homeless people near the Philippines' capital of Manila.

Pilger interviewed the great American linguist and political activist Noam Chomsky, whom he has admired for many years, in a special edition of *The Late Show* (1992). (Photograph: David Munro)

In *The Last Dream* (1988), Pilger and director Alan Lowery, a fellow-Australian, heard Leila and Arthur Murray tell the story of their son Eddie's death in police custody. The couple later explained, in *Welcome to Australia* (1999), that Eddie's body had been exhumed and his sternum was found to be smashed but they still awaited official answers. (Photograph: Patrick Riviere/Carlton TV)

Charlie Perkins was featured in three of Pilger's documentaries, after the Aboriginal rights leader took the journalist on a trip to the outback in 1969. Thirty years later, in *Welcome to Australia* (1999), Perkins lamented that conditions for his people were still unjust and they had not taken a 'big step' forward. Perkins died in October 2000, living into his sixties, unlike many Aborigines. (Photograph: Patrick Riviere/ Carlton TV)

Sydney Harbour was not the most welcoming of places when Pilger made his first documentary back in his homeland. While filming interviews there for *Pilger in Australia* (1976), the rain poured incessantly. However, when he made *Welcome to Australia* (above, 1999), the country lived up to its image of a sunny paradise. (Photograph: Patrick Riviere/Carlton TV)

Pilger has featured his home country of Australia in four single documentaries and a three-part series, *The Last Dream* (1988). A photograph he took on his first close-up encounter with Aborigines in 1967 has been featured in several films.

Black humour is evident throughout many of Pilger's documentaries, but he could afford a wider smile while making *Burp! Pepsi v Coke in the Ice Cold War*, about the intense rivalry for world dominance by two American multinationals. He even had a 'conversation' with a talking Coca-Cola vending machine in Atlanta, Georgia.

In *Nicaragua* (1983), director Alan Lowery and cameraman Noel Smart filmed Pilger interviewing the mother of two young Sandinistas who died in the 1979 uprising against the dictator Somoza.

The modern-day image of St Nicholas as Father Christmas was, reported Pilger in *Burp! Pepsi v Coke in the Ice Cold War* (1984), invented by Coca-Cola in the 1920s for an advertising campaign.

Bob Muller, a former US Marine who lost the use of his legs in Vietnam, featured in several Pilger films, notably *Heroes* (1981), about the struggles of the United States' veterans of the Vietnam War. (Photograph: Ken Regan)

John Pilger and David Munro returned to report on life for the Vietnamese twenty years after the end of the hostilities in *Vietnam – The Last Battle* (1995) and, in Hanoi, met Mrs Thai Thi Tinh, who lost her husband and five of her eight children during wars spanning half a century, against the French and Americans. (Photograph: Nic Dunlop)

In *Vietnam: Still America's War* (1974), Pilger reported that more than 70,000 soldiers and civilians had been killed since the Paris Peace Agreement of a year earlier and revealed that an American 'ghost army' had replaced those soldiers withdrawn under Richard Nixon's 'peace with honour'.

Pilger explored the Vietcong's network of underground tunnels at Cu Chi, which had kept the National Liberation Front one step ahead of the Americans, in *Do You Remember Vietnam* (1978). This Vietcong major, 'Minh No. 4', had fought in the tunnels. He is pictured with Pilger's longstanding friend, Eric Piper of the *Daily Mirror* (who died in 1982). (Photograph: David Munro)

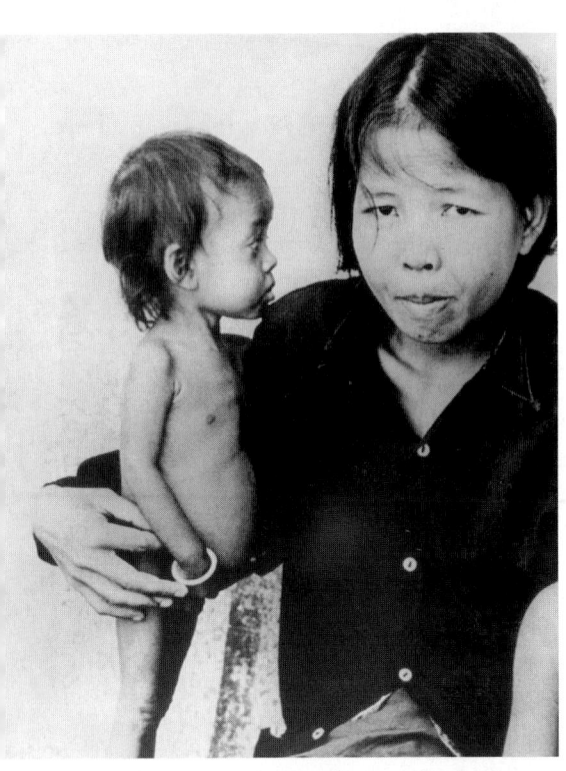

The graphic images of starving children in *Year Zero* resulted in $45 million of aid being sent to relieve the people of Cambodia. (Photograph: Eric Piper)

The complex story of Cambodia's journey into the abyss, laying the ground for the emergence of the Khmer Rouge, started with the country becoming an extension of the United States' war in Vietnam. In *Cambodia – Year One* (1980), Pilger found some of the many unexploded bombs dropped by American B-52s. (Photograph: Eric Piper)

Year Zero – The Silent Death of Cambodia documented Pol Pot's genocide with film of skulls dug from a mass grave (left) and found irony in the fact that banknotes discovered by orphans on the streets of Phnom Penh (below), after the retreating Khmer Rouge destroyed the national bank, were worthless. (Photographs: Eric Piper)

John Pilger's historic documentary *Year Zero – The Silent Death of Cambodia* (1979) revealed to the world the legacy of famine in the wake of Pol Pot's overthrow by the Vietnamese. Filming it was a harrowing experience for (left to right) sound recordist Steve Phillips, Pilger, director David Munro and cameraman Gerry Pinches. (Photograph: Eric Piper)

the Indonesian dictatorship's invasion and occupation of the small island, 400 miles north of Australia, in 1975. As many as 200,000 people, one-third of the population, had died – proportionately more than killed by Pol Pot in Cambodia. Only the Australian documentaries *Buried Alive* and *Shadow Over Timor*, and secret, dramatic footage of a 1991 massacre, had provided glimpses of Asia's other holocaust.

In 1991, British cameraman Max Stahl (a pseudonym) had asked Pilger to film in East Timor with him. Pilger had to say no, because he was then in the middle of a High Court libel action resulting from his documentary *Cambodia – The Betrayal* (see Chapter 8). On his trip alone, in November of that year, Stahl filmed shocking scenes of a massacre of up to 400 civilians by Indonesian troops in the Santa Cruz cemetery in the capital, Dili. His videotape, buried among graves before Stahl was arrested, was recovered and screened in Yorkshire Television's *First Tuesday* documentary *Cold Blood – The Massacre of East Timor*, broadcast on ITV in January 1992. Having established a close relationship with the Fretilin guerrillas, Stahl used a pseudonym so that he could return.

Pilger, who had never been to East Timor, now planned a 90-minute documentary with the intention of finding out what had happened to those who had 'disappeared' following the Santa Cruz massacre and telling the full story of the islanders' struggle since the 1975 invasion and the role of Western governments, notably the United States, Australia and Britain. Filming would take place in East Timor, Indonesia, Portugal, Australia, the United States and Britain. This meant that the documentary would be expensive to make. So, for the first time, Pilger sought a co-financed production with Central Television. He approached the Australian Film and Finance Corporation, which required a commitment from an Australian television channel to broadcast the film before it could agree to funding. None was forthcoming – despite its proximity, East Timor had attracted little interest in the Australian media – and the AFFC turned him down. He was told by an AFFC official, 'Timor is too much of a political hot potato in Australia while there is a Labor government in power.'[6]

In the event, Central Television fully financed the programme and Pilger and director David Munro planned to travel to East Timor in August 1993. They changed their identities and set up a fake company called Adventure Tours, 'specialising in Third World tourism', after dismissing more eccentric ideas for disguises. 'Priests was one rejected early,' recalled Pilger, 'followed by ornithologists, although we did acquire the latest volume of *Birds of Borneo, Java and Bali* in preparation for a period of study.'[7] Munro designed bags that each had a concealed compartment for a small Hi–8 video camera, with the lens concealed behind a gauze screen.

Max Stahl and a Birmingham doctor, Ben Richards (also a pseudonym), joined the team and flew direct to Indonesia. Pilger and Munro flew to Sydney, where they filmed an interview with Richard Woolcott, a former Australian ambassador to Indonesia, who had known in advance of the Indonesian invasion and had refused to accept that genocide had occurred. They also interviewed James Dunn, Australia's former consul in East Timor, who took a very different view, already declared in his 1983 book *Timor: A People Betrayed.*[8] 'By all demographic surveys, the loss of population was astonishing,' he said. 'It was worse than Cambodia.' In Canberra, Pilger interviewed Shirley Shackleton, whose husband Greg was among the five television newsmen murdered by Indonesian troops in 1975. She described the horrific fate they had met as they attempted to film the Indonesians invading.

Pilger and Munro then flew to Bali, where they caught an internal flight to Kupang, in Indonesian West Timor. There, as directors of Adventure Tours, they hired a four-wheel-drive vehicle and driver, hid the camera bags beneath the seats and headed for the border with East Timor. With Pilger lying face down in the back of the vehicle, they drove past the immigration post in the early hours of a Sunday morning. They then promptly got lost and strayed back into West Timor. This meant navigating the border all over again. Once safely across a second time, they drove into the mountains, away from Dili. Pilger and Stahl were to interview eyewitnesses to atrocities, some of them filmed in shadow to protect their identities. The film they brought out would reveal for the first time the full extent of the horrors that had been visited on the people of this other 'faraway country'.

After two weeks under cover, Pilger and Munro were made aware that they would soon be discovered by the Indonesian military. Filming on the beach at Dili was a particularly unnerving experience. 'When I recorded a "camera piece" that morning . . . near the pier, under the noses of a group of Indonesian soldiers and with the camera only partly concealed, I could hear an echo of my words and felt deep inside me a cold fear I had not previously known,' Pilger recalled.[9]

He and Munro decided to get out quickly. 'We sensed they were on to us,' explained Pilger. 'We were stopped at a road block and had to produce our false documents. Then, in the hotel, we ran into an Indonesian major who asked what we were doing. David turned on a virtuoso performance. He told him we were bringing hitherto undreamt of tourist dollars to East Timor, which would benefit the enlightened Indonesian administration.'[10] On the morning they left, Pilger and Munro burned their notes and taped the small video cassettes to their legs, bellies and crotches. They flew from Dili airport, having booked on a later flight. They had also filmed interviews with Timorese exiles in Australia, the United States and Portugal, and with Mario Soares, the president of East Timor's colonial master, Portugal, in Lisbon. In New York, Pilger interviewed Nugroho Wisnumurti, Indonesia's ambassador to the United Nations, who, clearly caught off guard, accused Amnesty International and Indonesia's other accusers of 'lying . . . no more than that . . . liars all of you!' The film's coup was an interview with C. Philip Liechty, a former senior CIA operations officer based in Jakarta. Pilger had traced Liechty, in retirement, after he had voiced his disenchantment with the Suharto regime in a letter to the *Washington Post*. It was the first time he had spoken out in eight years. Pilger and Liechty met in a hotel lounge in Washington and instantly found common ground. 'He is one of a school of CIA officers who joined during the Kennedy era out of a genuine, if thoroughly misplaced, sense of idealism – though sincere all the same,' explained Pilger. 'He had seen all the intelligence coming out of East Timor before and during the invasion, and was genuinely grieved by his government's part in the bloodbath. When I met him, he was seeking to make personal amends by telling everything he knew. He was the quintessential whistle-blower. I liked him.'[11]

Death of a Nation – The Timor Conspiracy was screened on ITV in February 1994. Two weeks before transmission, the Australian press reported that the documentary would reveal a second massacre in Dili following the Santa Cruz cemetery killings filmed by Stahl. The 'hot potato' remark by the Film and Finance Corporation official now made sense. Without having seen the new film, Australian Prime Minister Paul Keating condemned it. 'No evidence to back Pilger claims'[12] was one newspaper headline. Keating and his foreign affairs minister, Gareth Evans, even questioned the scale of the original massacre, which Evans referred to as an 'incident'. Australia's only national newspaper, *The Australian*, owned by Rupert Murdoch, mounted a campaign to smear the film. It started with a feature discrediting witnesses to the second massacre, written by foreign editor Greg Sheridan, who had admitted discussing with top Indonesian officials at a private function in Jakarta how their version of the original massacre might be represented.[13] The Suharto regime in Jakarta mounted its own offensive against *Death of a Nation* by presenting an Indonesian-Chinese priest, Marcus Wanandi, to the foreign press. Wanandi had been installed in Dili as an assistant to East Timor's bishop, Carlos Belo. He told journalists that there had been no second massacre.

In 1998, the *Sydney Morning Herald* published damning

evidence from official documents showing that Australian officials had known that a second massacre had taken place. Ten days before he had declared that 'the balance of the available evidence' was against 'Pilger's claim that a second massacre had taken place', Gareth Evans was sent a top-secret letter from the Australian ambassador in Jakarta, Allan Taylor. This disclosed that Taylor's predecessor, Philip Flood, had met the head of Indonesia's feared Special Forces, Kopassus, who confirmed that the second massacre had happened and bodies had been 'burnt and some dynamited'. This information was suppressed until the appeareance of advance press stories about the revelations in *Death of a Nation*. Ambassador Taylor wrote that Canberra ought now to be given all the details 'in the light of the allegations by Pilger'.[14]

Death of a Nation – The Timor Conspiracy opened with 'headline' eyewitness accounts of East Timorese who had lost relatives, some executed in front of them by the Indonesian military. In part of a long opening piece direct to the camera, Pilger said:

> [These people] were killed resisting the invasion. They were murdered without reason. They died in concentration camps and starved. Perhaps [the word] 'genocide' is too often used these days but, by any standards, that's what's happened here and it happened mostly beyond the reach of the TV cameras and the satellite dish, and with the connivance and the complicity of Western governments, the same governments that were prepared to go to war against Saddam Hussein but were not prepared in almost parallel circumstances to stop a rapacious invader that had broken every provision in the United Nations charter and had defied no less than ten United Nations resolutions calling on it to withdraw from East Timor.
>
> 'We should keep our heads down,' said a British ambassador to Indonesia, 'and let matters take their course.' 'Letting matters take their course', the governments of Britain, the United States, Australia and others supplied the means by which the regime in Jakarta has bled East Timor. This film is the story of that

bleeding and of a cover-up that tells us much about the selectivity
and aims of great power and how the modern world is ordered.

One exile, Abel Guterres, told Pilger what life was like in East
Timor before the invasion. 'The Portuguese very much left
people alone in their traditional lives,' he said. Jose Ramos-Horta,
the foreign minister in exile, said the Portuguese had adopted a
benign attitude towards the East Timorese. 'And they were lazy,'
he added, with a laugh. Black-and-white film followed of book
burnings following General Suharto's military coup in Indonesia
in 1965. 'In the West, Indonesia was seen as an investors'
paradise,' said Pilger, 'a huge market rich in oil and other natural
resources. Richard Nixon called Indonesia "the greatest prize in
South-east-Asia". Suharto and his generals were welcomed to the
free world.' Over film shot by Stahl of Indonesians secretly
digging up a mass grave of some of the victims of Suharto's
coup, estimated at half a million, Pilger said that the United States
had actively supported the generals, according to declassified
documents. 'These people are finding the bones of relatives
whose murder almost thirty years ago was the precursor for
the coming genocide in East Timor,' he said.

Pilger related Australia's support for the Indonesian dictatorship.
Labor Prime Minister Gough Whitlam had regarded relations with
Suharto as vital to his country's strategic and economic interests and
believed that East Timor, the Portuguese colony, ought to be part
of Indonesia. Richard Woolcott, the former Australian ambassador
to Indonesia, agreed but insisted that Whitlam only wanted
integration if the East Timorese consented. However, Australia's
former consul in East Timor, James Dunn, revealed that he had
been aware for more than a year before the invasion of an
Indonesian organization that had been formed to bring about this
integration 'regardless of the wishes of the people'.

Three independence groups had emerged in East Timor,
explained Pilger. The largest, Fretilin, and its more conservative
opponents, UDT, formed a coalition, which fell victim to

infiltration by Indonesian agents, and this led to civil war. After two weeks of fighting and 1,500 deaths, Fretilin emerged as the victors with considerable popular support. The Indonesian invasion that followed was foreseen by Western intelligence, which monitored events from a shared intelligence base near Darwin, in Australia.

Pilger recounted how Greg Shackleton, the Channel 7 television journalist from Australia, set out with his crew and another from Channel 9 – including two Britons – to find evidence of the coming invasion. There followed excerpts from Shackleton's final report, filmed the day before his murder by invading Indonesian troops. The Australian government never publicly asked Jakarta for an explanation of the television crew's deaths. When former ambassador Woolcott was pressed by Pilger on why an official protest was not made, he answered, 'I'm not even to this day precisely sure what happened, except they [the television newsmen] were very unwise to be where they were.' (In 2000, Australian foreign minister Alexander Downer released official documents showing that the government of Gough Whitlam had known that an attack was about to take place in Balibo, where the journalists were.)

Standing on the edge of what was said by local people to be a mass grave, Pilger read a selection of diplomatic messages sent from Jakarta by the British, Australian and US ambassadors, which showed that Western governments were fully aware of the Indonesian invasion. Film of US President Gerald Ford and secretary of state Henry Kissinger arriving in Indonesia in December 1975 was followed by former CIA officer C. Philip Liechty telling Pilger that he had seen his own government 'very much involved in what was going on in East Timor and what was going on was not good'. Over pictures of Ford and Suharto, Liechty said, 'You can be one hundred per cent certain that Suharto was explicitly given the green light to do what he did.' In voiceover, Pilger said, 'The Americans persuaded the Indonesians to delay the invasion until after the president had left and on 7

December, as the presidential jet climbed out of Indonesian airspace, the bloodbath began.'

Jose Ramos-Horta, the foreign minister in exile, described how hundreds of people were massacred during the first days of the invasion. Standing on the beach at Dili, with the wrecks of Indonesian landing craft behind him, Pilger said, 'The Indonesian troops had been told that the East Timorese were communists and primitives, who threatened the very existence of Indonesia itself. The strategy was clearly to terrorize an entire nation.' Philip Liechty disclosed that the United States provided 'most of the weaponry, helicopters, logistical support, food, uniforms, ammunition – all the expendables that the Indonesians needed to conduct this war'.

In 1981, thousands of civilians died when the Indonesian military forced them to march across the island in human chains – the 'fence of legs' – in an attempt to flush out Fretilin guerrillas who were captured or killed. A witness told Pilger that he had seen the corpses, some of which were decapitated, castrated or raped. Pilger reported that an international blackout of news from East Timor was broken only when two nuns in Portugal received a letter from a priest in East Timor. The letter read:

> The invaders have intensified their attacks in the three classic ways, from land, sea and air. The bombers do not stop. Hundreds die every day. The bodies of the victims become food for carnivorous birds. Villages have been completely destroyed. The barbarities understandable in the Middle Ages, justifiable in the Stone Age, are an organized evil that has spread deep roots in East Timor. The terror of arbitrary imprisonment is our daily bread. I am on the persona non grata list and any day I could disappear. Fretilin soldiers that gave themselves up are disposed of. For them, there is no prison. Genocide will come soon.

Rare film followed of Fretilin guerrillas. 'We filmed them under the noses of the Indonesian army, which claims to control all of

East Timor,' said Pilger. 'They get no outside help from any government. All their weapons are captured from the Indonesians. Some have not seen their families for years and every man here has lost members of his family.' Filmed by Max Stahl, one guerrilla with the *nom-de-guerre* of 'Delfin' said he became a resistance fighter after witnessing a massacre in which sixty-six people died. All but two men in his village were murdered and the women were raped and many killed. 'Cristiano' pointed out the site of a village razed by the Indonesians in 1983. According to lists kept by the local priest, 400 were murdered and buried in a mass grave. The list, meticulously hand-written, was shown. The names and ages of murdered villagers were accompanied by the method of their killing and the Indonesian battalion responsible.

Famine had claimed thousands of lives in resettlement camps in the late 1970s and early 1980s, said Pilger. 'Although we saw no starvation, a great many people were terribly malnourished,' he added. Filming at the Hotel Flamboyant, in the former resort town of Bacau, he described how the hotel had been used as a place of torture. An Indonesian military manual stated that 'interrogation should be repeated over and over again until the correct conclusion is drawn'.

The film revealed that many East Timorese women had been forcibly sterilized, with injections of a contraceptive drug, Depo Prevera. The investigation was carried out by Dr Ben Richards, who found a clinic in which many women were sterilized. Pilger added that, in 1983, Suharto had received a United Nations prize in honour of his 'support for family planning'. James Dunn, who had conducted his own population survey of East Timor, explained that in 1993 the country should have had a population of almost a million, but it was 650,000.

In Lisbon, Dr Mario Soares, president of Portugal, told Pilger that genocide had been committed in East Timor – 'a cold destruction of a people, their complete identity, destroying their habits, their traditions, language and religion'. But Nugroho Wisnumurti, Indonesia's ambassador to the United Nations, denied systematic killing and insisted that his government was not responsible for occasional abuses by the military. 'I don't know why you ask these questions,' he said.

The film then cast the spotlight on Britain's involvement with the Jakarta regime. Over film of the Queen and Margaret Thatcher with Suharto, Pilger listed the missiles, helicopters, frigates, armoured vehicles, mine-disposal equipment and military communications sold to Indonesia. The Jakarta regime had guaranteed that British Aerospace Hawk fighter aircraft would not be used for internal suppression, the Tory armed services minister, Archie Hamilton, had told Parliament.

However, a candid Alan Clark, a former minister of defence responsible for the sale of the Hawks to Indonesia, said that he had never asked for guarantees. 'That must have been something the Foreign Office did,' he said. 'A guarantee is worthless from any government as far as I'm concerned. I wouldn't even bother with it, but it may look good in the formula.' Clark dismissed the idea that Hawks were being used by the Indonesians simply as 'trainers'. 'That's just a label you put on it,' he said. 'The Hawk's a training aircraft, but it's actually an exceptionally effective aircraft and can be used in a whole variety of different roles . . . It can be converted anyway. The Hawk is dual-use with a capital "D".' An article from the magazine *Jane's Defence Weekly*, shown on screen, illustrated that part of the deal was for 'conversion training' to a light attack aircraft. In one of the most memorable lines from any film, Pilger asked Clark, a vegetarian, if he ever worried how humans, like animals, were killed by equipment supplied by his government. 'Curiously not,' he replied.

Filmed secretly on the balcony of his hotel in Dili, Pilger delivered his final piece to camera. He said that Western politicians and diplomats 'not only encourage a lawless bully but condemn a whole nation to a slow cultural death'. But there were signs of optimism:

In 1993, the United Nations Human Rights Commission voted on a landmark resolution condemning the Suharto regime. This was due to the extraordinary efforts of those Timorese and their allies who refuse to allow the unthinkable to be normalized and whose tenacity is reflected in the eyes of people here, eyes that speak a resistance and defiance and courage. There is also a wider question: Are international relations at the close of the twentieth century to be dominated by euphemisms and lies that override justice and make small nations expendable? The fate of the people of East Timor is pivotal to this. For, if we allow our governments to arm their oppressors and steal their resources, and to do so in our name, how can we then claim the universal rights that are denied them?

A 'helpline' telephone number followed, inviting viewers to call for more information about East Timor. The response was unprecedented, according to British Telecom, which recorded more than 4,000 calls a minute to the number. This continued into the early hours of the morning. Several thousand people wrote to their MPs. Following a showing of the film at the Palais des Nations, in Geneva, members of the UN Human Rights Commission said that it had influenced them in their subsequent decision to send a Special Rapporteur on Extrajudicial Executions to East Timor to investigate massacres such as that at the Santa Cruz cemetery.

Jose Ramos-Horta said, 'Our struggle for the recognition of our human rights was in the doldrums until *Death of a Nation* was shown around the world. It changed everything for us; it gave us a visual and factual point of reference: something we could show to governments and say, "Do you find *this* acceptable?" I have no doubt it was crucial in bringing forward our liberation and saving countless lives. We shall never forget what John Pilger and David Munro did, what their brave film did; it is part of our history.'[15] In the preamble to the awarding of the Nobel Peace Prize for 1996, to Ramos-Horta and Bishop Belo, the contribution of *Death of a Nation* to the 'struggle of the East Timorese people for their freedom' was mentioned.

'Max Stahl's film, so courageously shot in 1991, really broke the silence on East Timor,' said Pilger. 'What *Death of a Nation* did was place his work in context, explaining the complicity of Western governments. Together, they probably helped to put East Timor on an international human rights agenda and to complement the years of work by Noam Chomsky, Carmel Budiardjo, James Dunn and countless other activists who spoke for the heroic resistance in East Timor. Whereas the first Cambodia film, *Year Zero*, contributed to a rescue operation, *Death of a Nation* raised awareness. However, it is important not to overstate this. Remember that East Timor had to endure five more years of blood-letting before the United Nations took significant action – and before the media declared it newsworthy. All a documentary like this can hope to achieve is to add to the drip-drip effect of change.'[16]

Pilger pursued the theme of British arms sales to Indonesia in his next documentary, *Flying the Flag – Arming the World* (see Chapter 2). In January 1999, *Death of a Nation* was shown again in an edited and updated form, and under its subsidiary title of *The Timor Conspiracy*. 'Suharto had been overthrown in Indonesia and events were moving very quickly,' said Pilger. 'Suddenly, East Timor was an issue.'[17]

The 52–minute version (in an hour-long slot) was preceded by Pilger's explanation of the public's response to the original documentary. He opened by quoting Neville Chamberlain's description of Czechoslovakia as 'a faraway country . . . a people of whom we know nothing', recalling his documentary about Charter 77 dissidents. The same could be said of East Timor, said Pilger. 'We are showing this updated version because the people of East Timor are in the news at last, once again fighting for their lives, and because their murderers continue to receive arms from this British government, contrary to its boast about an ethical foreign policy.'

The programme described the new Labour government's record of selling arms to countries with poor human rights records, in spite of a claim to an 'ethical' dimension in foreign policy. Jose Ramos-Horta accused the Blair government of hypocrisy. Pilger's encounter with Alan Clark from the original documentary was intercut with a new interview with a government minister, this time Derek Fatchett, minister of state at the Foreign Office. Pilger asked him, 'Would you dispute this statement, and I quote, "Hawk aircraft have been observed on bombing runs in East Timor in most years since 1984"?' 'I've seen those statements,' replied Fatchett. 'They have been challenged by the Foreign Office, by British Aerospace previously . . .' Pilger interjected, 'As you know, Robin Cook made that statement.' Fatchett's excruciating silence was followed by film of Cook, as shadow foreign affairs spokesman, making the statement to the House of Commons in May 1994. 'It may well be true you haven't granted new licences,' Pilger told Fatchett, 'but you've let Hawks go on to Indonesia. Isn't there a huge irresponsibility there somewhere?' Fatchett replied, 'No, because we had no power to stop the licences. The legal advice we had was that we had no power to revoke the licences, there was no good cause to do so.'

Pointing out that the arms trade had actually prospered under the Labour government and that Britain was the second-largest weapons supplier in the world, Pilger asked, 'Do you still claim to have an ethical foreign policy?' Fatchett replied, 'I would challenge your figures. I would say that we are ethical in terms of the fact that we have very clear criteria for the sale of defence equipment. Those criteria are different from the previous government and that is that they are criteria that will stop us selling or granting licences in the context of where there is a risk to regional stability and where there's a risk of internal oppression.' When Pilger quoted a 1998 Amnesty International report on human rights showing that the Labour government had approved licences for sixty-four contracts to sell arms to Indonesia, Fatchett simply reiterated that the government had new criteria for sales.

Britain was still Indonesia's biggest weapons supplier, pointed out Pilger, and the Foreign Office's human rights report for 1998 failed to mention that it was a major arms supplier to the regime. Fatchett said the government could pride itself on working with the Human Rights Commission in helping to establish a free press and democracy. 'The United Kingdom's record on human rights and pro-democracy activity is a very, very strong and impressive one,' said the minister, probably leaving few viewers convinced.

Pilger also interviewed Portugal's new president, Jorge Sampaio, who pledged to stand by the East Timorese if they voted for independence in a referendum. 'If the negotiations in the United Nations get to a point where a referendum was taking place and that will be the solution coming out of the referendum, we have to defend that solution because it has been internationally accepted,' he said.

The reaction in Britain to this updated programme was even greater than to the original documentary. Cable and Wireless, whose lines took telephone calls to a new 'helpline' number, registered 80,000 calls within seconds of the closing credits, 200,000 calls within half-an-hour and stopped counting when the figure passed half a million. This incredible response proved that, although the documentary started at the late hour of 10.40pm and attracted an audience that fluctuated between three and four million, 'ratings' – the yardstick for measuring the popularity of television – are, alone, seriously inadequate. Sheer 'quality' of viewing and audience appreciation is not taken into account. Indeed, a fifth of those watching both the East Timor documentaries bothered to telephone their response, a remarkable demonstration of audience participation in a medium often criticized for the passivity it induces. The 'docu-soap' series *Neighbours from Hell*, while attracting more viewers (admittedly in a peak-time slot), seldom inspired more than a dozen letters. The response to Pilger's East Timor films ought to give television bosses pause for thought on how they gauge the depth of audience reaction. When BBC World showed *Death of a Nation*, the audience was an estimated 156 million.

In 1996, Pilger and Munro entered another country undercover, once again to expose the brutalities of a dictatorship. This was the former British colony of Burma, with a strikingly similar story and programme structure to that of the East Timor film. Since 1962, Burma had been controlled by the military, led by the tyrant Ne Win. Torture and forced labour were commonplace, but little evidence had been seen on television in the West. In 1988, ten thousand people were killed in a popular uprising. Eight years later, Pilger and Munro, again posing as travel consultants, flew to Burma and filmed secretly for two weeks, this time with a camera lens the size of a pinhole, concealed in a shoulder strap.

'It was a country I had wanted to see for a long time,' said Pilger. 'The problem was finding a way to get in to film. Our disguise fitted perfectly with the regime's ludicrous Year of the Tourist, during which it held out the hope of attracting hard currency.'[18] In a trip organized with extraordinary precision, Pilger and Munro arranged for couriers to fly in and out of Burma to take their film to Bangkok, the Thai capital. 'As in East Timor,' recalled Pilger, 'we had a certain period of grace before our activities began to sink in with the authorities. In the south, we ran out of time quickly with the local military and had to leave in a hurry. I suspect that only poor communications prevented us from being expelled from Rangoon.'[19]

Arriving in the capital, Pilger and Munro had travelled south to find the 'death railway', from Burma to Siam, which had cost the lives of 100,000 Burmese and other Asians who built it alongside British and Allied prisoners of the Japanese during World War Two. Most of the south was not open to foreigners – understandably, because slave labour and child labour were common. Pilger and Munro found young children at work on an extension of the railway. 'Some were barely eleven years old,' said Pilger. 'We watched, horrified, as one child was almost buried in the cement he was mixing by hand.'[20]

A centrepiece of the film was an interview with Aung San Suu Kyi, the democracy leader and 1991 Nobel Peace Prize winner, who had spent six years under house arrest until 1995 and even then was denied freedom of movement. 'This was a moment when the authorities were allowing her to receive foreigners,' explained Pilger, 'but we were concerned we would be arrested once we had been to see her. So the interview was left until the day before our departure. The film was in the hands of our courier before we ourselves flew out.'[21]

Inside Burma – Land of Fear opened with the sun rising over a sublime Burmese landscape, a scene typical of Munro's style. His documentaries with Pilger on Mexico and Vietnam had opened as a dawning, but with a hint of menace. 'This is a film about the right of a people to freedom and the power of the human spirit to resist against overwhelming odds,' said Pilger. 'It's the story of Burma, once known as the golden land. On the surface, every-thing appears serene. It's a country of extraordinary beauty and gracious people. But Burma is also a secret country, isolated for the past thirty-four years since a brutal dictatorship seized power, the assault on its people all but forgotten. To tell their story, we had to go undercover. What we found was a land of fear.'

The film documented the panic on the streets as troops opened fire during the 1988 democracy uprising and witnesses told their stories. The 'harsh, bloody and uncompromising' regime in Rangoon bore comparison with that governing Indonesia and East Timor, said Pilger. More than one million people had been forced from their homes and, according to the United Nations, many thousands had been subjected to torture, massacre and a modern form of slavery. The Burmese regime was now hoping to win international respectability with foreign investment and tourism.

Tracing the country's history, including a hundred years of British imperialism, Pilger said that Burma and its population of forty-five million had 'a natural wealth perhaps unequalled in Asia – oil and gas and vast teak forests'. The military rulers had renamed the country Myanmar and turned it into one of the world's poorest. To Britain, which had colonized it in the early nineteenth century, Burma was simply an outpost of the jewel in its imperial crown, India. Rudyard Kipling had written a popular song romanticizing the imperial capital of Mandalay, a town he had never seen, while nearby his colonial compatriots were stripping bare the teak forests. In the 1930s, British companies were making profits of £12 million from exports of rice and precious stones. It was then that the Burmese independence movement began. In 1948, after occupation by the Japanese during World War Two, the Burmese were granted their freedom but had lost their leader, Aung San, to an assassin's bullet the previous year. Still, a golden age of sorts followed, with Buddhism, socialism and democracy flourishing.

In 1962, General Ne Win, 'a Stalin-like figure', seized power. Martin Morland, former British ambassador to Burma, described him as 'a control maniac . . . a very rigorous authoritarian' who removed the country from foreign influence. Newspapers, books and films were censored, and Ne Win ruled by astrology and superstition, ruining the economy by replacing the currency with banknotes that added up to or included the figure nine, his lucky number.

Filming a piece to camera on the White Bridge on Inya Lake, in the centre of Rangoon, shortly after dawn, Pilger looked uneasy, a reminder of his camera piece on the beach in Dili, East Timor. 'We're filming this with great care,' he said, 'because even at this hour it's almost certain we're being watched, which is a normal state of affairs for many Burmese. This causeway is known as the White Bridge. On 16 March 1988, hundreds of schoolchildren and students marched along it, singing the national anthem. Then, as they looked behind them, they saw the steel helmets of the army and they knew they were trapped. According to eyewitnesses, the soldiers beat many of them to death, singling out the girls. Those who escaped were pursued here into the lake, where they were caught and drowned one by one. Of the survivors, forty-two were locked in a waiting van and left in the noon-day heat, where all of them suffocated to death. In the meantime, fire engines were brought here to wash away the blood.'

Again, as in *Death of a Nation*, Pilger interviewed exiles as far afield as Norway. 'They kicked me in my ribs and punched my ears, many times,' said Kotun U in Burmese, with English subtitles on screen. 'Then they began to interrogate me. They told me to squat in a half-sitting position and made me face the wall. When I obeyed, they held a lit candle under my scrotum.' An exiled nurse, Ye Min Shain, filmed in shadow, said, 'The victims were made to kneel down, then the anus would be probed with nails. Cold water was dripped on to the victim's head for hours. The whole body would be beaten so much that, in some cases, internal organs like the lungs were damaged.'

At eight minutes past eight on the eighth day of the eighth month in 1988, the Burmese people began their democracy uprising. Dockers went on strike, followed by other workers, and students took to the streets. Accompanied by still photographs and pictures from a shaky, hand-held video camera, an exiled student, Soe Naing, recalled the terror when troops opened fire on a demonstration. 'Most of the people who died were young,' he said. 'The mothers who tried to save them were also shot. They spared no one.' Other exiles described the burning of bodies, dead and alive, in the city's crematorium. Several Burmese cameramen courageously recorded the atrocities, including the shooting of children. Soldiers opened fire inside Rangoon General Hospital, killing doctors and nurses, and the wounded.

Ne Win faced his first real opponent in Aung San Suu Kyi, daughter of the country's assassinated national hero, when she returned from her home in Britain in 1989 to lead the democracy movement. She called for elections, spoke at rallies and herself came close to assassination. In July 1989, she was placed under house arrest and, believing the opposition weakened, the generals called an election for the following year. When the National League for Democracy won 82 per cent of the parliamentary seats, the generals were stunned and refused to hand over power.

In her interview with Pilger, Suu Kyi spoke about her house arrest and enforced separation from her husband, Michael Aris, an

Oxford don, and their two sons. For almost two-and-a-half years, she had had no contact with her family. 'I would always remind myself that the families of my colleagues were far worse off,' she said.

Inside Burma showed 'the regime's great secret', the construction of an extension of the World War Two 'death railway', linking the towns of Ye and Tavoy. Munro's is the only film of the railway, on which 200,000 were forced to work. The railway was to transport soldiers and supplies into the area where a billion-dollar gas pipeline was being built for the regime by the French oil company Total, which is part-owned by the French government. The pipeline was to carry Burma's natural gas from below the Andaman Sea into Thailand. For the generals, the revenue of hard currency would allow them to re-equip their forces.

At the railway construction site, where children were building a viaduct across a riverbed, Pilger and Munro witnessed a scene that would have been commonplace. A wheelbarrow of clay tipped over into a hole beneath a grinder where a ten-year-old boy was already up to his shoulders collecting clay. Munro stopped filming and he and Pilger pulled the boy to safety.

They filmed other slave labour in Mandalay, where prisoners were working on a new tourist development. Pilger interviewed Australian lawyer Brian Whittaker, who in 1995 had witnessed slave labour in the north. 'We heard the clinking of chains and we went outside and noticed about thirty people crushing rock by hand,' he recalled. 'One of them raised his prison uniform at the legs to display manacles which were running across his ankles. He then quietly lifted his shirt, which showed a chain around his waist and, from my memory, he also had a manacle around his neck. One of the officials informed us that the prisoners were political prisoners . . . It was clearly not voluntary.' This was a clear breach of the UN Declaration of Human Rights, said Whittaker.

James Sherwood, American chairman of the Orient Express hotels group, which operated 'The Road to Mandalay' river cruise, told Pilger at the offices of its parent company in London that before entering business arrangements with the Burmese regime he had failed to find a single example of humans rights violations, although he admitted to a possible 'out of sight, out of mind attitude'. A 'senior CIA representative' had told him that allegations of abuse were untrue or related to the drugs war. Sherwood had made no attempt to meet the country's elected leader, Aung San Suu Kyi. 'I believe that the generals are in power,' he said.

'The generals' power is backed by foreign money,' said Pilger. 'One estimate is that since it crushed democracy in 1990 the Burmese regime has drawn 65 per cent of its financial support from oil companies. The main backers are the French company Total and its American partner, Unocal. The oil pipeline they are building in the south of Burma will allow the generals to sell the country's natural gas to Thailand. The deal will give them an estimated $400 million a year over thirty years.'

The British were back, too, said Pilger. Foreign Office minister Jeremy Hanley had told the House of Commons, 'Through commercial contacts with democratic nations such as Britain, the Burmese people will gain experience of democratic principles.' Mockingly, Pilger added, 'Of course. Just as the peoples of Saudi Arabia, Iraq, Iran, Indonesia and all the other modern tyrannies have gained experience of all the democratic virtues of British business. If the opposite wasn't true, this would be funny.' Repeated requests to interview British government ministers at the Foreign Office and the Department of Trade and Industry were turned down.

Then came the revelation that one British company to trade with the Rangoon regime was the arms company BMARC, a subsidiary of Astra, whose former chairman, Gerald James, had spoken in Pilger's 1994 documentary *Flying the Flag – Arming the World* about weapons sales to Iraq (see Chapter 2). Here, James showed Pilger a document revealing that BMARC had secretly shipped arms to Burma and other countries, which the company's receiver had been ordered to give him by Sir Richard Scott during the inquiry into arms sales to Iraq. The sale of weapons to Burma in 1990 contradicted the government's insistence that it would not grant such licences. Australia had also pursued a 'double-faced policy', said Pilger, before reporting that former Prime Minister Bob Hawke had led a trade mission to Rangoon. Japan's national broadcasting company, NHK, owned most of the only professional television film of the 1988 massacres but refused to allow its inclusion in this documentary, explaining that it might threaten Burma's stability.

On the verandah of his hotel, Pilger said, 'At the height of their epic struggle in 1988, the people of Burma produced a genuine popular democracy, then legalized it with an overwhelming vote. For this act of principle and courage, they've paid a terrible price. They deserve more than our complicity and silence.'

When *Inside Burma* was repeated in July 1998, under the same title, to mark the tenth anniversary of the democracy uprising, Pilger introduced it with the words, 'We are showing it again to break a silence, to call attention to the extraordinary uprising of a whole nation almost exactly ten years ago and which has since been virtually forgotten . . . Since I reported from Burma then, repression has deepened dramatically. You can get twenty-five years in prison now just for speaking privately against the government. The democracy leader, Aung San Suu Kyi, has been threatened day after day, her closest friends and allies tortured and imprisoned. She's once again alone in her house in Rangoon. After weeks of trying to phone her, I finally got through and, when she answered, the line went dead.'

A new interview was added with British Foreign Office minister Derek Fatchett, who was later grilled by Pilger for the updated version of his East Timor documentary (see above). The Labour Party was now in government in Britain and Pilger reminded Fatchett that in opposition he had declared support for Suu Kyi's sanctions call. 'Now you're in government, where are the sanctions?' asked Pilger. 'We've taken a tough line on the regime in Burma,' replied Fatchett. 'We have, for instance, toughened up our own position on trade and investment with Burma. We've made it very clear that the government discourages trade and investment . . . They're not sanctions in the sense that you've got the international legal justification for that and we always knew that would be the case.' Pilger asked how the government had discouraged the Premier oil company from building the pipeline and pouring millions of dollars into the regime. 'We have no sanctions against a company like Premier,' replied Fatchett.

Inside Burma was an example of a documentary that had no noticeable public effect, but it fulfilled Pilger's aim of bringing to television screens a country and an issue that might not otherwise be seen by viewers. Other Pilger films like this included those on Mexico and Japan (see Chapter 9). 'It's about telling viewers about a country, its past and present, and its people, somewhere that they would know little about, largely because television ignores it,' he said. 'I've always felt it a journalist's job to go to these places.'[22]

7. OUTSIDERS

ALTHOUGH HE SELDOM spells it out, John Pilger has always considered himself an 'outsider', someone who does not operate within establishment and institutional boundaries, accepting their 'consensus' and assumptions. When he wanted to make a series of half-hour interviews with similar 'dissenters', he came up with *The Outsiders*, a series for the fledgling Channel Four. This allowed him for the first time to make programmes for Tempest Films, which he had helped to form in 1969. With the start of Channel Four in 1982, the company that had been founded by those who themselves wanted to operate outside the existing television system at last had its chance as an independent.

The nine-part series, screened in three blocks of three episodes during 1983, came at a time when Tempest was undergoing a transition. Actor and manager David Swift, who ran the business, had lost all of his original team except Pilger and was in the process of selling the company to producer Jacky Stoller. Most of the episodes were filmed in her front room in North London, with views of Hampstead Heath, and directed by Alan Lowery, an Australian who directed more than a dozen of Pilger's subsequent documentaries, notably those on their native Australia. Pilger's introductions to each programme, summarizing direct to the camera each interviewee's achievements and 'outsider' status, were mostly filmed at his own home, in South London.

In planning the series and its subjects, Pilger had to decide who an 'outsider' was. He wrote in *TVTimes*, 'Loosely defining an outsider was not difficult; he or she "stood outside" or was

opposed to those institutions and orthodox ideas which lead most
of us in the same direction. We added one particular rider: our
outsider had to have demonstrated the courage of his or her
convictions. Such people, we thought, would not be hard to find.
How wrong we were. Outsiders, even by the fairly liberal
definition above, are rare.'[1] A difficulty for Stoller was having
to negotiate with the commissioning channel over those chosen
by Pilger for the programmes. 'We did have a certain amount of
trouble,' she recalled. 'We gave Channel Four quite a controversial list of people we were considering. They said they didn't
want too many Lefties. One of those thrown out was Darcus
Howe.'[2]

The series began with Sean Mac Bride, the former IRA leader
who became a founder of the human rights organization Amnesty
International. Born in 1904, into a household immersed in Irish
nationalism, he saw his father executed by the British when he
was twelve and joined the IRA three years later as a guerrilla
fighter in Dublin and gun runner for Michael Collins, whom he
accompanied to London for the 1921 partition treaty negotiations. In 1934, Mac Bride was made the IRA's chief of staff and,
through defending the rights of Republican prisoners, went on to
become Ireland's most distinguished lawyer. This led him to enter
politics as Irish foreign minister, before helping to draft the
European Convention on Human Rights and founding Amnesty
International.

Asked by Pilger when violence was justified, Mac Bride
revealingly answered that he believed it rarely achieved its aims
and thought the IRA's current battle used more than was required
to achieve its goals. Sidestepping the question of whether, as an
IRA member himself, he ever killed, he said, 'I've no idea. I
certainly threw hand grenades and fired machine guns in the
direction of British forces.'

A lawyer operating outside the law at times, Mac Bride
defended this with the explanation that the IRA was fighting a
'liberation war'. He saw force as necessary in South Africa under

apartheid. 'You have a right to resort to violence if you're being attacked,' he said. In Ireland, most of the population had not wanted partition of their country, which had been 'a political unit since the beginning of time', with 'a tradition, a history of its own, a language of its own'. He said a date should be fixed for British withdrawal and a federal constitution instituted in the North.

Mac Bride's major current concern was campaigning against nuclear weapons. Public pressure had forced US President Ronald Reagan to justify publicly his war policies, which he did by verbally attacking the Russians. Similar pressure had led to a strong anti-nuclear movement in West Germany. However, Pilger was doubtful about the effectiveness of such pressure in the case of nuclear weapons. This interview came shortly after the screening of his documentary *The Truth Game*, which showed how propaganda sought to justify that a build-up of nuclear arms was needed.

Another who had fought for rights for those in her own country, but in this case on 'the other side', was Helen Suzman, for years the lone voice speaking out against apartheid in the South African parliament. Pilger recalled that he had been banned from South Africa sixteen years earlier but had never met Suzman until now. For thirteen years, she had been the only representative of South Africa's Progressive Party. In the 104 days of her first session in Parliament, she made 66 speeches, moved 26 amendments and put down 137 questions.

A white liberal, Suzman told Pilger that Parliament was the major forum for change for anyone who was not part of a revolutionary movement. 'Courage is doing something when you are terribly frightened,' she said, 'and I can't ever say that I was terribly frightened in Parliament, because I was, after all, a duly elected member of Parliament and I have the right to talk and the right to enter debates.'

Suzman candidly revealed what life was like for a black South African. It often meant getting up at 4.30am, travelling from the black township of Soweto on an overcrowded train to Johannesburg and a job as an unskilled or semi-skilled worker earning a low wage, liable to be stopped by a policeman at any time and asked to produce a document showing that he or she had the right to be in the city. As one of the few people who could visit Nelson Mandela in prison, Suzman recalled him as 'a very forthright person and clearly very much in control of the situation'. She did not necessarily agree with his political views, but one of her jobs was to monitor prisoners, particularly political prisoners.

She did not believe that trade sanctions against South Africa were realistic, because they were too difficult to apply and could be counter-productive, with other firms stepping in and maybe treating blacks worse. Neither did she think revolution would bring about change. 'I believe change is going to come about via the economics of the situation,' said Suzman. 'In other words, as blacks take over the skilled work in South Africa or become the majority of the skilled workers, as I'm sure they will do in due course.'

Unlike Sean Mac Bride, she did not consider violence to be justified. 'I think the Soweto riots proved very conclusively that you cannot fight armoured cars with stones,' she said. The police and military strength, and the laws allowing detention without trial, were enormously powerful factors working against open rebellion among black people. Suzman believed there would be gradual change, with better living conditions for blacks, at least in the urban areas, over the next ten years. 'I hate to see defenceless people being knocked around,' she said. 'It's very upsetting indeed. You feel you want to do something about it.' Eleven years after Suzman's *Outsiders* interview, democracy finally arrived in South Africa. In 1998, Pilger returned to the country to reveal that the black population were still outsiders and little had changed for them since the apartheid years (see Chapter 9).

Another formidable woman to feature in *The Outsiders* was Martha Gellhorn, one of the great witnesses of the twentieth century and inspiration for Pilger's original reporting on the Vietnam War (see Chapter 1). The American, whose mother was a suffragette and father a distinguished gynaecologist, was the world's first accredited female war correspondent and a successful novelist. She was also Ernest Hemingway's third wife. In her journalism, she had always written from the point of view of the victims of war. She reported the Spanish Civil War from the defeated Republican side, whose cause she embraced, and later saw frontline action in China, Finland, World War Two, Vietnam and El Salvador.

Gellhorn's first successful novel, *The Trouble I've Seen*, was based on her experience of working for the Federal Emergency Relief Administration during the Great Depression of the 1930s. A story she told Pilger demonstrated her spirit and the sense of justice that she felt. In a town in Idaho, the unemployed shovelled mud from one place to another, then one day the contractor collected the shovels and threw them away, so there was no more work for them but he received from the government more shovels. Gellhorn recalled, 'I said to them, "The only way you will get any attention is to break the windows of the relief office . . ." They went off and broke the windows of the relief office. I, meantime, moved on, because I was going to look at something in Seattle. As soon as they broke the windows, everybody arrived at once to listen to their beef, so their beef was taken care of – it was very efficient. I was in Seattle and I was recalled to Washington by the FBI. I was inciting revolution and I was, in fact, fired.'

The Spanish Civil War left a deep impression on the journalist who had travelled to Europe to see the fight against Franco's fascism. Asked by Pilger for her lasting memory, she replied, 'The enormous bravery of the people, absolutely unbelievable bravery under appalling conditions, because the worst thing in Spain was increasing hunger . . . I think the hunger was what finished the country because the hospitals were full of starved children and people were so hungry that to walk across a room was an effort. Their bravery and their dignity always stay in my mind.' Gellhorn recalled, 'I remember Madrid, shells coming into the square in front of the hotel and . . . women were queuing up to get an orange and nobody moving because it was so important just to get an orange to take home to your underfed family.'

At the end of World War Two, Gellhorn entered Dachau on the day of liberation. Reaching this, the first German concentration camp, had been her personal war aim. 'It was a total and absolute horror and all I did was report it as it was,' she said. With her trademark, matter-of-fact style, she gave a graphic description of Germans digging out the bodies of people who had died in a death train and of skeletal prisoners at the camp still breathing, but admitted that this was one of the few occasions on which she had shed tears. 'It was a perfect circle of hell,' she said. 'I got out of Dachau in a state bordering on uncontrolled hysteria and went and sat in a field waiting to be removed with American prisoners-of-war.' She never forgave the Germans.

Gellhorn regarded America's war in Vietnam, from which she was effectively banned after her reports on Vietnamese victims, as 'criminal stupidity' and added, 'We should admit it was a mistake, it was a terrible mistake, it was a mistake against America as well as against Vietnam, and then make our policy on the basis of admitting mistakes. But perhaps governments never admit mistakes and perhaps that's what's wrong with government.'

Despite all the tragedies she had witnessed, Gellhorn insisted she still had hope. 'I think the world is just as awful as it can be at any given moment . . .' she said. 'There will always be a certain number of people fighting like hell from keeping it being unbearably worse.' Gellhorn died in 1998, aged 89, after a lifetime of campaigning in exactly that spirit.

Like Gellhorn, Jessica Mitford's political baptism of fire was in the Spanish Civil War, and, like Gellhorn and Helen Suzman, she did not allow her own privilege to prevent her campaigning for the rights of others. Jessica was the black sheep of the aristocratic Mitford family, sister of romantic novelist Nancy, fascist Oswald Mosley's wife Diana, and Unity, who was obsessed with Hitler. She left behind this charmed background by running away to Republican Spain, then stayed in the United States after the death of her first husband, married a Jew, joined the US Communist Party and became an object of Senator Joe McCarthy's witch-hunts. She was acclaimed for her book *The American Way of Death*, about the rackets of the undertaking business.

In her interview with Pilger, Mitford explained that Unity's attachment to the fascists and departure for Germany revolted her enough to become a communist herself. Her parents, too, were among those who appeased Hitler and Nazism; many of the British ruling class had supported Hitler's policies. 'He had crushed the trade unions, he had crushed the communists and he had crushed the Jews,' said Mitford, 'and don't forget there's a huge strain of anti-Semitism that runs through that class in England.'

She felt that anti-Semitism was still prevalent among the ruling class and considered the country had fewer freedoms than in the 1930s. However, Britain had seemed 'a haven of liberty' after experiencing the McCarthy-era United States, where the FBI established concentration camps to hold up to 100,000 'subversives'.

Living in the United States again, with 'Reaganism', Mitford said she saw a move there to reduce access to official documents under the Freedom of Information Act, which had been an important part of democracy. She had caused changes in the law herself with the book about sharp practices of US undertakers.

Another journalist who had railed against authority and the official line, like Martha Gellhorn, was Wilfred Burchett. In *The Truth Game*, Pilger had interviewed his fellow-Australian about his reporting of the human effects of radiation after the first atomic bomb was dropped, at Hiroshima, while other journalists were being shepherded by public relations officers (see Chapter 8). In this *Outsiders* episode, made on videotape in Pilger's South London home and directed by Hugh Munro, father of David, Pilger described Burchett as 'the only Western journalist to consistently report events from the other side', in the Korean War and the Cold War, and from China, the Soviet Union and

Vietnam. In his own country, Australia, he had been denied a passport and some denounced him as a 'traitor'.

Burchett recalled Hiroshima in 1945 as 'a city steamrollered' and the attempts by US public relations people afterwards to play down the effects of radiation on the population. This proved to him that there was 'no substitute for being on the spot' and influenced his future reporting. He then went behind the Iron Curtain to report from the communist bloc and discovered what was happening in the North when the Korean War began. 'What I saw was the danger of another world war developing out of that,' said Burchett.

During that time, he was accused of taking part in the brainwashing of Australian prisoners-of-war, resulting in his passport being confiscated by his own country's conservative government, which did not want him to return. However, the claim of brainwashing was false and, when Burchett instigated a libel action over an article repeating this allegation, the jury found it to be untrue but had to declare the libel 'privileged' because it was a faithful report of something that had been read into the Australian Hansard.[3]

Of his reporting from Vietnam, Burchett recalled Ho Chi Minh as 'the greatest man I've ever met, with all the modesty and simplicity that goes with human greatness'. Burchett believed that he himself had learned moral values growing up in Australia as the son of a Methodist preacher. 'I don't think I've ever departed from those,' he said. When Burchett died in September 1983, two months after his *Outsiders* interview was screened, Pilger wrote his obituary in the *Guardian* and pointed out that the journalist had recently told him that he had never belonged to a communist party.[4] This came towards the end of the television programme, where Burchett declared himself simply 'an independent radical'.

Another Australian, playwright and screenwriter David Williamson, was featured in *The Outsiders*. Best known internationally for his film *Gallipoli*, which told the story of futile sacrifices by Australian and New Zealand troops in that World War One battle, Pilger described him as someone who had 'sought critically to show Australians other than as caricatures beloved by Dame Edna Everage and English audiences'.

Asked by Pilger about the leap of Australia from a 'convict background' to 'the world's first and greatest suburban society', Williamson put this down less to the transportation of criminals than British working-class migration around the time of the gold rush, with concern for 'respectability' and 'suburban neatness'. The intellectual community in Australia were concerned that they had no artistic history. 'Australia has not got its impressionist painters, it has not got its William Shakespeares,' said Williamson. 'So, if you're an Australian, you don't have any of that cultural self-esteem to fall back on . . . You can be laughed at anywhere in the world.'

When Australian troops went into action at Gallipoli in World War One, it was presented as a victory to give the country self-esteem internationally, said Williamson, even though the exercise was 'shoddy, badly managed and a tragic waste of lives'. One way to get international self-esteem was to link itself to the mother-land, but new ways had to be found as Britain's own self-esteem began to slide. He described the Falklands War as 'a rather imbecilic exercise in old-fashioned shogunism on both sides' and said that Australians were shocked that, contrary to their concept of Britain as a moral country that 'stuck to the rules', it sank the Argentine cruiser the *Belgrano* outside the exclusion zone. The 'new wave' of Australian cinema in the 1970s had, said Williamson, given writers and directors the chance to tell their own stories, rather than British ones.

Australia was becoming a multi-ethnic society with the assimilation of many different cultures from other countries. With cable television coming from abroad, there was also more access to foreign media, said Williamson. 'It's a different Australia than I grew up in,' he added. 'Our children speak an American vernacular slang, mixed with an Australian one, now because they've watched *Sesame Street* . . . The unique distinctness of Australian society, at least on a superficial level, will get less.' The prospect for Aborigines seemed 'fairly bleak'.

Another writer, author Salman Rushdie, might be considered an 'insider', said Pilger, after the glowing reviews of his novel *Midnight's Children*. But he was born a Muslim in India, and lived as an Indian in Pakistan and, today, an Asian in Britain, making him an outsider on several counts. Rushdie grew up in a wealthy family and went to Rugby public school, where other children made it clear that they did not see him as part of their English, middle-class society. 'I wasn't one of *them* and there was really no point in my trying to *be* one of them, because I would never achieve it,' he reflected. Rushdie encountered his first racism at Rugby. 'The idea of myself as a foreigner was completely alien to me,' he said.

The author believed himself still to be considered a wog. 'So all I can do is to occupy the time-honoured role of the uppity nigger!' he said, with a laugh. However, he was no longer the object of racism, but he put that down to his class. The aim of *Midnight's Children* was to write a book in English that felt like the country that Indians knew, instead of a story about 'what happened to the West when it went east'.

Rushdie felt that British novels were not reflecting the social changes of the country in the way that they were represented in stage plays by writers such as David Hare, Trevor Griffiths and Howard Brenton. 'There has been a kind of reluctance in the British novel to confront the central issues,' he said. There was much in his adopted country that he enjoyed, although 'the Englands I enjoy are not at present the ones that are in charge', he added, referring to the Conservative government of Margaret Thatcher. 'You choose those bits of the country that you like to belong to. It's a kind of sadness that those bits are currently in retreat. I don't myself think that that retreat is anything like as irreversible and final as one is led to believe.'

Shame, Rushdie's latest novel at the time, was an attack on the military rulers of Pakistan for making the country the world's largest exporter of heroin, while at the same time returning to extreme Islamic principles. 'There are a large number of soldiers, of high-up figures in the military, who are making a killing out of heroin,' he explained. Rushdie himself was under attack eight years after this *Outsiders* interview, when his novel, *The Satanic Verses*, led Muslims to call for the author's death and resulted in his going into hiding, with police protection.

Greek-born Costa-Gavras, who had become a French citizen, had consistently reflected his opposition to repression and injustice in the films he had directed. The Oscar-winning 1969 picture *Z*, an indictment of the fascism of the Greek colonels, was the first to bring Costa-Gavras to international attention. 'His films leave indelible marks,' said Pilger, in his introduction to the *Outsiders* interview. He was attacked for *The Confession*, featuring the 1951 show trial of Czech communist Arthur London, which exposed repression under Stalin, and he turned down Hollywood's offer of *The Godfather* because he felt it was too soft on the Mafia. Costa-Gavras was being sued for $150 million after *Missing*, his 1982 Hollywood film set in Chile during the overthrow of Allende, implicated US officials in the coup.

'I see myself as someone who is always ready to fight for freedom,' he told Pilger. 'My movies are about victims because I like to be with them, to understand them, to see how they react.' Costa-Gavras grew up in poverty and his father was jailed as a communist several times. As a left-wing student in Paris, he never accepted the 'left-wing' politics of the Soviet Union, which he considered to be as right-wing as Franco's Spain and Hitler's Germany. In 1970, the Communist Party's reaction to *The Confession* was 'violent' and, in Chile, the film was portrayed as an attack on Allende for being Stalinist. He met Allende and recorded a Chilean television declaration to refute this claim.

Like Sean Mac Bride, Costa-Gavras insisted that violence was justified in certain circumstances and 'terrorism' would be acceptable in tyrannical countries such as Poland or Czechoslovakia. He did not believe that a film could in itself change the world but it could 'add a small piece' to a general movement and be used to discuss issues. 'It's my dream to make a musical – a political one, of course,' said Costa-Gavras. 'I personally think all musicals are political. *West Side Story*, in its time, was an extraordinarily political movie. For the first time in film, music and dance, the director and the authors were speaking about the racial problem in Europe, but [of] different societies, Chicanos and blacks and so forth.'

For the final episode of the series, Pilger introduced a representative of 'a large and often unseen minority who more than most others in our society are the true outsiders, the disabled'. In her teens, Patsy Spybey had been diagnosed as suffering from a rare disease called Friedreich's Ataxia, which affects the nervous system, like multiple sclerosis, and leads to loss of co-ordination, speech and heart problems. Told that her condition would only worsen, Spybey defiantly searched the world for treatment and believed she had found it in Germany. A year later, she was walking with the aid of a frame after ten years in a wheelchair and her speech was almost restored.

It took three years to get a correct diagnosis of her illness, during which time she had to endure the reactions of others to her symptoms while not being able to explain them. Once in a wheelchair, she had to put up with a different reaction in shops and other public places. 'They used to treat me as if I was a child and talk to me like a child,' she explained. 'They seem to forget that you're a woman.'

In a rehabilitation unit, Spybey met her husband-to-be, Peter, a member of staff who had to help her off the bedpan she needed each morning after waking up. 'I think there's more pressure on the able-bodied person in a relationship,' she said. 'A lot of people seem to think that Pete and I don't have a sexual relationship . . . I think a lot of people, in a lot of ways, pity Peter.' At one time, Spybey was extremely ill and tried to hide this from her husband because it made him worried, but this caused them to separate for ten months. 'I gave him an ultimatum in the end – you either come back today or not at all,' she eventually told him. 'I didn't really think he would take that ultimatum, but he did and we haven't looked back since.'

In Germany, she was given a treatment plan that involved cell implants from the glands of sheep and a diet that excluded packet and canned food and red meat and, unlike in Britain, she found the doctor more interested in her as a person. Spybey recalled, 'The doctor said, "When I've finished with you, you will walk." For someone to tell me that, I was speechless. I couldn't believe it.'

From not being able to dust her own home because of the need to move ornaments, and not being able to wash up, iron, pick up a drink off a table or use a knife and fork, she had recovered her co-ordination and now helped youngsters with similar problems. She felt hurt and anger at the fact that many were unable to have a normal childhood. 'All that rolled into one gives me motivation to at least try and do something,' said Spybey. Now, she faced opposition from people who accused her of giving false hope. 'To me, everybody's got to have hope and encouragement,' she said.

In 1992, Pilger's admiration for Noam Chomsky, the distinguished American linguist and political activist, led him to arrange an interview that took up an entire episode of BBC2's arts and media series *The Late Show*. 'I'd long been a fan of Chomsky,' explained Pilger. 'I corresponded with him and we became friends. I put the idea up to ITV, but they didn't have an interview programme, and Channel Four wasn't interested, so I phoned Michael Poole, executive producer of *The Late Show*, and asked how he would feel about a face-to-face with Noam Chomsky. He agreed to take it as a package, produced by Central Television for the BBC; I was then under contract to Central.

'My aim was to allow the Chomsky view to reach as wide an audience as possible. I challenged him on a number of issues that produced, I think, an interesting debate, especially on free speech, where I felt he was less certain than he usually is. His view is that you give this freedom, unfettered, to everybody, including fascists and racists. He and I disagree about that. Where does free speech begin and end? He said that, if a man with a gun threatened you, you should disarm him, if you can, while not denying the right to put his side – the right to speak. I thought the contradiction only made him more credible and quite endearing. I felt good about the interview, for the man's essential humanity came over.'[5]

The programme, co-produced by David Munro with David Herman of the BBC, was edited down to 45 minutes after recording a 70-minute interview on videotape in a BBC studio. Pilger introduced Chomsky as 'the man who has been described as perhaps the greatest American thinker of the twentieth century, a man whose unusual combination of intellectual brilliance and moral courage has attracted both a worldwide following and howls of rage'. In the 1960s, he became a critic of American foreign policy, especially the Vietnam War. He refused to pay taxes and supported young men in their opposition to being drafted to fight in Vietnam. Chomsky's attack on the United States' liberal establishment triggered the greatest response, as he branded fellow academics and journalists the 'ideological managers' of a system that caused death and destruction worldwide in the name of democracy, and held the media responsible for giving people the illusion of unfettered information when it was often the opposite of the truth. He described this in his book *Manufacturing Consent*.

Chomsky had berated both Cold War superpowers, the United States and the Soviet Union, for suppressing the aspirations and freedoms of small nations. 'His critics charge he is wedded to a simplistic view of the world based on imaginary conspiracies,' said Pilger. The questions that Pilger put to Chomsky in *The Late Show*, including the criticisms of his work, could easily have been those that might be put to Pilger himself in such an interview.

'My earliest childhood memories from the 1930s include people coming to the door and trying to sell rags to try to survive, scenes of police violently breaking up textile strikes in the city where I lived,' said Chomsky, who believed that 'the brutality and the violence and the suffering' would remain as long as there were disparities of power. His family were the only Jews in an Irish and German neighbourhood in Philadelphia that was pro-Nazi. Although he was only a child in the 1930s, Chomsky's view of world affairs was first coloured by the Spanish Civil War, as was that of Martha Gellhorn and Jessica Mitford. At the same time, he was anti-Leninist and sceptical about Marxism, whose name suggested an ideology, or 'form of organized religion', based on an individual. 'In any serious domain, you don't personalize collections of beliefs,' said Chomsky.

His description of himself as an 'anarchist and libertarian socialist' referred to a modernized form of liberalism. Any institution should be challenged, he said. Of claims that socialism was dead, Chomsky differentiated between that ideology in different parts of the world. In Eastern Europe, it had finished by early 1918, with all popular organizations wiped out after the Bolshevik revolution. In the West, there was a move towards a 'social democratic' system. True socialism would only come in the future, said Chomsky, explaining, 'Traditional socialism is based on the application of enlightenment ideals to an industrial society and it means that workers will control production, communities will control communities and so on.'

The Vietnam War had initially made no impact on his thinking, Chomsky revealed, but it did affect his actions, at a time when he was enjoying success as an academic. 'It seemed impossible to look in the mirror and continue with a very pleasant life that I was leading,' he said, admitting that he was a reluctant activist. Chomsky became adept at attacking the language and propaganda of the state, and he himself was frequently branded an 'extremist'. 'In the mid-1930s, Hitler was described as a "moderate",' he said. 'A moderate is anyone who supports Western power and an "extremist" is anyone who objects to it.'

Pilger pointed out that Arthur Schlesinger had accused Chomsky of 'betraying the intellectual tradition'. Chomsky happily replied, 'I agree with him. The intellectual tradition is one of servility to power and, if I didn't betray it, I would be ashamed of myself.' Neither did he worry about being labelled a dissident. 'It's a safe guess,' he said, 'that anyone who is called a dissident in their own society is probably an honest person. There are things that an honest person ought to be objecting to. Most people won't do it.'

In his book *Manufacturing Consent*, he had borrowed Walter Lippmann's theory that the general public were regarded as 'ignorant and meddlesome outsiders' and the small group who made the decisions had to protect themselves from this 'bewildered herd', ensuring that these meddlesome outsiders remained outside. The public were to remain spectators, not participants, but they could occasionally 'lend their weight to one or other of the responsible class' by holding elections, to create an illusion of democracy, said Chomsky. This could no longer be done by force, so it was necessary to manufacture consent. 'Indoctrination is the obvious means,' he said.

Pilger asked Chomsky how the Gulf War fitted into his theory of three bloodbaths – benign, constructive or nefarious? 'That was a constructive bloodbath,' replied Chomsky. 'It was done for a power purpose . . . It wasn't a war. A war is something where two sides shoot at each other. This was just a slaughter.' Following the Iraqi invasion of Kuwait, the public had not been presented with the possibility of a negotiated settlement, even though Iraq had offered one to the United States.

On the limits of free speech, Chomsky insisted, 'If we don't believe in freedom of expression for people we despise, we don't believe in it at all.' Pilger pointed out that Muslim extremists had the previous year called for the death of Salman Rushdie. Chomsky responded that people had a choice whether to follow such instructions. 'It's incitement to murder,' said Pilger. 'You have to ask whether it's incitement to imminent violent action,' retorted Chomsky. 'Freedom of speech is an important enough value so that you need an extraordinary argument to overcome it.' Such cases included someone holding a gun being told to shoot.

Since the 1960s, pressure from thousands of people had resulted in the United States becoming a very different country, Chomsky believed, but there were still major attacks on democracy throughout the world. In continuing his crusade against authority, he said, 'If I started to be praised by Establishment sectors, I would ask seriously whether I'm not doing something wrong.'

The *Late Show* Chomsky interview and the *Outsiders* series featured subjects with whom Pilger had an empathy. Where he has interviewed those in authority who are responsible for, or collude in, decisions that affect ordinary people, Pilger has inevitably shown a much harder, tenacious style. It is this that has undoubtedly given his television work popular appeal, as viewers have seen authority figures subjected to a style of questioning very different from the blustering that is often mistaken for adversarial. This is evident in all of his documentaries and has often succeeded in giving an insight into the way those in power work.

It is also sometimes apparent that he is better informed on the subjects at issue than those whom he is interviewing. A perfect example was his 1989 interview with Foreign Office minister Lord Brabazon for *Cambodia – Year Ten* (see Chapter 3), which was brought to an end – for all viewers to see – by a press officer protesting that he had not been warned that his lordship needed to be briefed for this particular 'line of questioning'. Pilger had pressed Lord Brabazon on Prime Minister Margaret Thatcher's assertion that there were 'reasonable' elements within the Khmer Rouge who could take part in a future Cambodian government:

LB: One thing we would not wish to see, above all else, is the return of the Khmer Rouge atrocities, which happened all those years ago. We would certainly not wish to see anything like that happen. That's why we took the view of Prince Sihanouk, whom we regard as the person most likely to succeed in forming national unity, that he felt that they should be a party to the quadrapartite process, he felt that they were better on the inside than on the outside. The fact is, they're there. You can't ignore the fact that they are there. It's better to try and get them on the inside than have them on the outside.

JP: Are you aware that Prince Sihanouk's army fights side by side with the Khmer Rouge?

LB: [Stumbling] I don't know what's going to happen once the Vietnamese troops leave.

JP: Well, no, I'm asking now. Are you aware that, now, Prince Sihanouk's army is fighting side by side with the Khmer Rouge?

LB: Well, that may well be the case.

Pilger then reported Margaret Thatcher's assertion about a 'more reasonable grouping' within the Khmer Rouge, before the filmed interview with Lord Brabazon resumed:

JP: Who exactly are these 'reasonable' Khmer Rouge?

LB: Who *exactly*? I don't know their *names*.

JP: Well, surely it's rather important, isn't it, if Britain is supporting their inclusion in a future government in Cambodia? Who are they?

LB: Well, there are obviously some more reasonable than others. These are the ones who Prince Sihanouk can work with.

JP: But you must know their names, surely?

At this point, Foreign Office official Ian Whitehead ended the interview.

Four years later, when Pilger interviewed Margaret Thatcher's former 'defence procurement minister', Alan Clark, about arms sales to Indonesia for *Death of a Nation – The Timor Conspiracy* (see Chapter 6), the politician was remarkably unfazed by the journalist's persistence, which had the effect of producing from Clark an extraordinary insight into how governments work and the way in which some politicians regard the public. Pilger began by asking Clark about armed services minister Archie Hamilton's assurance

to Parliament that Hawk aircraft sold to the Indonesian dictatorship would not be used for internal suppression:

> JP: Alan Clark, you were minister of defence when the sale of
> Hawk aircraft was being negotiated and finalized with the In-
> donesians, and your colleagues have talked about getting guar-
> antees from the Indonesians that Hawks would not be used for
> oppressive purposes against civilians and, in fact, in East Timor.
> What exactly are these guarantees?
> AC: Well, I never asked for guarantees. That must have been
> something that the Foreign Office did . . . a guarantee is worthless
> from any government as far as I'm concerned. I wouldn't even
> bother with it, but it may look good in the formula. That's a
> Foreign Office matter, not an MoD matter. We've never asked
> someone for guarantees.

In voiceover, Pilger reported that the Ministry of Defence had, in
fact, also accepted the guarantees. The government had insisted
that the Hawks sold to the Indonesians were simply 'trainers' and
would not be used against the Timorese. The interview continued:

> JP: As far as the Hawks were concerned, there was a great deal of
> talk from all the ministries and British Aerospace that they were
> merely 'trainers'. A lot has been made of that.
> AC: [Shaking his head] No.
> JP: No? They weren't telling the truth?
> AC: Well, that's just a label you put on it. They *are* 'trainers', but
> you said *merely* 'trainers'. The Hawk's a training aircraft, but it's
> actually an exceptionally effective aircraft and can be used in a
> whole variety of different roles.
> JP: It can be easily converted, too. As the Indonesians' Mr Habibie
> [Indonesia's weapons chief], a man you know, said, 'Oh, yes, it's a
> training aircraft,' with his tongue in his cheek, 'but we can easily
> convert it.'

AC: It can be converted anyway. The Hawk is dual-use with a capital 'D' . . .

JP: Did it ever bother you personally that this British equipment was causing such mayhem and human suffering?

AC: No, not in the slightest. It never entered my head. You tell me that this was happening. I didn't hear about it or know about it.

JP: Even if I hadn't told you it was happening, the fact that we supply highly effective equipment to a regime like that, then, is not a consideration as far as you're concerned, is not a personal consideration?

AC: No, not at all.

JP: I ask the question because I read that you were a vegetarian and you are quite seriously concerned about the way animals are killed.

AC: Yeah.

JP: Doesn't that concern extend to the way humans, albeit foreigners, are killed?

AC: Curiously not, no.

In untransmitted material, Pilger followed this up:

JP: Why not?

AC: Well, it's a philosophic field. I suppose there is a relationship with the doctrine of original sin and innocence and so on . . .

JP: In your view, are there categories of arms that should never be sold?

AC: Yes. Nuclear, ballistic missile technology, chemical biological precursors, things like that. But in the conventional arms market-place, as far as I'm concerned, it's open season.

JP: You have said that where a regime is oppressively outrageous, as the gassing of children is, an army supplier should back off. Do you consider the mass slaughter of children in East Timor oppressively outrageous?

AC: Do you mean lined up in front of a ditch?

JP: Yes. One of the examples used is of children and their mothers being burnt alive in a house, trapped there and burnt by the Indonesians. What's the difference?

AC: I think gassing is dreadful. It's one of those techniques that actually breaks through one's protective indifference and is upsetting. But the other things that you mentioned . . . they just occur in combat or violent occupation situations.

JP: I'm still not sure of the difference. Why is gassing any worse than shooting, burning, torturing?

AC: I can't tell. There's something about it that deeply offends one's natural instinct, I suppose. It's a different threshold of violence. The other things, the examples you've given . . . I'm not familiar with the situation in East Timor . . .

JP: You once asked a television audience, 'Does anyone know where East Timor is?' Am I right in taking from that rather contemptuous dismissal that [East Timor] is simply expendable?

AC: I don't understand the use of the word expendable.

JP: Of no consequence?

AC: If you want to get worked up about something, I can steer you in all sorts of directions, if that's your hobby, bleeding . . .

JP: Well, no, the bleeding has been done in East Timor . . . often because of British military equipment.

AC: I mean, you can look anywhere, so what's all this about East Timor suddenly? . . . I mean, how many people are there in the world? A billion or something? I mean, if you want to rush round and say, gosh, look how dreadful this is, whatever it is, you won't have any problems. British military equipment is being used in Kashmir, and British military equipment is being used in Sri Lanka. We don't live in an ideal world.

In another untransmitted section of the interview, Pilger followed up Clark's revelation about disregarding guarantees. He related arms sales to Indonesia to those to Iraq, which had used chemical weapons both in its war against Iran and to kill its own people:

JP: Shouldn't the public be cynical about all this after what happened over Iraq? Shouldn't the public be cynical about assurances, guidelines and denials from government about the sale of arms?

AC: Well, I don't know what you mean by the public, but I don't think the majority of people give a damn about it . . . unless those weapons are going to be used against our own troops.

JP: But it's the assumption that the public doesn't give a damn that allows ministers and officials to deceive. Isn't that correct?

AC: Why should they want to deceive if the public doesn't give a damn?

JP: You say they don't give a damn, but that's an assumption that has yet to be tested scientifically . . . I would have thought that ministers are public servants, are they not?

AC: Certainly, but you measure public opinion by dining-rooms in Hampstead.

JP: I've never been in a dining-room in Hampstead.

AC: Haven't you?

JP: No.

AC: Well, I'll accept your assurance. You see, there's a concept known as the chattering classes, and they get tearful about different issues, and talk to each other about them. I hold them in complete contempt. They tend to regard themselves in some way as being 'the public'. They get a lot of coverage in the *Guardian* and the *Independent*.

JP: Should a government lie to its people?

AC: No, certainly not . . . One must take very great care not to.

JP: Mislead its people, deceive?

AC: Well, deceive is the same thing. But misleading . . . you get into a very grey area of definition here. Misleading gets you into the territory of both semantics and gullibility. People often don't want to believe things. They feel more comfortable if they don't focus their attention on things . . .

JP: The fact remains that British aircraft kill and maim people in East Timor, and the government allows the sale of these aircraft on flimsy assurances that they won't be used there.

AC: Flimsy, no. I mean, they are given in a proper diplomatic context. I attach very little value to such assurances.

JP: Isn't all this, in broad terms, about the right of a small country not to be invaded by a large neighbour?

AC: Yeah, but they weren't British, were they?

JP: That makes a difference?

AC: Of course it makes a difference.

JP: So, if they're not British, you can then sell them aircraft to help a powerful neighbour get on with occupying the territory that it's invaded?

AC: I must caution you. In the way you express things [you] are constantly foreshortening these arguments and giving them a particular colouring . . .

JP: This is a regime that has perhaps one of the bloodiest records of the twentieth century.

AC: Well, that's a very competitive sphere.

JP: This regime has competed well in that league.

AC: Has it? There's Stalin, Pol Pot and others.

JP: In East Timor, it has killed more people proportionately than Pol Pot killed in Cambodia. By all credible accounts, it's killed a third of the population. Isn't that ever a consideration for the British government?

AC: It's not something that often enters my . . . thinking, I must admit.

JP: Why is that?

AC: My responsibility is to my own people. I don't really fill my mind much with what one set of foreigners is doing to another.[6]

When the East Timor documentary was screened in an updated form in 1999, Pilger added an interview with Labour MP Derek Fatchett, minister of state at the Foreign Office. Asked how the new government's 'ethical' foreign policy, declared by foreign secretary Robin Cook, squared with the reality of continuing arms sales to Indonesia, Fatchett was clearly on the defensive – a contrast to Clark's unashamed admission of a lack of concern about the use of weapons sold abroad. From the beginning, Pilger succeeded in wrong-footing Fatchett:

> JP: Would you dispute this statement, and I quote, 'Hawk aircraft have been observed on bombing runs in East Timor in most years since 1984'?
>
> DF: I've seen those statements. They have been challenged by the Foreign Office, by British Aerospace previously . . .
>
> JP: As you know, Robin Cook made that statement . . . [Pause and silence from Fatchett] He was then the frontbench spokesman on foreign affairs. He made it on 11 May 1994. Now, it may well be true you haven't granted new licences, but you've let Hawks go on to Indonesia. Isn't there a huge irresponsibility there somewhere?
>
> DF: No, because we had no power to stop the licences. The legal advice that we had was that we had no power to revoke the licences, there was no good cause to do so.
>
> JP: But under your government the arms trade has boomed. Your colleague, the defence secretary, recently congratulated the arms industry for a rise, I think, of 20 per cent in output, profits up, £5.5 billion worth of arms, the second-biggest arms salesman in the world. Do you still claim to have an 'ethical' foreign policy?
>
> DF: I would challenge your figures. I would say that we are ethical in terms of the fact that we have very clear criteria for the sale of defence equipment. Those criteria are different from the previous government and that is that they are criteria that will stop us selling or granting licences in the context of where there is a risk to regional stability and where there's a risk of internal oppression . . .
>
> JP: Shortly after Labour came to power, the Nobel Prize winner, Bishop Belo of East Timor, came to London and I heard him make a direct appeal to you and your colleagues, and he said, 'Please, I beg you, do not sustain longer a conflict which, without British arms sales to Indonesia, could never have been sustained for so long.' Aren't you ashamed by that statement?
>
> DF: No. Indeed, we've done exactly what Bishop Belo asked us to

do. We are working totally in line with the proposals put forward by Belo. Our approach is wholly sympathetic to that statement.

JP: Well, I'm not sure it's wholly sympathetic, because he was talking about stopping arms sales and since you came to power – this is the Amnesty report [Amnesty International UK's 1998 Human Rights Audit], which you know very well, of course – you have approved licences for sixty-four contracts for arms to the Indonesian dictatorship. They include small arms, machine-guns, ammunition, bombs, torpedoes, rockets, missiles, mines, riot-control agents, aircraft, and so on and so forth. Do you dispute these facts in the Amnesty report?

DF: We'll be publishing the first annual report on arms sales under the new criteria. That will come out in the next few weeks. There is a new set of criteria. We have put those criteria forward. They are open. They were published in July 1997. What you and others and Amnesty will be able to do is to judge the actions we've taken, the licences we've granted, against those criteria. There will be an annual report, a totally different departure from the previous government, more open, more transparent, greater accountability.

JP: Right. Well, we'll look forward to that. But, in the meantime, could you answer that question: do you dispute the Amnesty figures that your government has approved sixty-four licences? Have they got it wrong?

DF: Well, let me say to you that you need to look at that in the report when it comes out.

JP: Excuse me, minister, it's really a 'yes' or 'no'.

DF: No, it's not a 'yes' or 'no', because what you will see is that Amnesty are making judgements against previous . . .

JP: They're not making judgements – it's a list of facts.

DF: No, it's not a list of facts. Amnesty are making judgements against previous categories. Those categories may well change in the annual report. There may well be greater detail.

JP: So this Amnesty list is incorrect, it's wrong?

DF: I think the Amnesty people who compiled that list would recognize that there is greater detail that we can make available.

We hope to make that greater detail available in the annual report. When that greater detail *is* made available, then the categories make even greater sense than they do at the moment.

JP: But, in the meantime, people are being killed in East Timor. We're talking about what will happen and I don't understand why you can't explain what has already gone on.

DF: Well, we will explain. That will be in the annual report.

JP: Why not say it now?

DF: Because the annual report will bring it together. An annual report comes out, if I can just make this point, on a yearly basis. You don't need to have that on an weekly basis, otherwise it would subvert the purpose. It is an annual report, which will bring together all the licences that we've granted for each and every country.

JP: Jose Ramos-Horta [East Timor's foreign minister-in-exile], when I interviewed him the other day, described your government as hypocrites.

DF: Well, I think he's wrong in what he's saying there and fundamentally wrong, because we have been active, we have provided a lot of support for the diplomatic process, we've used whatever good offices we have to persuade the process to move forward. We will continue to take that active diplomatic role. I don't see any hypocrisy or inconsistency there. We have always had one very clear objective and we will continue to work towards that clear objective.

JP: The United Kingdom is still the biggest arms supplier to Indonesia. As Jose Ramos-Horta asked you to do, why not merely freeze arms sales?

DF: Well, there are different statements from individuals, but what individuals recognize is that the new arms criteria are tougher and more effective. You'll have to wait for the annual report, as I've already indicated, to make your judgement on that, but we have a new criteria [*sic*].

JP: You mention annual reports. Well, this is an annual report, your human rights report, published by the Foreign Office, for

1998. The section on Indonesia is striking for its omission. There's no mention here of the fact that you are a major arms supplier to that country. Isn't that a distortion?

DF: Let me say to you that we can point with pride to what we've done on the human rights side in Indonesia. We've worked with the Human Rights commission, we're helping to establish free press, to help the democratic process. All of those moves are going in the right direction in Indonesia, and the United Kingdom's record on human rights and pro-democracy activity is a very, very strong and impressive one.

This was Fatchett's second encounter with Pilger. In the updated repeat of *Inside Burma – Land of Fear* (see Chapter 6), he had fielded questions on Britain's failure to impose sanctions on a regime whose terrible human rights record was acknowledged by the United Nations. Pilger began by trying to match the Labour Party's policy while in opposition to the realities of it in government:

JP: Mr Fatchett, this is a statement made by you when you were an Opposition spokesman on foreign affairs, and I quote, 'The military regime in Burma has chosen to declare war on human rights. The Labour Party believes that a clear signal must be sent to the regime that their behaviour cannot be tolerated. That's why we support Aung San Suu Kyi in her call for sanctions.' Now you're in government, where are the sanctions?

DF: Well, what we've done in government is totally to live with that statement. We've taken a tough line on the regime in Burma. We have, for instance, toughened up our own position on trade and investment with Burma. We've made it very clear that the government discourages trade and investment. So there's very much a toughening-up, a sanctions approach, in relation to our trade . . .

JP: But they're not sanctions.

DF: They're not sanctions in the sense that you've got the international legal justification for that and we always knew that would be the case. You see, I think there is a danger of becoming obsessed by the word sanctions because, if you look at what we've done, we have discouraged trade, we've discouraged British companies, on the whole, from investing in Burma.

JP: How have you discouraged the Premier oil company, which is about to build a multi-million-pound pipeline and pour millions of dollars into the coffers of the regime? That's a British company. How have you discouraged *them*?

DF: We have no sanctions against a company like Premier, but what we have done . . .

JP: How have you *discouraged* them?

DF: Let me say . . . again, just look at the figures. What you're doing is to take the odd example to try to undermine . . .

JP: It's a *massive* example . . .

DF: . . . undermine the general case. The general case is a strong one and that is that we have taken a position of discouraging companies. I think that shows in terms of the result.

The Burma film also featured another revealing interview, with James Sherwood, chairman of Orient Express Hotels, which had started operating 'The Road to Mandalay' river cruise since the regime opened up the country to tourism:

JP: Mr Sherwood, last year your company signed a deal for $35 million with the Burmese regime. What does that involve?

JS: Well, it's basically an investment in ships and shore facilities for the development of river tourism in Burma.

JP: Did you consider all the implications of Burma's rather appalling record as far as human rights are concerned before you went in with this project?

JS: Well, I did and I've tried to investigate these allegations about human rights infringements, and it's very hard to pin them down. People make these accusations, or allegations. I immediately try to see if there's any proof to them but, of course, I accept that I cannot visit all of Burma and my visits are limited to the principal cities, so perhaps that's [an] 'out of sight, out of mind' attitude, so I can't speak any further than my personal knowledge.

JP: Did you make, really, any attempt before you invested in Burma to see this other side?

JS: Well, what I did do was that I contacted the senior CIA representative for Burma and had extensive discussions about the truth of all of these allegations and he confirmed to me that they were all untrue or, to the degree that they occurred, they were related to the drugs war.

JP: They're not allegations. You would think that the United Nations, Amnesty, Human Rights Watch, the United States government . . . The United States State Department says, for instance, forced labour is routine in Burma. I don't think these all come into the realm of allegations. There's a great deal of substance there, surely?

JS: Well, perhaps you can say so, but I don't have any personal evidence of it.

JP: Did you see the elected leader of the country, Aung San Suu Kyi, when you were there?

JS: No, I didn't, no. I think it would have been inappropriate or untactful for us to open a dialogue with the opposition leader.

JP: But she's the elected leader. Some would say that the generals who you saw were the opposition.

JS: I believe that the generals are in power.

Another instance of Pilger grilling a representative of an international business whose financial interests in a country sat alongside uncomfortable statistics came in *Apartheid Did Not Die*, a documentary about the continuing plight of black South Africans in the wake of democracy (see Chapter 9), screened simultaneously in Britain and South Africa. This was probably the first time that the corporate arrogance of the gold-mining giant Anglo American, whose profitability had grown during the apartheid years, was captured on television – in a country where television censorship had only recently been lifted. In untransmitted material at the beginning of his interview with Michael Spicer, the company's head of public affairs, Pilger probed the history of Anglo American in South Africa:

> JP: Your two most famous chairmen, Mr Harry Oppenheimer and Mr Gavin Reilly, opposed 'one man, one vote' and, indeed, Mr Oppenheimer made it clear that he didn't believe that apartheid was morally wrong . . .
>
> MS: I think that's completely erroneous.
>
> JP: It's in the official biography of him [Oppenheimer].
>
> MS: No, that's absolutely not correct.
>
> JP: He opposed 'one man, one vote' and so did Gavin Reilly.
>
> MS: 'One man, one vote' he opposed for a certain period of time . . . but, from the Seventies onwards, I think he recognized . . . that the system had to change.
>
> JP: But the South Africa Foundation [a powerful pro-apartheid group] had as its leading member Harry Oppenheimer . . .
>
> MS: Oppenheimer never had a high regard for the South Africa Foundation.
>
> JP: But he was a leading member of it. Are you saying he wasn't a member?
>
> MS: If you will do me the courtesy of a re-interview, I will come along with a number of different quotes.
>
> JP: Well, you're the public relations executive of Anglo American. Surely, you should have the evidence with which to answer these questions?
>
> MS: I don't carry them around in my head.

On screen, Pilger went on to ask Spicer about an estimate that every ton of gold mined in the country cost one life and twelve serious injuries:

> MS: Those are statistics that are of great concern. What we have always said is that South African mining has the most risks. There is no such thing as risk-free mining. What one has to do is to

mitigate the risk and that requires a number of interactions – technical interactions, human interactions and I think, as we would gladly accept now, those require co-operative manage-ment–employee interactions, which may not perhaps have always been there to the degree that was desired.

JP: You may be aware of the Business Report Study, which was taken from safety data of the Chamber of Mines. That's it [holding up the report for Spicer to see]. It says that, in 1995, Anglo American had the highest gold-mining fatality rate of all the major mining houses, even if you exclude the 104 men killed in the Val Reef accident of that year. Unfortunately, there is no response from the company in that. What would your response be to that?

MS: Highly regrettable. But perhaps one would have had a headline in 1994 that would have been different, 1993 that would have been different . . .

JP: What was the situation *then*?

MS: Anglo American did *not* have the highest. Some other company had the highest. After all, there has to be one that has the highest every year.

JP: To the lay eye – and you say these figures are regrettable – they're *shocking* figures. The government mining engineer, Mr Becker, said in almost every accident – he's talking about the whole industry, not just your company – one can find underlying causes: there is lack of management systems, supervision, training and negligence, and a lax enforcement of standards. And you say it's just mining. Does this man [have] it all wrong?

MS: No, I think that that's certainly part of a much broader issue . . .

JP: This man is the government mining engineer. He says that, in every accident, there are underlying causes and they have to do with negligence. What's the company's response to that? If it isn't a selective quote, what's the company's response?

MS: I've given you my response, John, to the entire subject. I've given it in general terms and I think that's what I have to say at the moment.

Pilger turned to the issue of compensation paid to injured miners and those with occupational diseases:

> JP: Some of the research that has recently been done in this country [South Africa] suggests that a third of all miners are suffering some form of quite serious . . . occupational disease, but they come away with very little. That's the point.
>
> MS: Certainly, levels of compensation have changed and are changing further.
>
> JP: *How* are they changing?
>
> MS: The amounts have been increased.
>
> JP: By what? Can you give me an example?
>
> MS: I'd have to give you a rough estimate. But, certainly, compared to the 1970s, they're in multiples of the levels then.
>
> JP: Can't you give me an example of a miner over a period of time – this is your field, really – and what he would have got and what he now gets?
>
> MS: I don't have the figures, John, no. I regret that . . .
>
> JP: Don't you find that extraordinary, for the public affairs manager of this company – I asked you a simple question, to give an example of the compensation. This is to do with mining and you don't have the information.
>
> MS: I don't find that extraordinary at all.

What followed, as Spicer attempted to walk out, was not seen on screen:

> JP: I wouldn't get up too quickly if I was you. The microphone might tear your clothes.
>
> MS: If I'd known it was you, John, I wouldn't have done the interview. [Your identity] was skilfully concealed.
>
> JP: It was a conspiracy, I can assure you.[7]

A similar, combative interview took place in *Paying the Price – Killing the Children of Iraq* (see Chapter 4), about the human cost of

UN sanctions on Iraq in the decade following the Gulf War. In 1999, as US under secretary of state, James Rubin was Madeleine Albright's deputy and the voice of US foreign policy. Not yet forty, he was considered a Washington high-flier, whose pugnacious way of dealing with journalists was a departure from the diplomatic style of the government spokesman. The tension between Rubin and Pilger produced memorable exchanges, not all of them included in *Paying the Price*. 'We couldn't use enough of Rubin,' said Pilger. 'Here was the authentic voice of power without the usual sophistry.'[8] The following includes untransmitted material:

JP: Mr Rubin, here's a current list of items that are delayed by the UN sanctions committee. There are eighteen holds on medical equipment, such as sixteen heart and lung machines, water pumps, agricultural supplies, safety and firefighting equipment, medicines, detergents, wheelbarrows. It goes on and on . . . how can that be justified?

JR: I'd like to give you a full and complete answer, if you'll permit me to do so . . .

JP: Sure.

JR: If it weren't for the United States, billions of dollars' worth of food and medicine would not be going to Iraq . . . there is no sanction on food and medical sales in Iraq. Any country can sell food and medicine to Iraq. There is no prohibition on that.

JP: But these are delayed, aren't they?

JR: Well, I'm going to get to that . . .

JP: . . . but they're held up.

JR: I've offered you 45 minutes of time. That means I need some time to answer your questions . . .

Rubin went on, at length, to claim that United Nations officials in Iraq backed US accusations that humanitarian aid was not getting through to people. He cited a recent UNICEF report as evidence.

JP: You're referring to the UNICEF report [but] UNICEF has rebutted everything you've just said. You didn't mention, for instance, the appendix to the report which said, and I quote, 'The difference in mortality rates between north and south cannot be attributed to the way the relief effort has been implemented.' A senior UNICEF representative in Baghdad was very clear. She said that there was no suggestion that there was a deliberate with-holding of supplies . . .

JR: I think you try to both ask the questions and give the answers . . .

JP: I'm asking you that because you didn't mention you were quoting a UNICEF report, did you?

JR: If you'd like to give a speech, we can switch chairs and you'll be happy to give your speech to the camera.

JP: I don't think it becomes a senior State Department represen-tative to speak like that.

JR: No, I'm offering you the opportunity to give a speech.

JP: Why don't you answer the question?

JR: I'll be happy to.

JP: Go ahead.

JR: If you would pose a simple, straightforward question.

JP: All right. Why have you misrepresented a UNICEF report which has rebutted the very charge that you've put forward?

Rubin went on to attack the chief United Nations humanitarian relief official in Iraq, Hans von Sponeck, who later resigned in protest at the sanctions:

JR: Mr von Sponeck is commenting on subjects beyond his competence . . . he's raising questions about whether it's wise for the Security Council to have imposed those sanctions.

JP: He's not saying that, with respect . . . he's commenting on the humanitarian situation, and he's the senior United Nations hu-manitarian official . . .

Pilger then moved on to an area he seldom strays from, that of official hypocrisy:

> JP: Don't you sometimes get a sense of irony . . . for years, the United States helped Saddam Hussein obtain weapons of mass destruction to use against his neighbours. The US did nothing when Iraq used chemical weapons against the Kurds . . . it was business as usual . . . isn't that all rather brutally ironic, especially for those children who are dying [as a result of sanctions]?
>
> JR: Iraq's regime is responsible for the depredations and deprivations in Iraq. That's who's responsible, not the United States. The United States didn't gas the Kurds . . .
>
> JP: You supplied seed stock . . . biological weapons were supplied by a company, the American Type Culture Collection, down the road in Rockville, Maryland . . .
>
> JR: Well, I'm sure they've been prosecuted for it.
>
> JP: No, they weren't. The Commerce Department gave its approval.
>
> JR: There is no [such] approval . . .
>
> JP: Those were the days you were backing Saddam Hussein.
>
> JR: There may be dual-use items that can be then used for other purposes . . . but to suggest that we were sanctioning the sale of chemical weapons agents to Iraq is ridiculous.
>
> JP: It's not ridiculous. It's true. The Senate Banking Hearings heard that this particular organization was given Commerce Department approval to sell these agents . . . it's brutally ironic?

Near the end of the interview, Pilger returned to his central theme, saying that, just as the outside world should have been alerted to the Holocaust, the genocide in East Timor and 'other atrocious happenings around the world', so the children of Iraq should not pay the price. Did Rubin not agree?

> JR: Well, the idea to compare what's going on in Iraq to the Holocaust, I find personally offensive.

JP: You may, but it's called a holocaust.

JR: That is an offence to the people who died in the Holocaust.

JP: The United Nations figures [are] half a million children [dead] . . .

JR: We've gone over this . . .⁹

A striking feature of Pilger's style of interviewing is that he is almost invariably polite, seldom raising his voice, but waiting for his interviewee − or quarry − to utter the specious or the downright untrue. Some interviews become almost philosophical debates. One example came in a long, polite interrogation of Peter van Walsum, chairman of the United Nations Security Council's sanctions committee, for *Paying the Price*:

JP: Why should the civilian population, including children born since the Gulf War, innocent people, be held hostage to the compliance of a dictator?

PVW: I think it is a difficult problem, but you have to think of one thing: a sanctions regime is not a form of development aid. Sanctions are part . . .

JP: [Laughing] Excuse me! Are you serious in saying that? I would think it's the very opposite, isn't it?

PVW: This is exactly my point. You should realize what sanctions are. Sanctions are one of the coercive measures that the Security Council has at its disposal under Chapter Seven. That is to say, it is part of this whole range of measures [and] at the very end of that scale you have the military action. Sanctions are the measure just short of action and obviously they hurt. They are like a military measure, they are like a military action.

JP: But *who* do they hurt?

PVW: Well, this is the first problem . . .

JP: Isn't this the key point − who they hurt?

PVW: With military action, too, you have the eternal problem of collateral damage . . .

JP: You have an entire nation of this collateral damage here.

Forgive me for interrupting, but let me just say this. Every UN agency dealing with health, food, agriculture and children have reported repeatedly that tens of thousands of the most vulnerable in the society have died and are suffering as a result of sanctions. Do you seriously call that collateral damage?

PVW: No, I didn't call it collateral damage.

JP: Well, you were drawing a comparison there.

PVW: No, I'm saying that military action has collateral damage. Sanctions are short of military action, but they also have, of course, effects that one doesn't want and I agree with you that we have to study this further and more extensively to see how we can improve the situation without letting the regime off the hook with regard to the excessive documented interest of the government of Iraq for weapons of mass destruction.

JP: Well, why aren't there sanctions on Israel, which has the only known nuclear weapons in the Middle East?

PVW: Well, Israel is a country that has been surrounded by countries that tried to wipe it out. It's not exactly the same situation.

JP: But it has nuclear weapons.

PVW: Well, yes, but we have not yet attacked or put sanctions on every country that . . .

JP: It [Israel] attacks Lebanon almost every day of the week. Why aren't there sanctions on Turkey, which has displaced something like three million Kurds and caused the deaths of perhaps 30,000 Kurds? Why weren't there sanctions on Turkey?

PVW: [After a long pause] Yes, well, there are many countries that do things that we are not happy with, but this is the situation which has come into being due to the invasion of Kuwait and that is the explanation for it . . .

JP: Do you believe that people have human rights, no matter where they live and under what system they live, [and] that the human rights belong to the individual?

PVW: Yes.

JP: Well, doesn't that, if you apply that to Iraq, don't, then, the effects that these sanctions have had, documented by the UN itself – aren't they violating the human rights of literally millions of people?

PVW: The human rights in Iraq are a very difficult subject. It is also documented in the United Nations that the regime has committed very serious human rights violations. You're aware of that?

JP: Of course.

PVW: So I think we are constantly concerned about human rights one way or the other.

JP: They're no different. You said they're a very difficult subject but, to an ordinary Iraqi, human rights belong to them – you would agree with that – regardless of the fact that they have been lucky or unlucky to have been born in Iraq. Doesn't hurting them violate those human rights?

PVW: Yes, but obviously this is exactly why I say that we do not want to hurt the population of Iraq and this is why we are trying to improve the system.

JP: The numbers of children – 4,000 under-fives dying every month – [are] terrible figures. This has been known for years. Why is it taking so long to deliberate on how to get over this so-called complex issue?

PVW: I think we could have solved the matter fairly easily if all members of the Security Council were determined to improve that situation but at the same time make sure that there are guarantees that Iraq would not again develop weapons of mass destruction. The fact that the major powers disagree on that makes it extremely difficult to solve this situation.

This was the first time that divisions on the Security Council over sanctions were admitted, and the ripple effect of this within government circles would have been considerable. For the public, the exchange between Pilger and van Walsum revealed not only the intransigence of the UN sanctions committee but its hypocrisy in singling out Iraq for trade embargoes while allowing the crimes of other regimes to go unpunished. It is this hypocrisy and selectivity of the application of power politics that Pilger has constantly strived to demonstrate to his viewers.

8. TRUTH GAMES

'TRUTH', 'OBJECTIVITY', 'impartiality' and 'balance' are notions that have figured prominently in examinations of John Pilger's work and how it fits into the framework of television. 'I think the "impartiality" and "objectivity" lost their dictionary meaning when they entered the mythology of liberal England,' said Pilger. 'They are code for the Establishment view of the world, against which most perspectives are measured. What I do perhaps offers a counter to the vast *imbalance* in the media that favours a consensual, essentially Establishment view. Of course, categorizing me as "committed", "crusading" and so on is often no more than a subtle way of discrediting.'[1]

To understand the limits of what is considered acceptable in broadcasting, their premises have to be traced back to the early days of the BBC, which was created a corporation by government charter in 1927, five years after its birth as the British Broadcasting Company. It was an élite organization right from the upper reaches of the English class system and its mission was to promote the view from on high through a fog of paternalism, so it clearly had no intention of upsetting the Establishment. Lord Reith, the BBC's founder, laid down rules intended to ensure 'impartiality', 'objectivity' and 'balance'. A defender of his friends and associates in the Establishment, what he really meant was soon vividly illustrated. During the General Strike of 1926, he wrote Conservative Prime Minister Stanley Baldwin's radio speeches, damning the strikes, while refusing to air the views of Labour leaders until after the dispute was over.

Reithian concepts seemed to be relaxed in the 1960s under the guiding hand of the BBC's more innovative director-general, Hugh Greene. *That Was the Week That Was* satirized politicians and socio-realistic plays by directors such as Ken Loach portrayed the underbelly of modern Britain. The documentaries of Denis Mitchell, such as *Morning in the Streets*, *Night in the City* and *In Prison*, allowed ordinary people to air their views in their own environment, without the interference of those in authority, who dominated so much media coverage.

Mitchell left the BBC in the early 1960s to join Granada Television and teamed up with a former BBC colleague, Norman Swallow, to make documentaries such as the Italia Prize-winning *A Wedding on Saturday*, set in a Yorkshire mining village. The pair went on to make the series *This England*, again allowing people to speak for themselves with little interference from an Establishment narrator. Similarly, Brian Moser's Granada series *Disappearing World* featured indigenous people all over the world who were allowed to tell their own stories.

With his concern for social justice and the oppressed, it might have seemed natural that Pilger should follow in the footsteps of these distinctive documentary-makers. But, by the late 1960s, Greene's liberal regime had run its course. The BBC was now under pressure to negotiate its licence fee with Harold Wilson's government, which appointed Lord Hill, a former Cabinet minister, as the Corporation's chairman. Lord Hill had previously held the same post at the Independent Television Authority (later the Independent Broadcasting Authority), where he ensured tighter control over ITV programmes. The Establishment connection was continued at the ITA when Lord Hill was replaced by Lord Aylestone, another former Cabinet minister.

Whatever the subject he chose, Pilger's intervention as a mediating voice, a journalist who looked at politics from the ground up, not the other way round, ensured that his move into television would not be easy. His first two documentaries for Granada (see Chapters 1 and 2) were both considered contentious by those in authority. (A programme is not in itself controversial. It becomes so only once someone quarrels with its content.) The second, *Conversations with a Working Man*, might have come from a Denis Mitchell film. However, Pilger's attempt to put one man's views into a wider political context fell foul of a Granada executive responsible for *World in Action*, despite that programme's track record of making programmes that did not always conform to the broadcasting authorities' rules of impartiality. Bemused, Pilger found himself under orders to change 'working class' to 'working heritage' and even to delete references to 'the people', which the executive insisted was a 'Marxist term'.

These were restrictions he had never experienced in print journalism. Working for the *Daily Mirror* had given Pilger a freedom to write for an audience that was broadly sympathetic to coverage of human rights struggles and left-wing politics. Whereas most other newspapers gave their support to the Conservative Party, the *Mirror* provided a journalistic home for the young Australian whose often subtle, descriptive writing won him the first of many awards, Descriptive Writer of the Year, within three years of joining the paper, then the biggest-selling in the Western world. (The next year, 1967, he became the youngest journalist to win the highest award of Journalist of the Year and, twelve years later, the first to win it twice.)

Television was different. It might have been argued that with only three channels at the end of the 1960s – BBC1, BBC2 and ITV – there was a case for strict regulation. However, there has since been no shift in the official notion of 'impartiality' as it is embodied in broadcasting law, despite the expansion of British television to five terrestrial television channels and scores more via satellite and cable.

Not surprisingly, as one who has always challenged authority, Pilger has often come into conflict with it. In the 1970s, the IBA dealt with his 'dissenting' voice in the *Pilger* series by adding a 'personal view' disclaimer at the beginning and end of each documentary. The BBC even extended this to drama when

Pilger's television play *The Last Day*, about the end of the Vietnam War, was broadcast on BBC2 in 1983. It was introduced as 'his personal view of those chaotic, final hours'. There is little doubt that Pilger confused the system. He was difficult to tag. Australian stereotyping seemed inappropriate. He belonged to no political party and his class was uncertain. A testy individualist, he wrote eloquently about popular movements. He was a talented and quite fearless reporter who saw himself as an agent of people, not power. That, above all, made him dangerous.

A long war with those who controlled television was beginning. His most public and longest-running battle with the IBA was over *The Truth Game*, a documentary about nuclear arms propaganda. The film argued that Western politicians used 'official truths' – propaganda – to justify spending money on more and more nuclear weapons, and that the 'unofficial truth' was that possession of these weapons made the prospect of nuclear war more likely. At the time, nuclear weapons was one of two subjects guaranteed to stir the British political class. With American Cruise missiles due to be deployed in Britain in the 1980s and a general election due in 1983, Pilger's contribution, of course, worried the defenders of 'official truth'.

The second subject, Ireland, Pilger had reported for the *Mirror*, but not television. By 1981, there was renewed debate about both Northern Ireland and nuclear weapons, but ill-defined limits were imposed. The apparently new climate allowed the screening of Robert Kee's BBC series *Ireland – A Television History* and ITV's potentially more controversial *The Troubles* without the censorial problems experienced by programme-makers over most of the previous twenty years.

'I can't remember a period when there's been such free reporting of Ireland since the British army went in,' said veteran Northern Ireland reporter Mary Holland at the time. 'This has happened because the political climate has radically changed. The government is trying to approach the Northern Ireland problem in a new way. By implication, what they seem to be saying is that the period of internal solutions in Northern Ireland is over and the road we're going down is some sort of loose federation of the two parts of Ireland. Although Mrs Thatcher may personally find programmes like *The Troubles* slightly hard to take, it reflects the policies she's trying to make. The parameters in which we are allowed to debate are those which are helpful to the government's present policy. The comparatively benign atmosphere is something which could be snatched from us very quickly.'[2]

And so it was when the Thatcher government allowed Bobby Sands and nine other IRA hunger strikers in the Maze jail to starve themselves to death rather than grant them political status. When *The Troubles* was repeated in 1989, twenty years after British troops were sent to Northern Ireland, the words of some interviewees were replaced by captions, in accordance with the government's new law, passed in 1988, which banned the broadcast of voices of members of paramilitary organizations. (The ban became farcical when broadcasters attempted to circumvent it by using actors' voices to speak the words of Gerry Adams and others. However, neither the BBC nor the ITV companies challenged the legal basis of the ban. This was left to Pilger and five other journalists whose action, backed by the National Union of Journalists, went all the way to the Law Lords.)

Finally, when *World in Action* made *The Propaganda War*, due to be broadcast in 1981, shortly after the death of the fourth IRA hunger striker, Patsy O'Hara, Granada Television withdrew the programme rather than adhere to the IBA's demands to remove footage of Bobby Sands's strike and a scene showing O'Hara's open coffin lying in state, guarded by hooded men. The window for 'debate' on Ireland, opened by the British government, was closed in less than a year.

Reporting of the nuclear arms race was equally fragile. In the autumn of 1981, Jonathan Dimbleby's documentary *The Bomb* was screened as part of his ITV series *Jonathan Dimbleby in Evidence*. Dimbleby had more of a reputation for questioning the 'official' viewpoint than his famous father, Richard, and elder brother,

David, and made clear from the beginning of *The Bomb* that the United States had started the nuclear arms race by developing the atomic bomb and dropping it on Japan, killing 70,000 people in Hiroshima instantly and many more with lethal doses of nuclear radiation. Dimbleby also questioned the need for the world's superpowers to stockpile nuclear weapons to the extent that they could obliterate countries many times over.

This was the first serious examination of the nuclear arms issue by television since *The War Game*, director Peter Watkins's remarkable 1965 dramatized reconstruction of the aftermath of a nuclear attack on London, which had never been shown by the BBC, claiming that it was too horrific. In truth, the programme was banned because it questioned the then Labour government's policy of nuclear deterrence – a revelation made by author and media academic Michael Tracey while researching his biography of former BBC director-general Hugh Greene. Tracey uncovered a letter from BBC chairman Lord Normanbrook to the Secretary to the Cabinet, Sir Burke Trend. 'The showing of the film on television might well have a significant effect on public attitudes towards the policy of nuclear deterrent,' wrote Lord Normanbrook.[3]

A 1963 *World in Action* programme about the government's defence spending had previously been banned by the ITA because it was said to contravene the Broadcasting Act's code of impartiality. This was the first recorded act of political censorship in British commercial television, although a talk show in which actress Siobhan McKenna referred to IRA internees as 'young idealists' and seven 10-minute reports by Alan Whicker for the current affairs programme *Tonight* had already been banned by the BBC.

The BBC had also censored an earlier programme about nuclear weapons. Until ITV arrived in 1955 and ITN began asking difficult political questions, the BBC had exercised the wartime Fourteen-Day Rule, which banned 'ex parte' statements on any issue for two weeks before it was due to be debated in Parliament. Not even MPs were allowed to debate impending legislation. The BBC appeared to assume that, once MPs were elected to Parliament, they were not to be questioned by the people who put them there.

As a result, a BBC programme called *In the News* was banned from discussing the hydrogen bomb in 1955 because the bomb was to be debated in Parliament within the following two weeks. The Fourteen-Day Rule was scrapped the following year. However, the feeling that it was not the broadcasters' job to ruffle feathers continued among many in television. So it is not surprising that Pilger's attack on successive British governments' nuclear weapons policies in *The Truth Game* should become perhaps the greatest controversy of his television career.

In the fifteen years up to 1980, the subject of nuclear weapons was not once debated in Parliament – which set the political agenda for most of the media – and rarely examined on television. Pilger's documentary highlighted the propaganda, which he contended was to persuade the public to support the government's policy of stockpiling more and more nuclear weapons. He revealed that Britain had more nuclear bases per square mile than any other country.

The Truth Game, a 90-minute programme that took eighteen months to make, was scheduled to be screened by ITV on 23 November 1982. It would start at 9pm, in peak-time, and continue after *News at Ten*. On 4 November, the film was withdrawn at the insistence of the Independent Broadcasting Authority after being viewed by the IBA's full board, on the recommendation of David Glencross, its deputy director of television. Glencross wanted what the IBA called a 'complementary' documentary made before *The Truth Game* was given the go-ahead, despite the fact that the Pilger film conformed to the IBA's guidelines on 'personal view' programmes – as did all his programmes. Some of Pilger's earlier documentaries had been 'balanced' by others. This was the first time that such a demand had been made *after* the production of a programme but *before* its transmission, and it extended the IBA's editorial control.

On the day the IBA's decision to postpone *The Truth Game* was announced, Pilger told *News at Ten*, 'I think the IBA is possibly afraid of what an audience might think of this programme.' But Lord Thomson, chairman of the IBA, denied that this was a case of backdoor censorship. 'John Pilger is perfectly entitled to his point of view but he mustn't feel that he has a monopoly of that point of view [*sic*],' he insisted.[4] However, Lord Thomson remained silent on the 'other' point of view, which largely echoed government policy and enjoyed a virtual monopoly on regular television news programmes. Indeed, the IBA at no time questioned *The Truth Game*'s adherence to its panoply of rules. Like *The War Game*, it was the film's 'unofficial truth' that was unpalatable, and the fact that Pilger's documentary provided a long overdue balance to the 'pro-nuclear' case. Moreover, most of those whom Pilger interviewed came from inside the West's military and political establishment.

On the anti-Establishment Channel Four current affairs programme *The Friday Alternative* – shortly before it was axed by the IBA, which claimed it contravened the Broadcasting Act – Pilger agreed that the Authority's action might not look like censorship but it meant that 'when a television company comes to make a programme about this subject again, it will have to think very hard because it means two programmes'. He added, 'What has happened to this film should be the final sequence in my film because it's a perfect example – it is backdoor censorship, it's nod-and-wink censorship, it's insidious censorship. It also says to the British public that your good sense is really not good enough for us – that you can't make your own conclusions on the basis of the evidence this programme is showing you.'[5]

The British public, as well as those with a vested interest, joined in a media debate on the postponement of *The Truth Game*. The letters page of the *Guardian* provided a lively platform. One correspondent suggested that Pilger's documentary should be shown, as planned, and 'balanced' by the Ministry of Defence's blatantly propagandist film *The Peace Game*, which was made to be shown in schools. 'CND might even be persuaded to show it with every showing of *The War Game*,' wrote Louis Mackay, from North London, 'because it is a perfect illustration of many of its points, and very funny in the manner of forty-year-old Movietone newsreels.'[6]

Pilger and director David Munro mischievously wrote a letter asking how *The Peace Game*, less than one-third of the length of *The Truth Game*, could possibly cost £70,000 to make – compared with the £90,000 spent by Central Television on their 90-minute film. 'Surely,' they added, 'as the £70,000 was taxpayers' money, the Ministry of Defence should explain: why such an amount of public money was spent on raw propaganda; and how exactly the money was spent?'[7]

As the argument proceeded, the IBA announced that the 'complementary' documentary would be presented by London *Evening Standard* writer Max Hastings, an Establishment journalist who, in June 1982, marched into Port Stanley with British troops at the end of the Falklands War and was later appointed editor of the *Daily Telegraph*. His participation seemed to guarantee that his film would broadly take the government line of maintaining a nuclear deterrence. However, Hastings refused to present a point-by-point rebuttal of *The Truth Game*, as the IBA had originally asked for, and even criticized the government's handling of the Cruise issue. With his film, *The War About Peace*, in production, the IBA allowed *The Truth Game* to be allocated a new transmission date – Monday 28 February 1983, again wrapped around *News at Ten*. Viewers would have to wait another two months before they could see the Hastings documentary.

The absurdity of the episode, which was also a fine example of the way those running broadcasting's bureaucracy saw no absurdity at all in their actions, was highlighted on the morning of *The Truth Game*'s transmission. TV-am, which had just taken to the airwaves as ITV's breakfast-time franchise holder, showed a clip from the documentary of pictures from the Hiroshima bombing with comments by the veteran journalist Wilfred

Burchett, who reported from Japan in the aftermath of the Second World War.

'They really are horrific pictures, aren't they?' said presenter Angela Rippon. 'And, in fact, we're only going to be seeing the programme that includes that clip tonight because a follow-up programme putting the other case has been agreed on and that can be seen in two months' time.' It was difficult to see what 'the other case', in this instance, was, but Rippon appeared to believe her own words.

She then turned to Pilger, in the studio, and said, 'John, what I have to ask is, what's a fine journalist like you doing a programme which, apparently, is so terribly one-sided?' Not surprisingly, Pilger did not agree. Conducted by someone who was clearly not a supporter of his brand of journalism, the interview continued rapidly downhill.

Pilger pointed out that government propaganda was not necessarily aimed at potential enemies but at the British public, to which Rippon retorted, 'I wonder if you aren't actually being a little naïve in saying that people don't realize that propaganda comes from our own side. We were well aware that that was what the government were doing during the Second World War.' Whether or not the British public knew they were being fed propaganda about nuclear weapons or not, *The Truth Game* sought to unravel truth from deception, the essence of propaganda. Without allowing Pilger to refute his alleged naïveté, Rippon asked about the 'many secrets' that had been kept from the public about nuclear weapons and were being revealed in *The Truth Game*. 'How can they have been secret if you're actually able to find out about them?' she asked. With the first hint of a smile, Pilger gave the examples of the previous Labour government secretly committing Britain to the £1 billion Chevaline Programme that had 'modernized' the nuclear arsenal and Tory defence secretary Francis Pym's admission of only twelve nuclear bases in 1980, when the real figure was 103.[8]

Rippon's interview with Pilger followed a preview of *The*

Truth Game in *The Sunday Times*'s television supplement, 'View', in which the BBC's David Dimbleby criticized Pilger's choice of 'friendly witnesses' and claimed that his failure to test his theories 'against the evidence of those who might disagree' amounted to 'a serenely unchallenged case from CND'.[9] As with Lord Thomson's earlier comments about Pilger's 'monopoly' point of view, Dimbleby chose to ignore the fact that this journalist was testing an issue whose one-sidedness had enjoyed a monopoly hearing on television.

At 9pm on Monday 28 February 1983, the viewing audience was finally allowed to make up its own mind about a film that had become news in its own right. The nuclear age began, said Pilger in his opening piece to camera, with the atomic bombing of Hiroshima in August 1945, followed three days later by the destruction of Nagasaki. Words such as 'experiment', 'success' and 'good results', used by American president Harry S. Truman to describe the 'unique and horrific carnage of nuclear war', were the first examples of a new kind of propaganda – reassuring language, and comic-book names for the bombs, 'Little Boy' and 'Fat Man', to distance the public from the horrors of nuclear war.

'Above all, we were conditioned to accept a so-called strategy for possessing nuclear weapons called deterrence, which no one could explain rationally and which blurred the fact that a massive nuclear arms race was well under way,' said Pilger. The secrecy, especially the failure of Parliament to debate nuclear weapons for fifteen years, was aimed not so much at a potential enemy as at the British people. Surely, he asked, in a democracy – unlike the Soviet Union – secrecy and propaganda should not control how we think?

There followed a catalogue of 'official' and 'unofficial' truths – propaganda compared with realities less known by the public and less liked by the politicians. Western governments claimed that the deterrence of a nuclear arsenal capable of wiping out everyone fifty times over had 'given us a generation of peace', but thirty-six

countries now had the bomb or the capacity to build it and war
between the superpowers had never been closer.

The Manhattan Project, which developed the atomic bomb,
continued even after Allied agents discovered in 1944 that
Germany did not possess such a bomb. Thus the fears of physicist
Albert Einstein, who originally urged President Roosevelt to
speed up uranium research, were unfounded, as Einstein himself
had agreed. The bomb was dropped on Hiroshima on the order of
Roosevelt's successor, Harry Truman, even though Japan was
defeated – the Americans had broken the Japanese codes, were
mining their harbours and had command of their skies.

Australian journalist Wilfred Burchett, who had reported exclusively from Hiroshima for the London *Daily Express* and
revealed the insidious effects of radiation, described 'a city
steam-rollered out of existence' and visited its two remaining
hospitals, where he found people dying in the most horrible way
from the after-effects of the bombing, while American public
relations officers kept other correspondents away from the victims. Burchett's front-page story, headlined 'The Atomic Plague'
and beginning, 'I write this as a warning to the world . . .', was
officially denied. Japanese film showing the terrible suffering was
secretly shipped to Washington and not released for twenty-three
years, as was the official American film, which confirmed
Burchett's reporting.

Pilger added that a secret Manhattan Project committee had
decided that the first Japanese target should be a city previously
spared from bombing so that the effects of a single atomic bomb
could be gauged effectively. The 'official' truth was that the bomb
was dropped to end the war, but the 'unofficial' truth was that it
was an experiment. New film showed a hospital in Hiroshima
where a thousand people a year were still dying of radiation.

Former American vice-president Henry Wallace revealed in
1946, reported Pilger, that he had warned Roosevelt during the
war that the US military had been planning a 'preventative atomic
strike' against the Soviet Union, three years before the Russians

exploded their first bomb. Arms technology now dominated both American and Soviet economies. In the late 1950s and the 1960s, the propaganda centred on a 'missile gap' between the United States and the Soviet Union after the Soviets put the first satellite into space. Former chief Pentagon scientist Dr Herbert York told Pilger that this was used to confuse the public at a time when the United States was technologically well ahead of the Soviet Union.

Admiral Gene La Rocque, director of the Center for Defense Information in Washington and a former Pentagon senior nuclear strategist, told Pilger, 'We have been three to five years ahead of the Soviet Union in the development of every strategic weapons system that has come down the pipe since we developed and exploded the atomic bomb at Hiroshima and Nagasaki, [and] the hydrogen bomb. We deployed our ICBMs first, we had the first jet aircraft to carry the bombs to the Soviet Union, the first nuclear-powered submarines, the first solar-propellered missiles in our submarines, we went to MIRV ten years before the Soviets came up with their Multiple Independent Re-entry Vehicles.' La Rocque added that the West had more strategic nuclear weapons than the Soviets.

Professor Lawrence Freedman, director of the Royal Institute of International Affairs in London, asserted that the Soviets had more weapons, although he conceded that the United States might have more warheads 'at the moment' and was certainly the 'pacesetter' on quality. For 'impartial analysis', Pilger turned to the Stockholm International Peace Research Institute's 1982 year-book, which stated that the United States was 'up to five years ahead of Russia'.

John Foster Dulles, US secretary of state in the 1950s, had spoken of creating 'an emotional atmosphere akin to a wartime psychology' and 'the idea of a threat from without' to persuade the public that it was necessary to build up a nuclear arsenal, adding that 'the manipulation of statistics, sometimes known as "disinformation", is one way of creating this wartime psychology'.

Describing this disinformation, strategic weapons analyst Dan Smith explained that Western statistics showing that the Warsaw Pact had more than three times as many tanks in Eastern Europe as NATO had in Western Europe did not tell the complete story because many of the Soviet bloc tanks were much older and less efficient. NATO had about 250,000 anti-tank weapons and other systems capable of destroying the Warsaw Pact's ground forces. The original figures told only 'half-truths'. 'From half-truths,' Smith said, 'one moves on to distortions, and from distortions one goes on to downright lies.'

In 1979, Greenham Common, near Newbury, in Berkshire, was chosen by a secret committee of NATO as the site for more than half of the American Cruise and Pershing missiles to be based in Britain, supposedly to balance Russia's SS-20 missiles aimed at Western Europe. However, said Pilger, Cruise was designed for a nuclear war in Europe and controlled by the United States. Outside the base, Joan Ruddock, chairperson of the Campaign for Nuclear Disarmament, examined a Ministry of Defence brochure that included graphs intended to convince the public that the Soviet Union had more nuclear weapons than NATO. 'But this is only one category of weapons,' she said, 'so this is an extremely dishonest presentation.' Dan Smith said that the published figures for NATO bombers capable of dropping nuclear weapons on the Soviet Union did not include at least four types of aircraft based in Western Europe. He dismissed this 'low-quality propaganda'.

'Now let's play a new television game called "Find the Missing Bases",' said Pilger, standing next to a map of Britain in the manner of a weather forecaster and clearly enjoying himself. There followed a humorous account of defence secretary Francis Pym responding to questions about the number of American bases on British soil. They rose from the twelve that Pym had admitted to in June 1980, in response to a question from Labour MP Bob Cryer, to 56 as a result of further questions – the 'scores' were illustrated by small bulbs lighting up on the map. The tally subsequently rose by another 47 bases – 'a long way from Mr Pym's dozen'.

Standing outside the Ministry of Defence in London, Pilger explained that his request to interview then defence secretary John Knott had been refused but that he had been offered an 'unattributable briefing'. 'Sorry,' he said, 'I've broken rule number one in telling you that.' Public relations officer Ian McDonald, best known for his televised press conferences during the Falklands War, had taken Pilger, director David Munro and researcher Nicholas Claxton to see an MoD official but instructed them afterwards that the meeting had effectively not happened and nothing discussed could be reported or attributed. An MoD public relations officer had offered film that was fourteen years old. 'The British public,' he said with a laugh, 'would not know the difference,' reported Pilger.

Access to the American base at Filingdales in North Yorkshire, which is intended to give early warning of a nuclear attack, gave Pilger and Munro the opportunity to film a thrice-weekly exercise reconstructing what would happen if a nuclear missile were fired at Britain during the minutes before impact. Over film of the early-morning London skyline, Pilger quoted a child survivor of Hiroshima who described the sudden flash he saw before 'fire broke out everywhere' and he and his family tried to find shelter under a bridge. The child's father died almost immediately, followed by his mother several days later.

A cartoon demonstrated how politicians and others in authority would get priority shelters in the event of a nuclear attack while the general public were already being offered mortgages on their own fall-out shelters. The soundtrack was the Abbey National Building Society's familiar 'Abbey habit' commercial jingle. Film of a shelter below a South London block of flats – designated not for the residents, but for police, the military and public servants – was juxtaposed with Pilger's voiceover quoting the government's *Protect and Survive* booklet, based on its civil defence plans. The public were to tape up toilet handles, stock up on tinned soup and put their heads in bags. Pilger said there were no evacuation plans, which meant that most of the population would be sacrificed while the Establishment was spared. 'What all this reveals,' he said, 'is that civil defence is simply a propaganda term and preparing us for war is the real aim.'

Footage of NATO exercises in Germany was accompanied by the theme from *M*A*S*H*, the long-running American comedy series set in the Korean War, with its memorable lyrics, 'Suicide is painless.' Reporting from the frontline of this potential German battlefield, Pilger pursued his theme of how language was used to distance people from reality. Terms such as 'death' and 'destruction' were no longer used, 'bombs' were now 'systems', 'soldiers' were 'human assets', 'civilians' were 'support structure' and 'dead civilians' were 'collateral damage' – 'that old favourite from Vietnam'.

Pilger asked General Bernard Rogers, US Supreme Allied Commander, Europe, at a press conference why he thought Europeans were increasingly frightened of NATO nuclear weapons on their own soil. 'If we're going to deter at all levels,' replied Rogers, 'they tend to be more frightened of our stationing weapons or modernizing our weapons system in order to accomplish that mission of keeping them from being used by the Soviet Union than they are frightened of those weapons that cause us to have to modernize in order to deter.'

A follow-up question by another journalist about Europeans' fears of a nuclear war appeared to enrage Rogers, who said, 'Listen, young man, don't talk to me about fear of war – I've been in 'em. And let me tell you, it's a stupid way to do business . . . None of us want to go back to war but, because we fear that there might be a war, it doesn't mean we shouldn't take the steps necessary to keep there from being one.'

Paul Warnke, the United States' chief negotiator in the Strategic Arms Limitation Talks between the superpowers in the late 1970s, told Pilger that the Soviet Union's leaders were genuinely afraid of nuclear war and their overtures for arms reduction should be assessed and taken seriously. To reject these would only bring war closer, although the American administration was divided between those who favoured arms control negotiations and others who simply wanted to 'out-compete' the Soviets. 'The idea you can fight, survive and win a nuclear war is calamitous nonsense,' added Warnke.

Summing up, Pilger said that the tide was turning in favour of those who questioned the build-up of nuclear arms, and opinion polls showed that a clear majority of the British people were opposed to the stationing of Cruise missiles on their own soil. The public were asking why their country had made itself a prime target for the Russians, who themselves had every reason to fear a nuclear war. 'In spite of our own insidious propaganda and secrecy,' he said, 'we live in a democracy and the Russian people do not. Surely, then, it is we who can and should take the initiative. Nuclear weapons were never an act of God. *Nothing* is inevitable.' As *The Truth Game*'s closing credits finished, an ITV announcer intoned, 'Max Hastings will be looking at another aspect of this important issue in eight weeks' time.'

Some of the press reaction to *The Truth Game* was predictable. Newspapers that had given unerring support to the nuclear arms build-up attacked it. Like parliamentary lobby correspondents, television critics usually follow a conservative agenda and do not like dissent. Peter Ackroyd, a television reviewer for *The Times* before finding acclaim as a novelist and the biographer of T.S. Eliot and Charles Dickens, tried to play down the programme. 'Most of last night's pictures were, in any case,' he wrote, 'familiar: the victims of Hiroshima, the absurd nuclear "defence" films, the talking heads from various defence agencies, even the by now ritual appearance of Petra Kelly, the garrulous and somewhat vapid leader of the German "Greens".'[10] This was a perfect example of Pilger's critics using other methods to denigrate his documentaries when they find it difficult to argue with the evidence presented.

More surprising was Stanley Reynolds's attack on Pilger in the

Guardian, whose editorial policies at least appeared to question the Establishment viewpoint. Almost half of Reynolds's review concentrated on Pilger's appearance – 'his popstar good looks . . . his affected speech pattern . . . his carefully ironed shirt . . . his out-of-fashion long hairstyle' – and concluded that he was 'some sort of macho version of the dolly bird, like Joanna Lumley in drag'. Reynolds also mounted personal attacks on the women in the film, Joan Ruddock and Petra Kelly. Whereas retired US Admiral Gene La Rocque and US arms negotiator Paul Warnke had spoken 'with a voice of authority – they were believable', those interviews were 'offset' by 'some housewife in England or Germany'. He added, 'The general, presumably, knows what he's talking about and yet John Pilger asked us to come down in favour of the housewife. It was this sort of emotional appeal that made you doubt the whole programme.'[11]

The *Guardian*'s letters page was bombarded with complaints. Referring to the paper's regular television reviewer, Claire Newton of South Croydon simply asked, 'Where, oh where, was Nancy Banks-Smith?'[12] Mary Dinsdale of Hastings asked, 'Should not your readers of Stanley Reynolds's opinions now demand an alternative and/or unbiased review of John Pilger's *The Truth Game*?'[13] Joan Ruddock (later to become an MP) wrote to point out that Conservative MP Michael Heseltine had just attacked her as 'a failed Labour candidate' and Stanley Reynolds 'calls me an English housewife'.[14] By the end of the week, the *Guardian* announced on its letters page: 'We have so far received 206 letters criticizing Stanley Reynolds's review of John Pilger's *The Truth Game* (ITV, February 28). In an attempt to mollify our postman we are closing this correspondence. – Ed.'[15]

However, the 'correspondence' on the saga was not quite closed. Max Hastings's 'complementary' documentary, *The War About Peace*, reached ITV screens on 21 April 1983. After its transmission, Stanley Reynolds was unrepentant, applauding this 'brilliant, low-key answer to Pilger's emotional approach' and the 'most distinguished group' of interviewees, who included

Michael Howard, Regius Professor of History at Oxford University, Michael Heseltine and George Bush. In an attempt to head off criticism of his concentration on Pilger's appearance, Reynolds began his *Guardian* review with a description of 'big, tall (6ft 5in), jut-jawed Max Hastings', with his 'clear, level gaze, that firm, old-fashioned square tone of voice and those big, black specs' that made him look like Clark Kent. 'I shouldn't apologize for all this,' he added. 'Television is television: important as what they say is the way they look and the way they say it. Supermax and Bondi looked the parts.'[16]

In reality, *The War About Peace* was a glossy 'Ministry of Information' job, at best just another television programme broadly promoting successive governments' nuclear deterrence policy, whereas *The Truth Game* contributed dramatically to an overdue public debate on nuclear weapons in advance of a general election. Indeed, it gave the issue a new lease of life on television. In May 1983, the BBC broadcast the American-made *Great Nuclear Debate*, which was notable only for its total exclusion of the opponents of nuclear policies. Channel Four launched its own 'Nuclear Week', including a studio debate equally bereft of opposition opinion. The point lost by these programmes was that the subject was now on a public agenda.

The IBA's unprecedented action in demanding a 'complementary' programme to *The Truth Game* after its completion was repeated in the same year, 1983, when the Authority sought to censor the airing of another taboo issue: the collaboration of the British trade union leadership with the Conservative government. Acclaimed director Ken Loach had made a documentary series, *Questions of Leadership*, in which rank-and-file trade unionists criticized certain right-wing trade union leaders for allegedly supporting the Thatcher government's assault on the power of shop-floor workers. Made by Central Television for screening on Channel Four, the four-part series was filmed in 1982 and scheduled to be shown in September 1983. However, during the previous summer, the IBA declared that the programmes contravened the Broadcasting Act. Channel Four asked Loach to edit them down to two 50-minute films and Central to make half-hour 'balancing' programmes to be shown after each one. When this was done, a Queen's Counsel consulted by Central Television asked for one small deletion from Loach's films, to which he agreed. At this stage, Loach believed that the programmes had finally been passed as a 'fair risk'. To his surprise, Channel Four and Central announced that they were still 'under discussion' because of 'legal difficulties'.[17]

The Directors Guild of Great Britain accused the broadcasting authorities of political censorship, presenting the extraordinary spectacle of the Guild's chief censorship officer, the right-wing Michael Winner, backing a documentary made by someone whose political views were the diametric opposite of his own. 'I am opposed politically to Ken Loach's philosophy,' he said. 'However, there have been many TV programmes suggesting lack of democracy in left-wing trade unions. Further, having investigated this matter fully, I am drawn to the conclusion that Ken Loach's views are basically correct.'[18] Such an alliance raised huge questions about official attempts to block the films. Eight days after the Directors Guild's accusation of political censorship, Central announced that the Loach documentaries were 'defamatory and would have no adequate defence at law',[19] and would not be screened. Loach replied that he had already conceded every request for changes made by an expert lawyer and any material still considered libellous could be replaced. 'The only explanation, therefore, is that this is not a legal, but a political decision,' said Loach, 'and, therefore, of concern to anyone who is concerned with freedom of speech.'[20]

Pilger had not seen the last of the IBA's censorship on nuclear matters. In January 1989, he presented *Reporting with John Pilger*, in *The English Programme* series of Channel Four schools broadcasts. It was one of four programmes under the title *Models of Writing*, aimed at fifth- and sixth-formers and discussing uses of language. Pilger put forward the idea of 'Nukespeak', the use of language to 'sell' the nuclear arms race (which would have been familiar to viewers of *The Truth Game*). The IBA insisted on cutting one sentence to improve the 'clarity' of the programme. Although each film in the series was personal, none of the others was censored. One featured Terry Jones, of *Monty Python* fame, talking about his writing for the *Guardian* and another discussed the art of reviewing.

In a letter published in the *Guardian* on the day his programme was broadcast, Pilger explained that an advance copy of his script had been sent by Thames Television to the IBA. In response, Christopher Jones, the Authority's deputy head of educational broadcasting, wrote that 'out of several possible cuts . . . one seemed quite unavoidable'. Pilger identified the cut:

> Today, bigger and more lethal weapons are described as 'modernized systems'. A nuclear war plan is known as a 'defence strategy' and the notion of attacking first with nuclear weapons is called 'flexible response'. With these words, many people, I believe, have been conditioned to accept the possession and stockpiling of nuclear weapons not only as normal, but necessary.

The final sentence was deleted. Pilger wrote that the IBA official had, in a letter to Thames Television, claimed that there was 'absolutely no evidence presented to justify the quasi-psychological word "conditioned", nor any to suggest that many people "accept" the situation, nor, if they did, that their acceptance was related in any way to the "Nukespeak" factor'. He pronounced, wrote Pilger, that 'it is not of course the job of this programme to tackle the more controversial themes in depth. Therefore the clarity of the actual aim of this programme is improved if the unsupported assertions are thinned out.' Pilger responded to this:

> I cannot find reference in the Broadcasting Act to the IBA having the power to dictate 'the job' of any television programme. Nor is there reference to schools programmes being prohibited from

tackling 'the more controversial themes'. Indeed, the Thames
series producer, believing that such themes are an integral part of
the education of mature students, encouraged me to tackle them.
In his dictum to Thames, Mr Jones referred to 'the requirements
for due impartiality and accuracy under the Act'. My programme
was clearly covered by the personal view guidelines of the IBA and
it contained not a single inaccuracy.[21]

One letter written to the *Guardian* asked why 'a known radical
journalist' was asked to make a programme if 'due impartiality
and balance' were required. In a further letter to the newspaper,
Pilger wrote:

> If the schools programme I made for Thames Television is to be
> considered 'radical', then that merely underlines the effectiveness
> of the Prevailing Bias which, in its crudest form, is establishment
> propaganda. My programme was 'radical' insofar as the media is
> now so influenced by establishment thinking and Thatcher's
> crusade that any serious departure from this bias, any seeking
> of truth through 'unacceptable' sources, any sustained attempt at
> diversity of analysis and viewpoint, appear almost extreme. Watch
> once bold reporters struggle through safe, pre-scripted formats . . .
>
> It is necessary only to examine the coverage of the two great
> upheavals of the 1980s, the Falklands War and the miners' strike,
> to understand how faithfully the Reithian code has been followed.
> Minutes of a BBC Weekly Review Board meeting during the
> Falklands War show that the BBC had decided that its reporting of
> the war was to be shaped to suit 'the emotional sensibilities of the
> public', and that the weight of BBC coverage would be concerned
> with government statements of policy and that an objective style
> was felt to be 'an unnecessary irritation'. War always gives the
> game away.[22]

Following *The Truth Game*, Pilger made *Frontline – The Search for
Truth in Wartime*, directed by Ross Devenish, who in 1972 had

made the ATV drama *The Siege of Dien Bien Phu*, a drama about the defeat of the French in Vietnam, which was notable for blending in with the action actual footage shot by the Vietnamese. *Frontline*, screened in July 1983, was inspired by *Sunday Times* journalist Phillip Knightley's book about the history of war correspondents, *The First Casualty – From the Crimea to Vietnam: The War Correspondent as Hero, Propagandist and Myth Maker*, the first casualty of war being truth. Pilger traced war reporting from the Crimea to the Falklands and explained how those journalists who diverged from the official view of their own government were often smeared.

The restrictions placed on reporters travelling with the Task Force to the Falklands had been covered as part of a BBC *Panorama* film entitled *The Media War*, screened in October 1982. Michael Cockerell examined the Ministry of Defence's manipulation of information, press photographs and television pictures, and the frustrations of British journalists.

The last third of *Frontline* dealt with the Falklands, but Pilger's film put the reporting of that war in a much wider context. He began by asking, 'What is the role of the media in wartime? Is it simply to record or is it to explain, and from whose point of view – the military, the politicians or the victims?' He then recalled the words of *The Times*'s correspondent in the Crimea, William Howard Russell, who wrote to his editor asking, 'Am I to tell these things or to hold my tongue?' His editor, John Delane, replied that he should go ahead and tell the truth. 'It was a rare moment of glory in the history of war reporting,' said Pilger. 'He reported the Charge of the Light Brigade as the disaster it was, he reported the waste and the blunders and the carnage of the whole British adventure. A government fell because of what he wrote, the Establishment grew to hate him, and Prince Albert called him "a miserable scribbler".' Crimea, added Pilger, was the last war before censorship.

Until the Crimea, the military had reported wars themselves. Phillip Knightley said that, in 1852, *The Times* decided to send a civilian for the first time 'and, of course, the army hated it'. This was Russell, who reported the Crimean War in a personal style – 'the truth as he saw it', said Pilger – and he was branded a traitor. The advent of the telegraph during the American Civil War meant that it was possible to get news straight from the front. This led to circulation battles, explained Knightley, and correspondents could be 'bought' by generals as they competed to get stories. Only a few wrote of the futility of war. Ned Spencer of the *Cincinatti Times* reported, 'As I sit tonight writing this epistle, the dead are all around me, the knife of the surgeon is busy at work and amputated legs and arms lie scattered in every direction. I hope my eyes may never again look upon such sights.'

Accompanied by newsreel film, Pilger said of World War One, 'It was the big lie. There was a deliberate, state-run conspiracy to lie to the British people about the futility of the war and its carnage. But what was significant was the extent to which the press and the reporters themselves took part in the conspiracy.' Philip Gibbs of the *Daily Chronicle*, who was later knighted, had said, 'We wrote the truth, apart from the naked realism of horrors and losses and criticism of the facts, which did not come within the liberty of our pen.' Pilger added, 'In other words, Gibbs was admitting that the correspondents wrote not what they knew to be true but what they were told was true. "There was no need for censorship," said Gibbs, "for we were our own censors."'

Knightley explained that reports of troops 'going over the top' and the sporting analogy of it as being the start of a cricket match served to take away the horror of the event being described. Goebbels based Nazi propaganda during World War Two on the British model of censorship, according to Knightley's book. During that war, censorship in Britain was tight and no correspondents were at Dunkirk. The story reported of military heroes obscured the real one of 'incompetence and disaster', said Pilger.

This prototype was used for the Korean War in the early 1950s, when reporting became 'a *Boy's Own* annual saga of good versus evil'. When BBC radio reporter Rene Cutforth described napalm being used as a new American weapon in that war, with its results on human beings reminding him of 'the smell of roast pork' from Sunday dinners back in Britain, his despatch was banned. Similarly, when journalist James Cameron and photographer Bert Hardy of *Picture Post* witnessed the brutal treatment of Koreans by Britain's South Korean allies, the magazine's owner, Edward Hulton, ordered editor Tom Hopkinson to drop their article. When Hopkinson refused, he was sacked, and Cameron resigned. 'Telling the victims' story,' said Hulton at the time, 'would give aid and comfort to the enemy.'

In Vietnam, generally regarded as an uncensored war, the US authorities used more subtle methods to manipulate journalists. Ralph McGehee, a former CIA intelligence officer, told Pilger that the Vietnam War was the agency's longest and most successful 'disinformation' operation, with the use of 'white', 'grey' and 'black' propaganda – all shades of lies. 'Black' propaganda was exemplified by a North Vietnamese junk being loaded up with communist weapons and floated down the coast of South Vietnam for international journalists to witness as 'proof' that the North was attacking the South, justifying the United States government's decision, in 1965, to send in Marines and begin bombing the North.

'Film such as this seldom appeared on television screens during the war,' said Pilger over pictures of carnage in North Vietnam. Morley Safer, of the United States' CBS network, had filmed the burning down of the village of Cam Ne by Marines using Zippo lighters. The military insisted that only a few houses had been razed, but reporters counted up to 400 destroyed. President Johnson personally tried to get Safer sacked, and the pressure on CBS meant that few reporters emulated Safer's uncompromising style. 'Even without censorship, it took almost two years for the massacre at My Lai to get out,' added Pilger. 'The reason was not lack of evidence, but a resistance to the story on the part of the media itself.'

Phillip Knightley compared the Americans in Vietnam with the

British in the Boer War in that 'the British government tried to remove from the Boer guerrilla forces their major source of sustenance – the Boer civilians – by putting all the women and children into concentration camps'. This made civilians legitimate military targets, and the strategy was pursued through-out World War Two and the atomic bombings of Hiroshima and Nagasaki. 'So, by the time we get to Vietnam,' added Knightley, 'the idea of civilians being killed in war has become acceptable.'

After the Vietnam War, said Knightley, the British government examined the effect of having reporters on the battlefield. As a result, the Ministry of Defence formulated a plan to control the media in a future war. This was put into operation during the Falklands conflict. The MoD did not want any journalists to accompany the Task Force to the South Atlantic but, under pressure from politicians, a few British reporters were eventually allowed to go. However, the celebrated war photographer Donald McCullin joked that, while there was space for a million Mars bars on the ships, there was no room for him.

Robert Harris, author of *Gotcha! The Media, the Government and the Falklands Crisis*, said that some American news organizations gave no credence to British reports as the war went on because they were regarded as 'a propaganda job'. Argentinian news sources won increasing influence. Reflecting that this was a war fought in the 1980s with modern technology, Harris pointed out, 'Television played very little part in actually covering the fighting. We saw virtually no pictures of fighting on the screens until the war was all but won . . . At the time of the Crimea, Russell's first despatch about the Charge of the Light Brigade got back to London in 20 days and some television pictures took 23 days to get back from the South Atlantic.'

John Shirley, of *The Sunday Times*, was convinced that pictures could have been transmitted sooner because the SAS had its own independent communications network and 'poached time on American satellites flying overhead' to relay messages back to its headquarters in Hereford. Frank Cooper, permanent under secretary of state at the Ministry of Defence during the war, insisted that the delay was for 'technical reasons' but added, 'I don't believe any democracy can win a war unless it has active public support.'

Pilger asked, 'Does the current war in Northern Ireland have active public support? The answer would seem to be no. But reporting the undeclared war in Ireland has special pitfalls, especially for television in Britain. For example, the guidelines of the Independent Broadcasting Authority say that any plans for a programme which explores the views of people who within the British Isles advocate violence for political ends must be referred to the Authority before filming. However, any programme giving the views of people who use violence outside the British Isles for political ends may go ahead without first consulting the Authority. The point is that life is made extremely difficult for any British journalist reporting any British war, in Ireland or the Falklands.'

John Shirley told Pilger that British reporters with the Task Force were 'prisoners of the Ministry of Defence', which controlled their movements and access to their news organizations. Anything that was 'damaging to morale' could not be reported. 'There was an incident on the *Canberra* when, after an evening's drinking, a few Paras climbed into one of the lifts,' recalled Shirley. 'Too many of them got into the lift on the *Canberra*, pressed the button and the lift broke and it fell three to four storeys through the ship. A couple of the Paras were quite seriously injured. We were not allowed to report that, because it was felt that it would be "damaging to morale" if it was seen that British troops were getting drunk and were having accidents on a ship.'

Shirley admitted that the proximity of journalists to the British troops and the relationships they built up affected his reporting, such as when he helped to unload bodies of dead Paratroopers after the battle at Goose Green. 'They were in an appalling state,' he said. 'There were just bodies with limbs all over the place, shirts piled over their heads to disguise them, blood and muck and filth, and it was just horrible . . . I wrote about that when the war was over. I didn't write about it at the time. Perhaps I should have done. I think I didn't feel it was fair, somehow, I just didn't feel it was fair . . . I actually knew some of those people. It affects you. We'd spent three months with them, really closely with them, by that stage. I just didn't think it was fair.'

However, one of Shirley's reports was subjected to blatant censorship. The advance on the Falklands capital, Port Stanley, from Teal Inlet was held up by bad weather. In one of his dispatches, the key sentence read, 'Only the weather now holds us back from Stanley.' It reached his newspaper in London as, 'Only the politicians now hold us back from Stanley.' BBC television reporter Brian Hanrahan's report that he heard 'the cries of men trapped below dying in the flames' after Britain suffered casualties at Bluff Cove was censored, said his BBC colleague Robert Harris.

The main source of 'news' was back in London. Each day, Ian McDonald, the MoD's deputy chief of public relations, held a press conference for newspapers and the broadcasting media. 'Mr McDonald knew that anything he said he said with the absolute confidence that no one in the room knew more than he knew or knew the truth if he was telling a fudge,' said veteran CBS correspondent Morley Safer, who recalled that in Vietnam the journalists sometimes went to the daily 'five o'clock follies' to see how closely the press briefings matched the reality they had seen. Safer called the Falklands War 'the most managed story in the history of journalism' and 'a censor's delight'. United States diplomatic and military contacts of his had been 'green with envy'.

Frontline was screened again in Channel Four's 'Banned' season in 1991. Although the documentary itself was not axed, delayed or censored, its content fitted perfectly into this package of television programmes and feature films that had been subject to such acts, including *The Propaganda War, World in Action*'s 1981 documentary about IRA hunger strikers, and a *Dispatches* interview with Sinn Fein president Gerry Adams, as well as the cinema pictures *Monty Python's Life of Brian* and *Brimstone and Treacle*. Also featured was *Death on the Rock*, Thames Television's *This Week* documentary investigating the murder of four unarmed IRA suspects by the SAS on Gibraltar. Although not censored when transmitted in 1988, it was subsequently subjected to a smear campaign, led by *The Sunday Times* and backed by the Thatcher government. Thames Television was eventually vindicated by a public inquiry chaired by Lord Windlesham.

For the repeat of *Frontline*, Pilger added a short postscript about the Gulf War:

> Looking at this film eight years on, in the aftermath of the Gulf War, I am struck by the relevance of some of the statements. So how will we view this latest search for truth in wartime in, say, thirty years' time? I think we'll have the same, uncomfortable feeling that we had when we watched some of those old newsreels, for little changed. Editors did as they were told by the Ministry of Defence, civilian casualties were played down. Yes, there was more information, but so much of it was repetitive and misleading. Perhaps the one difference was that censorship was aided by technology, which gave us the illusion that the war was almost bloodless, making war itself seem OK and preparing us for the next one.

Pilger returned to the theme of media coverage of the Gulf War in his book *Hidden Agendas*, published in 1998, describing it as 'the first real major action of the new Cold War', with 'a demon to fight, hi-tech weapons to fight him with'. He wrote that, unknown to most people in the West, up to 250,000 Iraqi civilians died in or as a result of the Allied attack, according to a largely ignored study by the Medical Educational Trust in London. International relief agencies reported 1,800,000 homeless.

In describing the BBC's 'objective' coverage of the war, Pilger referred to Greg Philo and Greg McLaughlin's highly critical study entitled *British Media and the Gulf War*. David Dimbleby's 'enthusiasm' for the 'surgical effect' of the American 'smart' bombs was singled out as typical of a media coverage that generally failed to question the accuracy of the new weapons. In fact, wrote Pilger, 'the first graphic result of the "surgical precision" was the American bombing of the Al-Amiraya bunker in Baghdad, in which between three hundred and four hundred women and children died'. Attempts to discredit this fact as Iraqi propaganda and portray the bunker as a military facility were later themselves discredited when unedited film from CNN of America and ITN of Britain was obtained by the *Columbia Journalism Review*. Pilger highlighted Dimbleby's interview with the US ambassador to Britain, in which the 'especially excited' broadcaster asked, 'Isn't it in fact true that America, by dint of the very accuracy of the weapons we've seen, is the only potential world policeman?' When this was published in the *New Statesman*, Dimbleby replied:

He [Pilger] claims that I and others reported on the new US 'smart' bombs as though they had somehow sanitized the war, guaranteeing that civilians would not be hurt. I remember the day the Pentagon first produced film of a 'smart' bomb. We discussed the implications of the new weapon with a variety of military experts, some of whom expressed scepticism about the claims being made. At no point did we suggest that the day of a painless hi-tech war had arrived, in which only objects, not people, were killed. Over many hours of broadcasting we dwelt as often on casualties as hardware. The BBC's own reporters gave us eye-witness accounts of death and injury in Baghdad and the horror of the retreat along the Basra road.[23]

To which Pilger replied:

Dimbleby seems to think he is regarded as the embodiment of BBC impartiality. He isn't. He is an establishment voice who barely disguises his own conservative views. He writes that 'at no point' did he suggest that a 'painless, hi-tech war had arrived'. Who can forget Dimbleby's performance on the first day of the bombing, 18 January? Barely containing himself, he lauded the 'accuracy' of the bombing as 'quite phenomenal' – which of course was nonsense. Most of the bombs missed their targets. Growing ever more excited, he interviewed the American ambassador and declared that the 'success' of the bombing 'suggests that America's ability to react militarily has really become *quite extraordinary* [his emphasis] despite all the critics beforehand who said it will never work out like that'. He told the grateful ambassador: 'You are now able to claim that you can act precisely and therefore – to use that hideous word about warfare – surgically.' Without offering a shred of independent evidence, Dimbleby pronounced himself 'relieved at the amazing success' of what turned out to be the slaughter of more than 200,000 people.[24]

Dimbleby had previously objected to Pilger's nuclear arms propaganda documentary *The Truth Game* (see earlier in this chapter) and to his receiving the prestigious Richard Dimbleby Award from the British Academy of Film and Television Arts (BAFTA) in 1991. The presentation of this award, for his contribution to factual television over the years, came shortly after Pilger had written critically in the *Guardian* and *New Statesman* about the Allied campaign in the Gulf and David Dimbleby's coverage of that war. Dimbleby failed to mention this. He told the *Sunday Telegraph*, 'BAFTA has taken leave of its senses. The award is intended to be given for an outstanding contribution to broadcasting. In his forays into television, John Pilger has shown that he stands for a kind of broadcasting which is the antithesis of everything my father believed in. As a family, we have no say in who gets the award. But if we had, I would have vetoed this.'[25] On the same day, *The Sunday Times* published an interview in which Dimbleby said, 'Pilger is not a broadcaster in the sense that the award was meant. It is for serious, continuous broadcasters. It's not for someone who makes occasional broadcasts, what I would call forays into television.'[26] These 'forays' had, in fact, produced almost forty documentaries in twenty years, a feat unequalled by any television journalist outside regular current affairs programmes.

Three days before the presentation of the award, veteran broadcaster Robin Day – who had refused to present Pilger with the award – wrote to the *Daily Telegraph*, 'By all means, let BAFTA honour Pilger or whoever they want for campaigning, polemical television. But the Dimbleby Award, if it is to retain its prestige, should be kept for practitioners of the "due impartiality" which is still a fundamental tradition of television journalism in Britain.'[27]

Like Dimbleby, Day failed to mention a certain vested interest in criticizing Pilger. In his book *Heroes*, Pilger had noted Day's failure to ask Prime Minister Margaret Thatcher, in a *Panorama* interview during the 1983 British general election campaign, why the government had vetoed or ignored dozens of opportunities for 'multilateral disarmament' presented to the United Nations over the previous two years. Pilger referred to Day's confession to *The Times* that he had 'handled [the interview] badly' and 'failed to ask a number of important questions to which the viewers were entitled to have answers'.[28]

Melvyn Bragg stepped in to present Pilger with the award during the BAFTA ceremony, at the Dorchester Hotel, London, on 17 March 1991. After mentioning the controversy, Bragg said, 'John Pilger is always looking for a truth. We know where he's coming from and the broad church of British television should be well able to hold and to celebrate such a man and such commitment. He is a valuable, independent voice, a voice which over the past few years has been particularly strong in ITV, despite rather testing times. Pilger is a man who, in the best sense, bears witness.'

Accepting the award, and a standing ovation, Pilger thanked Central Television, 'which has been foremost in promoting the

kind of courageous, popular documentary-making that has
brought home vital issues to a great number of people in this
country'. He paid tribute to David Munro, 'with whom I've
made all the Cambodia films. Certainly, without David's extraordinary talent I would never have made the films I have.' He
added:

> Apart from the personal pleasure this award gives me, I hope that
> BAFTA, by giving it to me, will encourage young journalists and
> young broadcasters to believe and not to lose faith that a dissenting
> voice is every bit as legitimate, if not more so, than one respectful
> of authority. Of course, there are many different kinds of broadcast
> journalists, and so there should be, but I think we all have one
> important role in common, and that is to show the effects of the
> decisions of those with power on the lives of ordinary people and
> that is what I've tried to do throughout my career.

The Late Show, BBC2's arts programme, featured a special report
on Pilger two days after the BAFTA awards ceremony. With fine
irony, it was a striking example of false BBC balance. Instead of a
reasonable discussion about Pilger's work, it produced two
polarized 'teams', dominated by the 'anti' team of William
Shawcross and Auberon Waugh, both right-wing commentators
who had long personalized their vehement opposition to Pilger's
work. ('The Trouble with John Pilger' was the headline over a
Shawcross feature in the *Observer* on the day of the BAFTA
awards.)

In the 1970s, Waugh had attacked Pilger for his campaign to
compensate children who were victims of the drug thalidomide.
Then, in 1982, he inferred that Pilger had invented an investigation into child labour in Thailand, a country that Waugh visited
frequently as a writer for *Business Traveller* magazine. In fact,
Pilger, who had arranged to 'buy' a Thai child in order to expose
the profitable trade in child workers in Thailand, was hoaxed.
Pilger sued Waugh, withdrawing the action when the *Spectator*,

which had carried the accusations, published a statement confirming the hoax and insisting that the magazine had not intended
to cast doubt on Pilger's integrity. In *The Late Show*, Waugh
claimed to have invented the verb 'to Pilger', which meant 'to
treat a subject emotionally with generous disregard for incon-
venient detail, to ham it up, always in the left-wing cause and
always with great indignation'.

The BBC's 'pro-Pilger' team consisted of Roger James, Central
Television's head of features, and the investigative journalist Paul
Foot, who had been a fellow columnist on the *Daily Mirror*. Foot
refuted Shawcross's claim that Pilger was 'anti-American'. Pilger,
he said, had many American friends and was simply 'anti-American imperialism'. Foot added, 'The point is that the people who
support the state of society as it is don't like journalists that upset
them. John Pilger is so good that he upsets them more than most
of us who do attack the Establishment and therefore his very
genius and his very ability is the thing that they detest most.
Therefore, they attack him where they think he's weakest, by
calling into question his ability, which is quite absurd because
anybody who knows John Pilger's work at all knows that he's in
the very top flight.'[29]

The receipt of such a prestigious honour as the Richard
Dimbleby Award was not to go unpunished. The following
week, *The Sunday Times* published a full-page article smearing
Pilger, just as it had smeared Thames Television's *Death on the
Rock* documentary three years earlier. Much of the 'evidence' was
a recycling of William Shawcross's public disagreements with
Pilger over Cambodia.[30] The newspaper's campaign against Pilger
ran into April and was joined by others when a High Court case
gave Pilger's opponents what they believed was the ammunition
they needed.

Following the screening of *Cambodia – The Betrayal*, in October
1990, two former British Army officers, Christopher Mackenzie-
Geidt and Anthony de Normann, brought a libel action against
Pilger and Central Television. In the film, Labour MP and

shadow overseas development minister Ann Clwyd told how she had met the two men when she was in Cambodia to witness the final Vietnamese withdrawal from the country. The men were officially listed as representatives of the Ministry of Defence, she said. In their libel action, both claimed that the programme had accused them of being among those who trained the Khmer Rouge to use landmines.

'Central Television and I made clear that it was never our intention to suggest that the two men referred to in my Cambodia documentary had trained Khmer guerrillas,' wrote Pilger after losing the libel action. 'We accepted unreservedly that they had not and we have never attempted to justify any such allegation.'[31] He pointed out that the words he used 'did not carry the meaning the plaintiffs put on them' and that the programme was commenting on British government intervention in Cambodia, which was of public interest.[32]

A vital witness for the defence was Simon O'Dwyer-Russell, of the *Sunday Telegraph*, who had close family and professional ties to the SAS and who, with Pilger and David Munro, had investigated British support for the Khmer Rouge. He died shortly after *Cambodia – The Betrayal* was broadcast. Pilger and Central Television's attempts to subpoena five witnesses – three government ministers who had, according to Pilger, made misleading statements to Parliament about the SAS operation in Cambodia and the SAS's present and former commanding officers – were overruled by the judge after the government's counsel claimed that national security would be threatened by their evidence. Pilger and Central withdrew from the case, with the television company paying 'substantial damages' in an out-of-court settlement with the two men.

The defence counsel, Desmond Browne, QC, likened this case to the *Spycatcher* trial four years earlier, in which the government intervened in an attempt to ban former MI5 officer Peter Wright's book. This time, the issue of a Public Interest Immunity Certificate – or 'gagging order' – by the government ensured that evidence relating to the SAS, the security services and 'national security' would be ruled out of court.

However, one revelation that emerged from the case was an extraordinary admission by armed services minister Archie Hamilton, one of those subpoenaed, that the SAS *had* operated in Cambodia but not, he claimed, since 1989. This came in the form of a written parliamentary reply and was among government documents sent to the solicitors acting for Pilger and Central Television by the Treasury Secretary. In its statement following the libel settlement, Central Television explained:

> Our film was principally concerned not with individuals but with governments – and especially the secret aid given by Western governments, including the British Government, to one side in the Cambodian civil war. Not only was Britain's role made clear by the government's admission last week about SAS training – but it was demonstrated again this week in the High Court, where the government was represented by two counsels, and others, who intervened in the libel case in an extraordinary way . . .
>
> In open court this week the government's representatives made clear that no evidence would be permitted that went beyond the statement last week by the Armed Services Minister, Archie Hamilton, confirming British military training of Cambodian guerrillas.
>
> Certain evidence regarding the SAS and the security services, such as MI6, which might be brought by our defence counsel would be challenged and a ruling sought that it not be allowed. The government counsel spoke in open court about 'national security' being at stake with the disclosure of evidence that 'travels into the area that the Secretary of State would protect'.[33]

What was demonstrated by this episode and Pilger's BAFTA award was the eagerness of his Establishment opponents to seize the opportunity to discredit him and, by implication, the threat he posed to their dominance of much of British politics and journalism. A decade and a dozen award-winning documentaries later, their total failure is evident. The 'valuable, independent voice . . . always looking for a truth', in the words of Melvyn Bragg, continued to make some of the most important documentaries produced anywhere in the world, helping to shape the international agenda with path-breaking films such as *Death of a Nation – The Timor Conspiracy*, *Apartheid Did Not Die* and *Paying the Price – Killing the Children of Iraq*.

9. PEOPLE'S JUSTICE

A S THE GREAT American reporter Martha Gellhorn wrote of John Pilger, 'He has taken on the great theme of justice and injustice.'[1] Indeed, justice is the continuous thread throughout all of Pilger's work. This is most evident in his campaigns, such as those for the thalidomide victims and the stricken in Cambodia who were denied aid because of power politics. He has also made single documentaries highlighting how governments deny the profit of material resources to the majority of their people, who often live in poverty while subsidizing the rich, especially big business. He once called this 'socialism for the rich and capitalism for the poor'.[2]

In 1978, Pilger presented a one-hour film, *The Selling of the Sea*, for the ITV company Westward Television and screened only in that region. Produced in association with UNESCO, the programme looked at the wealth beneath the oceans and how technology had made it possible to exploit it. This modern gold rush included fish and valuable minerals, as well as oil, and the richest nations had most to gain. Oil companies could drill for black gold, multinationals were able to sweep up millions of tons of valuable minerals lying scattered on the sea bed, and huge factory trawlers were used to scoop up whole shoals of fish in one net.

'Westward Television asked me to present it,' recalled Pilger. 'The budget wouldn't stretch to travel, so a lot of archive footage was used. At that time, the ocean boundaries were being re-defined and there was a proposal to reduce the limits around Britain, which opened up important ocean shelves for exploitation, both in fishing and natural resources. It was both a controversial subject and something of a "sleeper". I confess, I hadn't thought a lot about it, but it appealed to me.

'I learned that the exploitation of the sea was simply an extension of everything else. It was also a target for rapacious power. Look at the way the great fishing conglomerates of Japan have destroyed so much of the fishing ecosystem. Look at the way the people of East Timor and Burma have suffered partly because great multinational corporations have done criminal deals with dictatorships to exploit the oil and gas resources beneath their coastal seas.'[3]

Oil was also at the centre of Pilger's 1980 documentary about Mexico, in which he contrasted the beginnings of a bonanza that was to be enjoyed by the rich and powerful of that country with the poverty of most of its people. Pilger filmed in Mexico with director David Munro early in 1979. His report appeared in the *Daily Mirror* in May of that year, but their documentary, *The Mexicans*, was not broadcast until June 1980, having been overtaken by the urgency of *Year Zero – The Silent Death of Cambodia*.

The Mexicans, Pilger's second documentary with Munro, was not one of their most successful. Although beautifully filmed by John Davey and carrying a clear and previously neglected message, the pair expected too much of the hour-long slot and packed in excessive amounts of history. Perhaps this was because it suffered from Pilger having had little previous first-hand knowledge and experience of the country, although this did not affect future documentaries on Nicaragua and East Timor.

'I had been to Mexico, but it was a part of the world I knew little about,' he said. 'The film reflected my own discovery and I felt I had a responsibility to dispel the stereotypes: to give a glimpse of Mexico's amazing history and popular struggles. I was moved by the magnificent Diego Rivera murals in Mexico City, and the artist's depiction of the the colonial period, that I tried to do something not dissimilar on film! Indeed, we filmed the murals, over which I told their story. But it was too much. The viewers would have suffered from acute historical indigestion, and that was a lesson I learned. History is a critical component of all my films, but it is there not as a lecture, but to make sense of the contemporary.'[4]

Perhaps, too, *The Mexicans* suffered from not having as hard an edge as many of Pilger's documentaries. In Nicaragua, East Timor and Burma, there was visible struggle, often in the most brutal of circumstances. In the Mexico film, there was simply the plea to ensure that any future wealth from oil enjoyed by those in power should help to relieve the poverty of the common people. Munro very effectively brought a 'travelogue' quality of everyday normality to some Pilger documentaries that complemented the horrors being reported, particularly in Vietnam and Cambodia. Here, there was not the same content to establish a counterbalance to Davey's stunning photography.

Throughout the documentary, too, there was a significant lack of Pilger 'editorials' to the camera. Ironically, one aspect that his detractors criticize him for was hardly present, but perhaps this indicated that he had little of importance to say beyond the main theme of injustice. *The Mexicans* was an interesting observational documentary on a Third World country presented with the opportunity to climb out of its poverty. It was not a typical Pilger film, although Pilger himself would almost certainly challenge the notion of his own stereotyping!

He started by explaining that Mexico was discovered as an abandoned country by the Aztec Indians, who declared Mexico City their capital, and was then occupied by the Spanish until the two races merged, 'passiveness with aggression, a sense of betrayal with triumph'. Mexico was now approaching its second high noon, with the prospect of becoming the greatest oil producer on Earth. 'The pauper south of the border has literally won the pools,' said Pilger.

Scenes of peasants going about their daily business were accompanied by a frenetic Latin American song and guitar-playing. The Diego Rivera mural, a tableau of Mexican history in the National Palace, Mexico City, provided a backdrop. 'After

Spain had bled Mexico of its wealth,' said Pilger, 'the United States invaded Mexico in 1847 and took half of Mexico's territory. In 1862, the French intervened and installed the melancholy figure of Maximilian as emperor, until he was betrayed and murdered.' More betrayals followed and the dictatorship of Porfirio Diaz led to the bloody revolution that started in 1910 and lasted ten years.

Emilio Zapata and Pancho Villa led two of the main revolutionary groups but Zapata was lured into a trap in 1919, when he was invited to talk peace with the colonel of the federal army, and murdered, one of two million people who died in the Mexican revolution. Generals and despots assumed control of Mexico and today, said Pilger, the country was ruled by the Party of the Institutionalized Revolution, with the opposition allowed only 5 per cent of parliamentary seats, and big families continued to own vast areas of land. However, Mexico had remained relatively stable and many were depoliticized.

Children as young as six were put to work in the fields and extreme poverty lived side by side with extreme wealth in Mexico City. While the oil fields began to flow, half the population were without work and most lived in shacks in shanty towns, with rubbish strewn everywhere. Land reform had failed and cities were bursting with too many people. Recently, President Lopez Portillo had mounted a birth-control programme and succeeded in persuading 40 per cent of all women to use contraception, which was remarkable in one of the most fundamentalist Catholic nations on Earth. Relations with the Vatican had been broken off by Mexico's rulers 120 years earlier, although the Pope had recently visited. At an orphanage, Pilger heard the stories of some of the children there, including one whose mother was an alcoholic and another whose father killed his mother shortly before his own death.

A change of pace in the second half of *The Mexicans* gave the documentary new life. Over film of the wide, open spaces of southern California, Pilger commented that this land had been taken from Mexico by the United States in the war of the 1840s, creating Texas, New Mexico and Arizona. Pilger joined a US border patrol on the lookout for Mexicans trying to cross into the United States to get work. Every night, the patrols caught people, but many others evaded them and entered the country, assuming new identities and accepting a pittance for work that would enable them to send money back to their impoverished families.

Just across the Mexican border, Pilger visited the town of Tijuana and observed the hovels spilling down the hillside overlooking the country's rich neighbour. He recalled that 300 demonstrators had been killed in Mexico City when, in 1968, they took to the streets to protest at the divisions in their society. Some of those arrested were never heard of again and there was a campaign to find the 'disappeared'. Pilger conducted a long interview with a mother still searching for her son. At the end of the film, he said:

Mexico is not just a faraway country and what happens here may well affect us all. If you doubt this, you may recall events in other faraway countries in the Middle East that made us face our addiction to oil. Mexico is to become the most influential oil nation in the Western hemisphere, perhaps in the world. But Mexico is not just a name to be neatly dropped into this or that strategic camp; Mexico is people. And the 10 per cent growth rate that the economists say that the oil will bring is meaningless while children work at the age of six, while their parents have no work at all, while millions live beside open sewers, while people are kidnapped for seeking their rights under the law. In the economists' language, Mexico is a stable country. And so it is, for some. And how and when the rest of these extraordinary people determine their future is not known. But the roots and the life are there, as Lawrence wrote [in *The Plumed Serpent*], and if the forest should rise again it won't be just a faraway headache, like Iran or Chile, for it will happen just south of the border.

Following the film's transmission, Jose Juan de Olloqui, the Mexican ambassador to Britain, complained in a letter to the *Guardian* that he had never come across 'such a biased portrayal of my country'. He added, 'The programme only showed the poverty existing in Mexico, without taking into consideration a vast sector of Mexico's population: the middle class.'[5]

In 1980, when *The Mexicans* was broadcast, the country had been producing 2.5 million barrels of oil a day with proved reserves of 60 billion barrels. Placing their hopes on oil, the government borrowed huge amounts of money from international banks and ended up in a debt crisis. The currency collapsed, unemployment rose and capital spending was cut back. Mexico negotiated a deal with the International Monetary Fund for a $3.4 billion loan and the rescheduling of half of its $96 billion external debt. An earthquake in Mexico City in 1985 saved the government from having the debt called in and eventually, five years later, with no prospect of the oil revenues paying back its creditors, it agreed to the Brady Plan, under which it would receive $3.6 billion a year for thirty years. The debt burden that today weighs on so many Third World countries began in Mexico. In 1992, in his film *War by Other Means*, Pilger took this apparent abstraction of economics and turned it into popular television (see later in this chapter).

After Mexico, he turned his attention to the other countries of Central America. Newly elected US President Ronald Reagan was propping up the right-wing El Salvador junta, whose death squads and National Guard murdered 75,000 of their own people between 1980 and 1991. The Americans were also 'secretly' destabilizing the Sandinista regime in Nicaragua, which had unseated the US-backed dictator Somoza in 1979, by financing the Contras without the approval of Congress. It was the latest instalment in the United States' long history of intervening in its own 'backyard', to control its resources.

Pilger reported from El Salvador for the *Daily Mirror* and the *New Statesman* in 1981. In less than two years, he wrote, 20,000 civilians had been killed and the US government justified its aid by claiming that the Soviet Union and Cuba were sending arms to those who opposed the junta. Like the 'evidence' planted by the CIA to justify a full-scale war in Vietnam, these claims were bogus.

In 1983 Pilger travelled to Nicaragua with director Alan Lowery. In October of that year, just a few weeks before the screening of their documentary about Reagan's attempts to oust the Sandinistas, the United States invaded the country's Caribbean neighbour, Grenada. 'That came during post-production and gave the film an added edge,' recalled Lowery. 'We had originally planned to look at what was happening in the Central American countries of El Salvador, Honduras and Nicaragua, but we realized that was going to be too big to handle in one programme, so we decided to focus on Nicaragua. In Central America, the only successful revolution that had pushed aside US interests was there. It seemed there were lessons to be learned about how this country had created primary health care and education for everyone.'[6]

Before Pilger's and Lowery's documentary came to the screen, they faced familiar pressure from the IBA over what had suddenly become an international news story. 'During the last two weeks before transmission, the IBA tried to lean on the programme in terms of its content,' said Lowery. 'In the end, maybe one or two words changed, but nothing significant was lost. John was adamant about that. I remember phone calls backwards and forwards from the IBA to the dubbing theatre where we were editing. Richard Creasey, Central's controller of features, was fielding calls from them questioning parts of the commentary.'[7] In the last few days before transmission, after the programme's original title of *Nicaragua – A Nation's Right to Life* had been circulated to the press, Lowery was told that it had to be reduced to just *Nicaragua* and a 'warning' would have to be added before the programme alerting viewers to the fact that this was a 'personal view'.

The film opened with black-and-white still photographs of the

US invasion of Grenada. 'It was, some believe, a forerunner to a much bigger invasion, Nicaragua,' said Pilger, describing the American-backed repression imposed on Guatemala, El Salvador and Honduras. He said:

> Until 1979, it also happened in Nicaragua. Then, almost all the people of Nicaragua rose up against a tyrant called Somoza, whose family had been in power for more than forty years, put there by the United States Marines. That uprising cost 50,000 lives, almost as many as died for America in Vietnam, but out of a population of less than three million people. This film is about the people of Nicaragua and their unique struggle to end a cycle of poverty and humiliation. It is also about a threat which, according to President Reagan, this tiny country presents to the most powerful and richest nation on Earth.

From the start, Pilger had a topical story to get his teeth into and a subject that was both controversial and hopeful because of his emphasis on the democratic nature of Nicaragua's revolution, which contrasted the notion of a 'communist threat' as claimed by the United States and echoed by Margaret Thatcher's government.

Over film of children at newly opened schools and peasants taking part in the government's literacy programme, Pilger said, 'The real threat is this: children once denied education under the Somozas now have the same right to school as do children in Britain . . . In the past four years, 2,500 new schools have been built. And this is the threat: these middle-aged peasant women can read and write for the first time in their lives. In the past four years, illiteracy has been cut to less than 10 per cent of the population. And this is the threat: polio has been wiped out, infant mortality has been cut by a third, serious malnutrition has been dramatically reduced, a national health service has been established, in spite of pitifully meagre resources. And this is the threat: open roads, freedom of movement. In a region of turmoil, there's no curfew, no menace from within. It is ironic that Nicaragua is one of the few countries in Latin America where the United States ambassador is able to stroll in safety through the streets.'

Pilger traced the country's history back to 1823 and the Monroe Doctrine, proclaimed by President Monroe as a means of 'protecting' Latin America from Europeans. This became known as the United States' 'manifest destiny', a God-given right to control its own hemisphere – later extended, as Pilger has often pointed out, to the rest of the world. In 1912, US Marines landed in Nicaragua 'to protect democracy and to hold elections', but the people did not want a foreign army to organize their democracy. They lined up behind the nationalist Augusto Sandino, who questioned the United States' right to invade a small country. Film included previously unseen footage of the Marines in the 1920s. On 16 July 1927, after Sandino attacked the US barracks in the northern town of Ocotal, US planes bombed the town. It was the first ever use of dive-bombing, long before the German Luftwaffe's attack on Guernica, in Spain. Sandino subsequently adopted guerrilla warfare tactics and drove the Americans out, then signed a peace treaty in 1933. A year later, he was assassinated and the long Somoza tyranny followed.

Recalling the Somozas' forty-four-year rule as he stood next to a volcano in Masaya, Pilger described how a National Guard was formed to keep them in power. It was paid for and armed by the United States. The volcano had a terrible symbolism; Somoza despatched his victims there. Over film of a 'blood factory', he explained that Nicaraguans sold their blood for a dollar a litre, which Somoza sold to the United States for ten times as much. After a 1972 earthquake destroyed the capital, Managua, the National Guard looted and diverted aid from abroad.

Film of a children's playground built on the rubble of the earthquake immediately after Somoza's fall was accompanied by Pilger's comments that Somoza had refused to build parks or playgrounds, just as he had done nothing about the 83 per cent malnutrition or diseases affecting young children. He looted the country's banks, including most of the $65 million lent by the International Monetary Fund.

The victorious Sandinistas were left with 40 per cent of Nicaragua's infrastructure destroyed. Father Xabier Gorostiaga, director of the Nicaragua Economics Institute, told Pilger that after four years of what the Americans called 'communism' 60 per cent of the gross domestic product was in the hands of the private sector and land had been distributed to both co-operatives and private peasants. More than 3,500 co-operatives had been established and would soon be self-sufficient. 'Production is part of the defence system,' he said. 'If we are able to provide food to the people, health, education, this country is invincible.' Father Xabier explained that the revolution had been born out of nationalism, Christianity and Creole or Latin American Marxism.

At the maximum security prison in Tipitapa, Pilger was joined by minister of the interior Tomas Borgé, who had been tortured there under the Somoza regime while his wife was raped and murdered. Borgé talked about the National Guard's brutalities but explained that he chose to exercise compassion rather than 'bitterness and grudges'. This attitude, said Pilger, underwrote a penal reform system. Film followed of Somoza's former body-guard on a farm that doubled as a prison with no guards, where his rehabilitation was almost complete. The price of this latitude was that 2,500 National Guardsmen who were released by the Sandinistas had fled to Honduras, where they were signed up and armed by the CIA.

The cold-blooded killing of US television correspondent Bill Stewart in June 1979 was shown as his camera crew carried on filming when a National Guard officer aimed a gun at the head of the reporter, who was lying on his front. 'His murder on television shocked many Americans and helped to break an historical pattern,' said Pilger. 'For the first time, Washington found it very difficult to justify sending troops to intervene on behalf of their man Somoza.' A monument to Stewart's memory had been erected on a street corner in Managua on the first anniversary of his death, lauding him as 'part of free Nicaragua'. Mothers talked to Pilger about their sons who died in the fight against Somoza.

Now, there was the threat of invasion again. Pilger listed US intervention in 'its own backyard' since 1898 – in Cuba, Honduras, Nicaragua, Haiti, Panama, Guatemala, Chile and Grenada – resulting in a military encirclement of the region on land, sea and air. Since Reagan had come to power, there had been bombing raids on Nicaragua by insurgents from Costa Rica in the south and the Contras, former members of the National Guard directed and paid for by the CIA, had attacked from Honduras in the north. Over film of the Contras, Pilger reported that 15,000 of them were mounting hit-and-run attacks from Honduras and many were being trained illegally in camps in Florida. Meanwhile, US Naval task forces had arrived off the coast of Nicaragua. He compared this with an antiquated defence force of Eastern bloc tanks and Korean war jets 'poised against them' inside Nicaragua, plus two helicopters, a few patrol boats, a regular army of 22,000 and 25,000 reserves, and a militia. Susana Veraguas, who trained midwives, recalled that in one area of the country six of her students had been murdered by the Contras.

The United States' declared aim was to stop the flow of Sandinista arms to the guerrillas in El Salvador but, said Pilger, there was no proof of this. He asked the US deputy assistant secretary of defense, Nestor Sanchez, a former CIA officer who had helped to mount the abortive invasion of Cuba in 1961, about the Nicaraguan government's popular support. Sanchez claimed that there was 'sufficient evidence' to show this was untrue. He referred to a poll taken the previous year by the Catholic Church. When pressed, he admitted this had been a 'rather informal' survey. Of the Contras, he said the 'democratic freedom fighters' had found that Nicaraguans freely joined them in areas they had entered. Asked about US intervention, Sanchez said that his government wanted to redress the people's years of poverty, 'but we certainly don't see the solution in letting them become a country under communist domination and rule'. He insisted that the support of other countries' leaders such as Margaret Thatcher was 'vital', adding, 'I wish we could see the same, strong support that we are getting from our British allies from all our other allies in Europe.'

Having established the British connection, Pilger reported that delegations from Parliament in 1982 and the World Council of Churches in 1983 had praised the apparent pluralism in the Nicaraguan government and popular support of it. In contrast, on a recent visit to Nicaragua, Pope John Paul II had refused to bless the government there, although he had done so in Poland and El Salvador. 'It is ironic that the Vatican, together with the Reagan administration, appears to be doing to the Sandinistas in Nicaragua what Moscow is doing to Solidarity in Poland,' said Pilger. In El Salvador, after three nuns had been murdered by that country's National Guard, Jean Kirkpatrick, the US representative at the United Nations, suggested that they had been communist sympathizers. Death squads had killed 35,000 people in El Salvador since 1980 and the US ambassador, Robert White, was sacked for saying publicly that the security forces were 'the chief killers'. President Reagan wanted to give $200 million in aid to El Salvador, while there was no aid to Nicaragua, where there were no death squads.

'The British government is one of the few Western governments to enthusiastically support President Reagan's policy in Central America,' said Pilger in his summary, 'policies which are leaning towards a war against a small country whose crime has been to cut the death rate of its young children, to teach its people to read and write, and to let them live as human beings with dignity. Surely it's fair to ask this: How impoverished, how helpless does a country have to be before it's no longer seen as a threat by the United States? Or perhaps President Reagan understands that the real threat of Nicaragua is simply that of a good example and one desperately sought after from Central America to the Philippines, to Poland – the example of a society inspired by neither the United States nor the Soviet Union. The generosity of spirit you have seen from Nicaragua will not be sustained by more suffering. If governments won't help them, why can't they leave them alone?'

After the film's screening, in November 1983, *The Sunday Times* carried a thousand-word hatchet job on Pilger by Frank Barber, described by the newspaper as 'a writer and broadcaster, and author of a novel of African guerrilla warfare, *The Last White Man* (1981)'. In the article, Barber asked, 'Can one of our television networks legitimately give up an hour of its time to the transmission of a political propaganda film presenting a foreign government's case?' The Nicaragua documentary, wrote Barber, contained 'a string of questionable assertions delivered by a succession of mouthpieces and agit-prop figures on behalf of the Sandinista-dominated government of Nicaragua'.[8]

He noted that this was Pilger's ninth programme to be broadcast during 1983, including his documentary *The Truth Game*, Channel Four interview series *The Outsiders* and television play *The Last Day*. (In fact, the final three episodes of *The Outsiders*, screened in December, brought the total to twelve.) With this link, Barber took the opportunity to weigh in, late, with his stinging criticisms of *The Truth Game* and smear Pilger for 'ignoring or suppressing all contrary evidence' after taking a particular standpoint on issues such as nuclear weapons.[9]

The Sunday Times was deluged with letters defending Pilger and the veracity of his films, and asking who was Frank Barber. Many noted that since Rupert Murdoch had taken over the paper two years earlier, and Andrew Neil was made editor, hatchet jobs on perceived enemies were commonplace, as well as a campaign against ITV. Twice, Murdoch had been thwarted in his attempts to buy into the profitable network. In spite of the support for Pilger, *The Sunday Times* featured a letter from Gordon Smith, of Market Harborough, 'congratulating' Barber on 'performing a long-overdue public service in exposing the disgraceful policy of the IBA in presenting John Pilger's political propaganda as if it was fact-finding documentary'. However, a letter from Martha Gell-horn refuted Barber's claim that Pilger was a propagandist who featured 'questionable assertions' by outlining the credentials of those who were interviewed in the film, and described his statement that Pilger ignored or suppressed evidence as 'outrageous slander'. Director Alan Lowery wrote about 'Frank Barber's unprofessional personal view, thinly disguised as a television review', pointed out that 'every fact in the programme is supported by detailed documentation' and added that 'the researcher [Elizabeth Nash] was a former university lecturer in Latin-American politics'.[10]

Two weeks later, Pilger himself wrote to the newspaper that Barber's article was 'a contrived, bigoted and, above all, inaccurate attack on me and my work . . . in the spirit of Senator Joseph McCarthy'. Responding to Barber's charge that his films peddled propaganda, he added, 'I wonder how Barber's written words would stand up to two and sometimes three civil servants of the IBA combing through them up to six weeks before publication? I wonder how his "facts" would stand up to a researcher with an MA in Latin-American politics double-checking and double-sourcing? That is how it works for me in television.'[11]

Barber's allegation of 'political propaganda' was all the more remarkable for the fact that Barber himself had for several decades worked for BBC radio and been involved in broadcasting propaganda. He headed a special unit set up, at the behest of the Foreign and Commonwealth Office, to relay programmes to Rhodesia (now Zimbabwe) after Prime Minister Ian Smith made his white-minority government's Unilateral Declaration of Independence in 1965. For many years, alongside his work at the BBC, latterly as head of current affairs talks, Barber was a freelance sub-editor for *The Sunday Times*, dealing with major news stories, often in close consultation with editors Harold Evans and Andrew Neil.

As a result of the Nicaragua documentary, Robert Todd, a viewer in London who had been moved by the programme, began an extraordinary project. He bought a derelict house in Vauxhall for £18,000 and set about restoring it with free labour and £9,000 worth of materials, with the aim of selling it and sending the money to the people of Nicaragua. In 1985, Oxfam published a book, *Nicaragua – The Threat of a Good Example?*, by Dianna Melrose, who wrote that, from the charity's experience of working in seventy-six developing countries, Nicaragua proved exceptional in its government's commitment to improving the condition of the people and encouraging their active participation in development. In the same year, money from illegal American arms sales to Iran was being redirected to the Contras and the United States imposed a trade embargo against Nicaragua, in an effort to bring the Sandinistas to their knees.

In 1990, when Nicaraguans went to the polls for the second time after Somoza's overthrow, the Sandinistas were narrowly defeated. Although they won more votes than any other single party, a coalition led by the US-backed Violeta Chamorro, daughter of the murdered newspaper editor, took power. The Nicaraguan people were exhausted – from the effects of the blockade and the war against the Contras. Some regarded the Sandinistas as having become too arrogant. Since then, under unrestrained 'free market' policies, Nicaragua has risen to the top of the Latin-American league in poverty, illiteracy and preventable disease. The 'good example' is no more.

In 1986, Pilger moved to a part of the world that he had known well in the late 1960s, Japan. He wrote an award-winning series for the *Daily Mirror* in 1967 on the rise of Japan as an economic power. In researching this, Pilger lived with a Japanese family (and 'almost', he says, fell in love with their daughter).[12] He returned frequently to Japan when he was in Asia and reported on the rise of the Soka Gokkai, the huge, quasi-religious cult that became the third-biggest political force in the country. In 1977, he made the documentary *An Unjustifiable Risk*, showing the legacy of the atomic bombing on Hiroshima (see Chapter 2). He returned nine years later to make *Japan – Behind the Mask*, which argued that the Japanese 'miracle' was based largely on the work, and often deprivation, of the majority, who did not fit the stereotypes of a nation of 'suited automators'. He described the intense pressure on children to do well at school and the crushing of trade unions. Glossy images of commercials for Japanese goods were seen alongside film of sweatshops and pollution sufferers, as Pilger spoke to academics, authors and journalists about the state of modern Japan.

He said, 'You are more than likely to be watching this on a Japanese television set. If you're out, you may have recorded it on a video – Japanese, of course. And you may have checked the programmes by your Japanese watch, perhaps at the weekend you drove to the park in your Japanese car and took snaps with your Japanese camera. And yet most of us know very little about the people who make these things.'

If, as Pilger has written, journalism is about the stripping away of official masks, this film exemplified it. 'Whoever thought of the Japanese as being poor?' wrote Martha Gellhorn. 'Suddenly, like a revelation, the Japanese became human: a gently smiling giant, John bent to listen to tiny, wrinkled old people, and it turns out that the Japanese can be poor, neglected and out of it, in rich Japan, as anywhere else.'[13]

Since his first trip to Japan, Pilger had been fascinated by what he saw as 'public truths' and 'private truths', another form of the 'official' and 'unofficial' truths that he highlighted in his nuclear arms propaganda documentary *The Truth Game* (see Chapter 8). *Japan – Behind the Mask* asked how the country had achieved such economic success after suffering from World War Two more than any nation except the Soviet Union.

The images of hi-tech perfection and happy workplaces, with employees going through daily physical exercises, were only part of the story. Shigeru Wada, of the National Railway Workers' Union, told Pilger that the Ministry of Labour's statistics excluded about 42 per cent of workers, who had no legal protection. Pilger and director Alan Lowery highlighted a man whose factory was subcontracted to do work for companies such as Sony and Seko, employing part-time women who worked for less than £2 an hour, six days a week, with no sick pay or pension and only three days' annual holiday. Women made up 40 per cent of Japan's labour force but received less than half the pay of men and none of the fringe benefits, said Pilger. Most Japanese businesses were actually subcontractors for the large companies and surviving precariously.

For the first time since the war, unemployment was an issue in Japan as the yen gained in value and export prices rose. In 1985, about 1,600,000 were without jobs, but the unofficial figure was said to be much higher and the dole ran out after ninety days. In one area of high unemployment featured in the film, men queued up daily for work at subcontractors' factories and attempts to organize unions had ended in bloodshed. Although Japan's post-war labour laws gave workers the right to organize themselves and negotiate with management, US General MacArthur, who ran post-war Japan as a viceroy, cancelled the right of public workers to strike. This resulted in high wages for the post-war élite while most Japanese remained low paid.

'Today, the outside world sees only the mask of a docile workforce and a consensus society,' said Pilger. The recent railways privatization had been intended to break one of the last unions to maintain its independence since 1945. More than 70,000 workers had already been made redundant from the railways, with another 100,000 jobs threatened. 'That's the equivalent of wiping out British Rail altogether,' said Pilger.

Many Japanese travelled up to four hours a day by train to go to work. Years of property speculation by large companies had left little room in cities for housing. Almost half of homes had no flush lavatories, some still had no running water and most no central heating. Film showed a dustman, his wife and four children living in four rooms, totalling 30 feet by 18 feet, on a huge housing estate. As the dustman faced redundancy, the couple did piece-

work in the evenings for a multinational company, earning up to
£7 a day. Pilger visited Kawasaki, the world's largest industrial
city, where two-thirds of the country's goods were produced.
However, one million people lived alongside petrochemicals,
power stations and thousands of small factories. He described it as
Japan's 'invisible city . . . pollution-ridden, desperately overcrowded', with antiquated equipment and poor working conditions. In one hospital, 400 recognized pollution victims were
being treated, but the real figure could be as many as ten times
higher.

Not only was Japan's trade geared to the West, but it had an
American-style constitution, a British-style cabinet and a constitutional monarchy. What made the modern Japanese different
was a strong anti-militarist feeling, a legacy of the millions lost in
its twentieth-century wars and conquests. One shrine contained
most of the 2,500,000 names from the country's long war that
began in 1931 with its invasion of China and ended fourteen years
later with its surrender at the end of World War Two. However,
military spending was increasing, despite the constitutional sti-
pulation that only one per cent of Japan's gross domestic product
could be spent on a self-defence force. Behind the mask, said
Pilger, was the second-largest military power in Asia, after China,
and the seventh-largest in the world. Spending on the military had
increased as GDP rose while still maintaining the same ratio.

'Far from renouncing war,' said Pilger, 'Japan today is host to
119 American military facilities and is America's unsinkable aircraft carrier in the East. Despite this, the Reagan administration
wants Japan to completely re-arm and to be a full regional power.'
Prime Minister Nakasone had agreed to take part in the development of Star Wars technology. A journalist, Yumi Kikuchi,
explained that World War Two was not taught in history lessons
apart from the bare facts that it was fought and lost. 'It's an
embarrassment for older generations and I think they feel very
guilty,' she said. 'They want to forget about it.'

The government continued to censor textbooks, reported

Pilger. The 1937 Nanking massacre, in which 100,000 civilians were slaughtered by Japanese troops, amounted to no more than a footnote. Pilger and Lowery visited a kindergarten in Tokyo run by a liberally minded woman who allowed free expression, but this was a type becoming increasingly rare in Japan. The pressure on children to pass exams was intense and more than 35 per cent went to university, compared with less than 5 per cent in Britain. To achieve this, and 'a job for life', many were sent to 'cramming' schools. Although Japan's suicide rate among young people was far from the highest in the world, 'waves' of suicides resulted from the pressure of exams and bullying at school.

However, the 'most enduring' mask in Japan, said Pilger, was that of the women, who since 1945 had enjoyed some of the most favourable legislation anywhere in the world but had gained little compared with those in other developed nations. Female broadcaster Yoshiko Sakurai said that women were still expected to 'look prettier, speak soft and behave well' and not to express their opinions 'in a blunt way'. Pilger reported that many women in employment had to sign pledges to leave when they became pregnant and all were paid less than men. In April 1986, an equal opportunities law was passed, but women still received less pay. 'Custom in Japan is stronger than law,' Pilger said he had been told by a Labour Ministry official. Spelling out the threats posed to one of the world's major industrial nations, Pilger finished:

Today's Japan is vulnerable because it imports much of its food and most of its energy and is tied to the fortunes of the United States. If the American economy further weakens, causing anti-Japanese sentiment to grow in threatened American industries, restrictions on Japanese imports are likely and the effects in Japan will be unpredictable. What are now ripples on a tranquil surface could become raging waves. Of course, Japan is luckier than Britain, whose history of imperial success gives modern British leaders an inflated sense of Britain's power and significance. Many Japanese are not burdened by such nostalgia. They know that their imperial adventures brought them only pain and suffering, and it's this awareness that is the key to Japan's survival. But, despite all the pressures that they live under, it seems to me that their everyday kindness, modesty and grace remain unaffected. Of all their achievements in recent years, this may be their greatest.

Another Asian country, the Philippines, was the subject of *War by Other Means*, directed by David Munro and screened in 1992. It was about the fact that debts owed to the rich world by the Third World were far greater than the aid or charitable donations they received.

'I always find it immensely satisfying to take an issue that seems dry and endeavour to articulate it for a wide audience,' said Pilger. 'In this case, it was debt and showing how it affected people's lives. The film was set on Smoky Mountain, a horrific mountain of rubbish in Manila Bay. There, I met an amazing man, Eddie, and his family, who lived on the rubbish heap, and the film told of his struggle to get out. The bigger picture was that 60 per cent of the Philippines' budget went in paying off the interest on an unrepayable debt incurred by the Marcos regime. There was no money for housing and public services. Again, people were being punished for the crimes of a dictator, as well as the crimes of the banks such as the British high street banks and the World Bank, which poured money into Marcos's pockets and saw the country go into debt. When Marcos was overthrown, Cory Aquino should and could have repudiated the debt. But she came from the same élite and the poor, people like Eddie, are paying off a debt that is not theirs.'[14]

In *War by Other Means*, Pilger brought the issue home to a British audience in this way. He said:

Remember Live Aid in 1985, that symbol of concern and generosity? Did you know that during that year the hungriest countries in Africa gave twice as much money to us in the developed world as we gave to them? There was another famine last year. Perhaps you were one of those who took part in Red Nose Day. Did you know that, before that day was over, the equivalent of all the money that Comic Relief had raised in Britain, about £12 million, had come back to the rich countries, for every day this amount is given by the poorest to the rich as interest payments on loans that most of them never asked for or knew existed. In other words, contrary to a myth long popular in the West, it's been the poor of the world that finance the rich, not the other way round, and this film sets out to explain why.

It's also a film about war, a war you don't see on your television screens, for it's seldom news. It's been described as a silent war. Instead of soldiers dying, there are children dying, more than half a million in one year, according to the United Nations. That's more than twice the number of dead in the Gulf War. Instead of the bombing of bridges, there's the tearing down of forests and other natural resources, the bulldozing of farmland and the running down of schools and hospitals. In many ways, it's like a colonial war. The difference is that, these days, people and their resources are controlled not by viceroys and occupying armies but by other, more sophisticated means, of which the principal weapon is debt.

The power and politics of the World Bank was one way in which the rich countries of the world controlled the poor. The World Bank was set up after World War Two to finance the reconstruction of Europe, then to develop the Third World, explained Pilger. In the Philippines, 44 per cent of the national budget was used to pay interest charges to foreign banks while only 3 per cent was spent on health services. This was the legacy of the dictator Ferdinand Marcos, who had left a huge national debt, much of it from the World Bank. Cory Aquino pledged that she would 'vigorously renegotiate the terms of our foreign debts' but gave priority to paying off the banks. More than $6 million was paid back each day. 'Poverty now stands at 70 per cent of the population,' said Pilger, 'a rise of more than 10 per cent since she came to power.'

Eddie, from Smoky Mountain, and his wife, Teresita, each worked at least twelve hours a day to earn little more than £2, which paid for basic meals of mostly rice for them and four of their surviving six children. Everyone at Smoky Mountain lived without clean water or sanitation. John Cavanagh, of the Institute of Policy Studies in Washington, told Pilger that 'one Filipino child dies every hour because of the increase in debt service payments'. Film of headstones showed that many children indeed had short lives.

Over film of homeless children on the streets of Manila, Pilger explained that this 'could be anywhere in the indebted world'. He joined a police unit that rounded up these children and tried to find institutions to take them, although there were few. The National Economic Development Authority estimated that 500,000 workers would lose their jobs in the Philippines that year as a result of International Monetary Fund policies. 'That means more children on the streets,' said Pilger. Some used drugs, others turned to prostitution.

The country was abundant in food, but that did not pay back foreign investors. New factories funded by Japan would produce food for export, creating new revenue and profit for foreigners – and new debt for the Philippines. These factories would destroy food-growing land, on which eight million people depended. The destruction of the Philippines' rainforests was also complete. In 1991, a typhoon had left 6,000 people dead and 43,000 homeless in an area where previously the forest had protected the people from floods and mudslides. So the environment was a victim of the debt crisis, too.

Travelling to a World Bank/IMF conference in Bangkok, Thailand, convened to discuss ways of eradicating poverty worldwide, Pilger asked why World Bank officials spent $45 million a year flying first-class and staying in five-star hotels, and why the conference chefs were flown in from Paris to a country where children still died from malnutrition, and why 'they need to be shadowed by more doctors than most people in South-east Asia see in a lifetime'. Across the road from the conference venue, the Holiday Inn, were people living in poverty. Fences had been erected so that the delegates would not have to look at them.

Pilger described how 'debt was crucial to the pressure exerted by the United States in building the so-called coalition against Saddam Hussein'. The United States had been able to 'tailor the UN Security Council to its war plans by using debt and the international banks'. Egypt was told that $14 billion would be wiped off its national debt if it joined the coalition, Iran was rewarded for its support with its first loan from the World Bank since the 1979 Islamic revolution, and China received its first World Bank loan since the Tiananmen Square massacre. Syria was promised a 'special' one billion-dollar arms deal brokered by Washington.

Votes of the non-permanent members of the Security Council were critical. 'Minutes after Yemen voted against the resolution to go to war,' reported Pilger, 'a senior American diplomat was instructed to tell the Yemeni ambassador, "That was the most expensive 'no' vote you ever cast,"' meaning that $70 million in American aid to one of the poorest countries in the world would be stopped.' This had echoes of Pilger's 1976 documentary *Zap!! The Weapon Is Food*, which told how food aid was withheld from countries that did not vote with the United States in the United Nations (see Chapter 5).

Britain's influence on the international banks was relatively small, said Pilger, but in 1990 poor countries transferred more than £6 billion net to British banks. On top of this, the banks were allowed tax relief on making provision for so-called doubtful loans and, between 1987 and 1990, this relief amounted to £1.6 billion, the equivalent of ten times what the British public gave in charitable donations to the Third World. All of Britain's high street banks had refused to take part in this programme.

Many debtor countries were rescheduling – postponing – their debts. The only solution, said Pilger, was for these debts to be written off completely or at least their loan repayments channelled back into genuine development that put food-growing, health and education before so-called economic growth. 'The World Bank and the IMF should be abolished and replaced by a real development agency that is non-profit-making and entirely free of political strings and can help nations develop on *their* terms, meeting *their* needs,' Pilger suggested. Cancelling debt unconditionally would hardly affect the banks, he added. The debts of poor countries accounted for less than 5 per cent of loans from commercial banks.

In Britain in the 1990s, the rich had got richer and the poor poorer. No other country in Europe had seen such a dramatic rise in those living below the breadline. 'One in five British children now lives in poverty,' added Pilger. 'And, as in the Third World, poverty kills, says Professor Peter Townsend, a world authority.'

War by Other Means provided plenty to ponder. 'The film has been used in schools,' said Pilger. 'When you think of that collective audience, especially in the post-VCR world, documentaries become educational aids. In one sense, my films are meant to educate, presenting a complex, seemingly abstract issue and saying, "There is no reason why you, the viewer, should not understand this, because you have a right to understand it, and it is important, because it affects you." '[15]

The struggle of people against poverty, set against a backdrop of big business, was the theme of *Apartheid Did Not Die*, Pilger's report on the 'new' South Africa, screened in 1998. With director Alan Lowery, he set out to discover what this freedom meant to the majority of South Africans four years after Nelson Mandela and the African National Congress had assumed power in the wake of apartheid. The film caused great discomfort among white South Africans and the new black Establishment because of Pilger's description of a new, economic apartheid, which meant that most blacks remained in poverty while 5 per cent of the population controlled 88 per cent of the nation's wealth. The documentary, however, struck a chord with many of the black majority in whose name the struggle against apartheid had been waged.

It was Pilger's return to the country from which he was banned in 1967 for his newspaper reporting of apartheid. His articles on the iniquities and absurdities of 'race classification' had especially upset the white supremacist regime. He had never filmed in South Africa, although he had interviewed Helen Suzman, a lone voice against apartheid in the South African Parliament, in his 1983 Channel Four series *The Outsiders* (see Chapter 7). The uprising of the United Democratic Movement in the black townships, together with pressure from abroad, had finally ended white minority rule. Television coverage of the apartheid years had expressed the differing sympathies of those in the West. In 1963, *World in Action* revealed the squalid living conditions of blacks in South Africa and Angola, causing protests from the ambassadors of both countries. This led the Independent Television Authority, as it then was, to declare that *World in Action* had not been 'impartial' and all future Granada Television current affairs programmes were 'vetted'. It is instructive that British commercial television's long era of censorious intervention emanated from, effectively, a defence of apartheid.

Pilger opened *Apartheid Did Not Die* by quoting the Freedom Charter of the African National Congress that 'our country belongs to everyone and that all the people shall share in the wealth'. With Table Mountain behind him, he said:

This is Robben Island, off Cape Town, where Nelson Mandela and thousands of political prisoners were banished. It seems the right place to ask why those freedoms for which so many fought and died are still missing in South Africa. Yes, apartheid based on race is outlawed now, but the system always went far deeper than that. The cruelty and injustice were underwritten by an economic apartheid which regarded people as no more than cheap, expendable labour. It was backed by great business corporations, in South Africa, Britain, the rest of Europe and the United States, and it was this apartheid, based on money and profit, that allowed a small minority to control most of the land, most of the industrial wealth and most of the economic power. Today, the same system is called, without a trace of irony, the free market. This film will ask why apartheid continues, by other means.

A former Robben Island prisoner, the ANC resistance fighter Ahmed (Kathy) Kathrada, showed Pilger round the prison, where he spent almost as long as Nelson Mandela. For the first fourteen years, he said, he and Mandela slept on the floor in their cells, which had merely a couple of mats. Mandela had worn shorts, indicative of how whites classified blacks as 'boys'. Recalling the international pressure on the apartheid regime, Pilger said that white police firing on hundreds of Soweto schoolchildren in 1976 had led to international sanctions. By the 1980s, white privilege was at risk. Finally, in 1990, as the white economy began to slide, the new president, F.W. De Klerk, lifted the ban on the ANC and freed Mandela.

Over film of De Klerk with British Prime Minister Margaret Thatcher, Pilger said, 'The white Establishment and its backers in Washington and London wanted, above all, to maintain power over the economy and keep South Africa safe for international capital, regardless of the colour of its government. Behind these very public meetings, the ANC met secretly with the regime. A special relationship developed in which accommodating the demands of the old apartheid order began to take precedence over the support of the Freedom Charter.'

The ANC agreed to what it called 'historic compromises', including a policy of reconciliation. 'How was it possible for the victims of a form of genocide to reconcile with their oppressors?' asked Pilger. 'One of the deals was amnesty for the killers, torturers and collaborators. All they had to do was take part in a Truth and Reconciliation Commission, a kind of public confessional in which they didn't have to say sorry and there was no justice and people got away literally with murder. By broadcasting its evidence on national radio and television, the Truth Commission's greatest achievement has been to give white South

Africans the opportunity to come to terms with the horrors of the crimes committed in their name. No one can now say, "I didn't know." ' This was accompanied by film of black people weeping as they gave evidence to the Commission. Cosmas Desmond, author of *The Discarded People* and a former priest in the East End of London, told Pilger that apartheid had not been on trial because it was what one system did to a whole nation of people, not what one person did to another. One woman spoke of the death of her son, shot in the head by a police officer who had confessed to the murder and asked for amnesty.

Pilger was welcomed back to South Africa by Nelson Mandela, who told him, 'You should understand it was an honour to have been banned from my country.' He asked Mandela why not a single member of the apartheid regime had shown remorse. Mandela insisted that some members of the white cabinet had 'apologized generally' but the public wanted admissions that certain people had ordered others to carry out atrocities. He said, 'I think it's a great deal of concern that people like De Klerk have tried to avoid responsibility. I think it's a tragedy.' Throughout the interview, Pilger showed great respect for Mandela but did not spare him the questions he believed he should ask and his audience expected of him. Thus, Mandela's unease was visible when Pilger compared his specific promises to his people with the harsh reality of their lives as the ANC had shifted to a 'market' economy, with all its familiar divisions and effective abandonment of those in greatest need of social justice.

Roger Ronnie, general secretary of the South African Municipal Workers' Union, felt that true reconciliation would not be found in a truth commission but in the redistribution of wealth from those who benefited under apartheid to those who suffered. 'The failure to do that has made the whole reconciliation process a bit of a farce,' he said. An aerial view of the Sandton area of Johannesburg, home to some of the richest people in the world, with Pilger's comment that 'they've been asked to give up nothing, not even a modest wealth tax', was followed by film of the Alexandra township, literally across the road, where half a million people lived in an area of less than one-and-a-half miles, most of them without jobs and up to fifteen families living in one 'slum'.

White privilege was embodied in Edith Venter, captioned as a 'socialite and charity patron', who tried on designer dresses at a leading store, with Pilger looking on, barely containing his amusement. She told him that she had been nominated Best Dressed Woman of South Africa, and admitted to having an 'Imelda Marcos wardrobe' of shoes. There was far greater awareness of how blacks lived, she said, but her designer was less ingenuous as he chipped in his observation of the whites' view of the black townships: 'We know but we don't go.' She added that black people who could afford to had moved into white areas since the abolition of apartheid, 'which is fabulous for them'. In the voiceover, Pilger said, 'The jewellery she's wearing is worth more than £100,000. Half the African people of South Africa have an income of less than £12 a week.'

Another vivid example of white privilege came from a property agent, Pam Golding, who told Pilger that the market had actually improved for whites since the ANC came to power. She enthused about selling a house to Margaret Thatcher's son, Mark. 'I know that Baroness Thatcher liked the house,' she said. 'She was there and admired the view and thought it was a lovely home for her son and for her grandchildren.' Pilger chipped in, helpfully, 'Of course, she's a great friend of South Africa, she's been supportive over the years.' Golding replied, 'She is – she's fantastic.'

Pilger traced the roots of gold-mining, staple of South African capital, to Cecil Rhodes, first prime minister of the Cape in the late-nineteenth century. It was then that black people were first used as cheap labour on a massive scale. Today, he said, democracy had made little difference to the lives of the 70,000 miners on the gold fields at Carletonville. The local miners' union representative was seen making his daily phone calls to find out how many workers had been killed or injured overnight. Since mining had begun in South Africa, 69,000 men had died. 'It has been estimated that the human cost of every ton of gold mined is one life and twelve serious injuries,' added Pilger.

Michael Spicer, head of public affairs for Anglo American, the giant corporation whose business interests in the country ranged from minerals and tourism to property and retailing, admitted that these were 'statistics of great concern' but insisted that 'all mining has risks, South Africa has the most risks', referring to the fact that it was the deepest mining in the world. Spicer had no answer to Pilger's evidence, taken from official sources, of negligence by the mining companies. 'A third of all black miners have succumbed to deadly lung diseases, with little compensation,' said Pilger. Human rights lawyer Richard Spoor said that these did not kill people in the same way as a rock fall. 'It's an insidious, slow killer,' he explained. It was killing people far away out in the countryside, poor, rural people who had no voice.

From the former trading floor of the Johannesburg Stock Exchange, Pilger said that the five companies that controlled almost three-quarters of all listed shares in South Africa represented one of the greatest concentrations of corporate wealth in the world. He compared these underwriters of apartheid with the great German companies that ran the economy of the Third Reich. Over film of sixty-nine peaceful demonstrators being murdered by the South African police in the Sharpeville massacre of 1960, he noted that this did not stop foreign capital from pouring into South Africa. Britain was the biggest single investor in South Africa, followed closely by the United States. During the apartheid years, both saw their capital return higher profits than anywhere else in the world.

Pilger negotiated sale of *Apartheid Did Not Die* to the South African Broadcasting Corporation (SABC), which then threatened not to show it. Allister Sparks, the South African journalist described by Pilger as the country's 'great chronicler' during the apartheid years[16] and now the SABC's head of news and current affairs, insisted on screening a disclaimer similar to those demanded by the IBA in Britain in the 1970s. Replying to Sparks in the Johannesburg *Mail & Guardian*, Pilger wrote, 'Once it was agreed at the SABC that suppressing my film would be difficult as it was being shown simultaneously in Britain, [Allister] Sparks wrote a sheaf of disclaimers that ran as words on the screen. These were rather like the health warnings on packets of cigarettes. They warned viewers that the film they were about to see had nothing to do with SABC and was "a highly critical view of the new South Africa".'[17] Pilger also asked, 'Why did the SABC suppress a long interview with me, in which I explained the genesis and aims of the film? This was due to be shown on the eight o'clock news on the night before *Apartheid Did Not Die* was scheduled.'[18]

Sparks, who said he was offended by the film's criticism of the ANC, looked for flaws in the documentary. Taking issue with Pilger's assertion that foreign investment had increased after Sharpeville, he wrote, 'As everyone who was around at the time knows, there was a massive outflow of capital.' Pilger countered that this was a myth, that the outflow was 'short-lived' and 'in the 1960s, foreign investment was unprecedented, with foreign liabilities almost doubling'.[19]

Said Pilger in the film, 'The ANC's most important historic compromise was to reinforce the economic power of these pillars of apartheid. The ideals of the Freedom Charter were replaced by a policy favouring big business and the free market.' Under democracy, foreign investment had tripled, profits had risen and jobs had disappeared at the rate of 100,000 a year. Nelson Mandela told Pilger that the best way to introduce transformation was 'to do so without the dislocation of any aspect of our public life and we do not want to challenge big business in a way where they can take fright and take away their money'. Questioned on the Freedom Charter's aspiration to the people of the country owning its wealth, Mandela replied, 'They are already beginning to share in that wealth.' Some blacks were involved in major companies, he added. In voiceover, Pilger said that, since the ANC had come to power, inequality among blacks had risen and the class gap had opened up. 'People power is being taken over by a black élite, an extension of the black middle class created by the apartheid regime as a buffer to real change,' he said.

Challenged by Pilger about the ANC's willingness to deal with any government, regardless of their human rights record, Mandela replied, 'There is no country anywhere in the world where discrimination and oppression is part of the legal system . . . racism was entrenched in the constitution of the country.' Mandela said that some blacks were being returned to their own land. Pilger replied that this amounted to less than half of one per cent of those dispossessed. 'Today, wealthy white farmers continue to control more than 80 per cent of the agricultural land and their existing property rights are guaranteed in the constitution,' he said. The author Cosmas Desmond pointed out that only 60,000 of the white population, out of a total of four to five million, were farmers, most of them mortgaged by the Land Bank, effectively the government. 'If the government simply foreclosed on those loans, they would have the land back,' he explained. Most of the farmers were 'hardly productive at all', so the country did not depend on them.

One of the government's success stories, reported Pilger, was in health care, which was now available free for pregnant women and children under the age of six. Also, clinics had been built and youngsters were immunized against diseases such as polio. Another achievement was in providing access to running water to more than one million people, but up to fourteen million still had no reliable water supply, with many blacks walking a long distance simply to get polluted water, 'while whites continue to irrigate their gardens and fill their swimming pools'. Pilger highlighted a project of homeless women near Cape Town who were building their own homes. 'We are going to change South Africa,' said one. 'It is better to do it ourselves.' The woman, who had previously lived in a shack, added, 'The first time I flushed my toilet, I was frightened!'

In the closing sequence, Pilger described his film as a tribute to the resilience of those who had survived the apartheid regime. He asked, 'Did people vote to exchange apartheid for a democracy of privilege and poverty? Did all that celebration take place so that the new South Africa might be slotted into a predetermined economic system: a global apartheid whose only certainty is that the rich get richer and the poor poorer? . . . It was the ordinary people of South Africa who set the pace of change. It was their humanity and their courage that triumphed here, proving that fundamental change is possible. It will be a tragedy for all of us if their continuing struggle goes unrewarded, for its inspiration and lessons are universal.'

Apartheid Did Not Die was a telling example of Pilger exposing the reality behind the media images and carefully deconstructing the received wisdoms. In South Africa, it had an enormous impact, angering many whites while being taken up by blacks as a *cause célèbre*. Returning to that country, Pilger attended a meeting of people expelled by the apartheid regime from District Six, the 'coloured' area of Cape Town. He was asked to stand and was clapped enthusiastically for his documentary.

'It was, for me, one of the most important films I've made,' he said. 'We are all being drawn into a world of global apartheid, and the example of South Africa is crucial to our understanding of the dangers that lie ahead.'[20] After making *Apartheid Did Not Die*, Pilger began researching a book, *Freedom Next Time*. 'I am interested in the way ideals are squandered when they need not be,' he said. 'The ANC has become the party of big business, yet its mandate was the economic priorities of the majority of the people. Nelson Mandela is a great man, but he, too, has been adopted by the economic enemies of his people. Above all, and for all the violence that is apartheid's legacy, the generosity of character of the majority of people remains intact. It is a tremendous resource on which to build a truly new South Africa.'[21]

10. AUSTRALIA

'**PERHAPS THE MOST** compelling and difficult assignment for any journalist is the rediscovery of his own country, especially a country he left without ever really knowing it,' wrote John Pilger in *TVTimes* when ITV screened his first one-hour documentary, *Pilger in Australia*, in 1976.[1] It was then fourteen years since he had left Sydney to carve out a career in British journalism. He had returned on several occasions – 'always drawn back,' he said, 'by all the forces of longing and nostalgia that one's homeland can impose on an expatriate'.[2]

Pilger had grown up in the Bondi area of the city, close to an Aboriginal reserve, but had little idea of the Aborigines' history, which was not part of the school curriculum in Australia. In 1967, the year in which he was banned from South Africa for reporting on a Race Classification Board, one of the symbols of apartheid, the *Daily Mirror* sent Pilger home to report on Australia for British readers. 'I was a young Australian reporter in Britain,' he recalled, 'and Australia was finally becoming interesting to a British audience beyond the "corks on the hat" view.'[3]

During the trip, Pilger travelled to the far west of his home state, New South Wales, and the Northern Territory – the outback – for the first time. There, he discovered his country's own form of apartheid, which had rarely been mentioned by his parents. 'Although my family was politically enlightened and progressive, I think that they had, at best, paternalistic attitudes towards the Aboriginal people,' explained Pilger. 'As a child, I no doubt grew up with the same stereotypes of Aboriginal people as anyone else, albeit benign ones. My father travelled extensively throughout Australia and I think it is fair to say that he didn't have a high regard for Aboriginal people, whom he saw as idle and feckless. It was a common view: that of the "poor old Abo".'[4]

When Pilger made his first television documentary on Australia, in 1976, it was an inquiry into the country he had left at the beginning of the previous decade. The expatriate cast his eyes over a wide range of issues and produced a 'postcard'-type account of the changes. He sought to debunk some of the myths about 'the lucky country', such as Australia's reputation as a truly classless society and its loyalty to the Queen. He interviewed Prime Minister Malcolm Fraser and his predecessor, Gough Whitlam, as well as authors, journalists, Turkish-Australians, Italian-Australians and many others. At the time, Australia was settling down after the dismissal of reforming Prime Minister Whitlam by the governor-general, an issue that Pilger covered in a later documentary, adding evidence to the theories that British and US intelligence agencies had manipulated the sacking because of their fears for the future of US nuclear bases in the country.

However, the 1976 trip was not the happiest journey home for Pilger. 'The programme was a critical but affectionate look at Australia,' he recalled, 'but it rained all the time and the film ended up with a visual rising damp. During the interviews on idyllic Sydney harbour, the rain sheeted down. The postcard image, bless it, deserted us completely!'[5] Also, producer-director Charles Denton, who had long wanted to make a film about Australia, had a problem. He had hired a cameraman and sound recordist in Australia who were both members of the British technicians' union ACTT, but the sound man's membership had lapsed six months earlier. As a result, the crew and Denton were blacked by the union. John Ingram, who had made several episodes of the *Pilger* series, took over from Denton, arriving from London with another film cameraman and sound recordist.

Cameraman Ivan Strasburg, a British-based white South African, recalled filming an interview with Charlie Perkins, who had accompanied Pilger on a trip to Aboriginal Australia in 1969. 'I thought I would rather be a black South African at the time than an Aborigine in Australia,' said Strasburg. 'At least the future was with them, but there was no future for the Aborigines.'[6]

Despite Pilger's sodden memories of this Australian trip, the documentary was not so badly received. Although Stanley Reynolds, of *The Times*, regarded it as 'disappointing' and found it strange that it 'did not mention cricket and the great, thunderous fast bowling of the incomparable Dennis Lillee and the deadly swift Jeff Thomson',[7] Peter Lennon of *The Sunday Times* praised *Pilger in Australia* for having 'that truly high-class quality of going over old ground and making new connections in such a way that the entire image of his country was reshaped for us'. Lennon added that Pilger gave Australians credit for integrating many nationalities, such as Filipinos, Poles and Britons, 'but he gave them no quarter for their treatment of the Aborigines'.[8]

In 1981, Pilger was commissioned by the *Sydney Morning Herald* to make a film to commemorate the newspaper's 150th anniversary, to be screened in the New South Wales area by the Sydney station Channel 7, owned by the newspaper's parent company. 'Instead of making a rather gentle film about the historical journey of the *Sydney Morning Herald*, I decided to make one that would look at Australia through a different lens,' said Pilger. 'I did what I had set out to do in *Pilger in Australia*. *Island of Dreams* told the brutal history of convict Australia and the Aboriginal experience. It was during its making that I researched my own family's antecedents and discovered "the worst" – the fact that my great-great-grandparents were both convicts. The family myth was that my great-great-grandfather was a landowner. In fact, he was an Irish labourer transported to Australia for "uttering unlawful oaths": a political offence.

'*Island of Dreams* was one of the first documentaries on television to combine that critical and affectionate view of Australia. Some critics have found that difficult to analyse. My book *A Secret Country*, which I wrote to tie in with the 1988 bicentenary celebrations, also works from the base of a very affectionate view of Australia, perhaps some would say idealistic, but it's also highly critical. I like my homeland physically and I've also always appreciated the fact that Australia has been essentially a working-class country that celebrated working-class culture long before this became fashionable in Britain. A French friend who moved there in the 1970s said to me recently, "I love it here, the weather is magnificent, the food is magnificent, my children love it, the people are so friendly – and it's run by crooks." He exaggerated, but not by much.'[9]

David Bowman, editor-in-chief of the *Sydney Morning Herald* at the time that *Island of Dreams* was made, recalled that the idea to commission Pilger came as the traditionally conservative newspaper was experiencing a period of rejuvenation. 'It ran against the grain,' said Bowman. 'The *Herald* had been very much the domain of one family, the Fairfaxes, and there had been recent changes at board level. The chairman's son, James Fairfax, had taken over in the late 1970s and he turned out to be something of a fresh breeze. John had made a considerable name for himself in Britain and he was being noticed in Australia, although they probably didn't know about his radicalism. To James Fairfax's credit, though, he was given a free hand.'[10]

It was while making *Island of Dreams* that Pilger first met Alan Lowery, a fellow-countryman who had graduated from the Australian Film & Television School in 1974 with others such as Phillip Noyce and Gillian Armstrong, who went on to become successful feature film directors. Lowery moved to London in 1980 and was asked by executive producer Tony Culliton to film a 'camera piece' to slot into *Island of Dreams*. When director David Munro started making his mammoth documentary *The Four Horsemen*, Pilger approached Lowery to work with him. As well as the Channel Four interview series *The Outsiders* (see Chapter 7), they made *Burp! Pepsi v Coke in the Ice Cold War* and *Nicaragua* together before joining forces to film a documentary about their homeland.

'I said to John early on that it would be great if we could do a story about our own country,' recalled Lowery. 'There was a whole period of history being rewritten by historians such as Henry Reynolds and an untold story that most Australians didn't know, let alone people overseas.'[11] Pilger was inspired to make his 1985 film *The Secret Country – The First Australians Fight Back* after seeing *Lousy Little Sixpence*, an Australian documentary made by Alec Morgan two years earlier. It told the story of 'the stolen generation', Aboriginal children of mixed parentage who were taken away from their mothers and put away in institutions or used as bonded labour. Pilger was also able to draw on some of the material that he had used in *Island of Dreams*. His aim was 'to look behind the benign historical view of Australia and tell of the rapacious history of the Aboriginal experience since the whites arrived in the eighteenth century'.[12]

The Secret Country was subsequently embraced by many Aboriginal communities and used as a teaching aid by them and white educational groups throughout Australia. 'I heard a touching story about an Aboriginal elder dying in a remote part of the Northern Territory and leaving to his son, among his personal effects, a VHS cassette of *The Secret Country*,' said Pilger.[13]

The documentary opened with black-and-white newsreel film from 1938 marking the 150th anniversary of white settlement in Australia. The landing of the first ships in Sydney was re-enacted and, explained Pilger, Aborigines were press-ganged into playing roles. In his first piece to camera, he described Australia as 'a secret country with a secret history'. It was a 'frontier country', with on the one side the English poor and Irish political prisoners sent by Britain as slaves and on the other 'a mysterious and remarkable nation whose people could trace their roots back 40,000 years'. Pilger continued:

Britain waged war against this nation. Massacres as systematic as those practised against the Jews in the twentieth century were carried out in the name of God, king, anthropology, money and land. The jolly swagman was not especially jolly, the billabongs ran with blood. Few or none of these events were recorded or remembered by white Australians and, as the cities grew, the descendants of the white slaves, Australians like myself, seldom glimpsed the other side of the frontier, the outback as we called it. As children, we were given to understand that we were merely innocent bystanders to the slow and natural death of an ancient people, the first Australians, rather than the inheritors of a history every bit as rapacious as that of the United States, Latin America, Africa. All that was unmentionable and secret.

First, Pilger concentrated on the ways in which Aborigines still suffered. In Queensland, their deaths from preventable, infectious diseases had been found to be up to 300 times higher than the white average in 1983 and among the highest in the world. In New South Wales, one-quarter of the Aboriginal males who survived to the age of twenty were dead within another twenty years. 'These are Third World statistics,' said Pilger. The Third World disease trachoma, which caused blindness, was widespread, as was leprosy. Many black Australians lived in tin shelters and they had one of the highest prison populations in the world, for crimes relating to homelessness, alcoholism and unemployment.

However, there were signs of a fightback. In the past fifteen years, reported Pilger, the nation on the other side of the frontier had 'risen from its death bed' to claim back its share of Australia. He outlined what had been taken by the British after declaring the country 'an empty land', even though there were Aboriginal tribes of up to 300,000, perhaps even a million, people. Following Captain Cook's arrival in Botany Bay in 1770, white diseases such as smallpox caused many deaths, but there were also massacres. 'The early convict ships had brought thousands of white slaves, mostly English and Irish transported for crimes of poverty and politics,' said Pilger, 'and they became the instruments of massacre, directed by Christian gentlemen who had brought with them attitudes of racial superiority that were the staple of empire.

Ironically, their cruelty was at odds with liberal reformers in Britain who were then seeking to end the slave trade.'

The Aborigines were declared 'sub-human, little more than animals', and this was used to justify the seizure of their land and their extermination. 'They were hunted and raped and massacred, and few doubted at the time that genocide was the official policy,' said Pilger. A government report in the 1850s recorded incidents of their being poisoned. A war of resistance lasted more than a century and Pilger visited the banks of the Hawkesbury river, north of Sydney, scene of one such battle. 'In the 1930s, my father built a cottage here on the beach of an Aboriginal place called Patonga,' he said. An entire nation, the Durag, had lived all around for thousands of years, but he had known nothing about this during his childhood. The Durag had inflicted on the British 'a casualty rate greater than that sustained by the Australian armed forces during all of World War Two'. After twenty-two years, outnumbered and without guns, they were defeated.

To the camera, Pilger added, 'Today in a land of many cenotaphs and war memorials, on which is invariably written "Lest We Forget", not one of them stands for those who fought and fell in their own country.' The genocide continued into the twentieth century and, by the 1920s, at least 250,000 Aborigines had died. Marcia Langton, of the Central Lands Council (later to become a professor at Northern Territory University, in Darwin), recalled hearing white men only five years earlier referring to 'nigger hunts' in which they had taken part and justifying murder with the excuse that the Aborigines did not use the land in the same way as they did.

Pilger explained that to Aborigines the land was sacred, whereas Europeans saw it as something to be 'bought and sold, built on and exploited', an idea incomprehensible to black Australians. Pictures painted 10,000 years before the pyramids, and older than the cave paintings in France, had been discovered and were recognized as the longest historical record of any human beings. In the mid-1960s, Aborigines had revolted and Charlie

Perkins led 'freedom rides' of black and white students into the outback, based on the earlier 'freedom rides' into the segregated states of the American South. When they were confronted by an angry white crowd at a swimming pool, an Aboriginal woman pointed to a white man who had fathered children with a black woman. That evening, Aboriginal children were allowed into the previously whites-only pool.

This led Pilger into the issue of 'the stolen generation'. He spoke to two victims, Bobby Randall, whose song *My Brown Skin Baby* was heard on the soundtrack, and Vince Forrester. An interview from the Alec Morgan documentary *Lousy Little Sixpence* spelled out the human reality of separating children from their mothers. Margaret Tucker explained that, years after she had been taken away, her aunt told her that she had heard a moaning sound like an animal. 'They discovered that it was my mother lying under this tree and in the tall grass moaning,' she said. 'She couldn't cry any more. They had to care for her and look after her. I often wonder how many other children were taken like that, just like animals, because our hearts were absolutely broken.'

As the fightback continued into the 1970s, the first Labor government for twenty-three years was elected, led by Prime Minister Gough Whitlam and committed to a policy of justice for the Aborigines that included land rights legislation. An Aboriginal renaissance saw the rise to public prominence of people such as Pat O'Shane, the first Aboriginal female barrister and head of a government department, Charlie Perkins, the 'freedom rider', who became head of the Department of Aboriginal Affairs, and stage and screen actress Justine Saunders. 'Self-determination is happening in many ways,' said Pilger, over film of Central Australia Aboriginal Media, the first radio network to be run by, and for, Aboriginals in their own languages. Pilger also visited Aborigines in the Northern Territory who had transformed a mission into a centre for the community that included a clinic and a school where the first black teachers were qualifying.

One threat to the Aborigines had been the mining industry, which had moved many off their lands. But they had begun to stand up to this and had some support from whites, which offered the prospect of reconciliation between people of the Third and First Worlds in one country. In the 1950s, the Australian government had not only allowed Britain to test its new nuclear weapons in its 'empty' central and western deserts, but supplied uranium for the atom bombs. Between 1952 and 1957, nine bombs were exploded in Maralinga, close to Aboriginal settlements. One eyewitness, Yami Lester, told Pilger about 'the bang' and the black smoke that followed the first explosion. 'After that,' he continued, 'most of the people were sick and we all got skin rash and diarrhoea and sore eyes . . . I believe that some people died because we didn't have any proper treatment.' He went blind four years later. Only when British and Australian servicemen working on the tests began to suffer and die from cancers, reported Pilger, did the real story emerge. Finally, in 1984, the government had agreed to appoint a royal commission to investigate.

The new Labor Prime Minister, Bob Hawke, pledged himself to introduce land rights legislation, but the powerful mining lobby persuaded him to cancel Labor Party policy that would have allowed Aborigines to control rights on their own land. With the 1988 bicentenary celebrations just three years away, Bobby Randall, one of those Aborigines interviewed in *The Secret Country*, asked, 'When are we going to celebrate justice? When are we going to celebrate just giving back what was taken wrongfully?' Marcia Langton insisted, 'Aboriginal people will not survive unless we have real land rights . . . The right to refuse entry to outsiders, the right to say no to mining if we have to, if we feel that it's too dangerous.' In his final piece to camera, Pilger said that in a 1967 referendum 90 per cent of the electorate gave the federal government special powers to legislate justice for Aborigines. Some justice, rights, land and pride had been won back, but:

In this rich country, Aboriginal children remain sick and mal-nourished, and their death rate from simple, preventable diseases is not very different from that of children in poor countries in Africa and Asia. This almost incredible situation is not a medical problem but a political one and the obstacles to overcoming it stem not from malevolence but from a lack of political will to match sympathy with action. Support for the underdog has always been a powerful myth in Australia, in a white society with the humblest of origins, and, like many myths, it's partly true. Radical reforms like voting rights, minimum wage and child care legislation were pioneered in Australia. But when do the benefits of this noble and fragile tradition reach those whose extraordinary generosity of spirit has been expressed in this film? And what will happen in 1988 when two hundred years of European settlement is cele-brated? What version of events will be told then, an acceptable version, a compromise version or the secret truth? It seems to me that, until a committed policy of reconciliation, of real nation-hood, is offered to the first Australians, those who came recently can never claim their own.

Pilger and Lowery returned to Australia in advance of the bicentenary festivities to make a three-part series, *The Last Dream*, reflecting on the two hundred-year history of white Australia. Naturally, they were critical, in what was certainly an antidote to the celebrations to come, but Pilger again retained an affection for his homeland and a hope for its future as one nation, of whites *and* blacks.

In *Heroes Unsung*, the first episode of the trilogy, he reported on the transformation of the country from a 'secondhand European' society, in which he grew up, to the second most culturally diverse in the world, after Israel. Mass deportation of 'the scum of England and the inflammable matter of Ireland' to 'an antipodean Siberia' started in the eighteenth century. From the quayside at Cork, in Ireland, Pilger recalled his great-great-grandfather, Francis McCarthy, a landless Irish farmer, being taken there in

1821 and convicted of 'uttering unlawful oaths', the political crime of which the Tolpuddle Martyrs were also found guilty. McCarthy was sentenced to fourteen years' penal servitude in New South Wales, taken by boat in leg irons, but he never returned. At the same time, eighteen-year-old Mary Palmer was given a life sentence. Pilger said she was an Irish scullery maid in a London house whose crime probably involved property, 'perhaps as trivial as stealing a loaf of bread'. (His subsequent researches revealed that she was a prostitute in the East End of London, one of a gang of impoverished teenaged girls who had robbed and roughed up a client: a crime for which three were subsequently hanged. Mary, spared because she was pregnant, was sent to New South Wales for life.)

On Sydney Harbour, where the barque *John Barry* arrived with McCarthy after almost five months at sea, Pilger described the awful conditions aboard the ship and the sight in front of its human cargo as they approached 'the white sand of perfect bays' on the other side of the world. McCarthy worked as a labourer in Sydney, and Palmer was sent to 'the female factory' where her head was shaved and she was harshly treated while serving her time in solitary confinement. 'I remember this place – as a mental asylum,' recalled Pilger. Women were placed on view and offered to male convicts on 'an extraordinary courting day', and McCarthy met Palmer in this way, with marriage following. When one of their ten children married a blond piccolo player from Germany, 'a bloody Protestant', it was considered a mixed marriage. More than 160,000 men, women and children were shipped to Australia in such conditions. 'Unlike the first white Americans, who imagined themselves on a mission from God, those first white Australians knew they were Godforsaken,' said Pilger.

Pilger recounted the vast differences between Britain and Australia that emigrants faced, with a 'harsh' land of muted colours and intense heat, the reality behind the 'secondhand Europe'. Film shot by missionaries in 1905 showed that white slavery was accompanied by black slavery, as boats brought in slaves from the Pacific islands. Faith Bandler told Pilger that her father had been a victim of the Pacific islands being 'heavily raided for labour to develop the cane industry in the north', forcibly taken to Australia at the age of thirteen, in 1883.

In the twentieth century, the so-called White Australia Policy was developed, reflecting or fuelling the racism of the majority population. An Italian-born member of the New South Wales Parliament, Franca Arena, said, 'Our whole history has been a history of racism.' Restrictions on entry into the country, such as a dictation test in a European language, ensured that few non-Europeans were assimilated. As a shipping reporter on the Sydney *Daily Telegraph* in the late 1950s, Pilger saw the arrival of immigrants from the other side of the world. To expand the seven million population, many came from Europe as bonded labour. Newsreels of the time trumpeted their arrival and hopes of starting life anew. Many saw Australia as 'the last dream'. Up to one-third of the British population considered emigrating when they were offered the trip Down Under for just £10, on condition they stayed for at least two years. The reality for many, illustrated by black-and-white film, was living in a corrugated-iron army hut in the bush. Pilger also recalled the 'bride ships' arriving in Sydney, filled with 'proxy brides' from Italy, having taken part in wedding ceremonies in their homeland without the bridegrooms, whom they now came to join.

Great public works, tunnels, dams, bridges and power stations were built during the 1950s by labour of more than sixty nationalities. Australia had always celebrated men's contribution to its history but had seldom recognized the contribution of women. Poet and novelist Dorothy Hewett told Pilger, 'Universities were all run by Englishmen and people who were not at all in tune with Australian culture in any way at all . . . and they thought that all literature, all "culture", came from the Old Country.' Despite some of the strongest anti-discrimination laws in the world, women in Australia earned less than two-thirds of men's wages on average, said Pilger. A report by the government of New South Wales stated that up to 60,000 women worked in sweated labour, often earning less than a dollar (40p) an hour and many of them immigrants.

At Bondi Beach, which he described as 'my beach', Pilger spoke of the 'pleasure' culture that took place there, 'a source of good life not known in Europe'. He added, 'Australia is not a classless society. The beach is.' Returning to the house he grew up in, Pilger noted that it now had an inside 'dunny' (lavatory). He clearly enjoyed telling the story of Jack Platt, the shark catcher, fighting a fourteen-foot tiger shark in his dinghy. Such 'contrived innocence' was interrupted when the Boat People arrived from Vietnam in 1975, beginning the transformation of Australia into a Eurasian society. Almost half of the country's immigrants were now from Asia. In some suburban communities, such as one filmed by Pilger and Lowery, English was a second language. They also filmed a naturalization ceremony at which Asians swore allegiance to Queen Elizabeth. In reality, said Pilger, they would be 'second-class citizens' because only the whites in politics and the media had power in Australia.

Similarly, the treatment of Aborigines was a cloud hanging over the country. He recalled as a child seeing Aborigines on the beach at La Perouse and lamented that black children still died from preventable diseases and were confined to the poverty of 'Australian apartheid'. He said they had never been offered justice and this cast a shadow over the bicentenary celebrations.

The treatment of Aborigines continued as the first theme of *Secrets*, the second part of Pilger and Lowery's *Last Dream* trilogy. It opened with sombre black-and-white photographs of Aborigines, including a group in chains, followed by an upbeat colour television advertisement featuring whites celebrating the forthcoming bicentennial. 'It reminds me of an Australian beer commercial, only flatter,' remarked Pilger. Australian history was full of secrets, 'an epic cover-up'. He likened film of the funeral of a black who had died from head injuries while being held by police to scenes in the black South African township of Soweto. There had been almost a hundred Aboriginal deaths in police custody in recent years, reported Pilger, at a rate of one every two weeks, proportionately more than in South Africa. Australia now had the highest rate of imprisonment for black people in the world. Pilger interviewed Arthur and Leila Murray, whose son Eddie had died in custody. Police claimed that he had hanged himself but admitted that he was so drunk 'he couldn't scratch himself'.

As in *The Secret Country*, Pilger produced a black–and–white photograph that he had taken on his first trip into the outback, in 1967. 'It was my introduction to the secret life of my own country . . .' he said. 'Today, they still live on rubbish tips and the apartheid is as strong as it is in South Africa, in practice if not in theory.' He recounted the preventable diseases that were still killing people and the number of dead children's headstones in graveyards. He also recalled those children forcibly taken from their families and taken to Christian missions or as bonded labour in cattle stations or servants to the middle class.

Dr Ross Fitzgerald, a historian, expressed his 'abhorrence' at the nation now celebrating 'the slaughter of Aboriginal people'. Henry Reynolds, one of Australia's most eminent historians, said that by the middle of the twentieth century they had been 'as effectively dispersed from the pages of our history books as they had been dispersed the century before from the inland plains of Australia'. It was partly seen as 'something that was not appropriate for history that was aimed at creating national pride'. Once the Aborigines were incorporated into the country's history, it became the story of man against man. Today, said Pilger, it was estimated that more than 500,000 Aborigines died as a direct result of the British invasion.

Visiting one of 'the killing fields', Pilger reported that government officials and gold miners 'cornered and shot' up to 150 Aboriginal men, women and children at Battle Camp, west of Cooktown, Queensland, in 1873, leaving their bodies floating in a lagoon. Returning to another theme of *The Secret Country*,

Pilger explained the Aborigines' 'pure democracy', seeing them-selves as custodians of the land that was taken from them. The 1967 referendum resulted in Gough Whitlam passing the first land rights legislation the following decade, but his successor in the 1980s, Bob Hawke, commissioned a confidential survey seeking whites' attitudes to the issue. The report was leaked to the *Australian* newspaper, owned by Rupert Murdoch, and it claimed that most whites were opposed to land rights. Pilger said this was untrue and the government had offered 'little more than gestures' to the Aborigines.

Much of white history had been similarly disregarded. Pilger cited the struggles that led to a legal minimum wage pre-dating that of most advanced countries. Arbitration, child benefits, pension, paternity allowance and the vote for women were pioneered in Australia and New Zealand. The world's first Labour government was elected in Queensland, the miners of Broken Hill won a thirty-five-hour week in 1920 and the secret ballot was invented in Australia. English social reformers Beatrice and Sidney Webb discovered that it was 'not a country of social miracles, but a place of social hardship and struggle, of some gains and many losses'. There followed film of farmers being evicted in 1987, which Pilger described as 'commonplace'. High interest rates and falling prices had driven farmers out of business, and the near-collapse of the currency was one factor. Almost one-third of all farms had no income and many had been deserted.

Pilger contrasted this with the casinos and tourists on Queens-land's Gold Coast, 'the Las Vegas of the South Pacific'. Million-aires and poverty were two of Australia's growth areas. Over black-and-white still photographs of caravans, Pilger reported, 'In the two-thirds society, 70 per cent own their own homes, but the rest are in trouble.' Many who had lost their homes or could not afford to pay rent moved into caravans and mobile homes on the outskirts of cities. Meanwhile, a 'new establishment' had come to power since the Labor government of Prime Minister Bob Hawke and treasurer Paul Keating deregulated the Australian economy, making it susceptible to the whims of the money markets. The combined wealth of the richest 200 citizens had increased from less than five billion dollars to twenty-five billion dollars since Labor had come to power. Meanwhile, two million people lived in poverty.

Media moguls such as Rupert Murdoch and Alan Bond borrowed more and more money but paid no tax on the interest. They also paid much less than the national tax rate on their profits. Over film of Hawke and another media magnate, his friend Kerry Packer, Pilger commented that Packer's wealth had risen by 1,200 per cent during the first four years of Hawke's government. Another entrepreneur, Alan Bond, was a friend of Keating and one of the world's biggest gold producers. Hawke had given an assurance during the 1983 election campaign that profits on gold would remain tax-free. Since then, Hawke had passed a Media Bill that allowed Packer and Murdoch to sell their television interests for one million dollars profit, tax-free, and gave Bond his first TV network. Film followed of the 'glitzy', half-million-dollar wedding reception enjoyed by Bond's daughter. Another of Hawke's 'mates', Peter Abeles, head of the international trucking company TNT, had been accused of working with the Mafia in the United States to establish his group of companies there, although he denied knowing with whom he was dealing.

Corruption was as Australian as Fosters beer. 'In state politics, Australia is one of the most over-governed countries in the world,' Pilger later explained. 'It has a small population, six states, each with two houses of parliament, a Northern Territory that has so few people in it they can't make it a state but it still has a government, and then, over this, they have a federal government working on a constitution that is a mess, a combination of the American and British constitutional systems. All of this is a breeding ground for corruption.'[14] Pilger reported that more than a dozen official inquiries had been held into political corruption and organized crime in New South Wales alone.

Cabinet ministers, judges and dozens of top policemen had been the subject of allegations.

At the State Library of New South Wales, in Sydney, he recalled that Australia had a history of a diverse press and campaigning journalism, but now Rupert Murdoch controlled almost 60 per cent of all newspaper circulation and Australia had 'the most concentrated press ownership and the least independent newspapers of any Western democracy'. To buy the Herald & Weekly Times group in 1987, having denounced his Australian citizenship, Murdoch circumvented laws that restricted foreign media ownership by meeting Hawke and Keating, before directing his editors to switch their support to the Labor government. The chairman of the Press Council described the sale as 'unparalleled outside totalitarian countries', he reported.

Brian Toohey, who had been editor of the *National Times*, was lauded as one of the few investigative journalists who had consistently uncovered and published stories of corruption. David Bowman, former editor-in-chief of the *Sydney Morning Herald*, said that politicians were afraid to 'cross' Murdoch because of his power of widespread newspaper ownership.

Investigation was at the heart of *Other People's Wars*, the final part of *The Last Dream*, which included an account of the overthrow of Gough Whitlam's Labor government in the 1970s. Revelations of CIA and MI6 involvement had already been made by Australian authors and journalists, but Pilger brought the evidence together and uncovered new facts. 'I worked closely with William Pinwill, a very fine journalist who had a great deal of information that he had not been able to get published in Australia,' recalled Pilger. 'We sent him off to the United States to investigate the CIA connection over there and he came up with some superb material. Perhaps more investigative work went into that film than anything else I've made.'[15]

Other People's Wars opened with more traditional battles. 'We Australians have a special relationship with war,' said Pilger. 'We fight mostly against people with whom we have no quarrel and

who offer no threat of invasion. Australians fought in China
during the Boxer Rebellion, in New Zealand against the Maoris,
in South Africa against the Boers, in Europe against Germans, in
Korea against Koreans, in Vietnam against Vietnamese.' At the
National War Memorial, in Canberra, Pilger stood next to row
upon row of names on the walls, lamenting that his country had
sent 'willing young men to be martyred for some imperial cause
that didn't concern them'. In World War One, Australia, with a
population of just five million, had lost more men than died for
the United States in that and the Vietnam War.

Over film of Anzac Day being celebrated in the town of
Villers-Bretonneux, northern France, Pilger recalled that Australian diggers had turned back the Germans there in 1918.
Unusually, this juxtaposition was slightly confusing, linking the
day that marked the defeat of Australian and New Zealand troops
by Turks at Gallipoli in 1915 to activity in France three years later.
Black-and-white newsreel film showed the reality of Australian
lost lives and Pilger noted that 200,000 had died in that war. He
recalled that his own grandfather, Richard Pilger, born in Germany but a naturalized Australian citizen, was driven out of every
job he could find during the war. As the son of a German, Pilger's
father was bullied at school.

During World War Two, the Japanese bombed Darwin, in the
Northern Territory, and the Labor Prime Minister, John Curtin,
enraged Winston Churchill by bringing home Australian troops
from the Middle East. Following film of General MacArthur in
Australia, William Pinwill explained that Curtin had not been
told when he would arrive. When Japanese submarines appeared
off Sydney in 1942, Pilger's family and others left for the bush.
Humorously, he recalled that shells were 'fired at my mother's
washing' and 'the great unthinkable became law – the brewing of
beer was restricted'. Jingoistic black-and-white newsreel film
followed of Aboriginal soldiers training: They fought in both
world wars, reported Pilger.

Recently released documents showed that Australia's post-war

Labor government was regarded by the United States as 'unsafe'. In 1949, a conservative, Robert Gordon Menzies, was elected prime minister and pledged to preserve all that the United States and Britain stood for. He became the country's longest-serving leader and Pilger recalled growing up during his era. 'Menzies loved the Queen so much,' he said over film of him welcoming the British monarch, instructing viewers to watch her face as the prime minister recited the words of a seventeenth-century poet, 'I did but see her passing by and yet I love her till I die.' The Queen's embarrassed smile was unmistakable.

Pilger returned to the theme of British nuclear testing in Australia during the 1950s, previously covered in *The Secret Country*. At Ground Zero, Taranaki, one of the British test sites, he said that the land was highly contaminated. James McClelland, the Australian judge presiding over the royal commission that investigated the effects of the tests, said that Menzies did not even consult his cabinet when asked whether his country could be used.

Exploding the myth that Australia had been 'dragged into' the Vietnam War by the United States, Pilger reported that recently declassified documents revealed that from 1962 'Australian governments were prime movers in starting the war in Vietnam' to 'draw the full power of America into the region and to maintain a Western colonial order in Asia'. Pilger recalled the destruction wrought on the Vietnamese and the 1965 announcement by Menzies that Australian troops were going there after receiving a request for 'military assistance' from the government of South Vietnam. But, said Pilger, there was no such request, only a letter – pictured – from that government confirming Menzies's 'offer' of troops. Almost 500 Australians died in the war. One surviving veteran, Brian Day, told Pilger, 'We invaded in the same way as the Japanese invaded Asia and the Germans invaded Europe – it was a criminal act by our government to involve us.' The Australian government's denials that it had taken part in chemical warfare, resulting in the births of deformed babies, had proved to be false, reported Pilger. Another veteran, Barry Wright, spoke of using insecticides. Although US veterans had been compensated for the effects of the herbicide Agent Orange on them, Australian veterans – like the Vietnamese – had not, said Pilger. In 1987, a parade for the veterans had been staged in Sydney – 'they got tears and cheers, but no public apology'.

Australians elected their first truly independent government since 1788 when Whitlam's Labor Party came to power in 1972, said Pilger. During his first hundred days in office, Whitlam ordered Australians to stop fighting in Vietnam, conscription was ended, those jailed for opposing the war were freed and royal patronage was scrapped; the government spoke up for the rights of small nations and Palestinians; it also passed equal rights legislation and doubled education spending. The United States feared that Whitlam's policies were a threat to its secret bases in Australia, notably those at Pine Gap, Nurrungar and the North West Cape.

Victor Marchetti, a former CIA analyst, told Pilger that Australia was important to the United States in Asia. Pine Gap was officially a joint US–Australian facility, but it was actually 'planned, set up and run by the CIA as the eavesdropping capital of the world', said Pilger. At nearby Nurrungar, information gathered from satellites spying on Russia was vital to President Reagan's Star Wars programme, and the North West Cape base was responsible for transmitting to US nuclear submarines 'the order to fire'. Through that third base, during the Middle East war of 1973, Nixon had put US forces on nuclear alert, and, when Whitlam found out, he said that World War Three could begin in Australia. 'Australians had been made prime Soviet targets and they didn't know it,' explained Pilger. 'There was no early warning, no protection. Whitlam made it clear to Washington that their bases were no longer sacrosanct and the treaty governing Pine Gap, due to expire in December 1975, might not be extended.'

On 2 November 1975, Whitlam demanded to know the

names of CIA agents working undercover in Australia. Six days later, said Pilger, the CIA's chief of East Asia, Theodore Shackley, described Whitlam as a security risk and threatened to cut off intelligence links with Australia. Sir John Kerr, governor-general of Australia, had been associated with CIA-connected organizations in the 1950s and 1960s, reported Pilger, and the US intelligence agency boasted contacts with an Australian civil servant who had the ear of Kerr. William Pinwill, who conducted investigations in the United States for this documentary, told Pilger that there were suggestions from his CIA contacts that the agency believed it could trust Kerr 'to act in the interests of the Western alliance'. (Pinwill added, 'Not necessarily in the interests of Australia,' but this line was cut by the Australian Broadcasting Corporation when it screened the programme. The ABC also added a disclaimer to the *Last Dream* series, dissociating itself from the 'opinions' contained in it.)

On 11 November, reported Pilger, Kerr sacked the Whitlam government on the pretext of the Senate's refusal to release budget resources, but many regarded the affair as a constitutional *coup d'état*. 'For the CIA, it was a repeat of their successful overthrow of the Chilean government just two years earlier,' said Pilger. American investigative journalist Joe Trento told Pilger of 'a call from the CIA to MI5, MI6, saying we have a security problem in Australia, we have a security problem with the prime minister – he's endangering national security for the United States and the Alliance'. Dozens of such calls took place, said Trento, adding, 'I don't think you could say that the CIA forced Kerr to sack Whitlam, but I think that decisions were made that led to his sacking based on what the CIA was telling the English.' He said he had it 'on authority at the highest levels of the US intelligence community that there was genuine concern at the loss of those bases'. Trento did not see this as an overthrow, but 'they made a recommendation' and Kerr 'stupidly did everything he could to co-operate with the set-up'.

Shortly afterwards, reported Pilger, a CIA briefing document described Bob Hawke as 'best qualified' to succeed Whitlam as Labor leader. He did so and, in 1983, became prime minister. 'Today, the American bases are no longer in jeopardy and nuclear ships can enter Australian ports again,' said Pilger. 'Australian politicians have learned their lessons and, once again, are all the way with the USA.' Returning to his recurrent theme of small nations determining their own futures without being influenced by the superpowers, Pilger cited nearby New Zealand as 'showing the way' by banning nuclear weapons from its waters. Australia could 'break free from its imperial past and present' by standing alongside that government – 'and breaking free is surely the only future'.

Other People's Wars was a fitting final instalment of *The Last Dream*. Like the rest of the series, it was critical of Australia's attachment to this imperial past but declared that there was hope for a different future. In a short piece to the camera at the end, Pilger reminded viewers of 'those who fought and fell in defence of their own country, on their own soil', the Aborigines, whose names did not appear on any cenotaphs or war memorials and who should be given land rights. Echoing his final words in *The Secret Country*, Pilger said, 'Until we give back their nationhood, we can never claim our own.'

Four days later, *The Last Dream* was reviewed in the BBC2 programme *Did You See?*, hosted by Ludovic Kennedy. Publisher Carmen Callil, a fellow-Australian, praised the portraits of Menzies and the removal of Whitlam but felt there was 'a petulant whingeing about his [Pilger's] programmes'. Comedian Spike Milligan was impressed by the accounts of white Australians being downtrodden and later used as 'cannon fodder', but writer Jonathan Meades said Pilger's view was 'so partial' that 'it makes you wonder' and declared him 'rather sanctimonious'. Referring to Pilger's reporting of Australia's entry into the Vietnam War and the fall of the Whitlam government, Kennedy insisted, 'He didn't produce evidence for all these things.'[16]

Clearly, Kennedy was choosing to ignore the copy of the South

Vietnamese government letter, shown on screen, confirming the 'offer' of Australian military assistance and the investigations of William Pinwill and Brian Toohey. 'I found Kennedy's dismissive remarks outrageous,' said Pilger. 'I wrote to him and he didn't reply, so I wrote again and said that I was prepared to give him all the source material. I challenged him to examine it and, if he was wrong, to say so. But, of course, these people never do. In Brian Toohey and Bill Pinwill, we had two of the best people in their field, who were top investigators. I sent their documentation to Kennedy.'[17]

The night before *The Last Dream* was broadcast in Australia, Pilger spoke to Whitlam on the telephone. 'We talked for several hours,' he recalled. 'He backed the film and said that this was the only time, to his knowledge, that there had been a comprehensive television investigation and he was grateful for it. Whitlam didn't believe that his overthrow had been directly engineered by foreign intelligence agencies but felt that they had played a significant part. In the end, he blamed the governor-general, whom he loathed personally.'[18] Shortly afterwards, on Australian radio, Whitlam said he believed there had been CIA and MI6 involvement and added a revelation made in his 1985 book, *The Whitlam Government 1972–75*, that President Carter had in 1977 sent an emissary to Australia who told him that 'the US would never again interfere in the domestic political processes of Australia'.[19]

Pilger's documentary caused a stir in Australia. It was debated in Parliament and Bob Hawke issued a denial of the 'coup' allegations. 'That delighted me,' said Pilger. 'One of my favourite dictums is from Claud Cockburn: "Never believe anything until it's officially denied." And it was being denied by all the right people!'[20] Pilger also pointed out that the chapter entitled 'The Coup' in his book *A Secret Country*, which was 'legalled' by top Australian QC Geoffrey Robertson, had never been challenged.

It was the end of the following decade before Pilger and Alan Lowery returned to Australia to make another documentary.

With the Olympic Games due to be staged in Sydney in 2000, their film *Welcome to Australia*, screened the previous year, again tackled the Aboriginal problem, but this time from a different angle. It was about those black sportsmen who had been denied places in the country's international teams. The idea was inspired by Australian professor Colin Tatz's book, *Obstacle Race – Aborigines in Sport*. While making the new programme, Lowery was shocked by the reversal of Aborigines' fortunes since the previous documentaries. 'Between *The Secret Country* and *The Last Dream*, much greater awareness of the Aborigine problem grew up,' he recalled. 'I wasn't prepared for how downhill the situation had gone by the time we made *Welcome to Australia*. You could find blatant Third World conditions in a First World country.'[21]

In *Welcome to Australia*, a glossy Australian television commercial promoting the Games was followed by a string of stories and interviews highlighting this inequality in sport, which Pilger compared to that under apartheid in the old South Africa. Over film of the last Olympics held in Australia, in 1956, he reported that there were no natives in the national team. A black-and-white photograph of an Aboriginal football team, taken shortly after those Games and shown on screen, featured players who mostly went on to die in their thirties and forties.

Pilger told the story of Wally McArthur, one of the 'stolen generation', whose prowess as a sprinter was never recognized in Australia. Charlie Perkins, who had taken Pilger into Aboriginal territory in 1969 and appeared in *Pilger in Australia* and *The Secret Country*, recalled growing up with McArthur in a boys' home and called him 'the greatest athlete I've ever seen in my life'. Moving to Britain, McArthur made his name as a professional athlete and Rugby League player, whose shared record of goals and tries for the Rochdale Hornets still stands.

Perkins had made a name for himself in English football before returning home and becoming only the second Aborigine to graduate from an Australian university. Recalling his early days, Perkins said he was not allowed to leave the Aboriginal reserve on which he lived and, at a birthday party, he had to stand outside at the window. Little had changed for the Aborigines, he said, as they were 'still getting trachoma, diabetes is rampant, there's poor water to drink and no employment opportunities on these settlements'. He added, 'Sure, education has improved in some areas here and there, we've got more employment opportunities, but we've not gone that big step that we should have taken. It's really a tragedy.'

In his book, Colin Tatz had listed 1,200 outstanding Aboriginal athletes, of whom only five were given access to the equipment, training and facilities available to white Australians. 'They are people who have shown sometimes twice, sometimes three times, as much talent in order to rate a place,' Tatz told Pilger. Sprinter Cathy Freeman, who won a gold medal at the 1994 Olympics, was, the author said, 'the greatest thing that has ever happened to white Australia in recent years' but she did not represent all black women. Tatz believed that a Nigerian member of the International Olympic Committee, who had examined conditions in the country before it awarded Australia the 2000 Games, would have been shocked at the 'Third and Fourth World sporting facilities' in Aboriginal areas if he had been taken there.

Accompanying the discrimination against Aborigines in sport was the government policy that led to the 'stolen generation'. Finally, in 1997, Pilger could now report, the truth was officially recognized with the publication of a Human Rights Commission report, *Bringing Them Home*. It was later estimated that more than 100,000 children had been stolen from their families. The report called for an official apology from the government and reparations for the victims. Conservative Prime Minister John Howard refused to give either.

In Kununurra, Western Australia, half a mile from the route that the Olympic torch would take, Pilger and Lowery filmed doctors doing a spot-check on children for the eye disease trachoma. One-third of all the children and adults had the disease, which causes blindness. Australia was the only developed country on a list drawn up by the World Health Organization, said Pilger, 'a shame list of countries where children are still afflicted by trachoma'. The federal health minister had, in 1997, made 'an extraordinary admission' that there was no evidence of improvement in Aboriginal health during the previous ten years. Dr Richard Murray, who worked at a clinic run by an Aboriginal self-help organization, explained that Aborigines suffered 'exotic diseases' that had been wiped out in the Edinburgh slums in the nineteenth century. 'Until the problems of poverty and social justice are really addressed, we will continue to just save people,' he added.

The life expectancy of Aborigines was twenty-five years less than whites, reported Pilger, standing in an overgrown graveyard. It was true that the Aboriginal child mortality rate had improved, but they now died 'only three times faster than white children'. Pilger said, 'Suicides among Aborigines have now become an epidemic, largely unrecognized in white Australia.' In the northwest of the country, the suicide rate had increased five-fold in a matter of months and most of the victims were young. Film showed awards won by a nine-year-old athlete who killed himself. Colin Tatz ventured the idea that many who committed suicide believed 'they're going to be around to watch who comes to the funeral and who gives them respect, who gives them a sense of care and a sense of love which many of them feel they don't have,' adding, 'It's a terrible reason for committing suicide.'

The number of Aboriginal deaths in police custody had increased since Pilger's previous documentary, according to Amnesty International. He returned to the death of Rugby League player Eddie Murray, whose parents he had interviewed in *The Last Dream*. Now, he likened this case to that of Stephen Lawrence in Britain. After an excerpt from the original interview with Arthur and Leila Murray, in which the twenty-one-year-old's father said he believed his son had been killed by a police officer, Pilger reported that they had succeeded in having his body exhumed in 1997 and his sternum was found to be smashed. In a new interview, the couple demanded an explanation from the state government. 'We need answers,' said Leila Murray. Robert Cavanagh, an Australian senior lecturer in law, insisted that a proper autopsy was not conducted on Eddie Murray and police were not thoroughly questioned at the time because 'he was black and poor'.

The Howard government denied that genocide of Aborigines ever took place, said Pilger, as he recalled the battles that occurred on the Hawkesbury river, previously related in his film *The Secret Country*. He also repeated the fact that Aborigines were not commemorated on cenotaphs. 'Last year, Prime Minister Howard vetoed a proposal to add black names to the national war memorials,' said Pilger. 'There were no wars fought in Australia, he said. If that's true, then those who were killed must have been murdered.'

Professor Tatz, who was director of the Genocide Studies Centre at Macquarie University, said that Australia had consistently and systematically practised genocide over 210 years instead of in 'neat, tight, compacted time frames, such as Nazi Germany from 1933 to 1945 or Stalin's genocide between the two world wars or Rwanda in 1994'.

Pilger reported that Pauline Hanson's 'racist' One Nation Party had won 10 per cent of votes in the last general election. Historian Henry Reynolds explained that the one million people who voted for that party had not all endorsed the 'one nation' policy, which included taking the property rights of a minority, but did not find it extreme enough to vote against it. 'That is one of the most disturbing things that's come out of this,' he said. Prime Minister Howard had much in common with Hanson, said Pilger. They both denied Australia's bloody past and her 'one nation' policy was similar to Howard's 'one Australia' one of the late 1980s. One of his first acts as prime minister was to cut $400 million from the Aboriginal budget and he had refused a treaty with the Aborigines. An 'unprecedented' number of international reports had condemned the Australian government for its human rights record. Howard had declined a request by Pilger for an interview.

In 1993, the government of Paul Keating had granted limited native title to Aborigines while protecting the interests of mining companies and big landowners. The High Court reinforced its original decision but the newly elected Howard government passed legislation effectively cutting back these gains. 'Who really owns this vast island continent?' asked Pilger. 'The richest land is controlled by just twenty-five powerful landholders.' Kerry Packer, pictured with his 'mate' Bob Hawke in *The Last Dream*, was now shown with his 'new mate', John Howard. Between them, Packer and Rupert Murdoch controlled much of the Australian media, with Murdoch owning almost 70 per cent of the capital city press. Aerial shots showed their luxury homes beside Sydney Harbour. 'While Aboriginal land claims are often disputed, the land rights of the wealthy never are,' said Pilger.

The boomerang was the motif of the 2000 Olympics. 'In my lifetime, this country has become one of the most culturally diverse societies in the world, and it's happened peacefully,' said Pilger. 'The exceptions are those Australians who were here before any of us.' Many people in this multicultural society wanted to make amends for 'crimes committed against the Aboriginal people' and one such example was the 'Sea of Hands' campaign, with each 'hand' put on Bondi Beach symbolizing white opposition to the government's policies on black land rights, 'part of a grassroots movement of regret and reconciliation'.

But symbols and gestures were not justice. 'White Australians should listen to Aboriginal survivors, to the writers, the teachers, elders, historians, artists and activists who are part of an extra-ordinary renaissance. What they demand is the political will for a treaty that will bring land and justice.' Summing up, Pilger said that 'civilizations are judged by how they treat all their people, especially the most vulnerable, who are often the bravest' and asked, 'Why is it not possible for a nation's leaders to behave honourably towards less than 2 per cent of the population? Set against this question, the issue of whether or not Australia becomes a republic in the twenty-first century is simply irrelevant, for, until the First Australians are given back *their* nationhood, the rest of us can never claim our own.' This, of course, was the same theme as Pilger's sign-offs to *The Secret Country* and *The Last Dream*. 'It was the same,' he said later, 'but that principle of justice is still unfulfilled in Australia. In that respect, little has changed.'[22]

Those two documentaries had, in fact, been largely responsible for the establishment, in Canberra in the mid-1990s, of a memorial to Aboriginal dead, another of his recurrent themes. Part of the Australian Museum, it was financed through money raised by Aboriginal groups who acknowledged the Pilger films as an inspiration for it.

Of the latest documentary, Joe Joseph wrote in *The Times*, '*Welcome to Australia* probably isn't the film Australia's Olympic Committee showed to the Olympic authorities when it was pitching to host the 2000 Games. It was a charge-sheet of racial injustice and government neglect . . . Pilger doesn't see shades of grey. He's a black-and-white man. You can find his manner irritating, but you can't help admiring his zeal. Unlike, say, Michael Moore, there is no tricksiness, no made-for-TV japes. You might even say Pilger wears his heart on his sleeve.'[23]

Fellow-Australian Phillip Knightley, the only other journalist to win the British Press Awards Journalist of the Year honour twice, is well qualified to judge Pilger's view of their shared homeland from Britain as an expatriate. 'Our views are similar,' he explained. 'He was certainly among the first to draw international attention to the shameful way in which Australia has treated the Aborigines. The attitude of Australians has changed and there's a strong mood in the country for reconciliation, but John has a slightly less optimistic view than I have. In *Welcome to Australia*, he concentrated on the bad things that were happening but not the good. He would say that's not part of his brief and it's covered elsewhere. He's a polemicist and, if you want to arouse people's passions and anger, the stronger the polemic, the better. His style is purely his own – it's not everybody's, as was clear with the controversy over his getting the Richard Dimbleby Award. If you put yourself in the public eye like John does, a polemicist with an aggressive manner, sooner or later there will be a backlash.'[24]

In fact, the only public objections to the British Academy of Film and Television Arts giving the Richard Dimbleby Award to Pilger came from the Murdoch-owned *Sunday Times* and Dimbleby's son, the conservative broadcaster David. Moreover, Pilger has always denied he is a polemicist but freely admits that he reports from a standpoint, which is a humanitarian one and, unlike most of the media, undisguised. Another Australian journalist, David Bowman, who was editor of the *Sydney Morning Herald* when it commissioned him to make *Island of Dreams*, outlined Pilger's qualities in the magazine *ABC Radio 24 Hours* in 1998, in a feature declaring that the Australian press needed a journalist such as Pilger. Bowman wrote:

He deals in facts, presents witnesses, excuses nothing and tells as plain as day what he knows. His themes are universal: justice and injustice, oppressors and oppressed, arms traders and land mine victims, state power and betrayed workers, plutocrats and democrats, innocence and guilt. Such themes, frankly presented, can enrage Jacks-in-office and make editors nervous. They can also galvanize the public. The reality of honest reportage comes like a clean sharp wind after the posturings of the professional provocateurs and other second-rate desk-bound columnists who waste good space. If the Australian press does not already have a Pilger, it is because the major newspapers, with rare exceptions, have preferred to employ writers who see the world from the vantage point of orthodoxy and power.[25]

NOTES

INTRODUCTION

1. John Pilger interviewed by the author, 8 February 2000.
2. John Pilger interviewed by the author, 29 December 1982.
3. Gerry Pinches interviewed by the author, 16 February 2000.
4. John Pilger interviewed by the author, 19 December 1999.
5. John Pilger interview, 19 December 1999.
6. John Pilger interview, 29 December 1982.
7. John Pilger interview, 19 December 1999.
8. David Swift interviewed by the author, 21 January 2000.
9. John Pilger interview, 19 December 1999.
10. John Pilger interview, 19 December 1999.
11. Richard Creasey interviewed by the author, 11 July 2000.
12. John Pilger, *Heroes*, Jonathan Cape, 1986.
13. Jonathan Morris interviewed by the author, 14 February 2000.
14. Jonathan Morris interview, 14 February 2000.
15. John Pilger interview, 29 December 1982.
16. Richard Creasey interview, 11 July 2000.
17. Steve Anderson interviewed by the author, 10 July 2000.
18. John Pilger interview, 19 December 1999.
19. John Pilger interviewed by the author, 19 January 2000.
20. John Pilger interview, 19 January 2000.
21. John Pilger, *Heroes*.
22. David Glencross in a speech to the Royal Television Society on 8 March 1994, extracted in *The Times*, 9 March 1994.
23. *The 1999 Annual Performance Reviews for Channel 3*, Independent Television Commission, May 2000.
24. John Pilger has been awarded the following honorary doctorates: D Litt, Staffordshire University; D Phil, Dublin City University; D Arts, Oxford Brookes University; D Law, St Andrews University; D Litt, Kingston University. He was awarded a Visiting Fellowship by Deakin University, Australia.
25. John Pilger interview, 19 December 1999.

I. VIETNAM

1. Martha Gellhorn's Vietnam features were published in the *Guardian* during September 1966.
2. Martha Gellhorn, *The Face of War*, The Atlantic Monthly Press, 1988.
3. Martha Gellhorn, *The Face of War*.
4. *Television*, 'News: The Power of Pictures' (Granada Television), ITV, 12 March 1985.
5. *World in Action* (Granada Television), ITV, 3 November 1964.
6. Phillip Knightley, *The First Casualty – From the Crimea to Vietnam: The War Correspondent as Hero, Propagandist and Myth Maker*, André Deutsch, 1975.
7. John Pilger interview, 19 December 1999.
8. John Pilger interview, 19 December 1999.
9. Jeremy Wallington interviewed by the author, 27 January 2000.
10. *The Sunday Times*, 11 October 1970.
11. *The Sunday Times*, 18 October 1970.
12. John Pilger interview, 19 December 1999.
13. Jeremy Wallington interview, 27 January 2000.
14. *World in Action – 30 Years* (Granada Television), ITV, 12 January 1993.
15. Jeremy Wallington interview, 27 January 2000.
16. Leslie Woodhead, quoted in Francis Wheen, *Television*, Century Publishing, 1985.
17. John Pilger interview, 19 December 1999.
18. John Pilger interview, 19 December 1999.
19. John Pilger interview, 19 December 1999.
20. John Pilger interview, 19 December 1999.
21. John Pilger interview, 19 December 1999.
22. John Pilger interview, 19 December 1999.
23. *The Sunday Times*, 27 March 1983.
24. The *Guardian*, 31 March 1983.
25. The *Daily Telegraph*, 31 March 1983.
26. John Pilger interview, 19 December 1999.
27. David Munro interviewed by the author, 11 January 1988.
28. David Munro interviewed by the author, 5 January 1983.
29. John Pilger interviewed by the author, 29 December 1982, originally published in *Screen International*, 26 February 1983.
30. *Time Out*, 29 September–5 October 1978.
31. John Pilger interview, 19 December 1999.
32. John Pilger interview, 19 December 1999.
33. John Pilger interview, 19 December 1999.
34. The *Observer*, 8 October 1978.
35. *Variety*, 18 October 1978.
36. The *Daily Telegraph*, 4 October 1978.
37. John Pilger interview, 29 December 1982.
38. As told to David Munro.
39. David Munro interview, 11 January 1988.
40. John Pilger interview, 19 December 1999.

2. BRITAIN

1. John Pilger interview, 19 January 2000.
2. Norman Swallow, *Factual Television*, The Focal Press, 1966.
3. John Pilger interview, 19 January 2000.
4. David Swift interview, 21 January 2000.
5. Jeremy Wallington interview, 27 January 2000.
6. John Pilger interview, 19 January 2000.
7. The *Guardian*, 27 May 1974.
8. John Pilger interview, 19 January 2000.
9. John Pilger interview, 19 January 2000.
10. John Pilger interview, 19 January 2000.
11. Peter Hain, *Mistaken Identity: The Wrong Face of the Law*, Quartet Books, 1976.
12. John Pilger interview, 19 January 2000.
13. John Pilger interview, 19 January 2000.
14. Campaigning Journalist of the Year, 1977, British Press Awards.
15. *Daily Mail*, 15 August 1975.
16. John Pilger interview, 19 January 2000.
17. John Pilger interview, 19 January 2000.
18. The *Daily Telegraph*, 15 August 1975.
19. *Evening Standard*, London, 30 August 1977.
20. *Daily Mail*, 13 September 1977.
21. The *Daily Telegraph*, 13 September 1977.
22. The *Daily Telegraph*, 23 September 1977.
23. A Gallup poll showed 75 per cent broadly supporting Enoch Powell's views on immigration.
24. John Pilger interview, 19 January 2000.
25. *The Four Horsemen* (Central Television), ITV, 2 and 19 April 1986.
26. John Pilger interview, 19 January 2000.
27. John Pilger interview, 19 January 2000.
28. John Pilger interview, 19 January 2000.
29. John Pilger interview, 19 January 2000.

3. CAMBODIA

1. Louise Vidaud de Plaud interviewed by the author, September 1989.
2. Jim Howard interviewed by the author, 3 February 2000.
3. John Pilger interview, 29 December 1982.
4. William Shawcross, *Sideshow: Kissinger, Nixon and the Destruction of Cambodia*, André Deutsch, 1979.
5. Jim Howard interview, 3 February 2000.
6. Jonathan Morris interviewed by the author, 14 February 2000.
7. John Pilger interview, 19 January 2000.
8. Jim Howard interview, 3 February 2000.
9. The *Daily Telegraph*, 31 October 1979.

10. The *Guardian*, 31 October 1979.
11. The *Observer*, 4 November 1979.
12. The *Observer*, 11 November 1979.
13. The *Guardian*, 29 September 1979.
14. The *Guardian*, 2 October 1979.
15. The *Guardian*, 5 October 1979.
16. The *Guardian*, 5 October 1979.
17. The *Guardian*, 6 October 1979.
18. *New Statesman*, 12 October 1979.
19. Letter from Lady Plowden to Sir Evelyn Shuckburgh, dated 19 November 1979.
20. John Pilger interview, 29 December 1982.
21. Jim Howard interview, 3 February 2000.
22. *TVTimes*, 6–12 September 1980.
23. The *Observer*, 14 September 1980.
24. The *Observer*, 21 September 1980.
25. John Pilger interviewed by the author, September 1989.
26. John Pilger interview, 19 January 2000.

4. FLASHPOINTS

1. Letter from Justice Abu Sayeed Choudhury to Anthony Miles, editor of the *Daily Mirror*, dated 7 July 1971.
2. John Pilger interviewed by the author, 19 January 2000.
3. John Pilger, *Hidden Agendas*, Vintage, 1998; cited Richard Falk, 'The Terrorist Foundations of Recent US Policy' in *Western State Terrorism*, ed. Alexander George, Polity Press, 1991.
4. John Pilger interviewed by the author, 8 February 2000; also published in *TVTimes*, 4–10 March 2000.
5. Steve Anderson interviewed by the author, 10 July 2000.
6. Alan Lowery interviewed by the author, 14 March 2000.
7. Steve Anderson interview, 10 July 2000.
8. Rubin on the eve of his retirement as US spokesman, as told to John Pilger in confidence by a mutual friend.
9. *The Sunday Times*, 12 March 2000.
10. The *Guardian*, 7 March 2000.
11. The *Guardian*, 8 March 2000.
12. The *Guardian*, 9 March 2000.
13. *New Statesman*, 13 March 2000.
14. *New Statesman*, 20 March 2000.
15. *New Statesman*, 27 March 2000.
16. *New Statesman*, 3 April 2000.
17. *New Statesman*, 17 April 2000.
18. *New Statesman*,1 May 2000.
19. As reported to John Pilger by Denis Halliday.
20. John Pilger interviewed by the author, 4 June 2000.

5. UNCLE SAM

1. John Pilger interviewed by the author, 19 January 2000.
2. Martha Gellhorn, *The Face of War*, Virago Press, 1986.
3. John Pilger interview, 19 January 2000.
4. John Pilger, *Heroes*.
5. John Pilger interview, 19 January 2000.
6. John Pilger interview, 19 January 2000.
7. John Pilger interviewed by the author, 8 February 2000.
8. John Pilger interview, 19 January 2000.
9. John Pilger interview, 19 January 2000.
10. John Pilger interview, 19 January 2000.
11. John Pilger interview, 19 January 2000.
12. J.C. Louis and Harvey Yazyian, *The Cola Wars: The story of the global corporate battle between the Coca-Cola Company and PepsiCo Inc*, Everest House, New York, 1980.

6. TYRANNIES

1. John Pilger interview, 19 January 2000.
2. John Pilger interview, 19 January 2000.
3. John Pilger interview, 19 January 2000.
4. John Pilger interview, 19 January 2000.
5. John Pilger interview, 19 January 2000.
6. John Pilger, *Distant Voices*, revised edition, Vintage, 1994.
7. John Pilger, *Distant Voices*.
8. James Dunn, *Timor: A People Betrayed*, Jacaranda Press, Queensland, 1983.
9. John Pilger, *Distant Voices*.
10. John Pilger interview, 19 January 2000.
11. John Pilger interview, 19 January 2000.
12. *The Age*, 21 February 1994.
13. See *The Australian*, 4 March 1997.
14. For a summary of this episode, see the *Guardian*, 2 November 1999.
15. As told to David Munro, September 1998.
16. John Pilger interview, 19 January 2000.
17. John Pilger interview, 19 January 2000.
18. John Pilger interview, 19 January 2000.
19. John Pilger interview, 19 January 2000.
20. John Pilger interview, 19 January 2000.
21. John Pilger interview, 19 January 2000.
22. John Pilger interview, 19 January 2000.

7. OUTSIDERS

1. *TVTimes*, 10–17 December 1983.
2. Jacky Stoller interviewed by the author, 2 February 2000.
3. After John Pilger's obituary of Wilfred Burchett was published in the *Guardian* (28 September 1983), Frank Barber wrote to the newspaper's letters page (published 3 October 1983) taking issue with Pilger's assertion that the charge was 'bogus'. Pilger responded with a letter (published 6 October 1983) relating the full story.
4. The *Guardian*, 28 September 1983.
5. John Pilger interview, 19 January 2000.
6. Transcripts of untransmitted interview published in *Distant Voices*, revised edition, Vintage, 1994.
7. Untransmitted material supplied by John Pilger.
8. John Pilger interviewed by the author, 4 June 2000.
9. Untransmitted material supplied by John Pilger.

8. TRUTH GAMES

1. John Pilger interview, 19 January 2000.
2. Originally reported by the author in *Broadcast*, 13 April 1981.
3. Letter from Lord Normanbrook to Sir Burke Trend, 7 September 1965, cited by Michael Tracey in *Sanity Broadsheet*, No 6, 1980.
4. *News at Ten* (ITN), ITV, 4 November 1982.
5. *The Friday Alternative* (Diverse Productions), Channel Four, 5 November 1982.
6. The *Guardian*, 11 November 1982.
7. The *Guardian*, 17 November 1982.
8. *Good Morning Britain* (TV-am), ITV, 28 February 1983.
9. *The Sunday Times*, 27 February–5 March 1983.
10. *The Times*, 1 March 1983.
11. The *Guardian*, 1 March 1983.
12. The *Guardian*, 4 March 1983.
13. The *Guardian*, 4 March 1983.
14. The *Guardian*, 5 March 1983.
15. The *Guardian*, 5 March 1983.
16. The *Guardian*, 22 April 1983.
17. Cited in a Directors Guild of Great Britain press release, 23 July 1984.
18. Directors Guild of Great Britain press release, 23 July 1984.
19. Central Television press release, 31 July 1984.
20. Ken Loach interviewed by the author, originally published in *Screen International*, 4 August 1984.
21. The *Guardian*, 9 January 1989.
22. The *Guardian*, 19 January 1989.

23. Letter to the *New Statesman*, 27 February 1998.
24. Letter to the *New Statesman*, 6 March 1998.
25. The *Sunday Telegraph*, 3 March 1991.
26. *The Sunday Times*, 3 March 1991.
27. The *Daily Telegraph*, 14 March 1991.
28. *The Times*, 2 June 1983.
29. *The Late Show* (BBC in association with Central Television), BBC2, 19 March 1991.
30. *The Sunday Times*, 24 March 1991.
31. *New Statesman*, 12 July 1991.
32. John Pilger, *Distant Voices*.
33. Central Television statement, 5 July 1991.

9. PEOPLE'S JUSTICE

1. *New Statesman*, 12 July 1991.
2. John Pilger, Edward Wilson Lecture, 'Reading Between the Lines: Truth and the Media Society', Deakin University, Australia, 26 October 1995.
3. John Pilger interview, 19 January 2000.
4. John Pilger interview, 29 December 1982.
5. The *Guardian*, 9 June 1980.
6. Alan Lowery interviewed by the author, 14 March 2000.
7. Alan Lowery interview, 14 March 2000.
8. *The Sunday Times*, 20 November 1983.
9. *The Sunday Times*, 20 November 1983.
10. *The Sunday Times*, 4 December 1983.
11. *The Sunday Times*, 18 December 1983.
12. John Pilger interview, 19 January 2000.
13. *New Statesman*, 12 July 1991.
14. John Pilger interview, 19 January 2000.
15. John Pilger interview, 19 January 2000.
16. The *Guardian*, 11 April 1998.
17. *Mail & Guardian*, Johannesburg, 30 April–7 May 1998.
18. *Mail & Guardian*.
19. *Mail & Guardian*.
20. John Pilger interview, 19 January 2000.
21. John Pilger interview, 19 January 2000.

10. AUSTRALIA

1. *TVTimes*, 24–30 April 1976.
2. John Pilger interviewed by the author, 29 January 2000.
3. John Pilger interview, 29 January 2000; Pilger had, in fact, reported from Australia for the *Daily Mirror* in 1965 with a humorous feature about 'Strine' (Australian language). This brought his talents to the notice of

editorial director Hugh Cudlipp after it was mentioned to him by the paper's legendary columnist Cassandra (William Connor).

4. John Pilger interview, 29 January 2000.
5. John Pilger interview, 29 January 2000.
6. Ivan Strasburg interviewed by the author, 7 February 2000.
7. *The Times*, 28 April 1976.
8. *The Sunday Times*, 2 May 1976.
9. John Pilger interview, 29 January 2000.
10. David Bowman interviewed by the author, 18 February 2000.
11. Alan Lowery interviewed by the author, 14 March 2000.
12. John Pilger interview, 29 January 2000.
13. John Pilger interview, 29 January 2000.
14. John Pilger interview, 29 January 2000.
15. John Pilger interview, 29 January 2000.
16. *Did You See?* (BBC), BBC2, 30 January 1988.
17. John Pilger interview, 29 January 2000.
18. John Pilger interview, 29 January 2000.
19. Gough Whitlam interviewed by Brian White, Radio 2UE Sydney, 22 February 1988; Gough Whitlam, *The Whitlam Government 1972–75*, Viking, London, and Penguin, Sydney, 1985.
20. John Pilger interview, 29 January 2000.
21. Alan Lowery interview, 14 March 2000.
22. John Pilger interview, 29 January 2000.
23. *The Times*, 1 September 1999.
24. Phillip Knightley interviewed by the author, 18 February 2000.
25. *ABC Radio 24 Hours,* September 1998.

GENERAL BIBLIOGRAPHY

Fred W. Friendly, *Due to Circumstances Beyond Our Control*, MacGibbon & Kee, 1967.

Phillip Knightley, *The First Casualty – From the Crimea to Vietnam: The War Correspondent as Hero, Propagandist and Myth Maker*, André Deutsch, 1975.

Michael Maclear, *Vietnam: The Ten Thousand Day War*, Eyre Methuen, 1981.

John Pilger, *The Last Day*, Mirror Books, 1975.

John Pilger and Anthony Barnett, *Aftermath: The Struggle of Cambodia & Vietnam*, New Statesman, 1982.

John Pilger and Michael Coren, *The Outsiders*, Quartet Books, 1983.

John Pilger, *Heroes*, Jonathan Cape, 1986; revised edition, Pan Books, 1989.

John Pilger, *A Secret Country*, Jonathan Cape, 1989; revised edition, Vintage, 1992.

John Pilger, *Distant Voices*, Vintage, 1992; revised edition, Vintage, 1994.

John Pilger, *Hidden Agendas*, Vintage, 1998.

Norman Swallow, *Factual Television*, The Focal Press, 1966.

Michael Tracey, *The Production of Political Television*, Routledge & Kegan Paul, 1977.

Francis Wheen, *Television*, Century Publishing, 1985.

Other books used for specific references are included in the Notes section.

APPENDICES

TELEVISION DOCUMENTARIES

The Quiet Mutiny ('World in Action', Granada Television) ITV, 28 September 1970. Producer-director: Charles Denton.

Conversations with a Working Man (also co-producer) ('World in Action', Granada Television) ITV, 7 June 1971. Producer-director: Michael Beckham.

Vietnam: Still America's War ('Pilger', ATV) ITV, 12 May 1974. Producer-director: Charles Denton.

Palestine Is Still the Issue ('Pilger', ATV) ITV, 19 May 1974. Producer-director: Charles Denton.

Guilty Until Proven Innocent ('Pilger', ATV) ITV, 26 May 1974. Director: John Ingram, Series producer: Charles Denton.

Thalidomide: The Ninety-eight We Forgot ('Pilger', ATV) ITV, 2 June 1974. Director: Christine Fox, Series producer: Charles Denton.

The Most Powerful Politician in America ('Pilger', ATV) ITV, 9 June 1974. Producer-director: Charles Denton.

One British Family ('Pilger', ATV) ITV, 16 June 1974. Director: John Ingram, Series producer: Charles Denton.

An Unfashionable Tragedy ('Pilger', ATV) ITV, 2 January 1975. Producer-director: John Ingram.

Nobody's Children ('Pilger', ATV) ITV, 9 January 1975. Producer-director: John Ingram.

Mr Nixon's Secret Legacy ('Pilger', ATV) ITV, 16 January 1975. Producer-director: Richard Marquand.

Smashing Kids, 1975 ('Pilger', ATV) ITV, 14 August 1975. Producer-director: John Ingram.

'To Know Us Is to Love Us' ('Pilger', ATV) ITV, 21 August 1975. Producer-director: Richard Marquand.

A Nod and a Wink ('Pilger', ATV) ITV, 28 August 1975. Producer-director: John Ingram.

Pilger in Australia (ATV) ITV, 27 April 1976. Producer-director: John Ingram.

Zap!! The Weapon Is Food ('Pilger', ATV) ITV, 6 September 1976. Producer-director: Richard Marquand, Producer: Richard Creasey.

Pyramid Lake Is Dying ('Pilger', ATV) ITV, 13 September 1976. Producer-director: Richard Marquand, Producer: Richard Creasey.

The Street of Joy ('Pilger', ATV) ITV, 20 September 1976. Producer-director: Richard Marquand, Producer: Richard Creasey.

A Faraway Country . . . a people of whom we know nothing ('Pilger', ATV) ITV, 'Personal Report', 5 September 1977. Director: Alan Bell (credited as Bella Lang), Series producer: Richard Creasey.

Dismantling a Dream ('Pilger', ATV) ITV, 'Personal Report', 12 September 1977. Director: Nigel Evans, Series producer: Richard Creasey.

An Unjustifiable Risk ('Pilger', ATV) ITV, 'Personal Report', 19 September 1977. Director: Alan Bell, Series producer: Richard Creasey.

The Selling of the Sea (Westward Television) ITV Westward Television region only, 18 August 1978. Producer-director: James W. Goulding.

Do You Remember Vietnam (ATV) ITV, 3 October 1978. Producer-director: David Munro.

Year Zero – The Silent Death of Cambodia (ATV) ITV, 30 October 1979. Producer-director: David Munro.

The Mexicans (ATV) ITV, 4 June 1980. Producer-director: David Munro.

Cambodia – Year One (ATV) ITV, 10 September 1980. Producer-director: David Munro.

Heroes (ATV) ITV, 6 May 1981. Producer-director: David Munro.

Island of Dreams (Channel 7, Sydney) Channel 7, New South Wales, Australia, 13 June 1981. Director: Geoffrey Burton, Executive producer: Tony Culliton.

The Truth Game (Central Television) ITV, 28 February 1983. Producer-director: David Munro.

Frontline – The Search for Truth in Wartime (Central Television) ITV, 19 July 1983. Director: Ross Devenish, Producer: Nicholas Claxton. (Repeated on Channel Four in the 'Banned' season, 13 April 1991.)

Nicaragua (Central Television) ITV, 15 November 1983. Producer-director: Alan Lowery.

Burp! Pepsi v Coke in the Ice Cold War (Central Television) ITV, 22 May 1984. Director: Alan Lowery, Producer: Nicholas Claxton.

The Secret Country – The First Australians Fight Back (Central Television) ITV, 21 May 1985. Producer-director: Alan Lowery.

Japan – Behind the Mask ('Viewpoint 87', Central Television) ITV, 13 January 1987. Producer-director: Alan Lowery.

The Last Dream ('Viewpoint Special' series, Central Television) ITV, Producer-director: Alan Lowery, Associate producer (Australia): Alec Morgan.
  1. *Heroes Unsung* ITV, 12 January 1988.
  2. *Secrets* ITV, 19 January 1988.
  3. *Other People's Wars* ITV, 26 January 1988.

Cambodia – Year Ten ('Viewpoint 89', Central Television) ITV, 31 October 1989. Producer-director: David Munro.

Cambodia – Year Ten Update ('Viewpoint 89', Central Television) ITV, 21 November 1989. Producer-director: David Munro, Studio director: Hector Stewart.

Cambodia – The Betrayal ('Viewpoint 90', Central Television) ITV, 9 October 1990. Producer-director: David Munro.

War by Other Means ('Viewpoint 92', Central Television) ITV, 19 May 1992. Producer-director: David Munro.

Return to Year Zero ('Viewpoint 93', Central Television) ITV, 20 April 1993. Producer-director: David Munro.

Death of a Nation – The Timor Conspiracy ('Network First', Central Television) ITV, 22 February 1994. Producer-director: David Munro, Co-producer, Timor: Max Stahl, Associate producers: Gill Scrine, Ana de Juan. (Re-edited and updated as *The Timor Conspiracy*, ITV, 26 January 1999.)

Flying the Flag – Arming the World ('Network First', Central Television) ITV, in 'The War Machine' week, 15 November 1994. Producer-director: David Munro.

Vietnam – The Last Battle ('Network First', Central Television/Carlton UK) ITV, 2 April 1995. Producer-director: David Munro.

Inside Burma – Land of Fear ('Network First', Central Television/Carlton UK) ITV, 14 May 1996. Producer-director: David Munro. (Updated repeat, ITV, 28 July 1998.)

Breaking the Mirror – The Murdoch Effect ('Network First', Central Television/Carlton UK) ITV, 18 February 1997. Producer-director: David Munro.

Apartheid Did Not Die (also co-producer) (Central Television/Carlton UK) ITV, 21 April 1998. Producer-director: Alan Lowery.

Welcome to Australia (also co-producer) (Central Television/Carlton UK) ITV, 31 August 1999. Producer-director: Alan Lowery, Associate producer: Gillian Coote.

Paying the Price – Killing the Children of Iraq (also co-producer) (Carlton) ITV, 6 March 2000. Producer-director: Alan Lowery, Associate producer, US/UK: Chris Martin.

TELEVISION PLAY

The Last Day (screenwriter) (BBC) BBC2, 30 March 1983. Director: Richard Stroud, Producer: Peter Wolfes.

OTHER TELEVISION

Trans-African Hovercraft ('The World About Us') (writer) (BBC-Bayerischer Rundfunk-Fernsehen) BBC2, 12 and 19 July 1970 (two parts).

Midweek (10-minute reports) (BBC) BBC2, 10 May 1973 and 25 July 1973.

Low (reading extracts from David Low's autobiography) (Brook Productions), Channel Four, 8 December 1985. Producer-director: Russ Karel, Producer: David Elstein.

The Outsiders (presenter-interviewer) (Tempest Films series) Producer: Jacky Stoller:
1. Sean Mac Bride, Channel Four, 17 April 1983. Director: Alan Lowery.

   2. Helen Suzman, Channel Four, 24 April 1983. Director: Alan Lowery.
   3. Martha Gellhorn, Channel Four, 1 May 1983. Director: Alan Lowery.
   4. Jessica Mitford, Channel Four, 10 July 1983. Director: Alan Lowery.
   5. Wilfred Burchett, Channel Four, 17 July 1983. Director: Hugh Munro.
   6. David Williamson, Channel Four, 24 July 1983. Director: Alan Lowery.
   7. Salman Rushdie, Channel Four, 4 December 1983. Director: Alan Lowery.
   8. Costa-Gavras, Channel Four, 11 December 1983. Director: Alan Lowery.
   9. Patsy Spybey, Channel Four, 18 December 1983. Director uncredited.
Models of Writing: Reporting with John Pilger (*The English Programme*, Thames
   Television) Channel Four, 'Schools', 9 January 1989.
The Late Show (interview with Noam Chomsky) (BBC in association with
   Central Television) BBC2, 25 November 1992. Studio director: Rena
   Butterwick, Programme producers: David Herman, David Munro.
Books of the Century (presenter, choosing Noam Chomsky's *Manufacturing
   Consent*) (Mentorn Films) Channel Four, 17 September 1996.

OTHER PRODUCTIONS

The Guardian Interview – Oliver Stone (interviewer) (BFI TV) Recorded
   18 January 1994.

AWARDS

Newspaper
Descriptive Writer of the Year, 1966, Hannen Swaffer Prize, British Press
   Awards
Journalist of the Year, 1967, British Press Awards
Reporter of the Year, 1967, Granada Television *What the Papers Say*
   Awards
International Reporter of the Year, 1970, British Press Awards
News Reporter of the Year, 1974, British Press Awards
Campaigning Journalist of the Year, 1977, British Press Awards
Journalist of the Year, 1979, British Press Awards

Television
John Pilger won the Richard Dimbleby Award for factual reporting,
   1990 BAFTA Awards, London, 1991

The Quiet Mutiny
The Golden Dragon, Cracow Festival of Short Films, 1971
Chicago International Film Festival award, 1971
Diploma of Merit, Melbourne Film Festival, 1971

Vietnam: Still America's War
Bronze Hugo in the Network Public Affairs category, Chicago International
Film Festival, 1974

A Faraway Country . . . a people of whom we know nothing
Certificate of Merit, Chicago International Film Festival, 1978

Year Zero – The Silent Death of Cambodia
More than 30 awards, including:
Best Documentary of 1979, Broadcasting Press Guild, 1980
International Critics Prize for best news feature, Monte Carlo International
Television Festival, 1980
Silver Plaque, Chicago International Film Festival, 1980
United Nations Media Peace Prize, Australia, 1979–80 (for *Year Zero – The
Silent Death of Cambodia*, *Cambodia – Year One* and his Cambodia press
reports)
TVTimes Readers' Award, 1979

Cambodia – Year One
United Nations Media Peace Prize Gold Medal, Australia, 1980–81 (also for his
Cambodia press reports)

Heroes
Silver Plaque in the Documentary category, Chicago International Film
Festival, 1981

Nicaragua
Peace Prize, Melbourne Film Festival, 1984
Highly commended at the United Nations Association Media Peace Prize
Awards, 1984 (also for his press report on Eritrea)

The Secret Country – The First Australians Fight Back
Director Alan Lowery won a Red Ribbon (2nd prize) in the Anthropology
category of the American Film Festival, New York, 1986

The Last Dream: Heroes Unsung
Gold Plaque (third prize) in the Documentary – Syndication category, Chicago
International Film Festival, 1988

Cambodia – Year Ten
Honourable mention in the Broadcast Television – Current Affairs category,
Golden Gate Awards, San Francisco, 1990

George Foster Peabody Award, Athens, Georgia, USA, 1990

Award for Best Achievement in Documentaries, International Monitor Awards, New York, 1990

Special Commendation of the United Nations Association, UNA Media Peace Prize competition, London, 1990

Trophy for Best News Report (highest award of the competition), plus the Reporters Sans Frontières prize awarded for the humanitarian values of the report, Adventure of Information Festival (The Great News Report competition), Bouches du Rhône, France, 1990

Gold Award (best of category) in the Investigative Journalism category (TV and Video Productions), Houston International Film Festival, 1990

Cambodia – The Betrayal

Director David Munro won the Blue Ribbon (first prize) in the International Issues: Asia category, American Film & Video Festival, Illinois, USA, 1991

International Emmy Award for Best Documentary, New York, 1991

War by Other Means

International de Télévision Genève Award (Geneva International Television Award), North–South Media Encounters event, Geneva, 1993

Gold Medal in the Best Documentary Production category, International Television Movie Festival, Mount Freedom, New Jersey, 1993

Gold Award (first prize) in the Political/International Issues category, World-Fest-Houston (Houston International Film & Video Festival), 1993

Silver Hugo Award in the Documentary – Social/Political category, Chicago International Film Festival, 1993

Return to Year Zero

Director David Munro won a Certificate of Honourable Mention, Chris Awards (Columbus International Film & Video Festival), Worthington, Ohio, 1993

Death of a Nation – The Timor Conspiracy

Gold Award in the Political/International Issue category (Film & Video Production division) at WorldFest-Houston (Houston International Film & Video Festival), 1994

Certificate for Creative Excellence (third place) in the Documentary, Current Events, Special Events category, US Film & Video Festival, Chicago, 1994

Silver Plaque for Social/Political Documentary (National) category, Chicago International Film Festival, 1994

Audience Award for Best Documentary, International Documentary Festival of Amsterdam, 1994

Certificate of Merit in the Documentary – Disputed Lands category, Golden Gate Awards, San Francisco, 1995

Flying the Flag – Arming the World

Bronze Apple in the Domestic and International Concerns category, National Educational Film & Video Festival, Oakland, California, 1995

Certificate of Honourable Mention in the International Relations category, Chris Awards (Columbus International Film Festival), Worthington, Ohio, 1995

Vietnam – The Last Battle

The Chris Statuette (the highest award given to film or video productions in each of the nine production divisions) in the Social Issues division, Chris Awards (Columbus International Film Festival), Worthington, Ohio, 1995

Silver Medal in the National/International Affairs category, New York Film & TV Festival, 1996

Gold Special Jury Award in the Film & Video Production division of WorldFest-Charleston, Charleston, 1995

Gold Apple (best of category award) in the International Social Issues category, National Educational Media Network Awards, Oakland, California, 1996

Silver Screen Award (second place) in the Politics, Government, Citizenship, World Relations, Civics category, US International Film & Video Festival, Chicago, 1996

Inside Burma – Land of Fear

International Actual Award for Risk Journalism, Barcelona, Spain, 1996

Bronze Plaque in the Social Issues – International Relations category, Chris Awards (Columbus International Film & Video Festival), Worthington, Ohio, 1996

Gold Special Jury Award, Film & Video Production division, WorldFest-Charleston, Charleston, 1996

Award for Best Factual Programme, RTS Midland Centre Awards, Birmingham, 1996

Gold Apple in the Politics: Social Organizations in Other Lands category, National Educational Media Network Film & Video Competition, NEMN Apple Awards, Oakland, California, 1997

The updated repeat won a Gold Special Jury Award in the Film & Video Production division, WorldFest-Houston (Houston International Film & Video Festival), 1999

Apartheid Did Not Die

Gold Award in the Film & Video Production: Political/International Issues category, WorldFest-Flagstaff, 1998

Certificate for Creative Excellence (third place), US International Film & Video Festival, Elmhurst, Illinois, 1999

Welcome to Australia
Gold Medal in the National/International Affairs category, 1999 New York
   Festivals TV Programming & Promotion competition, 2000
Gold Award in the Television Documentary & Information Programmes:
   Political/International Issues category, WorldFest-Flagstaff, 1999
Bronze Plaque in the Social Issues – Anthropology and Ethnology division,
   Chris Awards (Columbus International Film & Video Festival), Worthing-
   ton, Ohio, 2000.

Paying the Price – Killing the Children of Iraq
The Chris Statuette in the Social Issues – International Relations division, Chris
   Awards (Columbus International Film & Video Festival), Worthington,
   Ohio, 2000

INDEX

A NOTE ON THE TYPE

The text of this book is set in Bembo. This type was first used in 1495 by the Venetian printer Aldus Manutius for Cardinal Bembo's *De Aetna*, and was cut for Manutius by Francesco Griffo. It was one of the types used by Claude Garamond (1480–1561) as a model for his Romai de L'Université, and so it was the forerunner of what became standard European type for the following two centuries. Its modern form follows the original types and was designed for Monotype in 1929.